# HOLLAND
# GUIDE

## YOUR PASSPORT TO GREAT TRAVEL!

## CRITICAL ACCLAIM FOR
## OPEN ROAD TRAVEL GUIDES!

*Whether you're going abroad or planning a trip in the United States, take Open Road along on your journey. Our books have been praised by **Travel & Leisure, The Los Angeles Times, Newsday, Booklist, US News & World Report, Endless Vacation, American Bookseller, Coast to Coast,** and many other magazines and newspapers!*

*Don't just see the world – experience it with Open Road!*

# ABOUT THE AUTHOR

Ron Charles is the author of Open Road travel guides to Spain, Portugal, Bermuda, Holland, and Bahamas (Winter 1996 release). He makes his home in Montreal and New York.

## ACKNOWLEDGMENTS

I'd like to thank the following people: Henny Groenendijk (Netherlands Board of Tourism-Canada), Frances Dion (KLM Royal Dutch Airlines-Canada), Debbie Hubner (KLM Royal Dutch Airlines-Canada), Derek Mc Quarrie (Rail Europe-Canada), Cecile Campeau (Rail Europe-USA) Andrew J. Lazarus (A.J. Lazarus & Associates-USA), Lauren Perlmutter (Tierney & Company-New York), Imad Khalidy (Auto Europe USA), Kelly McGonagle (Auto Europe-USA), Gervaise Frings (VVV-Rotterdam), Marianne van der Zalm-Waterreus (VCB-The Hague), Jan C. Kappenburg (VVV-Groningen), Els M.J. Wamsteeker (VVV-Amsterdam), Math Stroes (VCB-Maastricht), Dita Oosterhuis (VVV-Arnhem), Rob Kaercher (Gemeente Amsterdam), Cas Spijkers (Restaurant de Swean-Oisterwijk), Meine Visser (Hinderloopen), Monique de Haas (Alliance Gastronomique Neerlandaise), Guy Thornton (Union of Foreign Journalists-Amsterdam), Michel Ordeman (Jopen Bier-Haarlem), P.H. Rem (Paleis Het Loo).

Rosann Valentini (Relais & Chateaux-USA), Brenda Homick (Relais & Chateaux-New York), Maryse Masse (Relais & Chateaux-Paris), Carole Poister (Leading Hotels of the World-New York), Nathalie Roet (Golden Tulip Headquarters), Carla Gaita (Jolly Hotels-USA), Irene Bieszke (Grand Hotel Amsterdam), Regien de Boer (NJHC-Amsterdam), Nina Chung (Hostelling International-Canada), Jules & Josephine van Gaalen (Hostellerie van Gallen), Marc & Peter Ritzen (Kasteel Wittem), Johan L.L. Agricola (Landgoed Lauswolt), Fons van Groeningen (Kaatje bij de Sluis), Andre Mol (Kaatje bij de Sluis), Petra van Gestel (Holiday Inn Maastricht), Manon Schenkel ('t Familiehotel Paterswolde), Hans van der Heijden (Carlton Ambassador Hotel), K. Louis Sohl (Hotel Derlon Maastricht), Robert P. Verhoeven (Hotel de Swaen), Marcel van Aelst (Hotel Okura), Greetje Bazuin (Parkhotel Den Haag), Kathrin Tschol (Amstel Hotel-Amsterdam), Juul Klumpes (Hotel Des Indes), Sebastian Dollenkamp (Hotel de l'Europe Amsterdam), Sandra M. Luurssen (Hotel Kurhaus), Charlotte Sparham-Snijders (Park Hotel Rotterdam), Lisbeth Vellekoop (Jolly Hotel Amsterdam), Christa Havekes (Carlton Beach Hotel), Peter Winters (Hotel de Bilderberg), Bram van der Hoek (Park Hotel-Amsterdam), and the hundreds of local VVV officers that showed me the places in their regions that weren't even listed on the maps.

# HIT THE OPEN ROAD - WITH OPEN ROAD PUBLISHING!

Open Road Publishing now has guide books to exciting, fun destinations on four continents. As veteran travelers, our goal is to bring you the best travel guides available anywhere! Here's what we offer:

• All Open Road travel guides are written by authors with a distinct, opinionated point of view – not some sterile committee or team of writers. Our authors are experts in the areas covered and are polished writers.

• Our guides are geared to people who want great vacations, great value, and great tips for both standard tourist sights *and* fun, unique alternatives.

• We're strong on the basics, but we also provide terrific choices for those looking to get off the beaten path and *experience* the country or city – not just *see* it or pass through it.

• We give you the best, but we also tell you about the worst and what to avoid. Nobody should waste their time and money on their hard-earned vacation because of bad or inadequate travel advice.

• Our guides assume nothing. We tell you everything you need to know to have the trip of a lifetime – presented in a fun, literate, no-nonsense style.

• And, above all, we welcome your input, ideas, and suggestions to help us put out the best travel guides possible.

# HOLLAND GUIDE

**YOUR PASSPORT TO GREAT TRAVEL!**

**RON CHARLES**

# OPEN ROAD PUBLISHING

1st Edition

*This book is respectfully dedicated to Henny Groenendijk-Baljet, Kenan Tas, Gervaise Frings, my research assistant Marieke Rietbergen, and all of the wonderful people of the Netherlands who helped make my travels and research so memorable.*

Cover photos courtesy of the Netherlands Board of Tourism, New York. Inside Photography by Ron Charles.

Maps by Rob Perry.

# TABLE OF CONTENTS

# contents

# contents

# contents

# contents

# contents

# 1. INTRODUCTION

When most people think of the Netherlands, images of wooden shoes, tulips, windmills, dikes, and Heineken beer come to mind. But Holland is so much more!

With many historic cities, traditional fishing towns, farming hamlets, and seaside resorts, it won't be easy to decide exactly how to best plan the perfect visit here. Every corner of Holland unveils another mysterious and enchanting sight. This guide will help you plan the type of travel experience tailored to your specific needs. After spending almost a year completing location research, I have based the chapters that follow on the places and events that have impressed me the most.

It's easy to cover a vast amount of the country in complete comfort by train, bus, bicycle, or rental car. The high season (April through September) is an exceptional time to see tulips blooming and enjoy fantastic weather. You can spend your vacation in a combination of castles, charming city center hotels, romantic bed and breakfast inns, and seaside resort hotels for less money than you might imagine. In the space of just one or two weeks, depending on your specific interests, you can enjoy visits through centuries-old castles and royal palaces, walks around beautiful gardens, day trips to old fishing villages, horseback rides along river valleys, and romantic picnic lunches in wonderful rolling countryside estates.

Or you can spend your days hunting for hand-made local crafts and antiques, strolling through historic city neighborhoods, visiting countless fine museums, engaging in every type of sport imaginable, shopping in Europe's finest designer boutiques, swimming and sunbathing on islands and pristine beaches, wining and dining in enchanting gourmet restaurants, trying your luck at a casino, partying all night long with the friendly locals, or just relaxing to your heart's content.

This book has been designed to give you all of the information necessary to create your own unique itinerary. With a little taste for adventure and this guide, your trip to Holland will be unforgettable!

# 2. EXCITING HOLLAND - OVERVIEW!

The following are brief descriptions of the major cities and rural areas that are covered in depth inside this book. For comprehensive walking tours, restaurant and hotel reviews, nightlife listings, excursion possibilities, and more specific detail, please consult each corresponding chapter.

## AMSTERDAM

Holland's largest and most visited city is its capital of **Amsterdam**. Surrounded by a series of picturesque canals lined by 16th through 18th century canal houses, dozens of interesting museums, countless monumental buildings, awesome churches, peaceful gardens, public market squares, world class designer boutiques, diamond cutting establishments, an amazing floating flower market, ethnic restaurants, a world famous red light district, and a thriving night life scene that lasts until sunrise, it's really a shame that most visitors choose to stay only a couple of days here.

It is fairly easy to visit a vast amount of the city in a limited time period since the many of the most famous historic, cultural, and architectural attractions can be found easy walking distance to each other. Just remember to be careful not to walk around alone after sunset, and don't even think about driving or parking your car here! I strongly urge you to leave you wandering around Amsterdam for the final days of your trip through Holland.

Make sure to see the hidden **Begijnhof** courtyard, the musical **Munt** tower, the **Rijksmuseum**, the **Van Gogh** Museum, stop off at the fragrant **Bloemenmarkt**, walk along the **canals**, and party in the **Leidseplein** and **Rembrandtplein**, or take in a movie at the famous **Tuschinski** theater before you leave town. You might also want to shop around for a cut and set diamond while you are wandering around.

## ROTTERDAM

**Rotterdam** is home to the world's largest port, and has been completely rebuilt after it was targeted by bombing raids during World War II. Now a showcase for modern architecture and new concepts in 20th century urban development, it is a truly fascinating city to explore. There are fine museums, great boutiques, water view cafes, excellent restaurants and night life establishments, and a population of hard working middle class residents that are among the most friendly in any major Dutch city.

Most sights and attractions are well within walking distance from each other, and with careful observation you can find charming little districts that are well worth exploring. Any visit here should include a visit via water taxi to the **Hotel New York**, and short hikes to the **Oudehaven** and **Delfshaven** historical harbors.

## DEN HAAG

**Den Haag**, seat of the Dutch government, is perhaps the most elegant cosmopolitan center to visit in all of Holland. Home to the Queen, The Hague is a safe and relaxing destination to spend at least a few days. In the space of a few blocks you can find fantastic mansions, palaces, museums, restaurants, and boutiques. As summer approaches, many residents shed their suits and ties before heading out (in various states of undress) to the nearby beaches of **Schevenginen**.

Make sure that during your stay you explore the **Denneweg** and **Noordeinde** shopping streets, the **Binnenhof** parliamentary complex, the amazing **Mauritshuis** museum, the 16th century **De Grote of St. Jacobskerk** church, the impressive old world **Hotel Des Indes**, the **Passage** shopping arcade, the **Plaats** and **Plein** squares, and the nearby beaches.

## DELFT

**Delft** is the place to head for unforgettable inner city walks past beautiful old canal houses and countless historic monuments. Known around the globe for its hand crafted "Delftware", this wonderful small city was also the birthplace of Golden Age artist Johannes Vermeer. While over 15% of the local population is comprised of university students, the town still has a life and ambiance of its own. There are dozens of bridges spanning the various romantic canals of Delft that can bring you past many of the fine structures, plazas, and tranquil side streets now famous throughout Europe.

Some of the most unique and memorable highlights here include visits to the popular café-lined **Markt** square with its bold **Nieuwe Kerk** and **Stadhuis** buildings, shopping in some of the region's best antique shops, enjoyable lunches on canal-side terraces, bargaining with the merchants for unusual objects found at memorable outdoor markets, quick stops inside as many as half a dozen great little museums, a tranquil canal boat cruise through the heart of the old town, and perhaps a visit to a **Delftware** factory before trying one of the city's many fine restaurants and night spots. Delft is especially enjoyable during the much less crowded low season months.

## MAASTRICHT

The sophisticated city of **Maastricht** continues to be greatly influenced by the culture and economic prosperity of neighboring Belgium and Germany. A short walk through any of downtown's unforgettably romantic and historic plazas and their adjacent side streets will soon reveal hundreds of rather well dressed citizens in the continual process of window shopping at fine designer boutiques and art galleries. A few days spend in and around town and its dramatic neighboring communities will reveal countless monumental castles and churches that were fortunately spared the perils of destruction from war raids.

Highlights of any trip to Maastricht are walks around the famous **Onze Lieve Vrouwe Plein** and **Markt** square, a stroll or boat ride the **Maas** river, hikes atop the ruins of the towering fortified walls, a fine meal in one of dozens of specialty restaurants, stop on an outdoor cafe on the **Vrithof** square, shopping on the historic **Stokstraat**, visiting medieval basilicas, checking out a typical outdoor market, and partying with the locals in unusual little cafes and pubs.

## VALKENBURG

The resort town of **Valkenburg** was once a quaint and peaceful farming village on the banks of the Geul river with roots dating back to the Roman era. Thousands of English, Belgian, and German tourists arrive each week of the high season, and fill up the town's tiny "Centrum". Most of the historic relics of the Valkenburg's medieval heyday now lie in ruins, but it's really worth a trip inside of the many strange underground Roman era quarries have been imaginatively utilized over the centuries.

Now that so many foreigners vacation here, literally dozens of amusing attractions and theme parks have sprung up within blocks of each other. Come prepared for crowds during the summer, and you'll need plenty of money. Make sure to also bike, drive, or catch a bus to a handful of incredibly friendly little hamlets such as **Wittem**, **Epen**, and **Mechelen**, (each with a couple of charming inns and rustic local cafes) within a 20 kilometer (12 mile) radius of downtown Valkenburg.

## LEIDEN

The university city of **Leiden**, birthplace of the master artist Rembrandt, is a great place to spend at least a day or two. It is the combination of the vast student population, and the presence of so many dramatic structures, that makes this small city a perfect place to wander around and discover you favorite museums, cafes, student filled restaurants, and great boutiques. Among the best places to visit are the **voor Volkenkunde**, **De Lakenhal**, and **van Oudheden** museums, the **Burcht** fortress, and the **Hortus Botanicus** gardens.

## ARNHEM

The working class city of **Arnhem** makes a delightful sight for a one or two day visit. North Americans may remember Arnhem as the sight of World War II's disastrous "**Operation Market Garden**" in September of 1944. The entire region around the city is filled with small towns such as Oosterbeek that regularly pay homage to this heroic effort, and are marked by the graves of the thousands of allied soldiers that were killed during this horrific 9 day battle.

Arnhem contains many sights well worth visiting, including the amusing **Koernmarkt** square with its many bars and cafes, the **Marktplaats** square which is home to a fantastic outdoor market and reconstructed church, several rebuilt medieval houses and monuments, some of the best shopping streets in the country, and a population of hard working people that go out of their way to be friendly to anyone from our part of the world. Also make sure to take the time to get to nearby sights such as **Oosterbeek**, **Apeldoorn**, the **Naational Park de Hoge Veluwe**, and the **Openluchtmuseum**..

## UTRECHT

**Utrecht** is the nation's forth biggest city, yet it has retained much of its small village ambiance. Graced by patrician mansion lined canals leading to the nearby Rhine river, this energetic university city has enough sights and amusing activities to keep anyone busy for a couple of days. As you stroll along the canals and side streets of the "Centrum", make sure to keep your eyes open for the many old wharves, almshouses, intimate cafes, and secluded inner courtyard gardens that help make Utrecht so enjoyable for locals and visitors alike.

Among the highlights of any trip here would be a stop at some of the city's great outdoor markets, a refreshing walk up to the viewing deck of the **Domtoren** tower, peeking inside several Gothic churches, a trip by canal boat along the nearby countryside estates, and fascinating tours through the **van Speelklok tot Pierement**, **Centraal**, and **Catharijneconvent** museums that display everything from antique musical instruments to masterpieces of medieval art and modern Dutch furnishings.

## HAARLEM

Known locally as the **Bloemenstad** (The City of Flowers), **Haarlem** is full of 18th century canal and town houses that display a beautiful assortment of window boxes and ceramic pots full of blooming multicolored flowers from April through October each year. There are dozens of worthwhile attractions, museums, quaint side streets, reasonably priced boutiques, fine restaurants, and friendly night-time venues to explore in complete safety here. Since this is one of the closest cities to Holland's main **Schiphol International Airport**, and is much more affordably priced than Amsterdam, Haarlem makes a perfect overnight destination to either begin or end your memorable vacation through the Netherlands.

Don't leave town without popping into the **Teylers** and **Frans Hals Museums**, a few of the **Hofje** almshouses, the **Grote Kerk** inside the middle of the entertaining **Grote Markt**, and perhaps a quick dip in the see at **Zandvoort**.

## GRONINGEN

The circular canal-bordered Centrum district of **Groningen** is only 1.2 kilometers (3/4 of a mile) in width, but still has dozens of fantastic places to visit. During a stress-free trip here you can mingle with thousands of interesting university students, shop in a wide variety of reasonably priced designer boutiques, enjoy one of the almost daily outdoor markets, find hidden gardens, stroll past countless 15th through 20th century monumental structures, chance your luck at a great casino, visit fine art museums, and drink with the locals until the sun comes up.

The people of this northernmost major city are really friendly, and will usually be glad to show visitors around the sights that only a native would even know about. Besides the city itself, there are several unusual attraction filled villages such as **Eenrum**, **Leens**, and **Houwerzijl** that can be accessed by car, bus, and bicycle from Groningen.

## HOW TO USE THIS BOOK

The chapters within this guide have been divided into logical and manageable sources for information on specific topics and localities. The first sections of this book deal with the vital information that a potential visitor must have before attempting to plan a great trip. You will find up-to-date information about entry requirements, customs regulations, passports, visas, climatic conditions, and other documents and details that may need to be either considered or actually obtained before you depart for Europe.

The next few chapters contain the necessary details which will help to explain the situations which they can expect upon arrival in Holland. There are detailed descriptions regarding local time, electricity, business hours, currency, climate, medical services, post offices, communications, holidays, and tourist information resources. Also included are special sections for the physically challenged, what to do in case of emergencies, entertainment prospects, and a brief history of the Netherlands.

After you know the basics, I have developed several chapters on how to best plan and book your vacation. You will find insider tips and detailed information on finding the best free tourist maps and brochures, booking the lowest international airfares, selecting the right travel specialist, and making sure that you end up with the kind of vacation that fits your needs. Additional sections will cover all of the facts about traveling by rental car, bus, train, or plane within Holland, as well as which method of transportation may be best suited to your tastes and needs.

After the previous chapters have provided you with the basic information needed to get you to Holland, I have moved on to describe and explain the sights and infrastructure of several of Holland's major cities and nearby charming rural historic villages. Each of these chapters will provide an in-depth look at what to see and do while you are in the Netherlands, and includes step by step walking tours to all the major attractions. There is also is an intensive chapter concerning what to expect from each classification of accommodations within Holland, including romantic deluxe castles, manor houses, seaside resorts, bed and breakfast inns, farm houses, villas, apartments, pensions, youth hostels, camp sites and even cheap rooms in private houses.

With some careful reading, you can easily determine which locations you wish to spend one night or more. Additional information such as local history and unique traditions is also be provided. The hundreds of listings and reviews in this publication will include directions by foot, bicycle, and/or public and private transportation to every notable attraction in and near the major cities of interest to visitors. I also point out the sights via self-guided walking tours, and direct you towards many enjoyable day trips and excursions, sporting activities, breweries, historical sights, wildlife zones, and charming off the beaten path adventures. I have added my own firsthand suggestions and reviews of terrific accommodations in all price ranges, regional restaurants, and evening diversions.

After reading this book, you will be a well-informed and culturally sensitive visitor who can travel throughout Holland with almost no stress. The best traveler is the well-prepared traveler, and that is what I am trying to achieve with this book. Remember that phone numbers and prices are constantly changing in Holland, and you should be prepared to ask for the assistance of the country's many helpful local VVV tourist offices during your vacation. With Holland Guide to assist you, I'm confident that you'll have the trip of a lifetime!

**WINDMILL IN ZEELAND**

# 3. SUGGESTED ITINERARIES
## FOR THE PERFECT HOLLAND VACATION!

### LONG WEEKEND IN AMSTERDAM
**(4 days/3 nights)**
   This tour is designed especially for those who have limited time in Holland and wish to focus on the area in and around Amsterdam.

**DAY 1**
Arrive in Amsterdam.
Check into your hotel.
Take a one hour canal boat cruise early in the morning.
Follow walking tour #1 as listed in the Amsterdam chapter.
Have lunch.
Follow walking tour # 2 as listed in the Amsterdam chapter.
Enjoy an fine Dutch dinner.
Overnight in **Amsterdam**.

**DAY 2**
Follow walking tour #3 as listed in the Amsterdam chapter.
Have lunch.
Follow walking tour #4 as listed in the Amsterdam chapter.
Enjoy an exotic Indonesian meal.
Visit some of the city's excellent night life venues.
Overnight in **Amsterdam**.

**DAY 3**
Depart Amsterdam on a half-day guided excursion by bus.
Return to Amsterdam.
Have lunch.
Shop and wander around all afternoon.
Stop off for a beer or a coffee at a brown café.
Go to a movie at the Tuschinski theater.

Enjoy a great dinner.
Visit some more of Amsterdam's excellent night life venues.
Overnight in **Amsterdam**.

**DAY 4**
Last minute shopping in Amsterdam before departure.
Have lunch.
Check out of your hotel – No Overnight.

## BASIC TOUR OF CENTRAL HOLLAND
**(8 days/7 nights)**
This is a good choice for those who want to see Amsterdam, and would like to also visit a few of the nearby major cities and attractions. (Minimal travel times).

**DAY 1**
Arrive in Amsterdam.
Take a 30 minute train or car ride directly to Leiden.
Check into your hotel.
Have lunch.
Follow the walking tour listed in the Leiden chapter.
Enjoy a fine dinner.
Overnight in **Leiden**.

**DAY 2**
Catch an early morning bus to Keukenhof gardens in Lisse (during high season).
Return to Leiden.
Check out of your hotel.
Take a 20 minute train or car ride to Den Haag.
Have lunch.
Follow walking tour #1 as listed in the Den Haag chapter.
Enjoy an great gourmet meal.
Visit some of the Denneweg's great bars and cafés.
Overnight in **Den Haag**.

**DAY 3**
Follow walking tour #2 as listed in the Den Haag chapter.
Have lunch.
Take a 15 minute tram ride to Scheveningen.
Follow walking tour #4 (Scheveningen) as listed in the Den Haag chapter.
Have a good fish dinner near the ocean.
Return to Den Haag.

Visit some of the city's good night life.
Overnight in **Den Haag**.

**DAY 4**
Check out of your hotel.
Take a 10 minute train or car ride to Delft.
Check into your hotel.
Take an early afternoon 45 minute canal boat cruise through Delft.
Enjoy a fine dinner at a canalfront restaurant.
Visit a few of the outdoor terraces and cafes.
Overnight in **Delft.**

**DAY 5**
Follow the walking tour listed in the Delft chapter.
Have lunch.
Shop and wander around Delft.
Enjoy a good dinner in a local restaurant.
Overnight in **Delft**.

**DAY 6**
Check out of your hotel.
Take a 40 minute train ride to Amsterdam.
Check in to your hotel.
Follow walking tour #1 as listed in the Amsterdam chapter.
Have lunch.
Follow walking tour #2 as listed in the Amsterdam chapter.
Enjoy an exotic Indonesian meal.
Stop for a beer or a coffee in on of the many brown cafés.
Overnight in **Amsterdam**.

**DAY 7**
Follow walking tour #3 as listed in the Amsterdam chapter.
Have lunch.
Follow walking tour #4 as listed in the Amsterdam chapter.
Enjoy an fine Dutch dinner.
Visit some of the city's excellent night life venues.
Overnight in **Amsterdam**.

**DAY 8**
Last minute shopping in Amsterdam before departure.
Have lunch.
Check out of your hotel – No Overnight.

## BIG CITY TOUR

**(10 days/ 9 nights)**
 If you are trying to see a fair amount of the Holland's most impressive cities, and have a reasonable amount of time, this is one good way to do it. (Moderate to long travel times).

### DAY 1
Arrive in Amsterdam.
Check into your hotel.
Take a one hour canal boat cruise early in the morning.
Follow walking tour #1 as listed in the Amsterdam chapter.
Have lunch.
Follow walking tour #2 as listed in the Amsterdam chapter.
Enjoy an exotic Indonesian meal.
Overnight in **Amsterdam**.

### DAY 2
Follow walking tour #3 as listed in the Amsterdam chapter.
Have lunch.
Follow walking tour #4 as listed in the Amsterdam chapter.
Enjoy a typical Dutch dinner.
Visit some of the city's excellent night life venues.
Overnight in **Amsterdam**.

### DAY 3
Check out of your hotel.
Take a 50 minute train or car ride to Den Haag.
Check into your hotel.
Have lunch.
Follow walking tour #1 as listed in the Den Haag chapter.
Enjoy an inexpensive local meal.
Visit some of the city's great clubs and bars.
Overnight in **Den Haag**.

### DAY 4
Follow walking tour #2 as listed in the Den Haag chapter.
Have lunch.
Take a 15 minute tram ride to Scheveningen.
Follow walking tour #4 (Scheveningen) as listed in the Den Haag chapter.
Have a good fish dinner near the ocean.
Return to Den Haag.
Visit some of the city's good nightlife.
Overnight in **Den Haag**.

**DAY 5**
Check out of your hotel.
Take a 25 minute train or car ride to Rotterdam.
Check into your hotel.
Have lunch.
Follow walking tour # 1 as listed in the Rotterdam chapter.
Enjoy an inexpensive local meal.
Visit some of the city's great clubs and bars.
Overnight in **Rotterdam**.

**DAY 6**
Follow walking tour #2 as listed in the Rotterdam chapter
Enjoy a fine meal.
Overnight in **Rotterdam**.

**DAY 7**
Check out of your hotel.
Take a two hour train or car ride to Maastricht.
Check into your hotel.
Have lunch.
Follow the walking tour as listed in the Maastricht chapter.
Enjoy a superb gourmet meal.
Overnight in **Maastricht**.

**DAY 8**
Use a car, bus, or bicycle to get to Mechelen, Epen, and Wittem.
Have lunch
Return to Maastricht.
Enjoy a hearty local meal.
Overnight in **Maastricht**.

**DAY 9**
Check out of your hotel.
Take a two hour train or car ride to Utrecht.
Check into your hotel.
Have lunch.
Follow the walking tour as listed in the Utrecht chapter.
Enjoy a good local meal.
Overnight in **Utrecht**.

**DAY 10**
Check out of your hotel.
Take a one hour train or car ride to Amsterdam.
Have lunch – No Overnight.

## EXTENDED TOUR OF CENTRAL HOLLAND
**(12 days/ 11 nights)**
    This route has been created for people that want to visit several unforgettable old cities in a fairly short amount of time. (Moderate travel times).

**DAY 1**
Arrive in Amsterdam.
Take a 10 minute train or car ride directly to Haarlem.
Check into your hotel.
Have lunch.
Follow the walking tour listed in the Haarlem chapter.
Enjoy a fine dinner.
Overnight in **Haarlem**.

**DAY 2**
Spend part of the morning relaxing in café on the Grote Markt.
Shop and browse through the city's unique galleries.
Enjoy an inexpensive local dinner.
Visit the bars of Haarlem.
Overnight in **Haarlem**.

**DAY 3**
Check out of your hotel.
Take a 50 minute train or car ride to Den Haag.
Have lunch.
Follow walking tour #1 as listed in the Den Haag chapter.
Enjoy an inexpensive local meal.
Visit some of the city's great clubs and bars.
Overnight in **Den Haag**.

**DAY 4**
Follow walking tour #2 as listed in the Den Haag chapter.
Have lunch.
Take a 15 minute tram ride to Scheveningen.
Follow walking tour #4 (Scheveningen) as listed in the Den Haag chapter.
Have a good fish dinner near the ocean.

Return to Den Haag.
Visit some of the city's good night life.
Overnight in **Den Haag**.

**DAY 5**
Check out of your hotel.
Take a 10 minute train or car ride to Delft.
Check into your hotel.
Take an early afternoon 45 minute canal boat cruise through Delft.
Enjoy a fine dinner at a canalfront restaurant.
Visit a few of the outdoor terraces and cafes.
Overnight in **Delft.**

**DAY 6**
Follow the walking tour listed in the Delft chapter.
Have lunch.
Shop and wander around Delft.
Enjoy a good dinner in a local restaurant.
Overnight in **Delft**.

**DAY 7**
Check out of your hotel.
Take a 55 minute train or car ride to Utrecht.
Check into your hotel.
Follow the walking tour as listed in the Utrecht chapter.
Enjoy a great dinner on a wharfside terrace.
Visit several great student bars and clubs.
Overnight in **Utrecht**.

**DAY 8**
Take a morning one hour canal boat cruise through Utrecht.
Go to one of the city's great outdoor markets.
Shop and bargain hunt in downtown's many odd little boutiques.
Enjoy a good inexpensive dinner.
Visit a few of the area cafés.
Overnight in **Utrecht**.

**DAY 9**
Check out of your hotel.
Take a 50 minute train ride to Amsterdam.
Check in to your hotel.
Follow walking tour #1 as listed in the Amsterdam chapter.
Have lunch.

Follow walking tour #2 as listed in the Amsterdam chapter.
Enjoy an exotic Indonesian meal.
Go to a movie at the Tushinski theater.
Overnight in **Amsterdam**.

**DAY 10**
Follow walking tour #3 as listed in the Amsterdam chapter.
Have lunch.
Follow walking tour #4 as listed in the Amsterdam chapter.
Enjoy an fine Dutch dinner.
Visit some of the city's excellent night life venues.
Overnight in **Amsterdam**.

**DAY 11**
Depart Amsterdam on a half-day guided excursion by bus.
Have lunch.
Follow walking tour #5 or #6 as listed in the Amsterdam chapter.
Enjoy a fantastic gourmet meal.
Overnight in **Amsterdam**.

**DAY 12**
Last minute shopping in Amsterdam before departure.
Have lunch.
Check out of your hotel – No Overnight.

## HIGHLIGHTS OF HOLLAND TOUR
**(16 days / 15 nights)**
This tour is perfect for those trying to find the most enchanting cities and villages in Holland and have plenty of time to run around. (Moderate to Long travel times).

**DAY 1**
Arrive in Amsterdam.
Take a 35 minute train or car ride directly to Den Haag.
Check into your hotel.
Have lunch.
Follow walking tour # 1 as listed in the Den Haag chapter.
Enjoy a fine dinner.
Overnight in **Den Haag**.

**DAY 2**
Follow walking tour #2 as listed in the Den Haag chapter.
Have lunch.

Take a 15 minute tram ride to Scheveningen.
Follow walking tour #4 (Scheveningen) as listed in the Den Haag chapter.
Have a good fish dinner near the ocean.
Return to Den Haag.
Visit some of the city's good night life.
Overnight in **Den Haag**.

## DAY 3
Check out of your hotel.
Take a 10 minute train or car ride to Delft.
Check into your hotel.
Take the walking tour as listed in the Delft chapter.
Enjoy a fine dinner at a canalfront restaurant.
Visit a few of the outdoor terraces and cafes.
Overnight in **Delft.**

## DAY 4
Check out of your hotel.
Take a two hour train or car ride to Maastricht.
Check into your hotel.
Have lunch.
Follow the walking tour as listed in the Maastricht chapter.
Enjoy a superb gourmet meal.
Overnight in **Maastricht**.

## DAY 5
Use a car, bus, or bicycle to get to Mechelen, Epen, and Wittem.
Have lunch.
Return to Maastricht.
Enjoy a hearty local meal.
Overnight in **Maastricht**.

## DAY 6
Check out of your hotel.
Take a 1 and 1/2 hour train or car ride to Arnhem.
Check into your hotel.
Have lunch.
Follow the walking tour as listed in the Arnhem chapter.
Enjoy a good local meal.
Overnight in **Arnhem**.

**DAY 7**
Use a car, bus, or bicycle to get to the Park Naational de Hoge Veluwe
Have lunch.
Return to Arnhem.
Enjoy a good local meal.
Visit some of the cafes off the Korenmarkt.
Overnight in **Arnhem**.

**DAY 8**
Check out of your hotel.
Take a 1 and 1/2 hour train or car ride to Groningen.
Check into your hotel.
Have lunch.
Follow the walking tour as listed in the Groningen chapter.
Enjoy a fine informal meal.
Overnight in **Groningen**.

**DAY 9**
Use a car, bus, or bicycle to get to Eenrum, Leens, and Houwerzijl.
Have lunch.
Return to Groningen.
Enjoy a good local meal.
Visit some of the bars near the Grote Markt.
Overnight in **Groningen**.

**DAY 10**
Check out of your hotel.
Take a 1 and 1/2 hour train or car ride to Utrecht.
Check into your hotel.
Follow the walking tour as listed in the Utrecht chapter.
Enjoy a great dinner on a wharfside terrace.
Visit several great student bars and clubs.
Overnight in **Utrecht**.

**DAY 11**
Take a morning one hour canal boat cruise through Utrecht.
Go to one of the city's great outdoor markets.
Shop and bargain hunt in downtown's many odd little boutiques.
Enjoy a good inexpensive dinner.
Visit a few of the area cafés.
Overnight in **Utrecht**.

**DAY 12**
Check out of your hotel.
Take a 50 minute train or car ride to Haarlem.
Check into your hotel.
Have lunch.
Follow the walking tour listed in the Haarlem chapter.
Enjoy a fine dinner.
Overnight in **Haarlem**.

**DAY 13**
Check out of your hotel.
Take a 20 minute train or car ride to Amsterdam.
Check into your hotel.
Follow walking tour #1 as listed in the Amsterdam chapter.
Have lunch.
Follow walking tour #2 as listed in the Amsterdam chapter.
Enjoy an inexpensive meal.
Visit some of the city's excellent night life venues.
Overnight in **Amsterdam**.

**DAY 14**
Follow walking tour #3 as listed in the Amsterdam chapter.
Have lunch.
Follow walking tour #4 as listed in the Amsterdam chapter.
Enjoy an fine Dutch dinner.
Go to a movie at the Tushinski theater.
Overnight in **Amsterdam**.

**DAY 15**
Depart Amsterdam on a half-day guided excursion by bus.
Have lunch.
Follow walking tour # 5 or # 6 as listed in the Amsterdam chapter.
Enjoy a fantastic gourmet meal.
Overnight in **Amsterdam**.

**DAY 16**
Last minute shopping in Amsterdam before departure.
Have lunch.
Check out of your hotel – No Overnight.

# 4. LAND & PEOPLE

The beautiful country of **Holland** (officially known as **The Netherlands**) covers 41,160 square kilometers (15,892 square miles) of northwestern Europe. Bordered by the **North Sea**, **Belgium**, and **Germany**, it encompasses 12 unique provinces that have a combined population of just over 15 million residents. While it is true that much of the country is flat, there are some scattered rolling hillsides, a handful of small islands, and a dramatic coastline that has played an important role in the history and development of this wealthy nation.

For such a small country, Holland has a surprising amount of diversity. While the big cities such as Amsterdam tend to draw the most tourists, travelers should make a strong effort to get out to the smaller cities, quaint villages, university towns, and of course the coastline. Much of the countryside is dotted by dikes that have allowed the Dutch to reclaim vast areas of land that were formerly submerged – and about 925 windmills. With over one-third of its land mass resting below sea level, without these (and more modern) tools Holland would face a constant series of catastrophic floods.

Over 95% of the people living in Holland are of Dutch origin. The few growing immigrant groups are those from Indonesia and Turkey, but hundreds of refugees arrive monthly from various war-torn nations. The country's official language is Dutch, an expressive but rather difficult language for non-natives to pick up quickly. Most of you will be relieved to know that English is spoken by the vast majority of people here, even in the most remote corners. Old World traditions and customs can still be found in some areas, including **Volendam** (Noord-Holland) where residents still wear wooden shoes, and **Middelburg** (Zeeland) where men wear round hats and black pants with silver buttons while women adorn themselves with hand made lace shawls.

The Dutch people themselves are polite, practical, liberal, modest, and extremely well educated. While some 40% of the population are Catholic, since Reformation the **Dutch Reformed Church** has been accepted by most of those living in the north and central regions. These

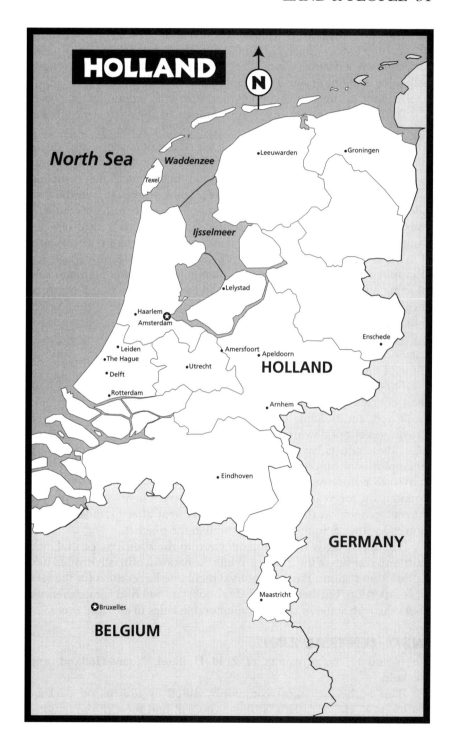

days, however, religion has a minor role in daily life. Social problems have become the focus of most conversations. The vast majority of people in Holland have a positive approach to life and usually combine hard work with a fair amount of fun. They tend to describe their lifestyle as "cozy," a term that can only be fully understood after a fair amount of time here.

Dutch people rarely cover the windows of their street-view living rooms, seemingly inviting any curious passer-by invade their privacy. They can be a bit frugal at times (a sale here is a major event!), and the so-called Dutch Treat means that on dates and social events all participants are expected to split the bill. No matter how much the locals may complain about not being paid enough, they somehow always seem to have the cash needed for partying and to take long vacations on the beaches of southern Europe (or beyond) during the winter. Since the credit card has not caught on big here, many people still use cash for purchases of every size.

While **Queen Beatrix** is the official head of state, most political decisions are made by the elected parliament. With rather high standard of living and heavy taxes imposed on all consumer goods and personal income, the Netherlands has been able to maintain one of the world's most generous social programs. All Dutch citizens are entitled to receive universal health care, free education, enormous unemployment insurance benefits, and much more. For some visitors from North America some of the Netherlands' domestic policies may seem strange.

For example, the open sale of marijuana, paying students to continue their education, creating thousands of strange jobs just to keep people employed, and building brothels on the outskirts of town to keep the prostitutes out of downtown areas. But the evidence seems to show that all of these efforts have paid off in fighting crime, drug addiction, and unemployment. Since the government needs to reduce its spending it has started to reduce many of these social benefits that their citizens have counted on for years. While it becomes increasingly difficult for the current generation to find gainful employment after graduating from university, they are among the first to feel the pinch.

The following is a brief introduction to the southern, central, and northern sections of the country. While the nation is officially divided into 12 different regions, I have combined them into larger areas for the sake of comparison. Further along in this book, you will find comprehensive tours through some of the most memorable cities in all these zones.

## WEST-CENTRAL ZONE

Including the provinces of **Zuid Holland**, **Noord-Holland**, and **Zeeland**.

This is the area most commonly visited by tourists on package vacations to Holland. This is where you will find most of the nation's largest cities, including **Amsterdam, Rotterdam, Den Haag, Delft, Leiden,** and **Haarlem**. The vast majority of this zone is made up of flat inland areas that have small agricultural zones, but there are also some nice coastal sections to the west where both sand dune beaches and major seaside resort developments can be found resting along-side each other.

If you head all the way north there are a handful of amazing little harbor villages with windmills that really take you back in time. Within the space of a week, touring west-central Holland you can wander through some of Europe's most enjoyable cities, find small traditional lakeside villages lined with windmills, cycle or sail around the giant Ijsselmeer man made lake, day trip to quiet little harbor towns of **Zeeland** where people dress in traditional costumes, hop on a ferry to a great island called **Texel**, and get a good view of the flowers in bloom at **Keukenhof** during the warmer months.

This is a good destination for the first time visitor, and from here you are usually less than one hour away from any of this zone's major cities, fabulous windmills, gardens, manor houses, cheese markets, and villages. Many people use Amsterdam as a base from which to take day trips through this whole area.

## EAST-CENTRAL ZONE

Including the provinces of **Utrecht, Flevoland, Gelderland**, and **Overijssel**.

This large chunk of land stretches between the giant **Ijsselmeer lake**, and heads eastward towards the German border. The important cities of **Utrecht** and **Arnhem** can be found in this zone, as well as hundreds of tiny communities that each have their own legends to tell. Since the Ijjselmeer itself affects a large segment of this zone, it is important to note that it did not exist as such some 80 years ago. The 296,000-acre man made body of water was formed after the construction of a massive dike cut off part of the Zuiderzee sea and created not only the lake, but also allowed the reclamation of over half a million acres of agricultural land.

This small section of east-central Holland that has the most interesting little villages and former pirate havens to discover, and is also a great destination for every imaginable water sport. Further towards the east is the huge **Naational Park de Hoge Veluwe**, the country's largest and most interesting park.

## SOUTHERN ZONE

Including the provinces of **Noord-Brabant** and **Limburg**.

These lower areas are bordered by Belgium and Germany, and have an ambiance that is much different than any other in Holland. The major city here is **Maastricht**, but there are also many charming villages that line the coastal areas and more interior parts of this zone. Of particular note are the limestone hills (the highest points in the Netherlands) and old half timber barns that cover many adorable little villages in much of Limburg and the historic cities of Noord-Brabant. Since this area is a bit far from the heart of Holland, many tourists never make this far south. Make sure to either rent a bicycle or a car and head out for some of the country's most memorable day trips. If you want my advice, I would not leave Holland without checking out the area just outside of **Valkenburg**.

## NORTHERN ZONE

Including the provinces of **Friesland**, **Drenthe**, and **Groningen**.

The topography of this more isolated and remote zone includes a large percentage of reclaimed land. While a few major cities such as **Groningen** can be found here, much of this area is covered by large farms. This is the part of Holland that was first settled by prehistoric peoples and is dotted with prehistoric Hunnebed megaliths. The enchanting coastal areas are packed with antique wooden sailing boats and there are even a few ferries to take you off on a journey to one of several great islands.

Few North Americans make it this far north, since its highlights are a bit far from each other. This is a peaceful part of the world where people are generally in no particular rush. Throughout the year it is an outdoor sporting paradise, and those seeking real adventure should make the effort to get up here, especially during the summer when the islands and lakes make for an idyllic setting.

**COME SAILING IN FRIESLAND!**

# 5. A SHORT HISTORY

## PREHISTORIC HOLLAND

Not much is known about the prehistoric residents who created small settlements in what is now eastern Holland as far back as about 30,000 BC. These seemingly tribal peoples have left us little evidence to document their existence. Sometime around 4600 BC, **Neolithic** peoples began to develop agriculturally-based settlements in what is now the southernmost province of Limburg.

The **Hunebeds and Nomads** took control over large sections of what is now northeastern Holland. Sometime around 275 BC, an influx of **Germanic** tribes begin to settle north of the Rhine river, while at about the same time **Celtic** tribes headed west and south of the Rhine river. Some of the most compelling artifacts from these rather different civilizations are the ancient megaliths, burial mounds, pottery, and early *terpen* (water retention walls) used in the northern coastal areas to protect settlements from the encroaching sea, and pottery.

## THE ROMANS COME & GO

Soon after **Julius Caesar** and his Roman troops arrived on the scene in 57 BC, they conquered the Celtic **Belgae** tribes. Now almost all of the land south of the Rhine river was absorbed into the Roman administered province of **Gallia Belgica**, and farming estates began to develop along important military routes. At the same time, Roman attempts to occupy the areas north of the Rhine River were unsuccessful, and the Germanic Frisians continued to flourish, learning the hard way how to tame both the coast and interior sections of the northern regions.

Things were rather stable for almost four centuries until the decline of the Roman empire began to set in. Villages were left undefended, fortresses were abandoned, and by 407 AD, the Germanic **Franks** were in control.

## THE FRANKISH (MEROVINGIAN) EMPIRE

By the middle of the 6th century, the Franks moved began to join forces with other tribes in Belgium and France and together formed the so-called Merovingian kingdom ruled by **King Clovis**. Then referred to as Austrasia, the Merovingian controlled regions of southern Holland soon began to accept Christianity. The Frankish nobles encouraged their rulers to try and capture lands up north that were still firmly in the hands of the Frisians. After years of bloody skirmishes, in 734 Frankish King Pepin was able to defeat the Frisians and extend his empire through northern Holland.

As King Pepin's son **Charlemagne** took the throne, powerful bishops made sure that even the northernmost reaches of this new empire were converted to Christianity, and the Franks now had power over the entire Benelux region (Holland, Belgium, and Luxembourg). From this point onwards a series of powerful counts were given large counties to administer, with churches and monasteries receiving secular jurisdiction to assure their unique powers and immunity from taxes. In the year 800, as Charlemagne boldly continued to expand his kingdom through other parts of Europe, he was crowned **Holy Roman Emperor** by the pope.

For several years after Charlemagne's death in 814, the empire was racked by years of brutal political and military infighting. It was during this same period of time that Viking warriors plundered many villages and raided their church's treasuries. The situation grew worse until finally in 843, the Treaty of Verdun enforced the empire's partition into three separate kingdoms, to appease each of Charlemagne's three battling grandsons. The new region of **Lotharingia** now included all of Benelux.

Soon after, the kingdom was split up yet again, this time with the north and eastern regions ruled by German-aligned Franks, with the southern and western regions now ruled by French-aligned Franks. This meant that most of the territory that now makes up Holland, with the exception of the southern regions, came under the indirect control of the German King (also crowned as the Holy Emperor of Rome).

## THE COUNTS TAKE POWER

Between the 10th and 12th centuries, powerful counts begin buy as much land as possible and establish their own feudal counties in various sections of the empire. As these new areas began prospering from their new industries and maritime trade routes, many important cities began to spring up or greatly expand along the major rivers' banks. At that point, the real power shifted to just a handful of greedy noblemen that start to rule their counties in a more autonomous manner. This did not sit well with the German King they were supposedly aligned to, so the king began to appoint carefully selected dukes and powerful religious leaders to try and retake political control of these merging counties.

The church was given a tremendous amount of land, power, and political immunity in exchange for their help to the crown, and soon became the dominant force in many regions. It was also during this era that many dikes, windmills, and polders were built to help reclaim formerly useless swamps and marshes, thus greatly increasing the amount of productive land in both coastal and inland counties..

## THE CITIES GAIN SOME AUTONOMY

In the south, the French-controlled area of **Flanders** (including what is now Limburg) began to expand its textile industries during the 11th and 12th centuries. Since not enough sheep were being raised in the region, several major factories and merchants became dependent on English ships to bring them raw materials. Of course this created a unique set of problems, since England was consistently at war with the French empire that was supposed to be ruling Flanders.

At around the same time, the German throne was too busy dealing with internal political problems to keep their eyes on this part of their European kingdom. After the **Concordat of Worms** was passed in 1122, the Germans could no longer appoint their own hand-picked bishops. Now these counties would be ruled by their own counts and bishops, instead of being controlled as part of the rapidly declining German empire.

As the larger towns began to grow at a much faster rate, they soon felt compelled to regain control over their own affairs, and reduce the high taxes they paid to their count. While this path occasionally lead to bloody 12th century battles between townspeople and the ruler's soldiers, it eventually helped to secure more freedoms for many towns. New local laws were established, professional guilds (trade unions) started to get politically active, and municipal taxes became commonplace.

## FROM THE BURGUNDIAN TO THE HABSBURG ERAS

Soon after, French Duke **Philip (the Bold) of Burgundy** married Countess Margaret of Flanders in 1369, he became ruler of Flanders. By 1473, Duke **Charles (the Bold) of Burgundy** aggressively extended French rule through most of what is now Holland. Once Charles had died, his daughter Mary took charge over the empire and soon married Maximillian **of Habsburg**, Austria. In 1482, Mary died in an equestrian accident and Maximillian became ruler of an even larger Habsburg empire that included the former Burgundian territories.

After being crowned as Holy Roman Emperor, Maximillian transferred leadership of his territories in the Low Countries to his son Philip (the Handsome). Upon Philip's death in 1515, his son Charles V takes over, and soon becomes both King of Spain and Emperor of Germany. **Emperor Charles V** extended the Habsburg empire further north into Friesland, Drenthe, and Groningen.

## RELIGIOUS UNREST

By the beginning of the 16th century, many European scholars began to question the role and legitimacy of the Catholic church in politics and daily life. Followers of reformists such as **Martin Luther** and **John Calvin** begin to spread Protestantism to the major cities, but were persecuted for their revolutionary ideas. As Philip II of Spain inherited the throne, he was faced with serious opposition from his subjects in the Netherlands. After fanatical Calvinists began to attack churches, the king sent in his top soldiers to quash any unrest.

With the stern **Duke of Alba** running the show here for Philip II, countless Protestants and Calvinists were tortured and killed by the Spanish mercenaries that occupied many cites, thus planting the seeds of revolt. For many years the Calvinists in the northerly provinces would continuously vow to abolish the Catholic church and its corrupt leadership.

## THE UNITED PROVINCES OF THE NETHERLANDS

**Prince William of Orange** returned to his native Netherlands after several years of self-imposed exile in Germany. Along with those sympathetic to the cause, such as radical Calvinists, Prince William started to organize a series of rebel attacks against the Spanish forces, and in doing so began the **Eighty Years War** in 1568. While the fight did not go all that well for Prince William and his troops at first, later battles eventually resulted in substantial victories. Beginning in 1579, the northern and central Dutch provinces of Friesland, Gelderland, Groningen, Holland, Overijssel, Utrecht, and Zeeland, came together to sign **The Union of Utrecht** that openly declared their intent to end Spanish rule.

These same provinces would again band together, this time in 1581, to declare their independence from Spain and form what they called the **Republic of the United Provinces of the Netherlands**. They also set up a governmental body called the **States-General** that controlled this new union of provinces in military and foreign affairs. The King of Spain refused to acknowledge this document and tightened his bond with Flanders – resulting in a huge rift between the northern and southern parts of the Netherlands. The States-General led to  the Reformation, a period during which the **Calvinist Dutch Reformed Church** became the republic's official religion, public practice of the Catholic faith became illegal for over 300 years, and almost all of the former Catholic churches were either closed or converted.

In July of 1584, Prince William of Orange was assassinated in his Delft residence by an angry Catholic, but the organized resistance to Spain continued under the authority of his son Maurice. As the rebel provinces conquered much of what is now Limburg, Spain's grip loosened. In 1648, the Spanish government finally recognized the independence of Holland in what became known as the **Peace of Westphalia**.

## THE GOLDEN AGE

By the start of the 17th century, the Dutch economy was growing at a rapid rate. The newly formed **Dutch East India Company** and **Dutch West India Company** had secured profitable trading routes throughout Europe and East Asia. New colonies were acquired in Sri Lanka, South Africa, Sumatra, Java, Brazil, Curaçao, St. Martin and Surinam. Powerful banks were set up in Amsterdam to handle the ever-growing flow of trade-related money, and arrange currency exchanges and loans to many Dutch merchants and shippers. After the English started to lose ground with their shipping trade, they got even with the Dutch by forbidding any shipping companies in the Netherlands from participating in the trade or transportation of English products. With tensions already mounting, a conflict known as the Anglo-Dutch war started in 1652 and soon left the poorly equipped Dutch navy in ruins. After accepting defeat two years later, the Dutch gave up many concessions to the English, and found their ability to trade seriously restricted by the English Crown.

There was a great feeling of revenge brewing in the Netherlands, and this period was marked by the expansion and rebuilding of a more sophisticated Dutch navy. In 1667, the Dutch navy attacked England and set afire most of their fleet, which was moored at Chatham.  Prince **William III of Orange** then took over leadership in 1672 and once again restore Dutch trading supremacy.

Calvinists, Jews, and Huguenots flocked to Amsterdam to freely pursue their religious freedom. These new residents brought great skills as world-class merchants and industrialists. Culture and the arts also prospered, as masters such as Frans Hals, Rembrandt, Jan Lievens, Jan Steen, Jacob van Ruisdael, and Johannes Vermeer began painting in their own unique styles during this time.

## THE REPUBLIC ENDS
## & A NEW KINGDOM IS BORN

The 18th century marked the beginning of a rapid decline for the republic. In 1795, only six years after their bloody revolution, French troops invaded the Netherlands and forever put and end to the Republic of the United Provinces of the Netherlands. The newly formed **Batavian Republic** controlled the Netherlands for the next 11 years, and was responsible for replacing the outdated States-General with a more efficient National Assembly, as well as finally ending the reformation. In 1806, the Batavian Republic was replaced by the **Kingdom of Holland** ruled by Napoleon's brother **Louis Bonaparte**, who was then installed in Amsterdam as the new king.

During the French occupation, the towns and citizens of Holland were forced to pay high taxes to their occupiers, and suffered through a depression as the English (who were now at war with the French) blockaded Dutch ports and devastated the kingdom's trade-based economy. He was rather sympathetic to the needs and wishes of Holland, and was forced to abdicate in 1810 after continually avoiding the stern directives sent to him by Napoleon. The kingdom was absorbed into the French empire for a few more years until it collapsed when Napoleon was defeated in Russia.

In 1814, Prince William VI of Orange came back from exile and was then declared as **King William I of the United Kingdom of the Netherlands** during the 1815 Congress of Vienna. During his first year in power. a new constitution was written and a constitutional monarchy was made official. In 1830, a revolution in Flanders led to the emergence of a new separate kingdom to the south (including areas that formerly were part of the Noord-Brabant and Limburg provinces) that we now know as Belgium.

### EUROPE AT WAR

In 1914, when **World War I** started, **Queen Wilhelmina** declared the country's neutrality. The nation unsuccessfully struggled to salvage its economy from the effects of allied blockades of northern European ports during the war. When the war was over, the great depression of the 1930's was equally devastating. As World War II broke out, Holland declared its neutrality once again. This didn't much matter to Germany, and in the matter of a week's time, the Nazis defeated the Dutch army, bombed Rotterdam to the ground, and started a brutal five year occupation of the Netherlands.

Queen Wilhelmina escaped into exile in England, and the Nazis went on to murder well over 225,000 Jews, resistance members, and hostages.

The allied counter-invasion of Holland started with the September 1944 battle known as **Operation Market Garden**, during which British troops were unable to secure a Rhine river bridge crossing in Arnhem. Once the Germans surrendered in April 1945, Queen Wilhelmina returned from her exile and began reconstructing the economy and city centers that had been severely damaged.

In 1948, **Queen Juliana** was crowned, and a year later the Dutch East Indies colonies become the independent Republic of Indonesia. In the 1950's, the Dutch Guiana colony was granted freedom and became the country of Surinam, and the colonies of the Netherlands Antilles also broke away from Dutch control.

## THE RECENT PAST

During the 1960's, Holland developed giant electronics and petro-chemical industries as it began to prosper once again. From now on, the elected government would be headed by coalitions of Catholic, Protestant, and Socialist political parties. In 1980, **Queen Beatrix** is crowned, and remains on the throne to this day.

Holland is a member of the **European Economic Community**, but faces pressures from its larger and more conservative neighbors due to Dutch policies on drugs and social issues. Holland is now one of the world's most liberal and tolerant nations, and maintains a high level of social services paid for by a multitude of taxes.

# 6. PLANNING YOUR TRIP

## BEFORE YOU GO

## WHEN TO VISIT HOLLAND

**High Season**

While Holland is a great place to visit anytime of the year, most people tend to arrive during the late April through mid-September (summer) high season. This is certainly the best time to enjoy great sightseeing weather in every corner of the Netherlands, and gives you the best opportunity to view plenty of incredible flowers.

Unfortunately, high season is also the time of year when the sights, attractions, and cities are at their busiest, so the hotels in resort and tourist related areas tend to charge their highest rates. If you are interested in visiting beaches to swim in warm ocean waters and bask under the heat of the sun, you may prefer the summer months of June, July, and August.

During these months, almost all of Holland's northern and western coastline (and islands) becomes burning hot and overcrowded with vacationing tourists from all over the globe. Since most Europeans receive a full month of vacation with pay (typically during August) the airlines and resort area hotels have no problem with increasing their rates by over 40% during these summer months. Although I have enjoyed the summers in Holland, they are typically not much of a bargain.

**Low Season**

The late March through early April (spring) and late September through mid-November (fall) times offer pleasant, but not always warm or sunny, weather. If you don't mind wearing a sweater or jacket, you can still comfortably run around the country and have an excellent time. While swimming in the sea is definitely out of the question, and about 10% of the major attractions close down, this is still a good time to arrive if you don't expect to see any flowers. Another benefit to these months is the abundance of available accommodations and airfare at low season rates.

The November through March (winter) time period is often filled with long strings of cold, rainy, and windy days. If you have to come here during these months, its best to stick to visiting the major cities. Rain and overcast skies are not uncommon, but you may still find several bright clear days to enjoy. As much as 20% of the country's major attractions close down during this off-off season. This is usually the quietest time to tour the country, and there are few tourists outside of Amsterdam.

## CLIMATE

Being so compact in size, the temperature difference between regions is usually within one degree Celsius. The amount of wind, rainfall, and snow may vary from region to region, but the most common weather systems affect the entire country in a similar manner.

| AVERAGE HIGH & LOW DAILY TEMPERATURES, & AVERAGE RAINFALL | | | |
|---|---|---|---|
| (Based on Amsterdam) | | | |
| | *Avg. High* | *Avg. Low* | *Days of Rain* |
| *January* | 40F | 31F | 19 days |
| | 05C | -1C | |
| *February* | 41F | 32F | 15 days |
| | 05C | 00C | |
| *March* | 48F | 35F | 13 days |
| | 09C | 02C | |
| *April* | 54F | 39F | 14 days |
| | 12C | 04C | |
| *May* | 63F | 46F | 12 days |
| | 18C | 09C | |
| *June* | 67F | 51F | 11 days |
| | 20C | 11C | |
| *July* | 70F | 55F | 13 days |
| | 21C | 12C | |
| *August* | 71F | 56F | 14 days |
| | 21C | 13C | |
| *September* | 66F | 51F | 15 days |
| | 19C | 11C | |
| *October* | 56F | 46F | 17 days |
| | 13C | 09C | |
| *November* | 48F | 37F | 18 days |
| | 09C | 04C | |
| *December* | 43F | 34F | 19 days |
| | 07C | 01C | |

## WHAT TO PACK

Most of you will have little need for suits, ties, expensive dresses, and formal clothing. Only a handful of expensive gourmet restaurants and equally snobby nightclubs will enforce a strict dress code. Any hotel will be pleased to welcome guests that are comfortably attired. The main concern about what to bring to wear should be based on the season which you will be arriving during, and it's typical climatic conditions. Since summers can be quite hot, I suggest lots of thin cotton clothing and a good bathing suit. In the spring and fall it would be wise to pack for mostly cloudy days, and chilly nights, with the possibility of rain at any time. In the winter you should be prepared for anything from rain and snow to an occasional unexpected heat wave.

In all seasons, pack a money belt or sac, an umbrella, bathing suits, a sweater, comfortable walking shoes, sneakers, a waterproof wind breaker, extra glasses or contact lenses, necessary medications with copies of the prescriptions, personal hygiene items, sunglasses, an empty nylon bag for gifts and shopping, an electric converter, hair dryer, sunscreen, lots of film and batteries, a waterproof key holder for swimming, photocopies of your passport, travel insurance documents, a list of travelers check numbers, good maps, this book, and the phone numbers of your travel provider and credit card companies in case of emergencies.

## VISA REGULATIONS

Typically, all US and Canadian citizens require only a valid passport to enter Holland. At the present time, no special vaccines are required to gain entry into the Netherlands. Visitors who intend to spend over 90 days within Holland may need to register with the government to receive official permission to stay here longer, please call the Dutch consulate in your own country before departure for exact details.

## CUSTOMS REGULATIONS UPON ARRIVAL

Customs and immigration officials are usually easy to deal with in Holland. I have rarely seen anyone be subjected to a luggage search at an airport here. The following are excerpted from the official Dutch customs regulations at press time. Please check with Holland's consulates if you need further details.

North Americans arriving into Holland are allowed to bring an unlimited amount of cash for means of payment for tourist or travel expenses.

Adults are each allowed to import into Holland the following amounts of these products:

| | |
|---|---|
| •Cigarettes | 200 |
| | or |
| •Cigarillos | 100 |
| | or |
| •Cigars 50 | |
| | or |
| •Tobacco | 250 grams |
| •Perfumes | 50 grams |
| •Cologne | half-liter |
| •Liquor | 1 liter  (over 44 proof) |
| | or |
| •Liquor | 2 liters  (under 44 proof) |
| •Wine | 2 liters |
| •Coffee | 500 grams |
| •Tea | 100 grams |

All North American visitors are allowed, for temporary importation, objects for personal use which must leave with them upon departure:

Personal jewelry, cameras and video cameras, a reasonable quantity of film and accessories, binoculars, sports equipment such as tents and camping gear, fishing gear, guns (check with airline for restrictions), non-motorized bicycles, tennis rackets, wind surfing boards, delta wings, musical instruments, sound recording equipment, radios and televisions, video recorders, typewriters, calculators, and personal computers.

If you have any additional questions, please contact one of the Netherlands embassies on this side of the ocean before you depart.

## DUTCH EMBASSIES IN NORTH AMERICA

• **Netherlands Embassy in Canada**, *350 Albert Street, Suite 2020, Ottawa, Ontario K1R-1A4, (613) 237-5030*
• **Netherlands Embassy in America**, *4200 Linnean Ave. N.W., Washington, D.C. 20008, (202) 244-5300*

## CUSTOMS REGULATIONS UPON YOUR RETURN

### Returning to the US

All US citizens can return to America with up to $400 without paying duty if you have left the USA for over 48 hours and haven't made another international trip within the last 30 days. Each family member is eligible for the same limits, and these amounts may be pooled together. Normally a 10% duty will be assessed on goods which have exceeded the $400 value, but are below $1400in total value. Above this point the duty will vary with the specific merchandise being imported. Each adult may also bring in up to 1 liter of wine or alcohol and either 100 cigars (except from Cuba) or 200 cigarettes.

There is no duty on antiquities or works of art which are over 100 years old. Bring all receipts with the merchandise to customs to avoid additional problems.

**Returning to Canada**

All Canadian citizens can return to Canada with up to $300 CD once each year if you have left Canada for over 7 days, or up to $1000 CD several times each year if you have left Canada for over 48 hours. Each family member is eligible for the same limits per person. Normally a combination of federal and provincial taxes will be assessed on goods which have exceeded the $300 CD value depending on the specific items involved. Each adult can also bring in 1.14 liters of alcohol, or 8.5 liters (24 cans or bottles each with 12 ounces) of beer.

Also allowed for those at least 16 years old are up to 50 cigars, 200 cigarettes, and 400 grams of tobacco. Bring all receipts with the merchandise to customs to avoid additional problems.

## OFFICIAL HOLIDAYS

• **New Year's Day**, *January 1*
• **Good Friday**, *in Late March or Early April*
• **Easter**, *two days in late March or April*
• **Queen's Birthday**, *30 April*
• **Liberation Day**, *5 May*
• **Ascension Day**, *May*
• **Whitsuntijd**, *two days in late May or early June*
• **Christmas**, *25th-26th December*

The government of Holland occasionally moves holidays around to form long weekends for it's citizens. Many additional regional holidays exist which are not included in this list as they vary with each province. During these days expect many museums, castles, restaurants, banks, government related offices, and several private companies to be closed. Trains and buses will tend to run on limited schedules during these time periods.

For more a more detailed look at regional festivals, celebrations, and special events, see Chapter 7, *Basic Information*, Major Festivals section.

## STUDENT TRAVEL & YOUTH ID CARDS

For full time students under the age of 26 who can provide documentation of their current status, take advantage of the **International Student**

**Identity Card** (I.S.I.C.), valid for one year. Get the card in North America before you depart for about $15. It allows its holder to have discounts on international flights, museums, public transportation, and other services. Included in the U.S. with the cost of these cards is a special emergency medical insurance which can cover around $3000 in medical bills as well as perhaps $100 a day in hospital bills for about two months. Another card, known as the **International Youth Card**, is also available with similar features for young adults under 26 who are no longer in school. To obtain one of these cards, contact one of the following student travel companies.

• **Council Travel**, *New York, (212) 661-1450*
• **Travel Cuts**, *Toronto, (416) 979-2406*

## VVV TOURIST INFORMATION OFFICES IN HOLLAND

Once you have arrived in Holland, there are almost 350 different **VVV** tourist information centers to pick up vital tourist information in several languages. Each major city, tourist destination, and rural town hall usually operates at least one VVV office to assist visitors to their region. These tourist information offices are usually marked with a blue and white "VVV" sign.

Many of these offices are open during typical business hours, so during Saturday afternoons and all day on Sundays they may be closed. These tourist offices are normally staffed by local residents who have the ability to communicate in multiple languages, and are individually managed and funded by the local and/or regional government. Most of the VVV staff members are extremely friendly, and helpful with handing out inexpensive maps, walking tour brochures, hotel listings, transportation schedules, and much more.

I suggest that when you arrive in a city or town you should first pop into the local VVV and find out if they can offer any suggestions to help you better enjoy and understand your visit. If you are both specific and nice to them, the staff of these tourist offices will often advise you of totally off the beaten path attractions and unique bed & breakfast or farm house accommodations that only a lifelong local resident would know about. The VVV can also help get you discounts on rental cars, book excursions, sell maps and guides for all regions of the country, recommend unusual restaurants and bars, arrange private guide services, find cheap rooms in private homes, sell you locally made souvenirs, and point you in the right direction.

In addition to the listing of the main regional and municipal VVV offices, you will also find more information in each city chapter later in this book.

**Major City VVV Listings**
- **Amsterdam** - *Stationplein VVV Tourist Office, Stationsplein,10, Tel. (20) 551-2512*
- **Rotterdam** - *Main VVV Tourist Office, Coolsingel 67, Tel. (10) 402-3200*
- **Den Haag** - *Main VVV Tourist Office, Koningin Julianaplein 30, Tel. (70) 361-8888*
- **Scheveningen** - *VVV Tourist Office, Gevers Deynootweg 1134, Tel. (70) 350-0500*
- **Maastrich**t - *Main VVV Tourist Office, Kleine Staat 1, Tel. (43) 325-2121*
- **Delft** - *Main VVV Tourist Office, Markt 85, Tel. (15) 212-6100*
- **Utrecht** - *Main VVV Tourist Office, Vredenburg 90, Tel. (30) 233-1544*
- **Groningen** - *Main VVV Tourist Office, Gedmpte Kattendiep 6, Tel. (50) 313-9774*
- **Arnhem** - *Main VVV Tourist Office, Stationsplein 45, Tel. (26) 442-0330*

**Head Regional VVV Offices**
- **Noord-Holland Provinciale VVV**, *Florapark 6, Haarlem, Tel. (23) 531-9413*
- **Zuid Holland Provinciale VVV**, *Delft, Tel. (15) 213-1942*
- **Utrecht Provinciale VVV**, *Europalaan 92, Utrecht, Tel. (30) 280-1111*
- **Zeeland Provinciale VVV**, *Middelburg, Tel. (118) 633-000*
- **Noord-Brabant Provinciale VVV**, *Tilburg, Tel. (13) 543-4060*
- **Limburg Provinciale VVV**, *Valkenburg, Tel. (43) 601-7373*
- **Gelderland Provinciale VVV**, *Oosterbeek, Tel. (26) 333-2033*
- **Flevoland Provinciale VVV**, *Lelystad, Tel. (320) 230-500*
- **Overijssel Provinciale VVV**, *Almelo, Tel. (546) 818-767*
- **Drenthe Provinciale VVV**, *Assen, Tel. (592) 351-777*
- **Friesland Provinciale VVV**, *Stationsplein 1, Leeuwarden, Tel. (58) 213-1343*
- **Groningen Provinciale VVV**, *Ged. Kattendiep 6, Groningen, Tel. (50) 313-9774*

## NETHERLANDS BOARD OF TOURISM

Before you begin to plan your vacation in Holland, it would be a good idea to contact your country's head office of the **Netherlands Board of Tourism** (NBT, or Nederlands Bureau voor Toerisme). If you ask a few questions relating to your specific interests, these offices will send you large manila envelopes full of maps, English language tourist information, artistically designed regional summaries, phrase books, and maybe even a few glossy brochures from the powerful and well-connected major tour operators.

The receptionists at these offices are usually very informative Dutch residents who are trying their best to keep up with the tidal wave of daily inquiries. If their line seems constantly busy, or if they don't seem to have the time to answer many questions, it's only because they don't have a large staff to keep up with such a large volume of calls. These are nice people who have a huge amount of work to do.

On the other hand, a personal visit to one of the NBT offices can result in a somewhat more intensive discussion and the chance to receive much more specific printed material. The NBT either prints or distributes hundreds of useful documents in several languages which are then eventually sent along to the tourist offices which they control throughout the world.

Via Internet, you can find their new web site at: **http://www.nbt.nl/ holland**

**NBT Offices in North America**
• **Netherlands Board of Tourism**, 355 Lexington Ave., *21st floor, New York, N.Y. 10017, Tel. (212) 370-7367, fax: (212) 370-9507*
• **Netherlands Board of Tourism**, *225 North Michigan Ave., Suite 326, Chicago, Illinois 60601, Tel. (312) 819-1636, fax: (312) 819-1740*
• **Netherlands Board of Tourism**, *9841 Airport Blvd., Suite 103, Los Angeles, California 90045, Tel. (310) 348-9339, fax: (310) 348-9344*
• **Netherlands Board of Tourism**, *25 Adelaide Street East, Suite 710, Toronto, Ontario, Canada M5C-1Y2, Tel. (416) 363-1577, fax: (416) 363-1470*

## BOOKING YOUR VACATION

I strongly advise that you consider prepaying for the airfare, rental car, and some if not all of your accommodations. If you are traveling to Holland between April and September, do not expect to find availability in many hotels and inns by just showing up. It is best advised to book your most desired high season accommodations well in advance. In the low seasons, I suggest that you book at least the first and last few nights in advance, and then try to find a few places along the way on your own.

I would like to point out the many advantages of using a travel professional to help with reservations. A good travel agent or specialty tour operator can provide detailed information on hotels, airfare, and car rentals without the need for travelers to spend hundreds of dollars calling. They also have access to special prices which are not available to the general public. If anything goes wrong and you need a refund or change to your schedule, a good travel professional with advance notification can often avoid certain penalties that would normally apply.

## TRAVEL AGENTS & TOUR OPERATORS

Travel agents are hard working consultants who usually get paid on a commission basis. If a client desires a normal package tour, no additional fee should be charged, as the agent's commission of between 8% and 12% is deducted from the package's list price. For special custom vacations (known in the industry as an **F.I.T.**), travel agents may charge as much as $150 in advance to cover the extra hours and long distance calls which will be required. Each advance revision or cancellation may be heavily penalized with stiff fees or just as often may be non-refundable.

Travel agents have access to computer databases which can search out the least expensive regularly scheduled airfares offered by international airlines, and also can look up information about over 8,500 hotels throughout the world. Travel agents (and a few savvy frequent travelers) also have access to large hotel information books like the **Hotel and Travel Index** published by the Reed Travel Group which gives great basic listings on tens of thousands of major hotels. Unfortunately, the best deals on airfare and most remarkable accommodations in Holland are not going to necessarily appear in a travel agent's computer. What distinguishes a great agent from a good agent is quite clear. A good travel agent will either know first hand about the country you are visiting, or will offer to make a few calls and find out more. A great agent (and they are around if you look!) will spend lots of time and energy researching their client's destination, and will work with you to book exactly what you want.

No matter who you pick to assist you with your travel plans, make sure you are at least as equally well informed. The more specific that you can be about what type of trip and price range you want, the closer you'll get to matching your dreams with reality.

### The NBT's Special "Holland Travel Professional" Program

One good way of finding a great travel agent that has been tested on their first hand knowledge about the destinations, hotels, and attractions of Holland is to contact the NBT office nearest you and ask for a **Holland Travel Professional** list. These computer printouts are available for free, and show the names, addresses, and office phone numbers for several dozen travel agents in your country that have recently participated in a special familiarization course and trip through the Netherlands, and have proven their ability to better council their clients about where to stay, and what to do in Holland.

### Tour Operators & Specialty Tour Operators

These are the wholesale sources for well over 75% of the packages and 25% of the F.I.T. custom vacations sold in North America. A good tour operator will specialize in just one or a few different countries, and have a staff of experts who have been to almost every hotel, inn, and cruise located in the countries that they represent. Unfortunately many tour operators do not sell direct to the public and prefer to deal with agencies to avoid lengthy phone calls and having to act like a government tourist offices. I have included a list of a few of these organizations who are quite willing to sell directly to the public. Because the staff of most tour operators do not get paid by commission, their suggestions tend to be honest evaluations of first hand experiences. Unlike travel agencies, these companies will often charge a much more reasonable penalty for each revision or cancellation made in advance, and usually offer discounted package rates on dozens of well known hotels in all price ranges.

I have called many different tour operators to research this guide book, and only the most honest, experienced, and informative tour operators are listed below in order of their helpfulness and accuracy. I have based these recommendations on the results of several cold calls I made to each company as a perspective client. On the first call I pretended to have with minimal knowledge about Holland. I later called again acting as a former visitor to the Netherlands that just wanted specific information about lesser known spots and accommodations for my next trip over.

The responses I got ranged from detailed answers on the phone with honest and informative follow up information in the mail from the companies on the top of this list, to no help at all (or totally slanted information) from a dozen or so others that do not appear below. While they tend to work more often with travel agencies, they will all allow direct bookings from well informed individuals that know what they want.

I'd recommend any of the following agents:

• **Abercrombie & Kent** *(800) 323-7308*

For those interested in living aboard a converted barge while it cruises along Dutch rivers and canals, this upscale adventure tour operator has several choices priced between $1000 and $1800 per person (land only) including all meals and plenty of special events.

• **Brooks Country Cycling Tours** *(800) 284-8954*

This New York City based travel company concentrates on unique week long high season Dutch barge cruises that visit cities such as Leiden, Delft, and Haarlem. Each morning after breakfast, participants will hop on excellent 21 speed hybrid bicycles and then proceed along enchanting bicycle paths for a few hours before returning to the barge to eat dinner and sleep. Prices for a relaxing week long trip through the pristine waterways and bike routes of central Holland start at around $900 per person (land only).

• **CBT Bicycle Tours** *(800) 736-BIKE*

Well respected for running affordable biking tours all over northern Europe, this Chicago based adventure bicycle specialist runs several 7 to 10 day bike tours that include about 55 kilometers (34 miles) per day of escorted rides at uniquely Dutch areas such as the North Sea Coast, Amsterdam, Gouda, and Zeeland. Prices start at $630 per person (land only) and include transfers, private guided tours, breakfast, several dinners, and accommodations in comfortable 2 and 3 star inns. Bikes are available for a surcharge if you don't bring your own.

• **Classic Adventures** *(800) 777-8090*

At least once a year during the summer, this well established bicycle touring company schedules a fantastic 6 day trip in Holland. After breakfast you will either be given an escorted tour of a local attraction, or set free to enjoy a 30 to 50 kilometer (19 to 31 mile) bicycle ride at your own pace to the next destination. They use a wonderful collection of charming little city center and rural hotels (many can be found listed in this book), and include a hearty breakfast, a full dinner, and special excursions. The price for this unique adventure costs $1398 per person (land only) plus bike rental if you don't bring your own.

• **Delta Dream Vacations** *(800) 872-7786,* & **American Express Vacations** *(800) 241-1700*

Both of these full service tour operators are managed by the same staff, and offer packages including airfare, Amsterdam hotels, rental cars, and a few other services. They also have the ability to sell refundable $120 open vouchers, each valid for 1 double room with breakfast in a series of good properties throughout the country. The service is pretty good for such a big company, plus you get even more frequent flyer points on Delta or KLM.

• **Grand Destination Management Inc.** *(770) 333-9396*

If you already know exactly when and where you stay in Holland, try giving a call to this Atlanta wholesaler. They book almost any custom package you design, and get good rates for countless hotels, bed and breakfast inns, castles, excursions, rental cars, and KLM airlines flights. They are staffed by Dutch-Americans that really know the Netherlands first hand, and have an affiliated office in Holland in case you need on sight assistance.

• **Holland Approach** *(800) 776-4655*

This east coast based Dutch run tour operator can book excellent customized (F.I.T.) packages and get you competitive prices on a wide variety of hotels in all price ranges, rural inns, castles, Rhine river cruises, excursions, rental cars, flights on several airlines. They have good firsthand knowledge of Holland, and have a solid reputation.

• **Tauck Tours** *(800) 468-2825*
   With many their years of experience in catering to an upscale bus tour market of mainly 45+ year old clients, the people at Tauck continue to receive my highest ratings for customer service and exceptional value for the money. At press time, for $3,775 per person (land only) they offer an all inclusive a 14 day Holland, Belgium, Luxembourg, France, and Switzerland trip with 4 days in the Netherlands. They use superb hotels, restaurants, guides, and narrated excursions. Highly Recommended as one of the best escorted bus tour operators in Europe!

## TRAVEL EMERGENCY & MEDICAL INSURANCE

One of the most important issues of any trip abroad is what to do in an emergency. Since the possibility of a medical problem is always a factor of risk, it is strongly advised that you take out an insurance policy. The best types of travel insurance are in the "Primary Coverage" category.

In an emergency, most of these policies will provide 24 hour toll free help desks, lists of approved specialists, the ability to airlift you to a hospital with the proper facilities for your condition, and much more valuable assistance including refunds on additional expenses and unused hotel nights.

## TRIP CANCELLATION & INTERRUPTION INSURANCE

Many special policies also cover vacation refunds if a family member gets ill and you must cancel your trip, if the airline you were supposed to be flying on goes out of business, if you must depart early from your trip due to sickness or death in the family, if the airline fails to deliver your baggage on time, if your luggage is stolen from your car, if your stay is extended do to injury, etc. One element which is normally not covered are airplane schedule changes, missed connections, and flight cancellations. Please check with your travel agent, tour operator, or the Canadian and American Automobile Agencies for further details.

**Travel Insurance Companies in North America**
• **Mutual of Omaha** *(Tele-Trip), (800) 228-9792 in the US; (402) 351-8000 in Canada*
• **Travel Guard**, *(715) 345-0505 in the US and Canada*
• **Crown Life Travel Insurance**, *(800) 265-0261 in Canada*
• **Access America**, *(800) 284-8300 in the US and Canada*

## GETTING THERE

## NON-STOP SCHEDULED FLIGHTS TO HOLLAND FROM NORTH AMERICA

**KLM Royal Dutch Airlines**
• *in the US, 1-800-374-7747*
• *in Holland, (20) 474-7747*
• *in Canada, (514) 939-4040. Check with directory assistance for additional local and toll free numbers for your province.*

By far, the best and most comfortable way to get to Holland from North America is to take **KLM Royal Dutch Airlines**, the superb international carrier of Holland. They offer a wide variety of excellent non-stop flights to Amsterdam daily or several times weekly from Montreal, Toronto, Calgary, Vancouver, New York, Los Angeles, San Francisco, Atlanta, Houston, Detroit, and other major hubs. For those in other cities, a special code sharing agreement with their global travel partner Northwest Airlines adds even more direct and non-stop flights from cities such as Boston, Washington, and Minneapolis, as well as connecting service via dozens of North American cities. Either way, KLM makes it easy to get you effortlessly to Schiphol International Airport near Amsterdam, and home again.

The lowest currently published (low season) midweek round trip prices (known in the travel business as promotional apex fares) to Amsterdam tend to start at around $499 plus taxes from New York, and $599 CDN plus taxes from Montreal and Toronto. High season rates tend

to run upwards of 30% extra. Additionally, when traveling with an adult, children under 12 years old may qualify for special rates, while infants under 2 years of age sitting on an adult's lap may be entitled to as much as a 90% discount. There are also special fares for senior citizens, groups, and young adults under 26 years of age. There are a limited number of discounted seats per flight, special advance purchase requirements, specific dates of validity, and cancellation & revision penalties that may apply to all of the above, so call KLM Reservations (open 7 days a week), or your travel agent, for exact details.

Passengers should give strong consideration to flying in the extremely comfortable World Business Class compartments. While tickets for these more spacious seats are obviously more expensive, the benefits are significant. Besides having 50% more room to stretch out in, you can also expect to have your own video screen with a choice of first run in-flight movies, specially selected meals with vintage wines, and a miniature blue and white Delftware canal-house filled with traditional Dutch gin as a special reminder of your trip. Those traveling in these specially designed sections are also pampered from the moment they arrive at the airport. Among the many perks for World Business Class flyers are special VIP airport lounges with open bars and complimentary snacks, available fax machines, special priority check-in and baggage services, and much more.

Travelers continuing on to other destinations around the globe can book connecting KLM flights, and make use of Schiphol Airport's modern and user-friendly international terminal. KLM also offers priority boarding for the physically challenged, a wide variety of special meals, an inexpensive express bus to the downtown Amsterdam hotels, and many affordable European hotel and fly/drive vacation packages. Once you've booked your flight with KLM, be sure to join Northwest Airlines WorldPerks frequent flyer program so you can earn valuable points on KLM flights, and use them towards free airline tickets.

The overall service and comfort level offered to all passengers on KLM flights is simply outstanding. Their highly professional (and friendly!) staff go well out of their way to ensure your complete comfort. Great films are shown on their flights, and the cabin crew will offer cocktails, snacks, meals, coffee, extra pillows, and blankets for your comfort. Duty free shopping is also available on board. I love flying on KLM, and I highly recommend them to all my readers!

### Delta Airlines
• *in North America, 1-800-221-1212*
**Delta Airlines** has daily non-stop service between their hub in New York and Amsterdam.

**Martinair**
· *in the US, (407) 391-6165*
· *in Canada, 1-800-387-2004*
    **Martinair** has an assortment of non-stop flights to Amsterdam from Toronto, Tampa, Newark, Oakland, Denver, Vancouver, and other cities.

**Northwest Airlines**
· *in North America, 1-800-225-2525*
    **Northwest Airlines** has many scheduled non-stop flights weekly to Amsterdam via their own hubs in Washington, Boston, Minneapolis, and Detroit, as well as via connecting KLM equipment from many other North American cities.

**Singapore Airlines**
· *in the US, 1-800-387-0038*
· *in Canada, 1-800-742-3333*
    If you are not flying on KLM, I suggest checking out **Singapore Airlines**, a fantastic luxury carrier that has great low prices on 3 non-stop flights per week between New York and Amsterdam.

**United Airlines**
· *in North America, 1-800-825-2525*
    With **United Airlines**, you can fly daily non-stop planes between Washington DC and Amsterdam. They usually match the going rate listed by other major carriers.

## FLIGHTS WITH CONNECTIONS TO HOLLAND

    Several international airlines offer connecting service through to Amsterdam from several North American cities. These flights take longer than the above mentioned airlines because the require a change of planes in Europe before continuing on to Holland. The fares are often the same price as non-stop choices, but sometimes a free stop over in the city where you change planes is allowed. The following is a partial listing of airlines with service to Holland via another European gateway.

**Air France, via Paris**
· *in the US, 1-800-237-2747*
· *in Canada, 1-800-667-2747*

**Alitalia Airlines, via Rome**
· *in the US, 1-800-221-4745*
· *in Canada, 1-800-361-8336*

**British Air, via London**
• *in the US,* 1-800-247-9297
• *in Canada,* 1-800-247-9297

**KLM Airlines, via Amsterdam**
• *in the US,* 1-800-374-7747
• *in Canada,* 1-800-361-5073

**Lufthansa Airlines, via Frankfurt**
• *in the US,* 1-800-645-3880
• *in Canada,* 1-800-645-3880

**Sabena Airlines, via Brussels**
• *in the US,* 1-800-955-2000
• *in Canada,* 1-800-955-2000

**Swiss Air, via Zurich**
• *in the US,* 1-800-221-4750
• *in Canada,* 1-800-267-9477

**TAP Airlines, via Lisbon**
• *in the US,* 1-800-221-7370
• *in Canada,* 1-800-221 7370

**TWA Airlines, via Paris**
• *in North America,* 1-800-892-4141

## CHARTER FLIGHTS

Several charter operators offer flights to Holland from New York, Boston, Chicago, Miami, Toronto, Vancouver, and other North American gateways. Be extra careful whenever booking a charter flight as they are not bound by the same regulations as normal scheduled carriers. It is not uncommon for these flights to be delayed for hours (or even days!) waiting for replacement equipment, while you are stuck sleeping at in the airport lobby. Charter flight tickets are normally non-changeable/non-refundable and are often not covered by travel insurance. For more details, call your travel agent.

## DISCOUNT TICKET CONSOLIDATORS

There are many discount ticket brokers who offer last minute and special advance purchase round-trip fares, for airlines who have not sold enough seats on specific flights. I only suggest this method when you have not been able to find a reasonable deal for tickets directly with major airlines for the desired dates.

While some of these companies are in the habit of ripping off clients, several large companies have been doing a fairly good job in supplying the traveling public with good deals on highly restrictive tickets. It is advised that you first ask your travel agent for their recommendations, or call the local consumer protection agency or Better Business Bureau about any complaints on file about the consolidator you are considering.

I strongly recommend that you either purchase your consolidated tickets from a travel agent or specialty tour operator, and be sure to use a major credit card to purchase this type of ticket. This way you will be better protected in case of any problems that may occur.

These are a few consolidators with a good reputation:
- **Travac**, *212-563-3303*
- **Air Travel Discounts**, *212-922-1326*
- **Auto-Europe**, *1-800-223 5555*
- **Unitravel**, *1-800-325-2222*
- **World Travel**, *1-800-886-4988*
- **Travel Cuts**, *416-979 2406*
- **New Frontiers**, *514-526-8444*

## COURIER FLIGHTS

In many cases, a large company may need to send documents to Europe on a specific day. Agencies exist that book passengers on flights to Europe and use their luggage allotment to transport several documents to European clients. Since you are giving up your rights to your luggage compartment space, you are only allowed to bring whatever you can carry aboard. Upon arrival, a representative from the courier company will take possession of the stored documents.

These flights can run as low as $249 round-trip and usually are valid for only one week. This is not the most recommended method of travel because you never know what is really in those suitcases, and you are completely responsible for their contents. Another major disadvantage is that you may be booked on a standby, or next available day basis. Travel agencies do not reserve these types of tickets, so please check the travel section of your local newspaper.

Some reasonably good courier agencies include:
- **D.T.I.**, *1-212-362-3636*
- **Now Voyager**, *1-212-431-1616*

## SCHIPHOL AIRPORT

The main international airport that services Holland-bound flights is the **Amsterdam Airport Schiphol**. Located 17 kilometers (10 miles) southwest of Amsterdam, this large and well- designed modern facility has just one terminal that is broken up into a downstairs arrival section, and an upstairs departure section. A total of 76 airlines operate from Schiphol and provide over 2,500 flights a week to more than 200 destinations around the globe. With it's current annual passenger load of over 20 million people, many of which are transferring to other European destinations, this is indeed a rather busy airport by any standard.

For a complete floor plan and service listing for Schiphol Airport, you can visit their sight on the World Wide Web at **http://www.Schiphol.nl** from your home computer.

More information about the airport, getting to the city from the airport, and other arrivals information in Chapter 13, *Amsterdam*.

## BOOKING YOUR HOTEL

The major international hotel representatives are listed below. These are among the very best hotel chains in the world. Holland boasts a wide variety of lodgings, and in this section I've also provided lengthy descriptions of the many different kinds of available accommodations.

## MAJOR HOTEL REPRESENTATIVES

Thousands of experienced world travelers help to plan their own hotel overnights after weeks of intensive research. The following is a partial listing of the best hotel groups and representatives that deal both with travel agents, and directly with the public in North America. There are hundreds of other good companies, but these are (in my experience of over 10 years in the travel industry) among the very best.

First decide what your budget really is going to be, what nights you wish to be in which city, and have a good idea of the specific location and ambiance you are looking for in a hotel. After everything is listed on a piece of paper, call one of these phone numbers to reach an agent who can send a huge color brochure, make a reservation with a major credit card, request specific room categories, and perhaps even offer a special (corporate, weekend, off season) rate that nobody else even knew existed. Once again, although these companies prefer to work via a travel agent, they will still help individuals book spectacular hotels all over the globe.

The following are hotel representatives I recommend:
• **Relais & Chateaux** *(800) 735-2478 or (212) 856-0115*

This magnificent collection of unforgettable gourmet restaurants and charming little luxury properties around the world is perfect for those travelers that are expecting the highest standards of quality and service. While most of the properties tend to fall in the higher price categories, you should consider spending at least a night or two in one of these truly memorable inns. Relais & Chateaux offers a half dozen fine inns, converted castles, and superb restaurants in Holland.

• **Leading Hotels of the World** *(800) 223-6800*
    With a wonderful selection of medium and larger sized famous 4 and 5 star hotels throughout the world, their name says it all! They represent 2 of the highest quality luxury properties Amsterdam. Both of these remarkable hotels offer a vast array of services and conference facilities, and provide a great setting for deluxe travelers and businessmen.

• **Inter-Continental Hotels** *(800) 327-0200*
    With just two member properties in the Dutch cities of Den Haag and Amsterdam (each more fantastic than the other), Inter-Continental is has a lock on the most deluxe properties in both Amsterdam and Den Haag. These are among the finest places to stay in Europe, and both have superb rooms and suites.

• **Golden Tulip Hotels** *(800) 344-1212*
    When I want to book myself into a really good full facility Dutch hotel in the moderate price range, I make sure to give a ring to this great resource. Among the dozens of carefully selected properties they either own or represent in Holland is a core group of excellent value 3, 4, and 5 star city center Golden Tulip and Tulip Inn hotels with huge rooms and extremely nice staff members.

• **Small Luxury Hotels of the World** *(800) 525-4800*
    This medium sized company offers a selection of romantic manor houses, boutique style 4 and 5 star luxury hotels, and enchanting resorts on every continent. The number of member properties in Holland are increasing monthly.

• **Utell International** *(800) 44-UTELL*
    This highly respected industry powerhouse offers instantaneous pricing, information, and reservations at well over 6,500 different 2 through 5 star hotels worldwide including at least 90 in Holland at every imaginable price point. Their hard working reservation agents just need to know what price range you are looking for, and their advanced computer system selects several choices for you to choice from.

**The Netherlands Reservation Center**

A special hotel industry organization in the Dutch city of Leidschendam, called the **N.R.C.** (**Netherlands Reservation Center**), can book budget hotels, bungalows, apartments, and other affordable accommodations for visitors. Send them a fax with the details of where, when, and what type of property you are looking and your maximum budget. A week or so later a fax will be sent to you including a suggested property. If this reservation is acceptable, you must reconfirm by faxing them your credit card information within 72 hours or it will be canceled.

The booking service is free, but cancellation and revision fees may apply. Contact the Netherlands Reservation Center, *fax (70) 320-2611.*

## ACCOMMODATIONS IN HOLLAND

There are well over 2,450 different government-licensed accommodation providers in Holland. For those of you who want to have a complete listing of almost every official accommodation in Holland, you will have to but a copy of the Dutch language-only *ANWB Hotels Nederland* book for 24.95 NLG (**NLG** is used throughout this book to denote the Dutch currency, the **Netherlands Guilder** – see Chapter 7, *Basic Information*, section on Currency & Banking, for currency conversion and other money information). Perhaps a better idea is to get free copies of the NBT-published *Hotels* and *Hotels in Amsterdam* brochures from your country's NBT offices. Although these books use ratings from 1 up to 5 stars for most of the properties in the country, the system cannot be fully trusted.

I have included brief descriptions in this book's regional chapters of more than 100 of the properties throughout the Netherlands that I have visited and can appropriately review. I have listed each destination's properties in up to four separate price categories that are relevant to the average room rate of that specific city. Within each of the price categories, I have listed the hotels from top to bottom in the order of my personal suggestion.

While the quality and facilities of accommodations may change from season to season, I have given you the most up to date information currently available to help you select the best places to fit your requirements. The price guidelines for all types of accommodations which I have used in my reviews are based on the lowest price room rate for two people staying in a double room, not necessarily including city taxes. In some cases, I have listed either a year round or weekend price. Please keep in mind that many hotels have up to 50% surcharges during special festival, high season, and holiday seasons. If you are traveling around Holland without all your nights already pre-reserved, any local VVV tourist information office can book a hotel room for you at a fee of about 3 NLG or so per night.

Also keep in mind that you will have to hand over your passport (and in some cases a credit card imprint) upon check in. All registered guests must be placed on the property's occupant sheets that the government then uses for statistical analysis. Make sure that you get back your passport later the same day, and walk around with a photocopy of it until the original is returned.

## HOTEL INDUSTRY TERMS USED IN THIS BOOK

**Low Season** – *Usually from about October through March, excluding holidays.*

**High Season** – *Usually from about April through September.*

**Rack Rate** – *The full retail price of a room, special rates may also be available.*

**Gourmet Packages** – *This price includes fine dining 2 or 3 times daily.*

**Corporate Rate** – *Available to almost anyone who presents a business card.*

**Weekend Rate** – *A limited number of discounted rooms Friday through Sunday.*

**Special Packages** – *Discounts given during quiet times of the year.*

**Double Room** – *A room designed and priced for 2 people staying together.*

**Apartment** – *A unit with cooking facilities built in.*

**Dormitory Room** – *A large room with bunk beds for many people.*

**E.P.** – *European Plan, no meals included in the price.*

**C.P.** – *Continental Plan, a small breakfast included in the price.*

**B.P.** – *Breakfast Plan, a full breakfast (typically a buffet) included in the price.*

**M.A.P.** – *Modified American Plan, full breakfast and dinner included in the price.*

**A.I.** – *All Inclusive Plan, all meals included in the price.*

## COMMON TYPES OF ACCOMMODATIONS

Hotels in Holland run the full gamut of quality and accommodation levels and are available in several types of classifications. Hotel properties throughout the country which can be housed in everything from centuries old convents and palaces, to brand new towering resort complexes on the sea.

Any property which uses the word "hotel" in its name will be officially rated by a series of stars. If a hotel is listed as having **1** or **2 stars**, chances are that it will have private bathrooms and facilities such as a breakfast room and central heating. Properties of **3 stars** or more will often be loaded with additional facilities including a restaurant, parking, cable TV, an outdoor pool, in room phones, elevators, and perhaps even mini-bars. Most **4** and **5 star** hotels may have gourmet restaurants, snack bars, lounges, air conditioning, health clubs, sports facilities, marble bathrooms, late night or 24 hour room service, business meeting rooms, garage parking, suites, multilingual staff, a concierge desk, and bell boys.

Also in the same general price range and quality range are the following sub categories. The so called castle-hotels (**Kasteelhotels**) that are usually 4 or 5 star hotels in historic castles. Vacation Apartment Complexes (**Vakantie-Appartementen**) are generally large buildings surrounding either the sea or a swimming pool that offer family sized apartments with kitchens and various special activities. Apartment-hotels (**Appartementen**) that are usually small buildings with rooms and suites that include cooking facilities and are often (but not always!) rented for a minimum period of 1 week. Pensions (**Pensions**) are similar to basic 1 and 2 star hotels, and offer minimal facilities besides a clean bed. Budget hotels and private hostels (**Budget hotels**) are usually found in the larger cities and are essentially privately operated hostels with huge dormitories and perhaps a few small and cheap private rooms.

There are also Bed and Breakfast Inns (**Logies met Ontbijt**) in either private homes or rural farm-houses in every province. They offer guests a chance to stay in traditional manor homes and farm houses. Some inns may also offer apartments and guest rooms with fireplaces, 4 poster beds, scenic patios, and even modern or antique style kitchens. Bungalows (**Bungalows**) are basic cabins with living quarters and are inexpensive alternatives to hotels when no luxuries are required. Summer houses (**Zomerhuisjes**) are seasonal rental homes that usually can be found in resort areas, and have minimum rental periods averaging one week.

Simple rooms in private houses are also available through contacting the local VVV tourist information office. Other private rooms may be offered to you, but keep in mind that most of these basic accommodations are not officially recognized by the government, and are usually part of the underground economy. I have not included listings of these units because they come and go each season and there is no quality assurance. The most common way to find a private room is to either inquire at a local VVV tourist office, or go to a local train station and look out for either signs or the hawkers who earn up to a 15% commission to each tourist they successfully bring in.

## YOUTH HOSTELS

For adults and youths alike, the vast network of excellent Youth Hostels (Jeugdherberg) provide a highly economical alternative to staying in budget hotels. There are well over 35 great hostels scattered through every major city and most rural areas of the country and its islands. I have reviewed hostels that I have stayed in and can fully recommend in several destination chapters of this book.

Many of these hostels are located in old castles and farm houses and provide both separate dormitory style accommodations for each sex, as well as a limited quantity of modern private double rooms for couples, and family sized multiple bedroom units. These properties welcome international guests of all ages, and are no longer used just by students and backpackers on budget road trips. The hostels tend to be located in major resort and population zones and are usually open from 9am until 12pm and from 5pm until sometime after 12 midnight when they lock the front door. If you need to stay out later, most will give you a front door key after paying a small deposit.

Each hostel is completely different, so expect anything from huge air conditioned rooms inside modern buildings in the city center, to spacious guest rooms with private bathrooms in old converted mansions. The current price range is from about 26 NLG to 36 NLG per person each night including a continental breakfast depending on the season and type of room requested. Many hostels offer inexpensive meals for a small surcharge. Many hostels also have sports facilities, bicycle rentals, electronic "Pin Safe" storage lockers, bicycle rentals, and in some cases even water sports and indoor tennis facilities available for a surcharge.

All guests of these hostels must hold a valid hostel membership card which is available for about $25 per year from any I.F.Y.H. office, or if necessary, from the hostel's front desk. These cards also enable their holders to receive discounts on the hostels themselves, as well as on restaurants and sports rental equipment. Special cards may be available for people under 17 and families at differing prices. To book reservations, it is best to contact the official member of the International Federation of Youth Hostels (I.F.Y.H.) in the country you live in.

Some hostels request a 10 day advance booking made via an I.F.Y.H. branch office, but if space is available you can just walk in and stay. A new computer system called the International Booking Network can often be used to reserve and print out confirmations for prepaid bookings in many hostels throughout the world for a mere $2.50 fee plus the price of the accommodation chosen. Many Dutch hostels are open year round, but it is not uncommon for several of them to be sold out well in advance for the summer season, so book early.

For specific location, pricing, and facility listings, order a copy of Hostelling International's multilingual handbook. Contact one of the following organizations or their many branches for more information:

• **American Youth Hostel Federation**, *Washington DC, (202) 783-6161*
• **Canadian Hostelling Association**, *Ontario, (613) 237-7884*

• **NJHC Dutch Association of Hostels**, *Amsterdam, (20) 551-3155*
• **Council Travel**, *New York, (212) 661-1450*
• **Travel Cuts**, *Toronto, (416) 979-2406*

## CAMPING

With hundreds of official public and private campgrounds throughout the country, the Netherlands is a great place to camp and caravan. If you follow normal precautions and don't leave anything valuable in your tent or caravan you will surely have a wonderful time. One of the most important issues besides security should be where you decide to stay. If you intend to avoid the official campsites and try to stay on private land you may end up with buckshot in your rear end.

If you attempt to illegally camp anywhere along the coast, you may very well be harassed (or even arrested) by the local police. To put it simply, the campgrounds are so numerous and cheap that there is almost no reasonable excuse to avoid them.

Most of the campgrounds and caravan sights are fairly attractive and located in areas which are close to tourism spots, city centers, beach resorts, and beautiful parks. Besides the typical almost hot showers and sanitary facilities, you may often find bungalows, mini-markets, snack bars, tennis courts, rental boats, laundry machines, telephones, on site parking, and swimming pools. Many sights are open year round and you can expect to pay between 4 NLG and 7.50 NLG per night for a tent site, and 12 NLG to 22.50 NLG for a caravan site. Parking, showers, meals, sports facilities, and electrical hook ups may be available at an additional fee. It would also be a good idea to get an **International Camping Card** from a local camping supply shop or from the US-based **National Campers Association**, *(716) 668-6242.*

Before departing for Europe, make sure that you have bought all the camping supplies that may be needed. Don't forget to bring extra waterproofed tent flies and strong bug repellent as they will be necessary. If you need to buy camping supplies within Holland, expect to pay double or triple of what they cost at home.

If you want specific information on every campsite in the Netherlands, you can ask in a Dutch book shop for a copy of the current ANWB camping guide which costs about 17.50 NLG. The local VVV offices may also offer either a listing of regional campsites, or a free copy of local campsite listings. In any case, you can always ask any NBT office in your country if they can send you some information before you depart.

# 7. BASIC INFORMATION

## BUSINESS HOURS

Most **retail stores** are open from 9:00am until about 6:00pm from Monday through Friday, and from 10:00am and 5:00pm on Saturdays. Among the most common exceptions to this schedule are Monday mornings, when a vast amount of stores open up at around 1:00pm. Many Dutch towns and cities now have one late shopping night per week, on either Thursday or Friday when shops close at 9:00pm. Sunday retail hours do exist, but only in selected shopping centers and a few boutiques in the most tourist related areas and larger cities. On every day of the week you can, however, find open restaurants, bars, corner grocers, pharmacies, train stations, bus stations, taxi stands, and cafes.

**Banks** and **Government offices** are generally open 9:00am until 4:00pm from Monday through Friday. Many **museums** are closed all day on Mondays, and take on Sunday schedules during public and religious holidays. Many of the country's 350 **VVV tourist information centers** are open 9:00am until about 5:00pm from Monday through Friday, and in some cases from about 9:00am until 4:00pm on Saturday (some, but relatively few, open on Sundays).

## CASINOS & GAMBLING

There are currently nine full service casinos operated by the government-controlled **Holland Casino** organization. They differ in size from one to another, but basically the interior design, selection of games, house rules, restaurants, and entrance fees are pretty much the same. To enter a Holland Casino establishment, foreigners must be over 18 years old, have a valid passport, wear suitable attire (no ripped jeans, Tee shirts, or sneakers!), and pay a 5 NLG per person cover charge. Many better hotels give their clients special vouchers for free admittance to one or more of these nine these casinos (ask your hotel's front desk for one!) Recently KLM Royal Dutch Airlines has also printed a free casino entrance voucher on the back of some of their international boarding passes.

Games of chance offered here include Blackjack, American and French Roulette, Punto Banco, a full assortment of slot machines, and in some facilities Sic Bo, Bingo, and The Big Wheel. Slot machines here accept multiple coins of 0.25 NLG, 1 NLG, 2.50 NLG, or 5 NLG, while other games have differing minimum bet level ranging from 5 NLG and way up. For exact details about any of their facilities, just pop into any of the establishments listed below and ask them for a free copy of Holland Casino's *The Rules of the Game* pamphlet.

- **Holland Casino Amsterdam**, *Max Euweplein 62, Amsterdam, Tel. (20) 620-1006*
- **Holland Casino Breda**, *Bijster 30, Breda, Tel. (76) 522-7600*
- **Holland Casino Eindhoven**, *Huevel Galerie 134, Eindhoven, Tel. (40) 243-5454*
- **Holland Casino Groningen**, *Ged. Kattendiep 150, Groningen, Tel. (50) 312-3400*
- **Holland Casino Nijmegen**, *Waalkade 68, Nimegen, Tel. (24) 360-0000*
- **Holland Casino Rotterdam**, *Weena 624, Rotterdam, Tel. (10) 414-7799*
- **Holland Casino Den Haag**, *Gev. Deynootweg, Scheveningen, tel (70) 351-2621*
- **Holland Casino Valkenburg**, *Odapark, Valkenburg, Tel. (43) 601-5550*
- **Holland Casino Zandvoort**, *Bashuisplein 7, Zandvoort, Tel. (23) 571-8044*

## CURRENCY & BANKING

The unit(s) of Dutch currency are called the **Guilder** and are officially referred to in plural as **Gulden**. I have used the abbreviation of NLG (Netherlands Guilder) to show how much things cost in Dutch currency. The Guilder can be divided into smaller units of **100 cents per NLG**.

Depending on what region of Holland you're in, these same monetary units may also be called by their old name, the **Florin**, and may also be abbreviated as **f**, **fl**, **Dfl**, or **Hfl**. This money comes in denominations of coins at 5 cents, 10 cents, 25 cents, 50 cents, 1 NLG, 2.50 NLG, and 5 NLG. Multiple colored bills are printed in denominations of 10 NLG through 1000 NLG.

Converting your currency and travelers checks into Gulden is quite simple, and can be done in several ways. Converting foreign currency at international airports in North America is recommended for small

### DOLLAR-GUILDER EXCHANGE RATE

*At press time, the value of $1 US is roughly equal to 1.7 NLG, while the value of $1 Canadian is equal to about 1.2 NLG. Be advised that these rates can fluctuate wildly, so check the exchange rate section of your newspaper to know what the value is.*

amounts only since the service charges and exchange rates are poor at best within America and Canada. If you're arriving into Schiphol Airport near Amsterdam and need cash for airport tips and taxis, or if you are arriving on a holiday or weekend, you can make your exchange at the Schiphol Airport's own full service banks, extend hours exchange booth (almost always open), or at the electronic exchange machines in the arrivals terminal. The banks throughout Holland give approximately the same exchange rate, and around the same service charge, even at the airport.

Most banks in Holland are open from Monday through Friday from about 9:00am until around 4:00pm, but some big city bank branches, private exchange companies, GWK train station-based bank offices, hotels, and credit cards service centers tend to open longer, and have limited weekend hours. All banks impose a very small commission (of up to 3.5% or so) for exchanges. In some cases, travelers checks will sometimes fetch 1% to 2% more than cash. If you want to exchange your travelers checks, you must present the teller with a valid passport (despite what your travelers check company tells you!). When entering a bank, look for the exchange sign and wait in line.

Private exchange bureaus also exist in the major city shopping and resort areas, although their exchange rate is not always good as it would be at a bank. There is no black market in Holland, so don't even try to look for it. Computerized ATM machines (Cirrus, Visa, Amex) and 24 hour automated currency machines are available in many downtown or tourist zones. Most hotels also will exchange currency for guests, but the rates are typically far below what a nearby bank would give you.

### Credit Cards

Credit cards have become a necessary part of most European trips. These days it is necessary in many cases to present a credit card at hotel front desks for an imprint to cover any unpaid phone calls, mini-bar usage, or room service fees charged to your hotel bill. Also, many rental car companies will not let you rent from them without a credit card deposit. Most 3 and 4 star hotels will accept Visa, Mastercard, and Eurocard, but several will not accept American Express or Diners Club because of the high usage fees and commissions they are billed. This situation also exists in many stores and restaurants throughout Holland.

Most people living here either use cash, or a so called PIN card or Chippenkaart card that takes money directly from their savings account balance. Even the post office here is in on the electronic banking craze, and has their own ATM machines throughout Holland. When using your Visa, Mastercard, or American Express Card abroad, the rate of exchange is seldom as good as the official bank rates would be for cash and travelers checks in Europe. It is a good idea to have a combination of cash, travelers checks and couple of credit cards during your travels. Another advantage to bringing your credit cards is that if you need a cash advance, this may be possible (depending on your specific credit card company's policy).

**Travelers Checks**
In most places travelers checks are readily accepted. Try to keep the denominations fairly small so the cashier will have enough Guilden to give you proper change. While Thomas Cook and Visa travelers checks are usually not a problem, **American Express Travelers Checks** are much more widely accepted. If you have American Express Travelers Checks, their offices in Amsterdam, Den Haag, and Rotterdam will exchange them with no service fees at all.

Another advantage to American Express is that if you have lost or stolen checks, their big **refund center** in Amsterdam can be reached from anywhere in Holland by dialing *(20) 520-7777*. You might also try to call American Express collect at *(919) 333-3211* to reach a U.S. travelers check refund and replacement office.

## ELECTRICITY
Dutch outlets are designed for 220 Volts AC and 50 Hertz, and the plugs are tipped by two round pins. If you are bringing electrical appliances or components, you should bring a transformer for the appropriate wattage, and the correct plug adapter (the largest European two round pin plug).

Many appliances such as hair dryers, razors, and personal computers already have a switchable transformer built in, and may require only an adapter for the plug. Check your owner's manual carefully.

## HEALTH & MEDICAL CONCERNS
Holland currently requires no inoculations or special immunizations for visitors from America and Canada. In fact, there haven't been any outbreaks of major infectious diseases here in many years. The best thing to do in case you worry about these things is to contact the **State Department Information Center** in the US (or your country's foreign ministry) and ask if there are any current travel advisories on the Netherlands. I am pretty sure you will find none.

If you are currently under medication, you should bring a copy of your prescription (with the generic name for the drug) along with your medicine. If necessary, a local **Apotheek** (pharmacy) may be able to either refill it, or refer you to a doctor who can write a new prescription. To find a 24 hour drug store or hospital emergency room, just call **directory**

**assistance** *(06-8008)* or look in on any drug store window or a local newspaper for listings. Hospitals are available in most major population areas; in case of an emergency, call *06-11* for an ambulance.

Every major city has at least a few medical centers that are open 24 hours a day, 7 days a week.

**Insurance Coverage in Holland**

Since you are not a Dutch citizen, at least in theory health care may not be provided to you for free. The one time when I needed emergency medical treatment in Holland, nobody gave me a bill or asked what type of insurance I carried. Americans with private insurance may be covered for reimbursement under their current policy, but that may only help you after months of detailed paperwork. Canadians may find that their provincial health insurance may cover or reimburse certain procedures, but don't count on it.

Check the Travel Emergency and Trip Cancellation Insurance sections in Chapter 6, *Planning Your Trip*, for important advice on this subject. For exact laws regarding the use of the Dutch government-controlled health care system as a foreigner, contact the **ANOZ-Verzekeringen** (Netherlands Public Health Service's Foreign Affairs Division) *in Utrecht, Holland, at Tel. (30) 256-5300 or fax them at (30) 256-5489.*

## MAJOR FESTIVALS

Every province and city in Holland hosts several festivals, fairs, concert events, religious processions, and special celebrations each year. The following list contains some of the most important religious, cultural, historical, gastronomic, sporting, and agricultural festivities. To receive information on the exacts dates of each specific event, contact the NBT offices in your country, or a local **VVV** tourist information office in Holland.

**JANUARY**
• **Leidse Jazz Festival** – A week long concert series in Leiden of respected jazz musicians .

**FEBRUARY**
• **Carnival** – A week of non–stop drinking and festivities throughout Limburg, especially fun during parades through Maastricht.
• **Elfstedentocht** – A fantastic 210 kilometer (131 mile) all day ice skating race along the canals of Friesland. Since the ice must be thick, it only takes place once every 15 or so years when it is a really cold winter.

## MARCH
- **Keukenhof** – Official late March opening of the famous gardens in Lisse.

## APRIL
- **2nd Passdag** – the second day of Easter in Holland is a family day, and they love to shop for good bargains on furniture (the only shops that are open!).
- **Passraces** – A series of high speed car races during Easter in Zandvoort.
- **Queen's Day** – During the last day of April the whole country parties with the excuse of celebrating Queen Beatrix's birthday. Amsterdam is literally covered with flea markets, and huge fireworks displays.

## MAY
- **Landelijke Feitsdag** – The national bicycle day when almost everyone goes out for a ride.
- **Scheveningen Sand Week** – The beaches of Scheveningen are filled with towering sand castles competing for awards.
- **Wadlopen** – The start of the season for mud walking treks in northern Holland. During moon low tides it is possible to walk from the mainland of Groningen to a couple of the Wadden Sea islands.

## JUNE
- **Holland Festival** – Amsterdam, Rotterdam, and Den Haag showcase concerts and live theater performances by mainly Dutch artists.
- **Fietselfstedentocht** – A 230 kilometer (143 mile) bicycle trip in one day between many on the cities in Friesland.
- **Rondje Texel** – The island of Texel hosts a catamaran race.
- **Pinkpop** – A huge open air concert festival in Limburg.
- **TT Assen Grand Prix** – A major car racing event in Assen.

## JULY
- **North Sea Jazz Festival** – For a week in and around Den Haag, the world's top jazz musicians start off their European tours with this great festival of concerts.
- **Dag Van Architectuur** – Every Dutch city gives tours of its proudest architectural monuments.
- **Middeleeuwse Burchfeesten** – A 2 day Medieval festival in Noorbeek.
- **Skutsjesilen** – antique sail boat race off the coast of Friesland.
- **Drentse Rijwielvierdaagse** – An assortment of bicycle races in Assen.

## AUGUST
- **Bloemencorso** – A series famous flower parades through some Dutch cities.

- **Festival Oude Muziek** – Utrecht schedules a week or so of special concerts of Medieval period music.
- **Preuvenemint** – A special weekend gastronomic street fair in Maasricht.
- **Visserijdagen** – The entire fishing fleet shows up for this harbor day in the northern city of Harlingen.
- **International Fireworks Festival** – Night after night of massive pyrotechnic displays in Scheveningen.

## SEPTEMBER
- **Prinsjedag** – The day when Queen Beatrix rides around Den Hague in a carriage to then officially open parliament.
- **Open Monumentendag** – Most major cities open monuments for free visits.
- **Kinderdijk Nachts** – The windmills of Kinderdijk are flood light at night for 1 week.
- **Haven Dags** – The port city of Rotterdam hosts a series of boat tours and maritime exhibitions.

## OCTOBER
- **Zuidlaardermarkt** – Europe's largest horse market takes place in Zuidlaren.

## DECEMBER
- **Gouda Bij Kaarslicht** – The city of Gouda's St. Janskerk church hosts a concerts and then the huge tree in the candlelit main square is illuminated.
- **Sintaklaas Dag** – Small children are given Christmas presents two and a half weeks before Christmas by St. Klaus and Black Peter, his faithful Moorish servant.

## NEWSPAPERS & MAGAZINES

There is a vast assortment of Dutch language dailies and weeklies available at any newsstand, hotel lobby, or local tobacco shop. If you search around the major cities and resort area newsstands, you may also find current copies of the *Wall Street Journal Europe*, *The London Times*, *International Herald Tribune*, *The European*, and *USA Today*.

Many public libraries and fashionable cafes also have at least a few of the above for free public reading. Special European editions of English language magazines such as *Time*, *Newsweek*, *Playboy*, *The Economist*, and *Penthouse* are also available at train station newsstands and at the gift shops in leading hotels.

## NIGHTLIFE

Each city and town in Holland has a vast assortment of evening entertainment. There are many establishments where you can enjoy rock concerts, jazz bands, symphonies, opera, theater, ballroom dancing, heavy drinking, casual conversation, disco action, raves, and even casino gaming. There are also thousands of establishments which are similar to the bars, discos, and nightclubs which you are already accustomed to back home.

Among the most typical places to hang out for Dutch people of all ages and backgrounds are each city's many bars (**Cafés**), old world-styled **Brown Cafes** with their dark wooden paneling, curious little **Proeflokal** gin tasting rooms, and of course the famous **"Smoking" Coffeeshops** where various strains of extremely potent hydroponic and outdoor marijuana and imported hashish are semi-legally sold by the gram.

Most younger Dutch residents tend to hit the bars and clubs by around 10:00pm on Friday and Saturday nights, and stay at just one or two different places until closing time (somewhere between 2:00am and 7:00am depending on local zoning regulations). Thursday night has now also become a popular evening for local students to drink heavily, and is often the best evening to go out. It's quite common for people between the ages of 17 to 34 or so to start off partying at 10:30pm and keep going at least until breakfast time the next morning, especially around Amsterdam and Groningen.

The bar scene here is among Europe's most exciting, and one night stands are a frequent occurrence here these days, and single Dutch women are liberated enough here to pick up men that they are attracted to. If you are going to spend the night with someone here, make sure you are smart and safe about it! I have included reviews of local nightlife in each regional and major city chapter, but you should always try to ask a local student or resident to fill you in on the most happening spots.

## PASSPORT PROBLEMS

Just in case you happen to somehow misplace your passport, or need the help and advice of your own government, contact your embassy. They can also provide other services which your tax dollars are paying for including travel advisories on other nations which you may wish to visit while overseas, lists of local English speaking medical specialists, and other valuable details.

• **American Embassy**, *Lange Voorhout 102, Den Haag, (70) 310-9209*
• **American Consulate**, *Museumplein 19, Amsterdam, (20) 664-5661*
• **Canadian Embassy**, *Sophialaan 7, Den Haag, (70) 361-4111*

## PERSONAL SAFETY & CRIME

After being in Holland dozens of times, I have run into only a few small situations (especially in Amsterdam!) that were problematic. I have also heard about theft of radios from parked cars, jewelry from suitcases, and of gasoline from unlocked gas tanks. To begin with, if you're driving around, make sure to remove or at least cover any visible items in the luggage or hatch area. If possible, avoid any rental cars with an open uncovered hatchback. Do not leave luggage, cameras, or any type of valuable item within the grasp of unscrupulous people.

Be extra careful around people that begin to surround you in the streets, and pay attention while in bus and train stations. If you have any special items you are traveling around with, leave them at the safety deposit box or in room mini-safe at your hotel. Always carry a wallet with 50 NLG or so inside, and keep the rest of your cash, credit cards, and important papers in a separate money belt. Be careful about walking around dark and deserted city neighborhoods at night. If you take these simple precautions, you are almost sure to avoid the possibility of a major problem.

In case you run into a thief, give up your wallet, let them run away, and then visit the nearest police station. To make an insurance claim, assuming you have coverage on either your homeowner's or a special policy, you must have a copy of a detailed police report. For emergency assistance anywhere in Holland, just call *06-11* from any phone, and an emergency response team will usually be dispatched within minutes.

## PHYSICALLY CHALLENGED TRAVELERS

For physically challenged people, Holland is about the most accessible country in Europe. Getting here is generally hassle-free as KLM and most other international airlines offer special seating assignments, wheelchair storage, and boarding assistance to anyone who requests so in advance. Upon arrival in Schiphol Airport, additional special airport assistance services are also offered free of charge by the airlines. Now that you have arrived in Holland, things can still get a little more difficult.

Although well-marked reserved so called "handicapped" parking spaces can be found in most cities and park parking lots, almost none of the major rental car companies offer specially adapted vehicles.

A heightened sense of public responsibility, as well as new regulations from the European Economic Community (E.E.C.) are really starting to have a positive effect on the availability of special services and facilities, especially in the larger cities of Amsterdam, Maastricht, Den Haag, Utrecht, and Rotterdam. Most cities know are proud of their own **Handicaptransportsystem** (special buses and mini-vans used for local rides by those in wheelchairs), but since these are designed for citizens of Holland, you must contact each city's municipal transit company to secure special permits to use these services. On the other hand, the **NS** national train system can arrange special assistance if you contact them at least a day or so before your rail journey. Their main office for this type of arrangement can contacted during weekdays, *Tel. (30) 235-5555.*

The **Netherlands Board of Tourism** offices in Los Angeles, New York, Toronto, and Chicago can forward you listings of hotels with specially adapted rooms, taxi companies that offer special mini van shuttles, and companies that book vacations for those with specific challenges. Wheelchair accessible bathrooms, entrance ramps, and well designed elevators with Braille and chime features are starting to become more common in the larger 4 and 5 star hotels in resort areas and business centers. Whenever possible, I have included a notation in hotel listings when special facilities are offered. Each regional VVV office may be able to direct visitors to additional transportation services, adapted accommodations, and restaurants which are properly equipped. There are also new daily dial-a-ride door to door bus services in some cities which must be arraigned in advance. For these dial-a-ride services, please call the VVV tourist offices in the city or region you will be visiting.

The offices of the **Stichting Dienstverlening Gehandicapten** in Utrecht can sell you a good booklet (in Dutch only for 7 NLG) that lists over five dozen places with specially adapted facilities for vacationing travelers that are physically challenged. Their address is *Postbus 222, 3500 AE Utrecht, Tel. (30) 231-3454.* Also in Utrecht are the main regional offices of the **Gehandicapenraad**, a government-sponsored organization that has some good information on this and other related subjects, located at *St. Jacobstraat 14, 3511 BS Utrecht, Tel. (30) 231-3454.*

## Helpful Organizations

- **Society for The Advancement of Travel for the Handicapped**, *New York, New York, (212) 447-7284.* A members-only service with basic information about travel needs for the physically challenged. Yearly membership is $45 for adults and $25 for students.
- **MossRehab Travel Information Services**, *Philadelphia, Pennsylvania, (215) 456-9600.* A free information and referral service with valuable hints and suggestions on companies which offer travel services for the physically challenged.
- **Flying Wheels Travel**, *Owatonna, Minnesota, (800) 535-6790.* A great full service travel agency and group tour operator which can provide helpful information and reservations for the physically challenged. Services include all forms of special transportation and accommodation reservations, and guided group tours.

## POST OFFICES & MAIL

Throughout the country there is a vast network of **Postkantoors** (post offices) which are open from around 8:30am until about 5:00pm from Monday through Friday, some with limited Saturday morning hours. Letters under 20 grams (3/4 ounce) sent via air mail from Holland to North America normally cost around 1.75 NLG and can take up to two weeks to arrive. Letters under 20 grams (3/4 ounce) sent between two Dutch addresses cost about 90 cents each and usually find their way to the addressee in about 3 to 4 days.

Most post offices sell **Postzegels** (stamps) and can help with normal postal needs. You can send and receive mail as well as make phone calls, international money orders, faxes, telegraphs, and wire money transfers at several of the larger branches. If you wish to have a main post office hold mail for you, general delivery can be arranged. I suggest letting the postal clerk know who you are and that you will eventually be expecting mail to arrive at his branch. Incoming letters must be marked *Poste Restante* and sent, with your last named boldly written and underlined, to the post office where you are nearest to. When letters arrive, they can be picked up at the post office as long as you present the clerk with a passport or other official ID. For details about these and other postage related topics, contact the state run PTT postal company's **information hot-line** in Holland, *Tel. (06)-0417.*

You can also receive mail and telegrams via the **American Express Travel Services** offices in Amsterdam, Rotterdam, and Den Haag if you contact Amex before you depart North America at *(800) 221-7282* and arrange this special service. These client letter services are free to American Express cardholders, vacation clients, and traveler's check holders, but can sometimes be obtained by others for a small fee. Both DHL and Federal Express can deliver packages between North America and Holland, and visa versa, within four business days.

## RADIO

The countless regional or major city AM and FM radio stations in Holland are wonderful sources of free entertainment, and most hotel rooms and rental cars have the equipment to receive them. There are hundreds of stations broadcasting every type of music and talk show imaginable. One of the funniest things about hearing the radio here is that after several sets of unfamiliar local music, you will then be pelted with old American songs like the Bee Gee's *Staying Alive.* The stations in large cities and resort areas will sometimes offer great classical, rock, blues, or jazz telecasts.

For those of you who are interested in English language radio, I suggest that you carefully search the dial for the hour or so long BBC

World Service and the U.S. Armed Forces Radio broadcasts. There are also daily programs geared towards tourists and expatriates from England, that are broadcast on some stations.

**Radio Netherlands** usually broadcasts in Holland on AM radio at 1440 khz.

You may want to purchase an inexpensive shortwave radio receiver before you depart. For under $200, you can get a great compact portable shortwave radio receiver, such as the top rated **Grundig Yacht Boy 400**, that will allow you to pick up a multitude of English (and other language) broadcasts originating from the country you are about to visit. This is a great way to be informed in advance of your vacation or business trip about special cultural events, weather conditions, festivals, important news, and other helpful tips. Once you have arrived in Europe, you will find it easy to keep in touch with the current events back home in Canada or the US.

Among the most enjoyable news, information, and entertainment programming in English on the shortwave bands are those broadcast several times daily by operations like **Radio Canada International**, the **Voice of America**, **Swiss Radio International**, **BBC World Service** (6195 kHz), and of course the superb **Radio Netherlands** (6045 kHz). For specific frequency locations for these and many other networks, ask your local book shop to order you a copy of *Passport to World Band Radio,* published annually by International Broadcasting Services Ltd. in Penns Park, Pennsylvania (ISBN 0-914941-37-2).

Also, consider sending a quick fax or letter to Marbian Productions International, *P.O. Box 1051, Pointe Claire, Quebec, Canada H9S 4H9 (fax. 514-697-2615).* This organization's president, Mr. Ian McFarland, a former shortwave radio program producer & host, will be glad to send you current programming and frequency schedules for a variety of shortwave stations, including the above mentioned networks, directly to your home or office for free.

## TAXES & SERVICE CHARGES

Almost every boutique, restaurant, hotel, taxi, excursion operator, and corner shop includes the Dutch Government's **BTW** (V.A.T.) tax in their price list. This tax can range from between 6% and 17.5% in total, and in some cases can be refunded to visitors only temporarily in Holland. For more information about BTW tax refunds, see Chapter 9, *Shopping.*

Most hotels will inform you at the time of booking if there are any additional service charges or city taxes not included in their quoted rate. If not, you should inquire before check-in time.

## TELEPHONES, TELEGRAMS, & FAXES

The phone system in Holland is more modern and convenient than any major telephone company's newest products are in North America. To begin with, most pay phones provide detailed multilingual instructions for local and international calling procedures. Of course you could always place a local or long distance call from your hotel, but you can expect to get hit with a surcharge of up to 250%.

About the only time I suggest using a hotel's equipment is when you need to send or receive a fax. Another possibility is to place calls (or even faxes and telegrams) from post office's telephone and communications department, private phone boutiques, or ask the nearest VVV tourist information center for the location of a Telecenter phone company consumer office, where you are shown to a small cabin and after making a call you pay at normal rates. Some of these telephone company offices will accept Visa and Mastercard.

The standard street corner digital screen pay phone accepts so called **Phonecards**, art covered plastic cards that can be purchased in quantities of 5 NLG, 10 NLG, and 25 NLG denominations that are available from VVV offices, tobacco shops, train station ticket counters, and the many so-called **Telecenters** operated by the state run PTT Telecom phone company. These cards keep track of every completed call, and show their balance, as well as the price of your current call, on a digital display on the phone. Most of these computer phone booths also accept Visa, Mastercard, and American Express Cards for international calls (for about a 2.50 NLG surcharge per call).

Only about 15% of the pay phones in Holland still accept coins, and most of these are found only in public establishments, hotel lobbies, and big city rail stations. Instead of taking a plastic card, these older devices accept only multiple coins of between 25 cents and 2.50 NLG, but some the newer 25 cent coins are occasionally refused. In most cases, these phones need a minimum of 50 cents before processing your call, in other cases you insert the coins after the person on the other end answers.

A typical call within one region or city should cost around 30 cents per minute, but if you are using coins, this amount will be rounded off (upwards to the nearest 25 cents). Calling outside the same city or region can bring the cost up to as much as 65 cents per minute. Calling internationally can cost 1.75 NLG or more per minute. In general, calling long distance or internationally from Holland is cheapest after 11pm on weekdays.

If you need to call internationally, you can use MCI, Sprint, ATT, Bell, and a variety of private phone company's access codes from within Holland to reach English speaking operators for collect, credit card, and third party calls. It is even possible to use these cards in the hotel's lobby pay phone. One thing to be careful about is that when you use your North American calling card from a hotel room, you may still end up paying a 5 NLG or surcharge on your hotel room bill.

Numbers and access codes are:
- **Netherlands Directory Assistance**, *06-8008*
- **International Directory Assistance**, *06-0418*
- **International Operator Assistance**, *06-0410*
- **US Country Code**, *001*
- **Canada Country Code**, *001*
- **ATT USA Direct Access Number**, *06-022-9111*
- **Bell Canada Direct Access Number**, *06-022-9116*
- **Sprint USA Direct Access Number**, *06-022-9119*

---

### PHONE TIPS

*To reach the US and Canada from Holland*
*Dial 001 immediately followed by the desired North American area code and phone number*

*To reach Holland from the USA and Canada*
*Dial 011-31 and then the area code and phone number*
*If the Dutch area code shows a zero (0) as a first digit, drop the zero.*

*To call between Two Dutch cities within the same area code*
*Drop the area code which is listed in parentheses.*

*To call between Two Dutch cities in different area codes*
*Use the area code (with the first zero (0) included) and then dial the number.*

*All Dutch phone and fax numbers in this book, except those with a prefix of 06, do not include the first zero of the area code! If calling from North America, dial 011-31 followed by the area code and phone number as it appears here. If you are calling from within Holland, first dial a zero, followed by the listed area code and number.*

---

### Cellular Telephones

Cellular telephones are quite popular in Holland, but your North American cell phones will not function on Europe's totally different **GSM** cellular operating system! If you're like me, and like to have some means of communicating while on the road, you best option is to rent a GSM cell phone to bring with you. I have even been able to connect to the Internet, and send most of my faxes via these phones and my notebook portable computer. While major rental car companies such as Europcar, Budget, Avis, and Hertz offer optional cell phones in their fleet of rental cars, they have always screwed up my reservation, and no phone was available when I went to get it.

In my experience, the best company to contact for GSM cell phone rentals is **Global Cellular Rental** in New York, London, and Paris. They can deliver a phone on time to your hotel (in just about any city in Europe) with a few days advance notice. Another advantage is that they can provide you with it's exact phone number before you depart North America so people back home will know exactly how to reach you while abroad.

Their rates are around $15 per day, $99S per week, or $249 per month for the rental itself, and a minimum usage fee of $80 will be put on your credit card. At the end of your rental, the phone can be picked up at your hotel for a small charge, or you can just drop it in a Federal Express envelope and ship it back to New York upon your arrival. The per minute incoming and outgoing charges vary depending on the hours and at which locations the service will be used, but a quick toll free call or fax to their offices can get you all the information you need.

• **Global Cellular Rental**, *New York, (800) 699-6861*

## TELEVISION

While you are traveling within Holland, I urge you to take advantage of the selection of media (plenty is in English) which is easily available. To begin with, a series of five Dutch broadcasting companies have their own TV channels. These stations transmit their signal to almost every corner of the Netherlands, and tend to offer a combination of locally produced new programming, documentaries, game shows, soap operas, talk shows, and subtitled international movies and mini-series.

Most cable subscribers and many of the better hotels also offer a selection of other European satellite TV programs from Europe, Germany France, Italy, and in some cases you will find CNN International. Usually at least one of these stations will be the SKY or BBC news networks from England which are quite entertaining.

The only word of caution that I should mention is that a couple of Dutch and German networks have a tendency to show porno flicks on weekend evenings. Most hotels also offer a movie channel that usually is billed at 25 NLG per 24 hour period of use, so try to catch as many different films as you can for this flat fee.

## TIME

Holland is in the **Central European Time Zone**, which is **Greenwich Mean Time** (GMT) + 1 hour from November through March, and GMT + 2 hours during daylight savings time from April through October.

Local time in all regions of Holland is 6 hours ahead of the North American Eastern Time Zone (New York, Boston, Montreal, Toronto), 7 hours ahead of the North American Central Time Zone, 8 hours ahead of the North American Mountain Time Zone, and 9 hours ahead of the North American Pacific Time Zone. Holland follows the same daylight savings time system as North America from April through October.

## TIPPING

There are many situations in which a gratuity may be appropriate. In most case you are free to use your judgment based on the quality of services rendered. These are the most common people and amounts to tip in Holland.

Many Dutch do not tip for some services which in our culture may be commonplace. If someone gives you back a tip, do not take it as an insult.

- **Taxi Driver**, 8% of the meter's rate
- **Hotel Porter**, 1.50 NLG per bag
- **Hotel Concierge**, 5 NLG per small favor, 25.00 NLG per big favor
- **Room Service**, 2.50 NLG per person per meal
- **Hotel Doorman**, 2 NLG per taxi
- **Bartender**, 1 NLG per round
- **Waiter**, 10% to 15% of the bill
- **Ushers**, 1 NLG per seat
- **Private Guides**, 2 NLG per person per day
- **Private Drivers**, 18.50 NLG per person per day
- **Tour Guides**, 15 NLG per person per day
- **Tour Bus Drivers**, 10 NLG per person per day.

---

### US DOLLAR LISTINGS IN THIS BOOK

*In this guide book, all dollar prices given are in US dollars unless otherwise noted.*

# 8. GETTING AROUND HOLLAND

## BY AIR

While there are a handful of small to medium sized commuter based airports within Holland, almost 98% of the air traffic here tends to be over at **Schiphol Airport** near Amsterdam. While connecting flights on small planes do exist to places such as Maastricht, I strongly suggest using less expensive methods of transportation such as the train system to get around the country. For more information, call your travel agent.

## BY BUS

For the most part, people use buses in Holland to get between various cities and suburban or rural towns within the nation's 12 provinces. Since there are literally dozens of separate municipal and regional bus companies, no one source can provide you with all the details you may need during your stay in Holland.

The two largest bus companies are **Interliner** and the **NZH**. They offer extensive and rather comfortable luxury motor-coaches that charge an average of 0.25 NLG per kilometer and have their own depots and stops near major train stations and downtown locations. Like the train system, they also have special same day return rates. The best suggestion I have is to visit the closest train station or VVV tourist office, and ask them for bus information. Each of these companies also have large but inexpensive system timetables for sale in their regional offices and bus station information booths throughout Holland.

• **Holland Mass Transportation Information**, *(06) 9292*

## BY BICYCLE

The Netherlands is one of the world's finest places to get around by bicycle. Not only is much of the country flat, but it is small enough to enable you to easily bike between many different cities and destinations in less than two hours. Almost every city, suburb, town, village, and remote hamlet is connected to each other by a vast network of over 14,500 kilometers (8,990 miles) of safe, separate, and intelligently designed **Fietspad** bicycle paths. These easy-to-find bike paths are indicated by a blue sign showing a white bike. Routes have their own well-indicated sign posts, and even traffic lights in big cities.

While this subject alone could fill whole books (and in fact does!) the basic idea is that the government tries to encourage bicycle use to help reduce automotive traffic and pollution. Also, with Holland's hefty 200% or so tax on new cars, most young people and students have little chance of affording a motorized vehicle of their own. Each day almost a million people all over the country ride to work, school, or local train station.

The first thing you will need to do is to decide if you are going to bring your own bike here, or to rent (or purchase) one in Holland. Most airlines will let you bring a bicycle instead of one of your two allowed suitcases, but you must call them in advance for exact details. Since bicycle theft in Holland is a major factor, my suggestion is to leave your brand new 21 speed hybrid at home! No matter how good your expensive "unbreakable" lock may be at home, it may not stand a chance in any Dutch city.

What most people do is rent a basic 1 or 3 speed black and white English style touring bike with no frills. While these take a little time to get used to, they are cheap and won't attract too much attention form the junkies and other thieves (if locked). Over 80 trains stations have a **Rijwiel** bicycle shop where you can rent a bike for around 10 NLG per day or 40 NLG per week, plus a refundable deposit. If you are using the train system, a special 2 NLG discount may apply.

If you are biking to various cities, or want to take a great ride through the countryside, make sure to buy some of the excellent **ANWB** (Royal Dutch Touring Club) **Fietsroute** bicycle route maps. There are also routes mapped out by the **Landelijk Fietsplatform** bicycle organization in Amersfoort. Most of these can be purchased for around 8.50 NLG each at most main city VVV tourist information offices and better Dutch book shops. Many local VVV tourist offices may also sell their own maps of regional bicycle paths with special historical or scenic importance.

· **ANWB** (**Royal Dutch Touring Club**), *(70) 314-1420*

## BY CAR

### Booking Car Rentals

Almost all major international airlines fly into **Schiphol International Airport** near Amsterdam. For those of you who want to immediately pick up a car upon arrival in Amsterdam, an abundance of well-known international rental car companies operate both airport kiosks and downtown offices all over Holland. Avis, Budget, National, Europcar,

Hertz, and several other lesser known companies maintain airport hours from early each morning until the last flight is scheduled to arrive. International drivers licenses are not required for North Americans driving in Holland, but it's not a bad idea to visit the CAA or AAA offices and get one for about $17.50. All that is required for car rental documentation is a major credit card, passport, and your valid US or Canadian driver's license.

If you intend to use a rental car in the Netherlands, it is advisable to book and prepay (in advance) from within North America so that you can save up to 45% of the normal locally available European rates. If you decide to rent a car only once you have arrived in Holland, rentals can be arranged from any Dutch travel agency or car rental company office. I strongly advice those desiring to rent a car for less than 3 days in a row to purchase a special voucher for 10 NLG at the VVV tourist information centers in Amsterdam, these certificates offers great reduced rates that are 50% off normal Dutch short term prices. There are rental locations within most major cities.

It is also important to call your credit card company before you leave for Europe to determine if any insurance is automatically included for car rentals in Holland. Most forms of insurance (collision damage waiver, liability, vehicle theft, personal accident injury insurance, property theft insurance) will be offered upon your pick up of the car and may add up to well over $35 per day additional. Make sure that you are covered one way or another, or else you may wind up with a big problem.

With advance booking and prepayment from the US or Canada, non-inclusive prices range from below $217 per week for a small 2 door manual car (Renault Twingo hatchback or similar) to well over $395 per week for any automatic or 4-door sporty car, plus insurance. Rates that include the 17.5 % tax and insurance can save you even more money. Specialty rentals such as Mercedes Benz may also be available. Also keep in mind that Schiphol airport car rentals will be charges an additional surcharge of about 30 NLG.

You can pick up a rental car in one major city in Holland and drop it off in another, usually with no extra drop-off charges. If you drop off your car outside of Holland, large drop-off surcharges of well over $125 will apply. Keep in mind that taking a rental car from the Netherlands into anywhere else in Europe is only allowed if you inform the rental company that you are doing so in advance, and ask the rental agent to provide you with a set of international insurance and registration documents.

## Major North American Car Rental Companies
• **AutoEurope**, *US, 1-800-223-5555*
• **AutoEurope**, *Canada, 1-800-223-5555*

• **Avis**, *US, 1-800-331-1084*
• **Avis**, *Canada, 1-800-879-2847*
• **Budget**, *US, 1-800-527-0770*
• **Budget**, *Canada, 1-800-268-8900*
• **Hertz**, *US, 1-800-654-1101*
• **Hertz**, *Canada, 1-800-263-0600*

### Discounted Car Rentals in Holland

If you want to save plenty of money and aggravation booking a rental car for use in Holland, or anywhere else in the world, give a call to a discount car rental broker who can provide you reservations through the above listed companies at up to a 40% discount if bookings are made before your departure from North America.

By far, the best and most serious of these firms is **Auto Europe**, based in Portland, Maine. This excellent company offers incredible discounts on all categories of rental cars through the world, and can even save you serious money on airline tickets and hotel reservations. As one of the travel industry's main suppliers of rental cars for package and customized tours, they have contracts with Budget, Avis, and Europe Car rental locations that allow them to get you a car for much less than these companies will quote you. The last time I went to Holland, Auto Europe saved me over $83 per week on my car rental (versus the best quote I had after calling everyone else) – plus I ended up with a much better car at no additional charge!

Their friendly and knowledgeable staff will beat any written quote on the market, and can provide repeat client discounts, AAA and CAA discounts, long-stay rates, low season super specials, and great deals on optional insurance against collision damage, theft, and even property loss. Their fully refundable car rental vouchers can be instantly faxed directly to you or your travel agent, and reservations usually only require a small prepaid deposit via credit card or check. Call all the others first, and then ring up Auto Europe.

• **Auto Europe**, *in US and Canada, 1-800-223-5555*

### Driving in Holland

Unlike some other countries in Europe, Holland is a relatively easy place to drive around. To begin with, the steering wheel and all other controls are placed exactly where they would be in your own car at home. While standard shift vehicles are most common, you can also get a car with an automatic transmission if necessary. Before arriving in Holland, it's best to pre-plan your driving route by using a good road map (available at any NBT office or your local travel book store) and an outliner. Ask the rental car company or your hotel's front desk to give you detailed directions to your next location, as maps may not point out serious construction delays.

A small percentage of Dutch people seem to drive faster than necessary. Expect a few other cars to pass on blind curves and sometimes even pull multiple lane changes at high speeds. If you drive very carefully, and stay in the appropriate lane for your desired velocity, you should be just fine. All of the roads here are in rather good condition, have no tolls to worry about, and have international road signs. I have driven over 6,500 km (4,030 miles) within Holland, and I have never had an accident or received a speeding ticket. Official **speed limits** (unless otherwise posted) are about 50 km/hr in towns and villages, 80 km/hr on most normal roads, and 120 km/hr on highways and motorways. Seat belts are mandatory, and should be used at all times while driving in Holland. Speed traps and radar have been popping up everywhere lately.

**Gasoline** is extremely expensive in the Netherlands. At press time, gas costs approximately 2.10 NLG and up per liter (about $5.50 per gallon). Since all of the rental vehicles are rather small in Europe, fortunately most car's fuel efficiency is very high. Over the last several years, many 24 hour 7 days a week service stations complete with repair shops, mini-markets, cafeterias, and bars have popped up throughout Holland and accept most major credit cards. Normal service station hours are from 8am until 7pm Monday - Sunday, but a small percentage of gas stations may close on Sundays.

It is important for me to explain that most roads in Holland are indicated by using letters and numbers. A super fast 3 or 4 lane in each direction motorway that is generally known as an **Autosnelweg** and is most commonly listed on maps and road signs with the letter "**A**" followed by numbers. A major 2 or 3 lane per direction European highway is normally referred to here as an **Europaweg** and are typically listed using the letter "**E**" followed by numerals. A smaller rural or regional roads of either 1 or 2 lanes in each direction is most often called a **Nationale Weg** and will usually have a prefix of "**N**" followed by a number.

Since crime is still an issue for tourists in any part of the world, a rental car is easy prey. Don't leave anything in your car when it is parked, and if possible it is advised to lock your gas cap. Since exposed hatchback cars have increased risks for potential pilferage, it is recommended to either cover the hatch or avoid renting these categories of vehicles (usually the less expensive cars). Many car rental companies maintain a rapid car replacement service in the event that you incur a breakdown or an accident somewhere in Holland. It is important to find out where the branch offices of your rental car company are located, and their emergency phone numbers.

The official automobile club and representative in Holland for members of the AAA and the CAA auto clubs is called **ANWB** (**Royal Dutch Touring Club**) and if necessary their emergency roadside assistance trucks can be reached by using any road-side emergency yellow phone, or by calling them from a normal phone at *(06) 8008* any time of the day or night.

In the event of an accident, you should call the police to come to the scene of the accident, write down the license plate of the other car(s) involved, and if possible hand copy his license and insurance information. If no police arrive on the scene within 45 minutes or so, pay a visit the closest police station, report the accident, and ask them to give you a copy of the accident report or the report number. Call your car rental company as soon as possible after you have obtained the above required documentation.

Perhaps the only major drawbacks to driving through Holland are the severe daily rush hours in and around big cities, and the expense and difficulty of parking. It seems that there are at least two cars for every parking space in most Dutch cities. Parking spots are typically indicated by a sign using a **black** "**P**" surrounded by a white circle and a yellow rectangular background. Most of the street side parking spots do not use coin meters, but rather you are expected to purchase a ticket from the nearby automatic machines. These spaces cost from 2 NLG to 4 NLG per hour and have a two hour limit.

**PARKING IN ROTTERDAM?**

The only time you may be able to park for free in these spots is indicated on the automatic ticket dispensers and is usually from about 7:00pm until around 9:00am Monday through Saturday (and either Thursdays or Fridays from 9:00pm for late shopping night) , as well as Sundays and holidays. After putting coins into the machine, it will print out a coupon with the hour of expiration printed on it. You must leave the automated parking coupon on the inside of the windshield so that the traffic police can easily see it when the come around to check. Tickets and tow trucks are often used for illegally parked cars, and can cost you upwards of 50 NLG per infraction (and much, much more if you are towed).

Several private and municipal parking lots (found by following the **white** "**P**" signs with blue backgrounds) can be found in each city, but some close rather early. Most of these garages cost at about 2.50 NLG per hour and somewhere around 26 NLG per 24 hours. Another good option are the Park & Ride garages near suburban train stations that are often free or inexpensive.

## BY FERRY

There are still more than a few ferry lines that run between various sections of coastal Holland. Besides a few tiny ferry boats in eastern Zeeland, there are several more (and much larger) vessels from northern Friesland and Groningen that service the beautiful little **Wadden Islands** (sort of the inexpensive Cape Cod of Holland). These trips take between 45 minutes and two hours each way, depending on which island you want to visit. All of these ferries operate in both directions year round, but have more frequent service in the April through October high season.

The **Texel Island** ferry departs the piers of Den Helder multiple times daily and a round-trip ticket costs about 11 NLG per passenger, 6 NLG per bicycle, and 50 NLG per car.

The **Terschelling Island** ferry departs the ports of Harlingen a few times daily and a round-trip ticket costs about 39 NLG per passenger, 16 NLG per bicycle, and 160 NLG per car.

The **Vlieland Island** ferry leaves from the ports of Harlingen a few times daily and a round trip ticket will set you back around 39 NLG per person, 16 NLG per bicycle, and cars are not allowed on the island.

The **Ameland Island** ferry leaves the harbor at Holwerd at least a couple of times (many more in the summer) each day and the round trip fare is currently 18 NLG per person, 9 per bicycle, and 135 per car.

Finally, the **Schiermonnikoog Island** ferry goes from the docks at Lauwersoog at least a couple of times (many more in the summer) each day and the round trip fare is currently 18 NLG per person, 9 per bicycle, and cars are not allowed on the island.

## BY TRAIN

The newly privatized national electric powered railroad company is called **Nederlandse Spoorwegen**, but is more commonly referred to simply as **NS**. They operate hundreds of train lines on well over 7,000 kilometers (4,340 miles) of tracks throughout the country. These train services are almost always on time to the minute, and are usually rather inexpensive.

Typical one way **Enkele Reis** fares cost somewhere around 0.40 NLG per kilometer in 1st class, and about 0.27 NLG per kilometer in 2nd class. Same day round trip **Dagretour** tickets are usually discounted at around 25% off of the price of 2 one way tickets. There are different categories of trains to choose from depending on your routing and desired time of arrival. The fastest and most comfortable **Intercity** express trains travel on several different routes that connect the country's 30 largest stations (while the **Eurocity** trains continue on past the borders), including Schiphol Airport. The reasonably fast **Sneltrein** trains have routes that cover some 80 or so stations with a limited number of stops. The **Stoptrein** trains stop rather often at small commuter stations and move at a snails pace sometimes. There are also several regional, and commuter rail lines which cover just about every corner of the country.

Most of the trains in Holland offer snacks and beverages in their via their so called Rail Tender cart service, are fully air conditioned, have a limited number of bicycle storage areas, smoking and non-smoking sections, both first and second class seating areas, small bathrooms, and even pay phones in some cases. To get exact fare information, schedules, advice, reservations, and tickets you must visit any train station in Holland. If you need these details before you depart, contact the **NBT** tourist offices in your country, or call the expert agents over at **Rail Europe** before departing North America. To bring your bike on board you must first purchase a special ticket costing between 13 and 26 NLG, and still may only be valid during off peak hours.

Any train station ticket booth in Holland will be glad to sell you inexpensive information books such as the yearly 9.75 NLG **Spoorboekje** Dutch train system timetable, the smaller 2 NLG **Intercityboekje** Dutch city express train timetable, and various other helpful multilingual publications. Another good source may be to purchase either the monthly *European Rail Timetables*, or the annual *On the Rails Around Europe* train travel guides published by **Thomas Cook** which can be found in travel book shops in major cities throughout the world (or by calling the Forsyth Travel Library toll free at *(800) 367-7984*). Trains don't always run on time, so plan your connections with enough time to still catch the next train.

All of the 80 major train stations in the Netherlands are staffed with patient clerks that speak great English, and feature facilities such as separate Domestic **Binnenland** and international **Buitenland** ticket booths, a nearby municipal and/or regional bus depot, a GWK bank with extended hours currency exchange desks, luggage storage lockers, public rest rooms, cafés, a few boutiques, vending machines, computerized pay phones that take phonecards and major credit cards, bike racks, short term car parking, nearby or adjacent hotels, and almost all contain a **Rijwiel** bicycle shop where with a passport or other official identification you can rent a bike for around 9 NLG per day or 35 NLG per week a plus refundable deposit (official ID such as a passport is required).

---

### TAKE THE TREINTAXI!

*A fantastic money-saving service known as the **Treintaxi** has been implemented at all train stations in Holland outside of the three big cities of Amsterdam, Den Haag, and Rotterdam. If you need to take a taxi somewhere in the city limits (and in some cases to the adjacent villages) of the station that you have just reached via train, for just a flat fee of 6 NLG per person you can be driven directly there via taxi. Considering that you could easily spend 18.50 NLG or more taking a normal private taxi for the same distance, this can save you a small fortune.*

*The only catch is that you must buy these tickets at the station of your departure, use them the same day, and wait until the taxi is full before it departs the well marked "Treintaxi" stand.*

---

NS also offers a unique series of some 85 special **Rail Idee** excursions that can be enjoyed via train. The offer packages including same day return train tickets and admission charges to such famous attractions as Keukenhof, the Museum Kroller-Muller near Arnhem, the Het Loo Palace in Appeldoorn, the beaches of Scheveningen, and Valkenburg's Thermae 2000 spa. These are a good way to save time, money, and aggravation. Inquire at any train station ticket window, or ask for a free copy of the multilingual *Exploring Holland by Train* brochure.

For those of you interested in scenic train rides, there are a few remaining scenic narrow gauge railways and riverfront lines left in Holland. Some of these railroads include antique and 1930's era steam engines and railroad cars. The most famous of these is the **Miljoenenlijn** that runs between the southern Limburg towns of Simpelveld, Schin op Guel, and Kerkrade. Operated by the ZLSM regional transit company in Simpelveld, it costs between 7 NLG and 18.50 NLG round trip (depending on the route) and departs Wednesday through Sunday between March and December, and daily during July and August. Reservations can be made by calling *(45) 544-0018*.

Finally, if you are in the mood to head out to an island, ask any Dutch train station ticket booth about the **Waddenbiljet** vacation package. For a reasonable sum you can book a combination of round trip train and ferry tickets to one of the Wadden Sea islands including  Vlieland, Terschelling, Ameland, or Schiermonnikoog. These packages also offer prepaid accommodations at your choice of several good hotels on the island you select. You can save about 35% of the normal cost for this type of excursion, and get additional savings once you arrive there.

**Discounted Holland-Only Rail Passes**

Several types of tourist train passes for Holland are available directly from the NBT tourist offices in Chicago. These Netherlands-only unlimited use (within a set number of days) first and second class train passes include the **Holland Rail Pass** that gives unlimited train service in Holland for 3,5, or 10 days in a 30 day period. For a small additional fee you can buy a **Public Transportation Link** supplement that allows you to use all Dutch municipal transit services such as trams, subways, and buses. These cannot be purchased separately and are valid only during the same 3, 5, or 10 days as the above-mentioned pass.

To order these passes, call the **NBT** in Chicago, *Tel. 1-800-598-8501.*

• **3 Day Holland Rail Pass**, *$88 1st Class, $68 2nd Class*
• **3 day tram & bus link**, *$13*
• **5 Day Holland Rail Pass**, *$140 1st Class, $104 2nd Class*
• **5 day tram & bus link**, *$21*
• **10 Day Holland Rail Pass**, *$260 1st Class, $184 2nd Class*
• **10 day tram & bus link**, *$33*

If you intend to do extensive train travel through Holland and didn't purchase a rail pass, at any Dutch station you can buy a 99 NLG **Rail Aktief Kaart** that is valid for one year and gets you a 40% discount on train tickets used during off peak hours.

• **Holland Mass Transportation Information**, *(06) 9292*

**Eurail Passes**

**Eurail** passes are accepted on the Dutch train system and must be purchased before your departure from North America, although some services may require a supplemental surcharge. There are several types of youth and adult Eurail passes available for travel within a specific amount of time through 17 different countries in Europe, or solely within one specific country. When using a rail pass you may be allowed to upgrade your journey by reserving seats, couchettes, and sleeping cars for a supplemental charge.

The best place to buy these passes is directly from the prompt and reliable staff of **Rail Europe** in both the US and Canada, from a specialty tour operator, or your favorite travel agency. Once you have your Eurail pass (which will automatically expire in 6 months from the date of issue), any upgrades, specific reservations, or sleeping car requests should be made directly with Rail Europe before you depart North America, or if already in Holland with any Dutch rail station's international ticket counter. Details of these passes are listed below.

Rail Europe's North American phone numbers are:
• **Rail Europe** *in the US:* 1-800-438-7245
• **Rail Europe** *in Canada:* 1-800-361-7245

### Eurail Youthpass

These are **second class** train passes valid for people under 26 years old. These passes can only be purchased within North America before departure, and are valid from the first day you use it in Europe. They allow for unlimited train travel in 17 European countries (as well as certain bus and ferry routes) within a maximum number of predetermined days.
• **15 day pass**: *$418 US*
• **1 month pass**: *$598 US*
• **2 month pass**: *$798 US*

### Eurail Pass

These are **first class** train passes which are valid for people of all ages. These passes can only be purchased within North America before departure, and are valid from the first day you use it in Europe.

They allow for unlimited train travel in 17 European countries (as well as certain bus and ferry routes) within a maximum number of predetermined days.
• **15 day pass**: *$522   US*
• **21 day pass**: *$678   US*
• **1 month pass**: *$838   US*
• **2 month pass**: *$1148 US*
• **3 month pass**: *$1468 US*

Accompanied children aged 4-11 can receive a discount of 50% off the above prices.

### Eurail Saver Pass

These are special **first class** train passes for people of all ages traveling on the exact same schedule of train travel in 17 European countries (as well as certain bus and ferry routes). They are valid for unlimited travel during a predetermined length of time. Between the months of October through March these passes requires a minimum of 2 people traveling together, between the months of April and September this pass is valid for a minimum of 3 people traveling together.

• **15 day saver pass**: *$452  US*
• **21 day saver pass**: *$578  US*
• **1 month saver pass**: *$712  US*

Accompanied children aged 4-11 can receive a discount of 50% off the above.

## Eurail Youth Flexipass

These are **second class** train passes valid for people under 26 years old. They must be purchased within North America before departure, and are good from the first day you use it in Europe. They allow for unlimited train travel in 17 European countries (as well as certain bus and ferry routes) within a maximum number of predetermined days within a given time period.

• **10 days of travel within a 2 month period**: *$438  US*
• **15 days of travel within a 2 month period**: *$588 US*

## Eurail Flexipass

These are **first class** train passes which are valid to people of all ages. They must be purchased within North America before departure, and are valid from the first day you use it in Europe. They allow for unlimited train travel in 17 European countries (as well as certain bus and ferry routes) within a maximum number of predetermined days within a given time period.

• **10 days of travel within a 2 month period**: *$616  US*
• **5 days of travel within a 2 month period**: *$812  US*

Accompanied children aged 4-11 can receive a discount of 50% off the above.

## Europass

These are **first class** train passes valid to people of all ages. They must be purchased within North America before departure, and are valid from the first day you use it in Europe. They allow for unlimited train travel in specific groupings of between 3 and 5 pre-selected European countries (as well as certain bus and ferry routes) within a maximum number of predetermined days in a given time period. Additional countries may be added to create a customized Europass valid for up to 9 pre-selected European nations in total, but the prices increase with the number of nations you choose. This one gets a bit complicated to explain, so call Rail Europe for the exact country groupings they are offering.

Also, if you travel with a second passenger on the exact same schedule, you can each save about 25%. Prices range from $316 US for one person traveling to 3 pre-selected countries on any 5 days during a 60 day period, and go up to $736 US for one person traveling to 5 pre-selected countries on any 15 days during 2 months.

**Europass Youth**

These are **second class** train passes valid for people up to age 25. They must be purchased within North America before departure, and are good from the first day you use it in Europe. They allow for unlimited train travel in specific groupings of between 3 and 5 pre-selected European countries (as well as certain bus and ferry routes) within a maximum number of predetermined days within a given time period. Additional countries may be added to create a customized Europass Youth valid for up to 9 pre-selected European nations in total, but the prices increase along with the number of nations you choose. This one is also complicated, so call Rail Europe for the exact country groupings they are offering.

Prices range from $210 US for one young adult traveling to 3 pre-selected countries on any 5 days during a 60 day period, and go up to $500 US for one young adult traveling to 5 pre-selected countries on any 15 days during 2 months.

**Rail Europe Offices in North America**
• **Rail Europe**, *US,* *1-800-438-7245*
• **Rail Europe**, *Canada,* *1-800-361-7245*

## INNER CITY PUBLIC TRANSPORTATION

Every city and region in Holland is serviced by one or more public transportation authorities offering a combination of either trams, buses, and sometimes underground metros (subways). I have listed local address and phone numbers of most of these in their corresponding city chapters. They all however have one thing in common: they utilize the same national fare by zones of travel system, and all accept the same **strip tickets** explained below.

Just keep in mind that buses can be entered via the front door, while most trams and all metros have several entry doors you can use. The normal hours of operation for most of the system is from about 6:30am until roughly 12:15am. After that your only choices are the more expensive and less frequent night busses that run from Centraal Station and various major stops through the city between 12:30am and 2:00am and again from 4:00am until 6:00am. All of these systems utilize the same types of tickets and passes.

To begin with, if you buy your tickets or passes in advance from a municipal transit office, a VVV tourist office, a metro station, post office, or one of many tobacco shops, you will save a lot of money. In these outlets, you can purchase the multiple use 15 and 45 unit **Nationale Strippen kaart** (strip ticket). These strip tickets allow for one or more people to each use two blank strips per zone of local travel.

Since most city's downtown (centrum) areas are covered in just one zone, this means that two blank strips must be stamped per person and all transfers made within one hour of the stamping are included. Locations outside of downtown zones and travel to neighboring cities may travel through several zones, so you must ask the driver how many blank strips are required. The current price for a 15 strip ticket is 11 NLG and for a 45 strip ticket is 32.25 NLG.

To validate your strip ticket, either present the strip ticket to the driver or conductor upon entry if he asks, or otherwise continue further into the bus or tram. As soon as you pass one of the several yellow validation boxes onboard, fold the card so that the top part being inserted into the machine is the second available blank strip, and push it into the validation box until you hear a ring or click. The strip is then marked in ink with the time and date, and upon your next use you will then fold the card down so that the next time it stamp once again on the second blank strip. When you use the metro, the validation machine is near the station's entrance. If two people are using the same strippenkaart for one ride, you must stamp the strip ticket on both the 2nd and 4th blank strips. If you need to use a night bus, you may find the need to stamp 3 strips per person.

Additionally, you can also consider buying a **Nationale Dagkaart** that gives unlimited municipal transit use for 1 day anywhere in Holland for 24 NLG per person, or a local **Dagkaart** full day unlimited use card (extra days available for a small surcharge) for either Amsterdam, Rotterdam, or Den Haag at about 12 NLG per person. If you have not arranged to buy an advance purchase strippenkaart or Dagkaart, you will then be forced to purchase your fare directly on the bus or tram. The drivers usually have 2 unit strip tickets for 3 NLG, 3 unit strip tickets or night bus tickets for 4.50 NLG, and 8 unit strip tickets for 12 NLG.

If you are caught on any bus, tram, or train without the properly validated tickets or pass, you could be fined upwards of 60 NLG plus the normal fare on the spot.

# 9. SHOPPING

Shopping in the Netherlands is a great pleasure! Each region produces different items, ranging from hand-painted wooden boxes and ceramics to traditional Delftware miniatures and South African cut diamonds. Fine European shoes, shirts, sweaters, dresses, handbags, belts, suits, linens, ceramics, tiles, embroidery, jewelry, and all sorts of additional items can be found at about 25% below their North American price. Most jewelry is made locally with 14 though 28 karat gold, and better quality sterling silver.

Remember that most retail stores are open from 9:00am until about 6:00pm from Monday through Friday, and from 10:00am and 5:00pm on Saturdays. Among the most common exceptions to this schedule are Monday mornings when a vast amount of stores open up at around 1:00pm. Many Dutch towns and cities now have 1 late shopping night per week on either Thursday or Friday when shops close at 9:00pm. Sunday retail hours do exist, but only in selected shopping centers and a few boutiques in the most tourist related areas and larger cities.

A tax of around 17.5% is already included in all posted retail prices. For tax-free shopping, try the huge mall inside of Schiphol airport.

Since Holland has joined the E.E.C., a program of tax refunds on selected export items has begun. What this **Tax Free for Tourists** program really does is quite simple and worth taking advantage of. Over 1,000 shops in Holland display the black and blue "Tax Free" sticker on their door. When you make a purchase of over 300 NLG, you can ask for a Tax Free voucher check for your refund. The unsigned check is made out to the tourist (you must have your passport with you) which can only be cashed at the airport upon exiting the country. The value of the check depends on what percentage of tax was placed on the specific item you have purchased. At the airport, go to the information booth and they will direct you to the cashier (7 days a week) before you reach the gates. My last refund check in Holland was for over 134 NLG (about 14% of the total price)!

For specific details either pick up a *Tax Free For Tourists* brochure at the airport, or at major downtown hotels.

Among the most impressive gifts to bring back home from Holland are diamond jewelry, gold bracelets, .925 sterling silver settings, antique or recently made Delftware items, Dutch porcelain dinnerware, typical beer glasses complete with golden logos, hand painted wooden items from northern villages like Hinderloopen, colorful wooden shoes, tulip bulbs and other export ready seeds, Dutch cocoa, and old Gouda type cheeses.

Each town and village in Holland offers many unique regional crafts which can easily be found in the shops, markets, craft fairs, and artisan's kiosks of each area. Several local VVV offices throughout the Netherlands have copies of pamphlets which give complete listings of all regional craft fairs and exhibitions each year. The most sought after examples of regional crafts include these fine products that are made and then sold in destinations that you should be visiting.

## EUROPEAN SIZE CONVERSIONS

*These sizes are approximate and may not be accurate in certain cases. Ask for a free measurement or try on items before you purchase them.*

### Men's Shoes

| | | | | | | |
|---|---|---|---|---|---|---|
| North America | 7 | 7.5 | 8 | 9 | 10 | 11 |
| Holland | 39 | 40 | 41 | 43 | 44 | 45 |

### Women's Shoes

| | | | | | | |
|---|---|---|---|---|---|---|
| North America | 4 | 5 | 6 | 7 | 8 | 9 |
| Holland | 35 | 36 | 37 | 38 | 39 | 40 |

### Men's Suits

| | | | | | | | |
|---|---|---|---|---|---|---|---|
| North America | 34 | 36 | 38 | 40 | 42 | 44 | 46 |
| Holland | 44 | 46 | 48 | 50 | 52 | 54 | 56 |

### Women's Dresses

| | | | | | | |
|---|---|---|---|---|---|---|
| North America | 6 | 8 | 10 | 12 | 14 | 16 |
| Holland | 36 | 38 | 40 | 42 | 44 | 46 |

### Men's Shirts

| | | | | |
|---|---|---|---|---|
| North America | 15 | 16 | 17 | 18 |
| Holland | 38 | 40 | 42 | 44 |

# 10. SPORTS

The following is a brief description of what types of sports you can expect to enjoy in Holland. Please keep in mind that by no means does this list go into every type of available participatory and spectator sport available throughout the country. Check with local VVV tourist information offices in each region for the locations and information regarding venues and outfitters for all types of sports.

## BICYCLE RIDING

Holland is a truly wonderful place to use bicycles, especially since much of it is flat. Every city, town, and village here is linked together by over 14,500 kilometers (8,990 miles) of specially indicated **Fietspad** bike paths. Most people rent a basic 1 or 3 speed black and white English style touring bike with no frills. While these take a little time to get used to, they are cheap and usually will not get stolen (if locked up).

Over 80 trains stations have a **Rijwiel** bicycle shop where you can rent a bike for around 9 NLG per day or 35 NLG per week a plus refundable deposit. The **ANWB** (**Royal Dutch Touring Club**) and the **Landelijk Fietsplatform** both produce special bicycle route maps that can be found for sale at VVV tourist offices and at many book shops throughout Holland. For further details on bicycles here, see Chapter 8, *Getting Around Holland*.

## CAR RACES & RALLIES

Among the many world-class racing events that take place on Holland's major raceways are the **Passraces** during Easter in Zandvoort, and the **TT Assen Grand Prix** during June in Assen.

## FISHING

With plenty of superb deep sea fishing possibilities, and well over 150,000 acres of inland rivers and lakes, Holland is a great place to fish. Flounder, pike, trout, cod, mackerel, and sea trout among the many fish commonly caught here. If you intend to sport fish on any inland area, you'll need to purchase an inexpensive Sportvis**karte** fishing license from any PTT post office in the Netherlands. Coastal and deep sea fishing do not require licenses, and can best be enjoyed from one of over 70 ports and harbors along the cost that offer year round fishing trips at about 40 NLG per person, plus tackle rentals and bait.

For a full listing of fishing boat operators in Holland, contact the national angler's association known as the **NVVS**, *Postbus 288, 3800 AG Amersfoort, Tel. (33) 463-4924, fax: (33) 461-1928.*

## HIKING

Nice walks can be enjoyed all over the Netherlands. You can choose between well over 350 separate and well-marked walking paths that pass lakes, national parks, tulip fields, coastal fishing towns, inland farming villages, game and forest reserves, and even sand dune beaches. The **Royal Dutch Touring Club (ANWB)** publishes many maps on this subject. Among the special facilities offered for hikers here are discounted **Rail-Idee** train excursion tickets with meal vouchers and route maps that can be purchased at any Dutch train station. There are also special foundations and government agencies that produce detailed route maps.

While special hiking path maps are available from almost any VVV tourist information office, the following are a list of organizations that can provide additional information on short, medium, and long range hikes.
• **Stichting Lange Afstands Wandelpaden** (Long Range Hiking Foundation), *Postbus 846, 3800 AV Amersfoort, Tel. (33) 465-3660, fax: (33) 465-4377*
• **Staatsbosbeheer** (The Dutch Forestry Commission), *Tel. (30) 692-6111, fax: (30) 692-2978*

### Mud Hiking

That's right, those wild and crazy people up in Friesland have a strange little sport called **Wadlopen** that you won't find back home! During exceptionally low tides, energetic Dutch people trek several miles across the receded Wadden Sea and head off for the islands of Schiermonnikoog, Ameland, or Engelsmanplaat. This is a downright dirty task, as most people end up sinking a foot or two into mud-flats that can feel like quicksand.

Don't do this alone, but if you really want to try something you can tell all your friends about for the rest of your life, give it a shot. Guided mud hikes are given between the months of May through September, and you must contact the following organization to make the arrangements for a day long outing: **Wadlopencentrum Pieterburen**, *Postbus 1, 9968 ZG Pieterburen, Tel. (595) 528-300.*

## HORSEBACK RIDING

Holland offers a wide variety of horseback and carriage riding facilities. Many stables, hotels, resorts, farms, and riding centers can offer hourly riding on wonderful pure and mixed breed horses for as little as 20 NLG per hour. Each region contains several different places to access horses, but you may have to ask your hotel of a local VVV tourist office for the best locations for scenic rides. Keep in mind that Dutch regulations on horse back riding may require you to purchase a special license for this activity, check with the stables about this!

## SOCCER - FOOTBALL

Like the rest of Europe, soccer (football) is a major national pastime in Holland. In the months between September and May there are many serious soccer league matches within the country (especially in the new stadium of Amsterdam's championship **Ajax** football club), drawing upwards of 65,000 spectators. Since these matches are so faithfully attended, the tickets which can range from 13.50 to 48.50 NLG per seat are often completely sold out well in advance.

If you are interested in seeing a match, you can check with the host stadium's box office to see if there are any seats available. Be extremely careful not to cheer too loudly for the visiting team, as fans can get a bit rough with their adversaries. Soccer matches are generally accompanied by a series of events, not unlike our pro football half-time and pre-game festivities.

## TENNIS

You can find both private and municipal tennis centers and courts in most major tourist resorts and large cities within Holland. Many hotels also offer a few courts for their exclusive use of their guests, but sometimes they can be persuaded to welcome others. If you are looking for lessons or court time, you can inquire at either the front desk of your hotel, or at a local VVV tourist office for details and suggestions. Typical court fees are 25 NLG per hour outdoors, and 35 NLG per hour on an indoor court.

## WATER SPORTS

With miles of superb coastline, nice lakes, and inland waterways, you'll find many opportunities to swim, sail, wind surf, water-ski, jet-ski, surf, dive, fish, and snorkel. Since there are so many different areas to enjoy water sports throughout the country, I have included a listing of the best facilities in each appropriate regional chapter.

For the most part, you can expect to find world-class water sports around Scheveningen, Zaandvoort, and coastal sections of Friesland, Groningen, Zeeland, and the huge Ijsselmeer man made lake. There are also countless spots for swimming, fishing, and sailing in lakes scattered around almost all of the interior regions of the country. Check with the local VVV tourist office for details on additional sights and equipment rentals.

Additional organizations that can provide information include the **ANWB** water sports department, *Tel. (70) 314-7720*, and the **Koninklijk Nederlands Watersport Verbond** federation, *Tel. (30) 657-1325.*

### Swimming

Most major Dutch beaches have seaside beach pavilions with rest rooms, changing facilities, beach chair rentals, snack shops, and more. For a few guilders per day you can use all their facilities. The larger beach resorts have lifeguards on duty in the June through August time period.

Nude bathing is not uncommon, but is often located on more desolate stretches of beach near the large resorts, as well as on more remote areas. The Dutch will sometimes sunbathe topless, and it is permitted on all public beaches. There are also dozens of lakes where you can swim, but not all have lifeguards and facilities. For more details, contact a VVV tourist information office in the area you wish to visit.

### Boats, Canoes, & Windsurfing

All sorts of water sports gear can be rented in various locations throughout the country. Many park areas rent out row boats, canoes, wind surfing boards, and in some cases electric powered motor boats. Some seaside areas also rent everything from small Boston Whaler type craft to cabin cruisers, catamarans, and yachts. For details about small boat and wind surfing board rental, check with any VVV office.

If you need information about canoe rentals, get in touch with the **Toeristische Kano Bond Nederland**, *Postbus 715, 2600 AS Delft, Tel. (15) 256-2792.* For details about renting motor boats, sail boats, cabin cruisers, and yachts, contact **Top of Holland**, *Stationsplein 1, 8911 AC Leeuwarden, Tel. (58) 216-0854, fax: (58) 213-213-6555.*

### Yacht Charters

During the warmer months there are thousands of modern and traditional sailing vessels of all types and ages available for rent with a full crew and skipper. These ships can range from barges and 35 foot pleasure craft up to antique schooners. If you look in the tour operators section of this book, you can also find barge cruises that don't require chartering an entire vessel, but instead offer space for individual passengers.

For more details about boat charters, contact one of the companies listed below:

- **Zeilvaart Enkhuizen**, *Stationsplein 3, 1601 EN Enkhuizen, Tel. (228) 312-424, fax: (228) 313-737*
- **Zeilvloot Harlingen**, *Noorderhaven 17, 8861 AJ Harlingen, Tel. (517) 417-101, fax: (517) 414-286*
- **Zeilvloot Muiden**, *Herengracht 49, 1398 AC Muiden, Tel. (294) 263-929, fax: (294) 262-307*
- **Zeilvloot Lemmer-Stavoren**, *Dwinger 19a, 8715 HV Stavoren, Tel. (514) 681-818, fax: (514) 681-847*
- **Zeilvloot De Zeeuwse Stromen**, *Nieuwe Bogendstraat 7, 4301 CV Zierikzee, Tel. (111) 415-830, fax: (111) 416-557*
- **Hanzestad Compagnie**, *Ijsselkade 62, 8261 AH Kampen, Tel. (38) 331-6050, fax: (38) 331-1577*
- **Hollands Glorie**, *Haringvliet 619, 3011 ZP Rotterdam, Tel. (10) 411-4994, fax: (10) 413-4843*

## GOLF

Golf is becoming a popular pastime for a growing number of Dutch people, as well as with visitors from Germany, Britain, France, and North America. Due to Holland's excellent climate from April through August, many courses have sprung up throughout the country, and several more are in the planning and construction stages. Some of these golf courses have been designed by the world's leading professionals such as Frank Pennick, and offer dramatic views and challenging fairways. Most clubs offer full range of services including access to opulent clubhouses, professional instruction, pro shops, driving ranges, bars, restaurants, and competitions.

You will find that many golf courses (even some private clubs) will offer rates for non-members to use their facilities, but the use of their greens may require buying a special golf permit. Also keep in mind that non residents may be asked for proof of membership at a golf club in their home country. The major cities and the coastal areas are studded with a vast array of choices for all levels of skill, and there are other courses in most regions of the country. Don't expect golf to be a cheap activity here, it can cost upwards of 65 NLG per person for a round of golf on a nice course this year.

Electric carts, equipment rental, locker rooms, lessons, and caddies are usually available at additional cost. Many hotels offer discounts and preferred tee times on local courses to their guests, so please at the front desk for details. Below I have also included a handy chart of some of the major 18+ hole golf courses and their vital information. For more details, contact the **Netherlands Golf Federation**, *Tel. (30) 662-1888.*

These are the major golf courses in Holland, arranged by geographic region:

## ZUID-HOLLAND
- **Alphen a/d Rijn**, *Zeegersloot Golfclub, 18 holes par 71, Tel. (172) 474-567*
- **Bergschenhoek**, *Hooge Bergsche Golfclub, 18 holes par 71, Tel. (10) 522-0052*
- **Brielle**, *Kleiburg Golfbaan, 18 holes par 71, Tel. (282) 417-809*
- **Capelle a/d Ijssel**, *Capelle Country Club, 18 holes par 69, Tel. (10) 442-2485*
- **Dordrecht**, *Merwelanden Golfclub, 18 holes par 71, Tel. (78) 621-1221*
- **Noordwijk**, *Noordwijkse Golfclub, 18 holes par 72, Tel. (252) 373-761*
- **Rhoon**, *Oude Mass Golfclub, 18 holes par 72, Tel. (10) 501-8058*
- **Rijswijk**, *Rikswijkse Golfclub, 18 holes par 72, Tel. (70) 319-2424*
- **Vlaardingen**, *Broekpolder Golfclub, 18 holes par 72, Tel. (10) 474-8140*
- **Wassenaar**, *Rozenstein Golfclub, 18 holes par 71, Tel. (70) 511-7846*

## NOORD-HOLLAND
- **Alkmaar**, *Sluispolder Golfbaan, 18 holes par 72, Tel. (72) 515-6177*
- **Amsterdam**, *Olympus Open Golf Club, 18 holes par 71, Tel. (20) 645-7431*
- **Amsterdam**, *Waterland Golfbaan, 18 holes par 72, Tel. (20) 636-1010*
- **Hilversum**, *Hilversumsche Golf Club, 18 holes par 72, Tel. (35) 685-7060*
- **Purmerend**, *Purmerend Golf Resort, 27 holes par 72, Tel. (299) 481-666*
- **Velsen Zuid**, *Spaanrwoude Golfbaan, 27 holes par 72, Tel. (23) 538-5599*

## LIMBURG
- **Brunssum**, *Brunssumerheide Golfbaan, 18 holes par 71, Tel. (45) 527-0968*
- **Geijsteren**, *Geysteren Country Club, 18 holes par 72, Tel. (478) 532-592*
- **Herkenbosch**, *Herkenbosch Burggolf, 18 holes par 72, (475) 531-458*
- **Mechelen**, *Zuid Limburgse Country Club, 18 holes par 71, Tel. (43) 455-2370*
- **Voerendaal**, *Hoenshuis Country Club, 18 holes par 72, (45) 575-3300*
- **Weert**, *Crossmor Country Club, 18 holes par 72, Tel. (495) 518-438*

## GELDERLAND
- **Arnhem**, *Edese Golfclub, 18 holes par 71, Tel. (26) 482-1985*
- **Arnhem**, *Rosendaelsche Golfclub, 18 holes par 72, Tel. (26) 442-1438*
- **Groesbeek**, *Rijk van Nijmegen Golfbaan, 36 holes par 72, Tel. (24) 397-6644*
- **Nunspeet**, *Nunspeetse Golfvereniging, 27 holes par 72, Tel. (341) 261-149*
- **Wijchen**, *Berendonck Golf Club, 18 holes par 71, Tel. (24) 642-0039*
- **Zoelen**, *Batouwe Betuws Golfcentrum, 27 holes par 72, Tel. (344) 624-370*

## NOORD-BRABANT
- **Best**, *Best Country Club, 18 holes par 72, Tel. (499) 391-443*
- **Valkenswaard**, *Eindhovensche Golf, 18 holes par 72, Tel. (40) 201-2713*
- **Molenschot**, *Toxandria Noord-Brabantsche Golfclub, Tel. (161) 411-856*
- **Oosterhout**, *Oosterhoutsee Golf Club, 18 holes par 72, Tel. (162) 458-759*
- **Wouwse Plantage**, *Wouwse Plantage Golf, 18 holes par 72, Tel. (165) 379-642*

## DRENTHE PROVINCE
- **Aalden**, *Gelpenberg Drenthe Golfclub, 18 holes par 71, Tel. (591) 371-784*
- **Havelte**, *Havelte Golf Club, 18 holes par 72, Tel. (521) 342-200*

## FRIESLAND
- **Beetsterszwaag**, *Lauswolt Country Club, 18 holes par 72, Tel. (512) 383-739*
- **Legemeer**, *Vegilinbosschen Golf Club, 18 holes par 72, Tel. (513) 496-111*

## UTRECHT
- **Leusen**, *Hoge Kleij Golfclub, 18 holes par 72, Tel. (33) 461-6944*
- **Maarsbergen**, *Anderstein Golfclub, 18 holes par 72, Tel. (343) 431-330*

## ZEELAND
- **Bruinisse**, *Grevelingenhout Golfclub, 27 holes par 72, Tel. (111) 482-650*
- **Oostburg**, *Brugse Vaart Golfvereniging, 18 holes par 72, Tel. (117) 453-410*

## OVERIJSSEL
- **Diepenveen**, *Sallandsche Golfclub de Hoek, 18 holes par 72, Tel. (570) 593-269*

## FLEVOLAND
- **Zeewolde**, *Zeewold Golfclub, 18 holes par 70, Tel. (36) 522-2103*

# 11. FOOD & DRINK

## TYPICAL DUTCH CUISINE

Each region of Holland offers a huge selection of unique traditional foods that are well worth a taste. The Dutch have traditionally cooked simple hearty meat, fish, and vegetable-based meals. For centuries, most Dutch people thought of seasonal local treats such as fresh oysters and mussels from Zeeland, or carefully aged Gouda cheese, as gourmet treats. Once exotic spices started arriving from far off Indonesia and distant parts of Europe, foreign restaurants started showing up everywhere.

Be open minded and try some odd sounding dishes. Every city has at least several great restaurants in all price ranges.

### COMMON REGIONAL DUTCH DISHES

**Apppelgebak** - *Apple pie with cinnamon*
**Boerenkool met Rookwurst** - *Potatoes with cabbage and sausage*
**Ertwensoep** - *Split pea soup with pork*
**Gerookte Paling** - *Smoked eels*
**Haring** - *Marinated herring*
**Hutspot** - *Traditional meat, carrot, and potato stew*
**Kapucijners** - *Potatoes, meat, pickles, onion, and molasses*
**Lekkerbekjes** - *Fried whiting*
**Maatje** - *Fresh seasonal herring*
**Oliebolen** - *Fruit filled doughnuts*
**Oude Kaas** - *Aged cheese*
**Pannekoeken** - *Dutch pancakes*
**Pofferties** - *Fried dough with powdered sugar*
**Rodekool met Rolpens** - *Pickled minced beef with apples*
**Stamppot** - *A stew with mashed potatoes and sausage*
**Uitsmitjer** - *Ham and cheese sandwich with a fried egg*
**Vlaamse (or) Patates Frites** - *French fries (often served with mayonnaise)*
**Zeeland Oesters** - *Fresh oysters from the province of Zeeland*
**Zuurkool** - *Sauerkraut*

Since Dutch food is fairly simple and hearty, the cuisine of the former Dutch East Indies colonies has become widely popular in Holland. Based on exotic spices like curry, coconut milk, peanuts, and sate, you must try to enjoy at least one rice table (**rijsttafel**) meal here before you go. Normally for one set price per person, you can select up to a dozen different medium-sized dishes with various sauces.

In most cities, there are also moderately priced Chinese-Indonesian restaurants (**Chinees-Indisch**) restaurants and take-out places where some of the following Indonesian dishes can be found:
- **Babi Pangang** – Pork in hot sauce
- **Bami Goreng** – Fried noodles with assorted meats or seafood
- **Gado Gado** – Assorted vegetables in peanut sauce
- **Kroepoek** – Shrimp crackers
- **Loempia** – Indonesian egg rolls
- **Nasi Goreng** – Fried rice with meat or seafood
- **Pisang Goereng** – Banana fritters
- **Sambal Oedang** – Shrimp in red chili sauce
- **Satay Ayam** – Chicken kebabs with peanut sauce
- **Udang Bakar** – Grilled jumbo shrimp

## BEVERAGES

Throughout Holland, you'll find the same selection of soon-familiar beverages. During breakfast, the most common drink is coffee (koffie) at 1.75 to 2.25 NLG a cup, and is usually served along with a special Dutch cream (**koffiemelk**). From 2 to 3.50 NLG or so, you can order an **espresso**; coffee with lots of frothy warm milk (**cappuccino**); or a coffee with just a bit of warm milk (**koffie verkeed**). Decaffeinated instant coffee is available in most larger cities and is often called by its brand name (**Nescafe**). The tea (**Thee**) here costs 2.50 NLG or so and is offered in both regular and herbal varieties and is quite good. Those looking to satisfy their sweet tooth may want to sample Dutch hot chocolate (**warme chocolademelk**) at around 3.75 NLG.

As the day progresses, a much more varied selection of beverages will be available for consumption. Water from taps in any foreign country can have its risks, so I suggest always drinking bottled water. There are many brands of great tasting European spring and mineral waters (mineraalwater). These waters cost about 1.75 NLG per liter in a store and as much as 9.50 NLG per liter in a restaurant. There is also an assortment of carbonated soft drinks like Coca Cola and Fanta (orange soda) and they cost about 2 NLG per can or bottle in stores, and around 3.50 NLG per glass in most restaurants.

## Beer & Wine

There are also some great brands of Dutch beer (**bier**). The most common type is pilsner (**pils**) and is close to what you normally can find at home. This medium strength (3.5% to 5% alcohol) beer typically costs between 1.50 NLG and 3.50 NLG per glass on tap or in a bottle, and included brands such as Heineken, Amstel, Grolsch, Brand, Oranjeboom, Leeuw, Ridder, Hertog Jans, and many other regional brews. Specialty beers cost between 4 NLG and 6.50 NLG a piece and include a light but powerful (5.5% alcohol) refreshing wheat-based white beer, served with a slice of lemon (**witbier**), with names like Wieckse Witte or Hoegaarden (from Belgium).

Other unique beers include Haarlem-made Jopen and Jopen Koyt beers that are based on a medieval recipe and have a good kick (5.5% to 8.5% alcohol), seasonal dark brews (wintervorst or bock**bier**), and microbreweries that have created all sorts of strange beers. There are also many Belgian beers here, and may include Trappist monastery brewed (**trappiestenbier**) bottles of Westmalle (7% alcohol), or even some strange offerings like Gulden Drak with a serious kick (10.5% alcohol). Almost every bar, café, and pub usually serves beer in special glasses and mugs that bear the logo of the beer you ordered. It is not uncommon for some bars to offer over 100 different types of beer.

Of course imported wine (**wijn**) from France, Italy, Spain, Chile, and California is commonly available anywhere you go in Holland. A bottle of good house wine or table wine should cost under 23 NLG in a normal restaurant, fancier labels start at around 48 NLG in a gourmet restaurant, though both cost and about half that much in stores. While a limited quantity of semi-sweet white wines are produced in southern Holland, they are not all that impressive.

**AAH ... THE WONDERS OF DUTCH (& BELGIAN) BEER!**

Try at least a small glass (borreltje) or two, at around 4.75 NLG each, of the unique regional Dutch gins (**jenever**) that are sometimes flavored with herbs. The older varieties (*oude jenever*) are truly impressive and can be found in normal bars and cafes, as well as in special old world styled gin tasting houses (**proeflokalen**) in many Dutch cities. Open during the afternoon and early evening only, if you have a half hour to before dinner, ask a local VVV office if they know of a "cozy" proeflokalen within walking distance. Its quite an experience to meet some of the people that stop off in these traditional spots on their way home from work.

## RESTAURANTS

In almost every city chapter of this book you will see listings of restaurants that I have enjoyed and can fully recommend, but I still suggest that you try to find a few gems of your own. It is easy to find great restaurants, serving either regional or various forms of international cuisine, by simply asking at your hotel's front desk for a suggestion. Many restaurants accept Visa and Mastercard and put their logo on the front door; American Express is often not accepted.

Breakfast (ontbijt) is served from 7:00am until 10:00am and usually consists of bread, cheese, sliced ham, jellies, yogurt, and occasionally eggs or delicious Dutch pancakes. Lunch (**lunch**) is normally taken somewhere between 12 noon and 2:00pm and may range from a French bread sandwich to a serious gourmet event. Dinner (**diner**) is a leisurely event that takes place somewhere between 6:00pm and 8:00pm and is when most Dutch people prefer to take multiple courses such as thick soup, a fancy salad, and a main dish followed by rich desserts and strong coffee.

Restaurants come in many types, each with a different typical ambiance. All cities will have dozens of good or great place to eat. You can choose between a full service restaurant (**restaurant**), a reasonably priced grand cafe (**café**) where a limited menu is served, or a popular and affordable local restaurant (**eetcafé**) that is usually the best bet for informal dining. For a better quality quick bite, head for an Arab-styled shwarma grill counter (**shoarma**) that can be found in every downtown zone and specializes in tasty and inexpensive kebabs and gyros until late at night.

Fast food here is usually fried and topped with heavy sauces. All the cities have American-style fast food joints, pizzerias selling by the slice, French fry stands, kiosks selling Indonesian egg rolls, carts selling herring and other fish, and in some cases a Feebo automat where croquettes with meat and other greasy items can be accessed all day and night with a few coins. You can also find snacks and sandwiches in many cheese and take out sandwich shops pastry shops. There are also some wonderful bars

(**bars**) serving great French bread sandwiches (**broodjes**) that come in a variety of fillings.

Usually a Dutch style breakfast in a local restaurant with bread and cheese with coffee will cost about 6 NLG, while a more filling version including Dutch pancakes and coffee costs about 11.50 NLG per person. If you instead choose an American style breakfast with an omelet, bacon, and toast a tourist restaurant or a hotel, expect to get hit for about 17.50 NLG for a sit down meal, or at least 27.50 NLG for a buffet. A simple sandwich lunch in a small restaurant can set you back between 9.50 NLG and 19 NLG a person, while a fancy 4 course gourmet lunch can easily cost upwards of 45 NLG a person. A Dutch, Indonesian, or Italian multiple course dinner without wine can cost from 32.50 NLG to well over 90 NLG per person, depending again on what you choose and where you eat.

In most restaurants you can find selections that are either totally a la carte, 2 or 3 course daily specials (dagschotels), and cheaper combination plates (**tourist menus**) with fixed prices. Vegetarians will have a limited selection, but can always find something in just about every restaurant and café in Holland. Several restaurants offer their shellfish items by the kilogram (2.2 pounds), so you may want to ask for a half of a kilogram at the very most.

When you have finished your meal receive the bill you will notice that a charge has added in at the end. The bills from all restaurants and cafes include all taxes, and a 15% service charge! If you have had a great meal. I suggest that you consider an additional 5% tip for good service and a 10% tip for extraordinary service to be left in cash on the table when you depart. If you put a tip on your credit card, I can assure you that your waiter will never get it.

I have included brief descriptions in this publication's regional chapters of more than 85 of the restaurants throughout Holland that I'm recommending to you in this guide. I have listed each destination's eating establishments in up to four separate price categories that are relevant to the average price, per person, of a full meal not including tax, wine, or tips for that specific city. Within each of the price categories, I have listed the restaurants from top to bottom in the order of my personal suggestion. All menu selections and prices are, as usual, subject to frequent change without notice.

## HOLLAND'S TEN MOST MEMORABLE RESTAURANTS

If you are looking for a special meal that you will never forget, these are among my personal favorites in Holland. I have included selections in the moderate through very expensive price category. Only a couple of these fine establishments prefer that you wear jackets, but reservations are a good idea at all of them!

Those few that are a fairly long trip away from the big cities have a small selection of opulent hotel rooms, and are certainly worth the trouble to reach by train or car.

### Very Expensive

**HOTEL & RESTAURANT DE SWAEN**, *De Lind, 47, Oisterwijk. Tel. (42) 421-9006. All major credit cards accepted. Member of Relais & Chateaux and also Les Patrons Cuisiniers.*

In every country in the world, there is always one restaurant that stands out among the very best. The famed Restaurant De Swaen, not far from Utrecht, is a great choice for those who want to experience the absolute finest cuisine available in Holland! This stunningly beautiful formal gourmet restaurant has helped set a standard from which all other dining establishments here should be measured against.

Their ever-present and extremely personable Dutch master chef, Cas Spijkers, has authored outstanding cook books and hosts a weekly television show. He is most often found in the kitchen that bustles with 18 chefs who labor for hours on end each day to create a spectacular array of culinary delights. The cuisine offered here is Mr. Spijkers' own unique blend of French influenced dishes. Dress well here, make a reservation in advance, and you can have an unforgettable 4 or 5 course meal for around 115 NLG a person and up, not including wine.

**RESTAURANT & HOTEL KAATJE BIJ DE SLUIS**, *Brouwerstraat 20 Blokzijl. Tel. (527) 291-833. All major credit cards accepted. Member of Relais & Chateaux and also Alliance Gastronomique Neerlandaise.*

Located in the charming little seaside town of Blokzijl in the province of Overijssel, this romantic little restaurant is among Europe's best kept secrets. Owners Fons and Anneke Groeningen have created an outstanding 40 seat restaurant in a beautiful old canal house near the village's picturesque harbor. Chef André Mol and his small team of skillful chefs create some of the finest gourmet seafood and meat menus imaginable. Just as Chef Mol to suggest and prepare what he thinks is most special that night, and you will have a 5 course meal to remember for the rest of your life. Dress neat but forget the tie, make an advance reservation, and expect the bill to cost upwards of 115 NLG per person plus wine.

**RESTAURANT HALVEMAAN**, *Van Leijenberghlaan 320, Amsterdam. Tel: (20) 644-0348. All major credit cards accepted. Member Les Patrons Cuisiniers.*

Located on a river in a peaceful park some 15 minutes ride away from downtown Amsterdam, this is my pick as the city's best place to dine. Chef John Halvemaan is a master of improvisation and really loves to invent new dishes with spices and recipes drawn from all over the globe. He is best known for fresh game, fowl, rack of lamb, lobster, and desserts that are all wonderfully prepared and presented. Dinner here can cost at least 120 NLG per person plus wine, you don't need a jacket or tie, and you should book your table in advance.

**MANOIR-RESTAURANT INTER SCALDES,** *Zandweg 2, Kruiningen. Tel. (113) 381753. All major credit cards accepted. Member of Relais & Chateaux and also Les Patrons Cuisiniers.*

For several years now this formal and elegant country style inn at the edge of a tranquil hamlet in the Zeeland province has been finding its way into European magazines. When I finally got here, I found that owner Maartje Boudeling really is one of the country's top chefs. Among their specialties are the fresh lobsters, oysters, and other seafood found in the famous nearby waterways. This is a serious and formal restaurant and is especially popular with rich Belgians that often drive well over an hour just to have dinner here. A typical 5 course dinner here will set you back around 130 NLG per person plus wine, and I recommend a jacket and tie, as well as advance reservations.

### *Expensive*

**RESTAURANT L'ORAGE,** *Oude Delft 111, Delft. Tel: (15) 212-3629. All major credit cards accepted.*

L'Orage is an exceptionally good gourmet French restaurant in the oldest part of historic Delft. You are seated in an intimate dining room or fireside lounge, and are given a wonderfully balanced menu of seasonal meat and fish specialties that have been prepared by a fantastic female chef. There is no strict dress code here, a reservation might be a good idea, and a multiple course dinner may cost you around 80 NLG per person, excluding wine.

**HERBERG ONDER DE LINDEN**, *Burg. van Barneveldweg 3, Aduard. Tel: (50) 403-1406. All major credit cards accepted. Member of Alliance Gastronomique Neerlandaise.*

Master chef Geerhard Slenema has created a rather good French restaurant in a picturesque 18th century farmhouse, in the village of Aduard near the northern city of Groningen. Besides an opulent formal dining room, they also have a nice outdoor terrace. The dining room features both classic and fusion creations based on fine meats and game, as well as some fish items cooked to perfection. People here tend to dress somewhat formally, make their reservations well in advance, and spend upwards of 90 NLG per person for a 4 course dinner, not including wine.

**RESTAURANT D'VIJFF VLIEGHEN**, *Spuistraat 294,* **Amsterdam.** *Tel: (20) 624-8369. All major credit cards accepted.*

This truly spectacular Dutch restaurant in Amsterdam's city center is housed in a series of fine 17th century mansions. The name of this famous establishment translates to "The 5 Flies," and its kitchen creates new Dutch-style cuisine that is both delicious and beautifully presented. Using a carefully selected assortment of fresh market ingredients in their hearty meat and fish dishes. The ambiance here is semi-formal yet relaxed. Dinner will set you back around 90 NLG per person plus wine, and reservations are required on most nights.

### Moderate

**HOSTELLERIE VAN GAALEN**, *Kapelstraat 48,* **Heeze.** *Tel. (40) 226-3515. All major credit cards accepted. Member of Relais & Chateaux and also Alliance Gastronomique Neerlandaise.*

It was a real gamble for chef Jules van Gaalen to take over a crumbling old inn in the Noord-Brabant village of Heeze and convert it in to a relaxed Mediterranean restaurant. He did such a good job that his affordable restaurant is often packed with casual families sitting next to rich local merchants dressed to kill. The wonderful menu here is unique, due to the chef's use of pastas, garlic scampis, basil sauces, aged cheeses, cold pressed extra virgin oils, and tangy imported ingredients that were not before found in Holland. A truly awesome 3 course dinner here usually costs around 55 NLG per person plus wine, and reservations are really important.

**RESTAURANT ZINC**, *Calandstraat 12,* **Rotterdam.** *Tel: (10) 436-6579. Cash only - No credit cards accepted.*

This small and down to earth little fusion restaurant near one of Rotterdam's harbors is my favorite place in the city to unwind. A well-known local chef serves up what may be the finest affordable gourmet cuisine in all of the region. Designed with a minimum of luxury and space, the interior of this amazing establishment seems to be based on an artist's studio, and is lined by crates of fresh seasonal vegetables, bare light bulbs, undecorated wooden tables, and a bustling open kitchen. Each night there is a totally different 3 or 4 course menu priced at around 50 NLG per person that will utilize a small selection of the day's freshest meat, poultry, and seafood specials. Check this place out, and let me know if you can find a better meal at even double the price anywhere in the region! Dress casually here and reserve several days in advance.

**LE HARICOT VERT**, *Molenstraat 9,* **Den Haag.** *Tel. (70) 365-2278. Cash only - No credit cards accepted.*

Master chef Herman van Overdam presides over this romantic yet casual little European country-style restaurant on an historic street in the heart of Den Haag. Just after walking through the front door you will be led to one of several tables surrounded by antique cooking utensils, stained glass windows, and hardwood paneling. The dress code is casual, and they always play great jazz music. Most of the faithful clientele here don't even ask to see the huge menu, they just tell Mr. Van Overdam to bring something special. At around 60 NLG a person for dinner, this is an excellent choice. I strongly suggest calling for reservations.

# 12. HOLLAND'S BEST HOTELS & INNS

After staying in or visiting over 425 different hotels, resorts, inns, farmhouses, apartments, bed and breakfast inns, and pensions throughout Holland, these are some of the places that I could never forget. I have based my selections on overall beauty, location, quality of service, value, cuisine, special features, attitude of the staff, and my own sense of what a hotel should offer.

There are plenty of other fine hotels throughout the country, but these were the places I feel would help anyone have a great experience. I have listed these hotels in a few different categories, each listing the properties in the order in which I would suggest them to a good friend. Not all of these fine properties are expensive, but most tend to be in the middle to upper end of the price range. Full reviews of the majority of the following selections can be found in their corresponding city chapters.

## DELUXE HOTELS

**AMSTEL INTER-CONTINENTAL HOTEL**, *Professor Tulipplein 1, Amsterdam. Tel: (20) 622-6060, Fax: (20) 622-5808. US & Canada Bookings (Inter-Continental) 1-800-327-0200. Special weekend rates from 500 NLG per double room per night (B.P.). Year round rack rates from 650 NLG per double room per night (E.P.). All major credit cards accepted.*

This is my choice as the finest hotel in all of Holland! Located on the banks of the Amstel river in a prestigious district of downtown Amsterdam, the superb 5 star Inter-Continental Amstel Hotel is simply magnificent. Since this property opened its doors in 1867, it has been the home away from home for some of the world's most famous celebrities and heads of state. After the completion of a massive two year renovation, there is certainly no more elegant place to stay while visiting Amsterdam. The staff here work extremely hard to assure that every guest, whether dressed in a designer suit or a pair of jeans, will become a repeat guest.

**AMSTEL HOTEL, AMSTERDAM**

The Amstel has 79 large and opulent air conditioned rooms and suites with huge marble bathrooms, imported amenities, antique or period style furnishings, fine Delftware, original artwork, satellite color television with VCR machines, stereos with CD players, direct dial telephones, mini-bar, fax and telephone answering machines, and large picture windows with remarkable river or city views.

Their facilities include a formal gourmet French restaurant, a fully equipped health club, indoor heated swimming pool, whirlpool, sauna, available massage, a beauty salon, elegant business meeting and reception rooms, underground valet parking, in house limousine service, video tape rentals, express laundry and dry cleaning, and the best 24 hour room service in town. The wonderful Amstel Hotel easily gets my highest rating of any hotel in Holland!

**KASTEEL WITTEM**, *Wittemer Allee, 3, **Wittem**. Tel: (43) 450-1208, Fax; (43) 450-1260. US & Canada Bookings (Relais & Chateaux) 1-212-856-0115. Year round rack rates from 210 NLG per double room per night (E.P.),. Special Gourmet Packages from 460 NLG per double room per night (M.A.P.) All major credit cards accepted.*

This is Holland's most enchanting and romantic small luxury property, and is among my favorite places to stay in all of Europe! Located in Wittem, a quiet town 15 kilometers (9 miles) away from either Valkenburg and Maastricht, this regal 12th century castle has been lovingly converted into an outstanding inn with a fantastic gourmet restaurant. As soon as you catch your first glimpse of the castle's dramatic facade, you know you're in for a great experience.

**KASTEEL WITTEM**

Affiliated with the famous Relais & Chateaux organization, the inn offers 12 luxurious double rooms that all have deluxe private bathrooms, hand-crafted furnishings, color satellite television, am-fm clock radios, direct dial telephones, and large picture windows looking out onto nearby rolling countryside. All of the public and dining areas are surrounded by priceless chandeliers, antiques, solid oak paneling, and priceless old Flemish paintings.

Owned and personally managed by Marc and Peter Ritzen, the hotel provides an exceptionally welcoming ambiance of casual elegance. Service here is simply outstanding, with all of the friendly staff members (including the owners) working together as a team to ensure that you will never want to leave. While here you can take nearby horseback rides, scenic rural drives, play golf or tennis, fresh water fish, bicycle around southern Limburg villages such as Epen and Mechelen, follow countless hiking trials, go wine tasting, or have an incredible picnic. The Kasteel Wittem receives my absolute highest recommendation, and should not be missed while visiting this part of Holland!

**THE GRAND - AMSTERDAM,** *Oudezijds Voorburgwal 197,* **Amsterdam.** *Tel: (20) 555-3111, Fax: (20) 555-3222. US & Canada Bookings (UTELL) 1-800- 44-UTELL. Weekend rates from 430 NLG per double room per night (C.P.). Year round rack rates from 595 NLG per double room per night (E.P.). All major credit cards accepted.*

The newly opened Grand is situated just in front of a picturesque canal within the walls of the former 15th century Amsterdam city hall. With a reputation for both personalized service and great rooms, this 5 star hotel is really trying hard to become the premier choice for deluxe

**GRAND HOTEL, AMSTERDAM**

guests visiting this famous city. There are 182 wonderful rooms, suites, and fully equipped luxury apartments, each with marble and tile bathrooms, impressive hardwood furnishings, remote control satellite television, direct dial telephones, mini-safe, mini-bar, and picture windows overlooking either the canal or the peaceful inner courtyards.

Facilities and services available include a casual yet elegant international bistro, outdoor dining areas, indoor swimming pool, whirlpool, sauna, gardens, valet and concierge services, 24 hour room service, the city's most impressive business meeting and reception rooms, express laundry and dry cleaning, and secured garage parking. Service here is excellent, and I strongly suggest giving this delightful property a try during your next stay in Amsterdam!

**HOTEL KURHAUS**, *Gevers Deynootplein 30, Scheveningen.Tel: (70) 416-2636, Fax: (70) 416-2646. US & Canada Bookings (SRS Hotels) 1-800-223-5652. Special weekend rates from 380 NLG per double room per night (B.P.). Year round rack rates from 440 NLG per double room per night (E.P.). All major credit cards accepted.*

The dramatic Hotel Kurhaus is a fabulous 5 star sea-front hotel in the popular resort of Scheveningen just outside of Den Haag. Since the late 19th century it has hosted countless members of royalty, heads of state, movie stars, and travelers from around the world. Besides having direct access to a long sandy beach, the hotel is also famous for its awesome two story fresco topped grand hall (Kurzaal), where meals or live orchestral concerts are often held.

There are 241 rooms and suites that contain private bathrooms, remote control satellite television, direct dial telephones, mini-bar, electric trouser press, mini-bar, and huge windows with tranquil ocean views in many cases. The facilities here include a great gourmet restaurant, a

**HOTEL KURHAUS, SCHEVENINGEN**

seaside terrace restaurant, a private beach area, available water sports rentals, private parking, nearby tennis and golf, plenty of business meeting and conference rooms, boutiques, an adjacent shopping center, and some of the friendliest staff members in town.

This is one of my favorite hotels in the Netherlands, and I highly recommend it to all of my readers that can afford a few nights of supreme luxury and comfort on the sea!

**LANDGOED LAUSWOLT**, *Van Harinxmaweg, 10,* **Beetsterzwaag**. *Tel: (512) 381-245, Fax; (512) 381-496. US & Canada Bookings (Relais & Chateaux) 1-212-856-0115. Year round rack rates from 275 NLG per double room per night (E.P.), Special Gourmet Package rates from 450 NLG per double room per night (M.A.P.). All major credit cards accepted.*

This stately hotel is located in beautiful Beetsterzwaag, a 20 minute drive southwest of Groningen. This superb 4 star Relais & Chateaux member property was originally built over a century ago as a wealthy family's elegant rural manor house. The estate has grown into a fantastic hotel and adjacent golf and country club that attracts travelers from around the globe.

All of the 58 dramatic rooms and suites feature marble or tile dual basin bathrooms, hardwood furnishings, remote control satellite television, am-fm clock radio, mini-bar, mini-safe, executive style desks, direct dial telephones, giant picture windows with memorable views, a selection fine art or antiques, fresh fruit baskets, and even panoramic balconies and working fireplaces in some cases. The public rooms are lavishly decorated with priceless 17th century Flemish paintings and soothing color schemes.

Facilities and services available here include an outstanding restaurant, a magnificent wood paneled bar and billiard room, conference and business meeting rooms, a large indoor/outdoor swimming pool, a beauty salon, a spa area, sauna, Turkish bath, solarium, two outdoor tennis courts, rental bicycles, walking trails, available nanny service, and a 18 hole golf course. The hotel can also arrange for you hot air balloon adventures, horse-drawn carriage rides, sailing trips on nearby lakes, indoor ice skating, and privately guided custom excursions.

The ambiance here is sophisticated yet and unusually welcoming do to the great service provided by a professional team working under manager Johan L.L. Agricola. There are no strict dress codes to deal with here, and you can walk around the property feeling like you are staying in a good friend's country house. The Landgoed Lauswolt receives my highest recommendation as the finest hotel in the north of Holland!

**HOTEL DE L'EUROPE,** *Nieuwe Doelenstraat 2-8,* **Amsterdam.** *Tel: (20) 623-4836, Fax: (20) 624-2962. US & Canada Bookings (Leading Hotels) 1-800-223-6800. Low season rack rates from 515 NLG per double room per night (E.P.), High season rack rates from 575 NLG per double room per night (E.P.), All major credit cards accepted.*

The old world-style Hotel de L'Europe is located alongside the charming Amstel river in the heart of downtown Amsterdam. This formal 5 star property is well within easy walking distance to the city's countless historic and commercial attractions. Guests are surrounded by opulent sun-drenched public spaces embellished with the finest marbles, hardwoods, rich fabrics, and chandeliers imaginable.

**THE OPULENT HOTEL DE L'EUROPE, AMSTERDAM**

There are 100 air conditioned rooms and suites each featuring marble bathrooms, exquisite furnishings, remote control satellite television, direct dial telephones, mini-safe, clock radio, mini-bar, views over the river front, the old city streets, or a tranquil inner courtyard. As a member of the prestigious Leading Hotels of the World, the Hotel L'Europe offers an excellent array of facilities and services including a formal gourmet restaurant, an elegant river-view brasserie, an indoor swimming pool, health club, sauna, private parking, 24 hour room service, business meeting rooms, and a good staff. This is a perfect choice for visiting executives and individuals who are looking to stay in the city center!

**INTER-CONTINENTAL HOTEL DES INDES**, *Lange Voorhout 54,* **Den Haag**. *Tel: (70) 363-2932, Fax: (70) 345-1721. US & Canada Bookings (Inter-Continental) 1-800-327-0200. Special weekend rates from 320 NLG per double room per night (B.P.). Year round rack rates from 505 NLG per double room per night (E.P.), All major credit cards accepted.*

Inter-Continental's deluxe 5 star Hotel des Indes is situated just across the street from the Paleis Lange Voorhout in the most charming section of downtown Den Haag. Once owned by an infamous local baron, this awesome hotel has some of Holland's most dramatic beautiful public spaces (especially its grand salon) that are filled with exotic hardwoods, imported marbles, fine wrought iron grillwork, hand cut crystal chandeliers, plush antique furnishings, and magnificent works of art.

The hotel has 76 period style rooms and suites that have private bathrooms, remote control satellite television, mini-bar, direct dial telephone, mini-safe, electric trouser press, period furnishings, and large windows. The property also offers a posh afternoon tea (especially interesting on Sundays), a fine gourmet restaurant, an elaborate bar, business meeting rooms, express laundry and dry cleaning, valet and concierge service, secured parking, room service, a serious ballroom, and a top notch staff. If only the best will satisfy you, this is definitely the place to stay while in The Hague!

## SUPERIOR HOTELS

**HOTEL DE SWAEN**, *De Lind, 47,* **Oisterwijk**. *Tel: (42) 421-9006, Fax: (42) 428-5860. US & Canada Bookings (Relais & Chateaux) 1-212-856-0115. Year round rack rates from 285 NLG per double room per night (E.P.). Special weekday rates from 200 NLG per double room per night (B.P.), All major credit cards accepted.*

This fine deluxe inn and simply amazing gourmet restaurant is located in the quaint village of Oisterwijk, a short distance by train or car from Utrecht. This centuries-old inn offers a special blend of charm, luxury, and hospitality. Every inch of this beautiful property is lined with opulent antiques, 17th century Flemish works of art, elegant carpets, awesome crystal chandeliers, marble tiles, and hand crafted wrought iron grillwork. The 18 individually designed rooms and suites all feature private marble bathrooms with gold fixtures, fine art and antiques, direct dial telephone, village or garden view balconies, remote control satellite television, electronic trouser press, mini-bar, and beautiful furnishings.

**THE WONDERFUL HOTEL DE SWAEN, NEAR UTRECHT**

Make sure to drop by Cas Spijkers' formal gourmet restaurant or informal bistro for the meal of your life. When weather permits, the hotel's perfectly manicured English gardens are the perfect place to relax and enjoy a sunny day off. If you are looking for a great little place to get away from the big city stress, and still enjoy all the services and facilities of an intimate luxury hotel, this impeccable Relais & Chateaux affiliated property is Highly Recommended.

**PARK HOTEL ROTTERDAM,** *Westersingel 70,* **Rotterdam.** *Tel: (10) 436-3611, Fax: (10) 436-4212. US & Canada Bookings (UTELL) 1-800-44-UTELL. Year round rack rates from 305 NLG per double room per night (E.P.). All major credit cards accepted.*

Located just a two minute walk away from the Museumpark and the Binnenwegplein in the heart of downtown Rotterdam, the wonderful Park Hotel is an ideal property for both travelers and businessmen. This stunning example of modern architecture has 189 rooms and suites located in both the original garden-side wing, and the famous modern styled towers. All rooms have private bathrooms, remote control satellite television, mini-bar, am-fm clock radio, direct dial telephones with computer modem jacks, executive style desk, as well as superb city views and air conditioners and mini-safes in most cases.

The facilities here include a gourmet French restaurant, a wonderful bar, free private parking, heath club, sauna, an Internet and computer work station, business meeting and conference rooms, 24 hour room service, express laundry and dry cleaning, an inner courtyard garden, available child care, and a great staff. I strongly suggest reserving one of the extraordinary deluxe corner rooms on the upper floors of the hotel's glittering silver tower. The Park Hotel is certainly the best hotel in Rotterdam!

**CARLTON AMBASSADOR HOTEL,** *Sophialaan 2,* **Den Haag.** *Tel: (70) 363-0363, Fax: (70) 360-0535, US & Canada Bookings (UTELL), 1-800- 44-UTELL. Special weekend rates from 193 NLG per double room per night (E.P.). Year round rack rates from 365 NLG per double room per night (E.P.). All major credit cards accepted.*

The comfortable Carlton Ambassador is found in the exclusive downtown embassy row section of Den Haag. This fine 4 star hotel has 80 charming rooms and suites in either English Tudor or Dutch Traditional style, that all contain private bathroom, hand painted hardwood furnishings, picture windows that open out onto adjacent gardens, executive sized desks with fax/modem and extra telephone ports, electronic mini-safe, mini-bar, complimentary coffee and tea, remote control color satellite television, and plenty of charm. The hotel offers a good restaurant, business meeting rooms, fireside lounges, room service, free morning newspapers, and a great staff. The Carlton Ambassador has become the most requested hotels in town for visiting diplomats, banking executives, and deluxe travelers from around the globe.

**HOTEL KAATJE BIJ DE SLUIS,** *Zuiderstraat 1,* **Blokzijl.** *Tel: (527) 291-833, Fax: (527) 291-836. US & Canada Bookings (Relais & Chateaux) 1- 212-856-0115. Year round rack rates from 270 NLG per double room per night (E.P.). All major credit cards accepted.*

Situated along-side a wonderful canal in the old pirate harbor town of Blokzijl on the awesome coast of OverIjssel province, this fantastic inn and gourmet restaurant is well worth the effort involved in getting here. The hotel offers eight giant luxury rooms, each with private bathroom, remote control satellite television, am-fm clock radio, hardwood furnishing, coffee and tea makers, mini-bar, nice art work, mini-safe, direct dial telephone, and plenty of sunlight streaming through the huge water-view windows.

The friendly van Groeningen family has run this famous inn since 1985, and make every guest feel at home. Just across the street is the inn's incredible gourmet restaurant, where André Mol continues to create some of Europe's finest cuisine. When visiting this area you can take short day trips to traditional villages, harbors filled with antique schooners, old castles, and quaint artisan workshops where delightful porcelain and hand painted crafts of the highest quality can be found. This is a fantastic place to get away from it all, and really see the heart and soul of Holland!

**HOTEL NEW YORK**, *Koninginnenhoofd 1, **Rotterdam***. *Tel: (10) 439-0500, Fax: (10) 484-2701. Year round rack rates from 180 NLG per double room per night (E.P.). Most major credit cards accepted.*

Imaginatively converted from the opulent turn of the century Art Nouveau style headquarters of the Holland America cruise ship line, and located across the river from downtown Rotterdam, this unusual hotel is best reached by water taxi. There are 72 unique rooms and suites with a variety of pretty views, all with modern private bathrooms, a bizarre selection of furnishings, direct dial telephones, remote control satellite televisions, and huge picture windows. There are also two dramatic towers that contain a small private museum as well as a truly wonderful deluxe room.

The complex also boasts a great affordable restaurant, an oyster bar, a tea salon, a cute gift shop, free parking, old world style business meeting rooms, 24 hour room service, a winter garden, boutiques, a nearby waterside park, and more. If you are looking for a romantic escape in an urban setting, this is certainly an interesting place to go!

**HOTEL NEW YORK, ROTTERDAM**

**THE JOLLY CARLTON HOTEL,** *Vijzelstraat 4,* **Amsterdam***. Tel: (20) 622-2266, Fax: (20) 626-6183. US & Canada Bookings (Jolly Hotels) 1-800-221-2626 or (212) 213-1468. Special package rates from NLG 290 per double room per night (B.P.). Year round rack rates from NLG 395 per double room per night (E.P.). All major credit cards accepted.*

This modern deluxe executive class hotel can be found just across the street from Amsterdam's Munt Tower and its adjacent floating flower market. This nice modern 4 star hotel far exceeds the competition with a high level of personalized service, beautifully decorated rooms, and plenty of facilities. There are 219 spacious air conditioned rooms and suites that all have large marble and tile private bathrooms, fine custom designed Italian furnishings, soundproofed windows, remote control satellite color television, mini-bar, electric trouser press, executive style desk, and direct dial telephones that can accept portable computer modem outputs.

There's a gourmet Italian restaurant, a terraced cafe and lounge, room service, business meeting rooms, secure underground parking garage, special dedicated non-smoking guest rooms, express laundry and dry cleaning, and many fine boutiques and entertainment venues just feet away from the front door. With an extremely professional staff from all over the globe, the Jolly Carlton Hotel represents a great value for the money in the moderate price range, and receives one of my highest recommendations for downtown hotels in Amsterdam.

## CHARMING, MODERATELY PRICED HOTELS

**GUESTHOUSE DIS***, Tafelstraat 28, Maastricht. Tel: (43) 321-5479, Fax: (43) 325-7026. Year round rates starting from 160 NLG per double room per night (E.P.). All major credit cards accepted.*

This romantic little downtown Maastricht inn, located on a tranquil side street full of 17th centuries townhouses, is one of the country's most unique properties. Situated just above a gallery of fine modern art, there are six enormous double rooms with private bathrooms, original exposed wooden beams, Italian designed leather sofas, parquet hardwood floors, antiques, remote control satellite television, direct dial telephone, mini-bar, incredible views out over historic side streets and private courtyard gardens, and a selection of modern paintings (from the gallery!) hung on the walls.

I strongly suggest calling well in advance for reservations, and don't forget to ask about their daily buffet breakfast served in an awesome 17th century Romanesque chapel – a real bargain. Highly suggested as one of the most charming and innovative small affordable inns in Holland!

**HOTEL LEEUWENBRUG,** *Koornmarkt 16,* **Delft.** *Tel: (15) 214-7741, Fax: (15) 215-9759. Year round rack rates from 158 NLG per double room per night (B.P.). All major credit cards accepted.*

Situated in a pair of beautifully converted canal-front patrician houses in the heart of Delft, this delightful 3 star city center hotel is a real gem! They have 38 spacious canal and courtyard view rooms with private bathroom, direct dial telephone, remote control satellite television, antique furnishings, fine art work, and plenty of charm. Facilities here include a good restaurant, one of the prettiest lounge and lobby areas found anywhere, nearby parking, business meeting rooms, an excellent friendly staff, and a great courtyard garden. For these rates the Leeuwenbrug is certainly a bargain, especially if you get one of their fabulous rooms with French or stained glass windows looking out over the quiet canal. Highly recommended as the most relaxing place to stay in all of Delft!

**PARK HOTEL DEN HAAG,** *Molenstraat 53,* **Den Haag.** *Tel: (70) 362-4371, Fax: (70) 361-4525. Special weekend rates from 155 NLG per double room per night (C.P.). Year round rack rates from 265 NLG per double room per night (C.P.). Most major credit cards accepted.*

Located in downtown Den Haag's old town section, this extremely welcoming 4 star full service hotel combines a blend of excellent facilities with an unusually good value for the money. The hotel also have the added benefit of being within easy walking distance to almost every major sight and attraction in town. The property's 114 medium sized single and twin rooms and suites contain marble bathrooms, remote control satellite television, electric trouser press, direct dial telephone, am-fm clock radios, hardwood furnishings, executive desks, artistic lithographs, and in most cases have great views out on to quaint centuries-old boutique and restaurant lined lanes.

Facilities include secure indoor parking, dual elevator service to all floors, a Mudejar style grand staircase, a peaceful dining room, business meeting rooms, display cases filled with unusual art and antiques for sale, a lobby bar, and a staff that will help you plan the perfect excursion or self guided walking tour. Don't forget to ask about their fantastic weekend rates, available in limited quantities during much of the year!

## QUALITY BUDGET ACCOMMODATIONS

**NJHC HOSTEL ASSUMBERG,** *Tolweg 9,* **Heemskerk.** *Tel: (251) 232-288, Fax: (251) 251-024. US & Canada Bookings (Hostelling International) 1-613-237-7884. Year round rack rates from 26 NLG per person in a dormitory per night (C.P.). Year round rack rates from 88 NLG per double private room per night (C.P.). Cash Only - No credit cards accepted.*

**NJHC HOSTEL ASSUMBERG, IN HEEMSKERK**

This magnificent 16th century castle is surrounded by a moat on the edge of Heemskerk, a 20 minute ride below Haarlem. While it may be off the beaten path, I still suggest staying here for a night or two and hitting the nearby North Sea sand dune beaches. The castle itself contains a series of large medieval salons that are frequently used by different orchestral music groups from neighboring colleges. A walk around the castle itself and the adjacent stables (now converted to hold private rooms) will normally reveal live music coming out from almost every window.

Inside the castle and stables, there are a series of rather nice yet basic double, triple, and quadruple rooms with private bathrooms, as well as a special section of dormitory rooms for up to 28 people each that have semi-private bathrooms and luggage lockers. Guests of the hostel are encouraged to use the available bicycles to visit the adjacent villages and attractions. Facilities include free outdoor parking, a nearby bus stop, storage lockers, conference rooms, a good cheap restaurant, a great and inexpensive bar, vending machines, and a nice staff. I really enjoyed my night here, and met plenty of interesting people from all over the globe.

**ARENA BUDGET HOTEL**, *'s-Gravesandestraat 51, Amsterdam. Tel: (20) 694-7444, Fax: (20) 663-2649. Year round rack rates from 25 NLG per person in a dormitory per night (E.P.). Year round rack rates from 90 NLG per double private room per night (E.P.). Cash Only - No credit cards accepted.*

Located on a small street near the southeastern edge Amsterdam, Arena is a low budget hotel, concert venue, dance club, cultural enter, hip café, and restaurant all wrapped up into one. Built in an old orphanage and an adjacent church, this bizarre establishment offers its young and casual guests rooms in both large co-ed and single sex dormitories with up to 80 bunk beds (some partitioned in sub-sections for 8 persons), as well as more private 2 through 8 bed rooms with private bathrooms. While far from deluxe, the accommodations are comfortable, there is no curfew, and the entertainment and inexpensive dining facilities here are among the most enjoyable in town. If you spend the time to look around, the older wings of this structure are laden with fine frescoes and antique hand-carved grand staircases.

**NJHC HOSTEL RHIJNAUWEN,** *Rhijnauwenselaan 14. Bunnik. Tel: (30) 656-1277, Fax: (30) 657-1065. US & Canada Bookings (Hostelling International) 1-613-237-7884. Year round rack rates from 26 NLG per person in a dormitory per night (C.P.). Year round rack rates from 74 NLG per double private room per night (C.P.). Cash Only - No credit cards accepted.*

That right, another hostel. This affordable riverfront mansion is situated just a 5 minute drive from downtown Utrecht. This superbly managed hostel offers a series of rather nice yet basic single, double, triple, and quadruple rooms with private bathrooms, as well as a special section of dormitory rooms for up to 20 people each that have semi-private bathrooms and luggage lockers. Guests of the hostel are encouraged to use the available bicycles to visit the adjacent old fortress and make their way into Utrecht via a beautiful winding country lane.

Facilities include free outdoor parking, a nearby bus stop, storage lockers, conference rooms, a good cheap restaurant, a great and inexpensive bar, vending machines, and a nice staff. Highly recommended as the most friendly place to stay, as well as the best value for the money, in the Utrecht area!

# 13. AMSTERDAM

Holland's capital city of **Amsterdam** has the largest population (720,493) of any city in Holland. Surrounded by a series of picturesque canals lined by 16th through 18th century canal houses, Amsterdam boasts dozens of interesting museums, countless monumental buildings, beautiful churches, peaceful gardens, public market squares, world-class designer boutiques, diamond cutting establishments, fine ethnic restaurants, a world-famous red light district, and a thriving nightlife scene that lasts until sunrise. It's really a shame that most visitors will choose to stay only a couple of days here.

The capital's rich and varied tapestry of history has been exceedingly well preserved, and is apparent everywhere. It is fairly easy to visit a vast amount of the city in a limited time, since many of the most famous historic, cultural, and architectural attractions can be found within easy walking distance to each other. Just remember to be careful not to walk around alone after sunset, and don't even think about driving or parking your car here if it is not essential. Amsterdam is also a great location from which to enjoy day trips to nearby towns and villages via bicycle, rental car, bus, train, and excursion bus.

## AMSTERDAM'S HISTORY

The first settlement of Amsterdam began around the year 1224, when a small hamlet with simple wooden cottages took shape on a hill at the mouth of the **Amstel** river. In 1264, a construction of a dam was begun on the same location, and the hamlet soon grew into the village of **Amstelledamme**. This area was originally under the control of the Lords of Amstel who took their orders from the Bishop of Utrecht. Then Count Floris V of Holland began to take over much of the bishop's territory in the late 13th century.

In 1300, Amsterdam was granted independent municipal rights, thus allowing it to install its own local government. To defend the area, members of the most powerful aristocratic families who controlled the local government formed groups of well-armed civil guard militia units.

From the 14th through 15th centuries, the city's port grew into an important center of maritime trade (for products such as beer) with nearby German-controlled cities along the Baltic and North seas. In 1345, the "Miracle of Amsterdam" occurred when a dying man was forced by tradition to swallow the Sacrament. When he then vomited and the Host was thrown on an open fire, it miraculously didn't burn. This event made Amsterdam a holy city and attracted thousands of Catholic pilgrims who traveled along the "Holy Way" route. In 1421 and again in 1452, great fires ravaged hundreds of wooden buildings, thus leading to a law that assured all new constructions be made of stone or brick.

By the 16th century Amsterdam became the sight of Europe's largest grain market and several new industries cropped up here, including ship building and textile manufacturing. Professional guilds then began to form for those involved in making furniture, clothing, and leather goods for the retail businesses that supplied an ever growing consumer base A fortified defensive wall was then set up to encircle the city and repel any unwanted visitors. In 1576, a group of Protestant rebels lead by Prince William of Orange besieged the city during a revolt against King Philip II of Spain, who had a tight grip on Holland. When the Calvinists finally took control of the city in 1578, the **Reformation** had begun and Catholicism went underground. As churches were looted and later converted, Amsterdam became the capital of the Dutch Republic.

**AMSTERDAM'S BEAUTIFUL CANALS**

Throughout the 17th century, Amsterdam began to greatly expand in size during its Golden Age, with the addition of three more ring canals designed by Hendrick Staets. Merchants continued to prosper and to build great canal houses and massive warehouses decorated with splendid gables and cornices. Artists such as Rembrandt came here to find rich patrons who supported their work.

As the struggle against Spain continued, new maritime trade routes to the Orient and Africa were established. Profitable organizations such as the **Dutch East India Company** took advantage of the recent colonization of Indonesia and made Amsterdam the European capital of the rare spice trade. A new commodities market soon was established, and a new type of bank was created to allow for currency transfers via check. This new influx of commerce from foreign lands helped the local economy grow, and brought with it the necessary funding to rebuild the city hall in stone. At the end of this period, the area's population had swelled to over 200,000, and the richest merchants began to build summer villas in the suburban countryside.

By the 18th and 19th centuries, Amsterdam was well known as one of the continent's most tolerant places. Hidden churches like "Our Lord in the Attic" were created by the Catholics, and prosperous immigrant Jews had begun construction of even more synagogues. After Napoleon's brother Louis Bonaparte was crowned King of Holland in 1808, economic decline racked the city. Even after the **House of Orange** returned from exile to form a monarchy in 1813, only a few new industries such as the importation and cutting of raw diamonds from southern Africa managed to flourish.

Holland remained officially neutral in World War I, the economy here continued to be in bad shape. As much as one-quarter of the 700,000 residents of Amsterdam found themselves without gainful employment. The new socialist government decided to create massive public works and housing projects, designed by architects of the so-called **Amsterdam School**, to help bring new jobs to the city.

When Germany invaded Holland in 1940, the Nazis began to deport Jews to concentration camps. Many citizens helped Jews (like Anne Frank and her family) to avoid capture for a while, but Nazi sympathizers eventually betrayed them to the Gestapo. After the war ended, the city became rather liberal and perhaps too tolerant. Radicals and the 60's hippie culture had soon brought hard drugs and hundreds of anarchist squatters into the heart of the downtown district. Things have finally quieted down a bit, and while the drugs, crimes, and hippies remain, the city has regained its status as a major European center for culture and economic stability.

## ORIENTATION

Amsterdam is located in the northwestern section of Holland, in the south-central section of the province known as **Noord-Holland**. From the center of the city, no town or village in this country is more than 250 kilometers (155 miles) away from here. In fact, most of the cities, villages, beaches, and attractions listed in this book can be reached from Amsterdam in well under four hours by car, train, bus, or ferry.

## ARRIVALS & DEPARTURES

**By Air**

The main international airport servicing Holland-bound flights is the **Amsterdam Airport Schiphol**. Located 17 kilometers (10 miles) southwest of Amsterdam, this large and well-designed modern facility has just one terminal that is broken up into a downstairs arrival section and an upstairs departure section. A total of 76 airlines operate from Schiphol and provide over 2,500 flights a week to 202 destinations around the globe. With its current annual passenger load of over 20 million people, many of whom are transferring to other European destinations, this is indeed a rather busy airport by any standard.

Among the many services offered in the airport are free luggage carts, wheelchairs for the physically challenged, 24 hour currency exchange machines, banks with extended hours and all night ATM machines, a VVV tourist information office, automated baggage lockers at 6 NLG to 10 NLG per day depending on size, staffed luggage storage for 5 NLG per bag each day, several restaurants and cafés, a juice bar, a baby care room, a fitness center, a golf practice range, available secretarial and translation services, a full service casino, credit card operated fax machines, press and conference rooms, V.A.T. refund areas, excursion and hotel booking kiosks, 24 hour medical care, two chapels, a beauty salon, over 4 dozen duty free shops and boutiques featuring designer goods, a pharmacy, a newsstand and cigarette shop, soda machines, dozens of pay phones that accept coins and credit cards, a train station and ticketing office, a full service post office, a multilingual airport information desk, car rental offices, VIP lounges for business and first class passengers, and modern executive class hotels on or near the premises with free airport shuttle service.

For a complete floor plan and service listing for Schiphol Airport you can visit their sight on the World Wide Web at **http://www.Schiphol.nl** from your computer.

For those of you trying to pick up or drop of passengers at the airport, parking near the terminals costs 2.50 NLG per half hour and 35 NLG per day. Long term parking is also available for 65 NLG for up to 3 days and

7.50 NLG per each additional day. If you want to leave your rental car at the airport while you explore Amsterdam for a few hours or days, ask your rental company's kiosk in the airport. Some of the major car rental companies will let you park in their officially assigned airport parking areas for free if you ask them for permission.

For airport general information, call *(20) 601-9111* or *(6) 350-34050*.

**Buses Between the Airport & Downtown**

The only express bus service that connects Schiphol Airport to downtown Amsterdam is the **KLM Airport-Hotel Shuttle**, operated by the NZH transportation company. The bus departs from in front of the arrivals area and leaves every half hour from 6:30am until 10:00pm daily and passes next to several of the city's major 4 and 5 star hotels, including the Amsterdam Hilton, Golden Tulip Barbizon Centre, Sheraton Hotel Pulitzer, SRS Grand Hotel Krasnapolsky, Holiday Inn Crowne Plaza, Ramada Renaissance, and the Golden Tulip Barbizon Palace.

The fare is 17.50 NLG per person one way or 30 NLG round trip, including luggage and can also be taken from these hotels back to the Airport on the same half hourly schedule. From the closest of these hotels, a taxi will only cost you 11 NLG or so per ride, not per person, to most other specific destinations in the downtown sector.

You can also take the public buses or trams from their stops near the above-mentioned hotels to almost any point in town for just 3 NLG per person if you do not have too much luggage. Tickets can be purchased from the bus driver who will be glad to make change of any small Dutch bill. To call the NZH company and find out if your hotel is near enough to walk from any of the scheduled stops, call *(20) 649-5651* during normal business hours.

**Trains Between the Airport & Downtown**

A well-marked train system ticket counter near the Schiphol Plaza shopping area on the arrivals level can sell you tickets for the 20 minute train ride from the airport to Amsterdam's **Centraal Station**, for 5.50 NLG one way or 9.50 NLG round trip. These trains depart every 15 minutes in each direction between 6:00am and 12 midnight, and then slow to one per hour.

After arriving at Amsterdam's Centraal Station, a taxi to most downtown hotels will only cost around 13 NLG or so per ride, not per person. You can also take the public buses or trams from the front of Centraal Station to almost any point in town for just 3 NLG per person, if you do not have too much luggage.

**Taxis from the Airport to Downtown**

Taxis are usually dark colored diesel or natural gas powered Mercedes-Benz, Renault, or Opel 4 door sedans marked with the "Taxi" sign on their roofs. They can be found in abundant supply at well-indicated taxi stands at the airport and throughout the city's main points of arrival and major shopping zones. Keep in mind that 99% of the taxis are medium-sized 4 door cars. Generally, their trunks can only hold three large sized and perhaps a couple of carry on bags inside as well. Unfortunately, almost no station wagon or van type taxis are available in Amsterdam.

The going metered rate for the 20 to 30 minute drive from Schiphol to the downtown area averages about 57.50 NLG per ride, not per person. Most Dutch taxi drivers are honest and usually do not try to rip off tourists.

**By Bus**

Most, but not all, of the bus lines between Amsterdam and other parts of Holland as well as the rest of Europe tend to stop at or near the **Centraal Station** train depot on the north end of the downtown section of the city. Be sure to call in advance to find out exactly where and when your bus comes in.

Connections between this station and any other point in Amsterdam can generally be made by the adjacent public bus, tram, or metro stations for 3 NLG per person each way, or via taxi for roughly 14.50 NLG or so, depending on where you are going.

**By Car**

Downtown street parking spots are impossible to find!

A vast array of high-speed national and international highways can bring you to Amsterdam from almost any point within Holland or even Europe. From the airport, it is easy to follow detailed directions via the correct exit on the **A-4** highway or the **A-10** ring road (ask for these instructions in advance!) into almost any part of downtown or suburban Amsterdam.

Amsterdam and its airport are also almost directly connected to several other major Dutch cities, such as Rotterdam and Den Haag, via the main **A-4** highway. From this highway, a series of other roads and highways cross-connect and spoke out to various destinations. There are no real road, bridge, or tunnel tolls on the excellent highway and smaller routes of Holland. With the recent abolishment of controlled border crossing points between most European Economic Community member nations, it may no longer be necessary to present passports or even wait on line while entering Holland via Germany or Belgium.

## By Train

As you can imagine, Amsterdam is linked to almost any other point in Holland and Europe by an exhaustive series of rail lines. This city has several different rail stations, each with its own series of daily arrivals and departures. The most common location for service to and Holland, as well as from other European countries, is at the large **Centraal Station** train depot at the north edge of the city's downtown section.

Connections between this station and any other point in Amsterdam can generally be made by the adjacent public bus, tram, or metro stations for around 3 NLG per person each way, or via taxi for roughly 14.50 NLG or so, depending on where you are going. To reconfirm in advance the exact time and station which you may need, *call (6) 9292.*

## By Sea

The Port of Amsterdam's **cruise ship passenger terminal** is located 1.3 kilometers (1 mile) away from the city center. Over 100 cruise ships from companies like Royal Caribbean Cruise Lines, Royal Viking Line, Costa Cruise Lines, P & O and others make this city a port of call during the warmer months. From the port, a taxi is the best way to reach any point downtown and will cost about 17.50 NLG per ride, not per person.

To find out more about cruses that stop in Amsterdam or elsewhere in Holland, contact your travel agent. Most ferries servicing Holland stop fairly close to, but not directly in, Amsterdam.

# GETTING AROUND TOWN

## By Public Transportation

The city of Amsterdam's **GVB** (Gemeente Vervoerbedrif) municipal transit authority offers a vast array of public transportation methods to get you safely and easily around town. There are two metro lines, 17 tram lines, over 30 bus routes, and nine night buses to choose from. Almost all of these vehicles stop in front of Centraal Station. Just keep in mind that buses can be entered via the front door, while most trams and all metros have several entry doors you can use.

The normal hours of operation for most of the system is from about 6:30am until roughly 12:15am. After that your only choices are the more expensive and less frequent **Nachtbus** night busses that run from Centraal Station and various major stops through the city between 12:30am and 2:00am and again from 4:00am until 6:00am.

All of these systems utilize the same types of tickets and passes. Besides using **Nationale Strippen Kaarts** (strip tickets that allow one or more people to each use two blank strips per zone of local travel; for more information, see Chapter 8, *Getting Around Holland*)) they can also sell you an unlimited use 1 to 9 day local **Dagkaart** (day card). The dagkaart allows one person unlimited travel on Amsterdam's public transportation system within a fixed number of days for the price of 12 NLG (1 day), 16 NLG (2 days), and 3.75 NLG for each additional day up to a maximum of 9 in total. Just bring this card with you during its validity day(s) and present it if asked by a driver.

To get free copies of the extremely useful GVB public transit system maps entitled *Lijnenkaart* and *Tourist Guide to Public Transport*, and the *Snelwijzer* tram map, or the even more accurate 3.95 NLG *GVB-Dienstregeling* public transportation system timetable, just pop into the GVB offices during regular business hours. For more information, contact the **GVB Information Office** at *Stationplein 14, Tel. (6) 9292.*

### By Canal Boat

You may wish to explore Amsterdam by way of its many canal waterways. There are several unusual options for those who want to hop on and off a boat all day long as it passes by several of the city's most important attractions. For more information about guided canal boat cruises (no getting on and off allowed), please check the *Excursions* section later in this chapter. Tickets for all of these services (except for the water taxi) can be booked and purchased at any Amsterdam VVV office.

The **Museumboat** run by Rederij Lovers offers glass-roofed boat service every 30 to 45 minutes or so between over seven different stops around the city from 10:00am until 5:00pm daily. The narrated tour includes stops at the Centraal Station, Prinsengracht, Leidseplein, Museumplein, Herengracht, Stadhuis, and Port areas where you can get off, walk around, visit a museum, and hop back on the boat to get to the next destination. A full day unlimited use pass is 22 NLG per person.

After 1:00pm each day, you can also get less expensive tickets that allow for fewer stops and are priced between 7 NLG and 15 NLG per person. All tickets include a 10% to 50% discount for many of the city's most important museums. The ticket office for this service is located at *Stationsplein #8 just in front of the Centraal Station, Tel. (20) 622-2181.*

Another good option is the **Canal Bus** Rembrandt tour that lets visitors get on and off every half hour from so for the entire day at stops near the Rijksmuseum, Leidseplein, Keizersgracht, Westerkerk, Centraal Station, and Stadhuis. This circuit runs from 10:00am until 6:00pm daily during the summer, and between the same hours from Friday through Sunday only during the low season. Tickets for this guided boat trip cost 17.50 NLG per person, and special combination passes that include free admission to the Rijkmuseum cost 25 NLG per person. Tickets can be purchased at *Weteringschans, 24, across the canal from the Leidseplein, Tel. (20) 624-1033.*

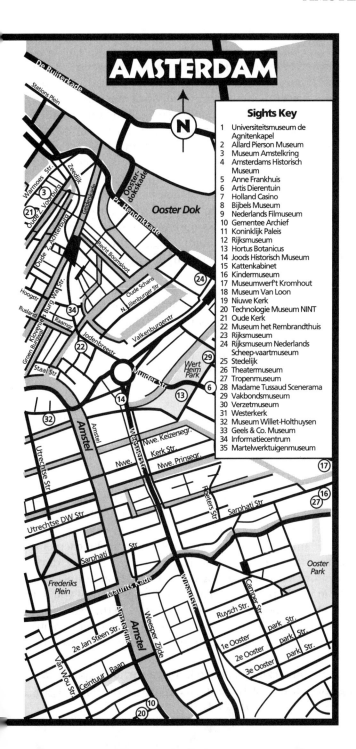

# AMSTERDAM

*Ooster Dok*

## Sights Key

1  Universiteitsmuseum de Agnitenkapel
2  Allard Pierson Museum
3  Museum Amstelkring
4  Amsterdams Historisch Museum
5  Anne Frankhuis
6  Artis Dierentuin
7  Holland Casino
8  Bijbels Museum
9  Nederlands Filmuseum
10 Gementee Archief
11 Koninklijk Paleis
12 Rijksmuseum
13 Hortus Botanicus
14 Joods Historisch Museum
15 Kattenkabinet
16 Kindermuseum
17 Museumwerf 't Kromhout
18 Museum Van Loon
19 Niuwe Kerk
20 Technologie Museum NINT
21 Oude Kerk
22 Museum het Rembrandthuis
23 Rijksmuseum
24 Rijksmuseum Nederlands Scheep-vaartmuseum
25 Stedelijk
26 Theatermuseum
27 Tropenmuseum
28 Madame Tussaud Scenerama
29 Vakbondsmuseum
30 Verzetmuseum
31 Westerkerk
32 Museum Willet-Holthuysen
33 Geels & Co. Museum
34 Informatiecentrum
35 Martelwerktuigenmuseum

The **Artis Express** has scheduled daily service connecting Centraal Station to the Artis Zoo via the Scheepvart Maritime Museum. This boat runs every hour between 10:00am and 1:00pm and again between 2:00pm and 5:00pm daily and costs 12.50 NLG per person. This ticket also includes a discount to the Tropenmuseum, Scheepvart museum, and the Artis Zoo. Tickets for this route can be purchased from their head office at *Prins Hendrikkade #25 just across from Centraal Station, Tel. (20) 622-2181.*

If you have strong legs, you may wish to rent a **Canal Bike** for a few hours. These self-propelled fiberglass pedal bikes cost between 19.50 NLG for a 2 person unit per hour or 29.50 NLG for a 4 person unit per hour, and can be rented and left off at any of their 4 canal jetties near the Leidseplein, Keizersgracht, Westerkerk, and Rijksmueum during the summer. During the winter, only the Rijksmuseum rental station is open. They are open daily around the year (I wouldn't suggest this activity in the winter!) from 10:00am until at least 7:00pm. Their office address is *Weteringschans #24 , Tel. (20) 626-5574.*

The last and most expensive way to get around various points along the canals is via the **Water Taxi** service. For 30 NLG per quarter hour (shorter time periods cost less) you can rent a water taxi boat to take you wherever you may need to go. You can either hail one down as it passes you along a canal, or call them a half hour in advance for a pick-up. The phone number for this unique service is *(020) 622-2181.*

### By Taxi

There are well over 5,000 licensed taxis which roam the streets and major passenger arrival points of this large capital city during all hours of the day and night. Drivers are typically polite, humorous, great sources of inside information, and quite honest in comparison to those currently found most other European or North American cities.

To find a taxi, either hail down an unoccupied cab driving by with its "Taxi" roof light illuminated, go to one of the dozens of obvious taxi stands throughout the city, or call *(20) 677-7777* for a radio response pick-up on demand. The main taxi ranks are located at the Leidseplein, Stationplein, Rembrandtplein, and Marnixstraat. During rainy days, festivals, trade fairs, or weekday morning and evening rush hours (8am until 10am and 6pm until 8pm) there may be a short wait until you get lucky. Taxi meters charge about 3 NLG per kilometer, so this works out to somewhere around 9.50 NLG to 16.50 NLG per ride (not per person) between most downtown locations depending on exact distance and traffic conditions.

For those who are physically challenged, you can arrange special taxi service by calling **Sneltax** at least 12 hours in advance of the desired pick up time, *Tel. (20) 655-6729 or (20) 613-4134.*

## WHERE TO STAY

*Very Expensive*

**AMSTEL INTER-CONTINENTAL HOTEL**, *Professor Tulipplein 1. Tel: (20) 622-6060, Fax: (20) 622-5808. US & Canada Bookings (Inter-Continental) 1-800-327-0200. Special weekend rates from 500 NLG per double room per night (B.P.). Year round rack rates from 650 NLG per double room per night (E.P.). All major credit cards accepted.*

Located on the banks of the Amstel river within easy walking distance to the Waterlooplein, the 5 star Inter-Continental Amstel Hotel is one of Holland's best grand hotels. Ever since this magnificent property first opened its doors in 1867, it has been the home away from home for some of the world's most famous celebrities and heads of state. Now with the completion of a two year total renovation of all the public rooms, guest rooms, dining areas, and facilities, it has become the finest deluxe hotel in all of Amsterdam. The staff here work extremely hard to assure that every guest, whether dressed in a designer suit or a pair of jeans, will come again and again.

Inside you will find 79 of the largest and most opulent air conditioned rooms and suites found in Europe, all featuring giant marble bathrooms with heated towel racks and imported amenities, a fantastic selection of antique or period style furnishings and Delftware, beautiful prints and original artwork, remote control satellite television with VCR machines and in-room movies, stereos with CD players, direct dial telephones, a large mini-bar, fax and telephone answering machines, and large picture windows with remarkable river or city views.

Their facilities include a formal gourmet French restaurant, a state of the art health club, indoor heated swimming pool and whirlpool, sauna, available massage, a beauty salon, several elegant business meeting and reception rooms, underground valet parking, in house limousine service, video tape rentals, express laundry and dry cleaning, and the best 24 hour room service in town. The wonderful Amstel Hotel easily gets my highest rating of any hotel in Holland!

**THE GRAND-AMSTERDAM**, *Oudezijds Voorburgwal 197. Tel: (20) 555-3111. Fax: (20) 555-3222. US & Canada Bookings (UTELL) 1-800-44-UTELL. Weekend rates from 430 NLG per double room per night (C.P.). Year round rack rates from 595 NLG per double room per night (E.P.). All major credit cards accepted.*

This recent addition to Amsterdam's selection of deluxe 5 star hotels has greatly impressed me during my last two night stay. Located alongside a picturesque canal within the walls of the former 15th century city hall, this extremely welcoming hotel is an excellent choice for those looking for personalized service and superb accommodations. You can choose from 182 fantastically designed rooms, suites, and fully equipped luxury apartments that all offer large marble and tile bathrooms with heated towel racks, impressive hardwood furnishings, remote control satellite television with movie channels, direct dial telephones, mini-safe, mini-bar, and sun-drenched windows overlooking the canal or the peaceful inner courtyards.

Among the many facilities and services available at The Grand include a casual yet elegant international bistro and outdoor dining area, relaxing lounges and public rooms, an indoor swimming pool and whirlpool, a great sauna, well-manicured gardens, full valet and concierge services, 24 hour room service, the city's most impressive business meeting and reception rooms, express laundry and dry cleaning, and secured garage parking. Service here is top quality, and the rather friendly and professional staff really go well out of their way to make sure your stay here is enjoyable.

**HOTEL DE L'EUROPE,** *Nieuwe Doelenstraat 2-8. Tel: (20) 623-4836. Fax: (20) 624-2962. US & Canada Bookings (Leading Hotels) 1-800-223-6800. Low season rack rates from 515 NLG per double room per night (E.P.). High season rack rates from 575 NLG per double room per night (E.P.). All major credit cards accepted.*

Now celebrating its second century of providing serious deluxe accommodations, the old world style Hotel de L'Europe is located alongside the charming Amstel river in the heart of the downtown Centrum district. This opulent 5 star property is well within easy walking distance to the city's countless historic and commercial attractions. Upon entering through the hotel's remarkable Renaissance style brick and stone facade, guests are surrounded by opulent sun-drenched public spaces embellished with the finest marbles, hardwoods, rich fabrics, and chandeliers imaginable.

There are 100 incredible air conditioned rooms and suites, all fully equipped with giant marble bathrooms stocked with imported amenities, exquisite furnishings, remote control satellite television with movie channels, direct dial telephones, plush designer fabrics, mini-safe, clock radio, mini-bar, wall to wall carpeting, more closet space than you will ever know what to do with, and a selection of great views over the river front, the old city streets, or a tranquil inner courtyard.

As a member of the prestigious "Leading Hotels of the World," the Hotel L'Europe prides itself in offering an excellent array of world class facilities and services including an award winning formal restaurant, an elegant brasserie with a beautiful riverfront dining terrace, relaxing bar and lounge areas, indoor swimming pool, health club with sauna and available massage treatments, private parking, 24 hour room service, fully equipped business meeting and private dining rooms, and a good staff. Perfect for visiting executives and veteran travelers.

### Expensive

**HOTEL OKURA**, *Ferdinand Bolstraat 333. Tel: (20) 678-7111. Fax: (20) 671-2344. US & Canada Bookings (Leading Hotels) 1-800-223-6800. Weekend rates from 400.00 NLG per double room per night (B.P.). Year round rack rates from 420 NLG per double room per night (E.P.). All major credit cards accepted.*

The famed 23 floor Hotel Okura is, without doubt, the best choice for visiting corporate and deluxe business travelers staying in Amsterdam. Located just a 4 minute walk from the giant RAI convention center in the city's lovely southern Zuid district, and a 5 minute ride to the center of downtown, this modern 5 star is also an excellent choice for upscale leisure travelers. Exceedingly well staffed by a team of 270 internationally trained professionals (one of the highest staff to guest ratios found in Europe!), every guest here is treated as a VIP from the moment they arrive.

Each of the 370 large air conditioned English-style rooms and suites offer large private marble bathrooms, electronic trouser press, remote control satellite television with movie channels, direct dial phones, mini-safe, am-fm clock radios, soundproofed windows with outstanding views, custom designed hardwood furnishings, mini-bar, and luxurious wall to wall carpeting.

Among the countless features here are 4 top rated restaurants, including an amazing Japanese grill-room and an opulent rooftop formal French gourmet dining room, great lounge areas, free parking, 24 hour room service, a wide array of business meeting and conference rooms, a shopping arcade with designer boutiques, available child care and secretarial services, beauty salon, available excursions and car rentals, express laundry and dry cleaning, the city's best health club equipped with state of the art interactive Nautilus machines, a full sized indoor swimming pool, Jacuzzi, massage rooms, solarium, saunas, and more than I could possibly list here. The Hotel Okura, a member of the famed "Leading Hotels of the World" hotel group, is Amsterdam's top business and convention hotel!

**HOTEL PULITZER**, *Prinsengracht 315. Tel: (20) 523-5235. Fax: (20) 627-6753. US & Canada Bookings (The Luxury Collection) 1-800-325-3589. Special Package rates from 260 NLG per double room per night (E.P.). Year round rack rates from 455 NLG per double room per night (E.P.). All major credit cards accepted.*

The charming Pulitzer is actually a series of two dozen authentic 17th and 18th century canal houses in the heart of the city that have been joined together to create a special hotel. With its prime location in front of two of the city's best known canals, this unusual property is well within walking distance to all of Amsterdam's most important sights and attractions. The most enchanting feature of the hotel are the many small secluded inner courtyard gardens where you can sit back and read while listening to the sounds of singing birds. If you can take advantage of their special package rates offered throughout the year, the Pulitzer is a good value.

All of the 230 rooms and suites here are totally different from each other, but each features modern private bathrooms, wood and wicker furnishings, remote control satellite television, direct dial telephone, mini-bar, picture windows with courtyard or canal views, and antique canal house architectural elements such as exposed beam or slanted ceilings. Facilities include a French patio restaurant, a breakfast room, a nice café, a tranquil piano bar, several business meeting rooms, 24 hour room service, express laundry and dry cleaning, a concierge desk, express check-out, excursion and car rental assistance, available nearby health club access, business meeting rooms, public areas lined with original art, indoor valet parking, quaint sculpture gardens, and more.

**JAN LUYKEN HOTEL,** *Jan Luykenstraat 58. Tel: (20) 573-0730. Fax: (20) 676-3841. Year round rack rates from 350 NLG per double room per night (B.P.). All major credit cards accepted.*

This cute little traditional Dutch family style hotel is situated just around the corner from the Rijksmuseum on a quiet residential side street. Comprised of several typical adjacent Amsterdam townhouses, the 4 star Jan Luyken offers 63 superbly decorated room that all have large tile bathrooms, remote control satellite television, am-fm clock radio, mini-safe, direct dial telephone, beautiful furnishings, executive style desks, and views out onto the surrounding old lanes. Facilities here include a great breakfast room, a 19th century style bar and patio, fully equipped business meeting rooms, private dining areas, and nearby parking. The staff here is outstanding.

This is one of my favorite small hotels in town. If you are looking for an alternative to the cold towering modern glass and steel hotels that are all too common in Amsterdam, this is a really good choice.

**AMSTERDAM RENAISSANCE HOTEL,** *Kattengat 1. Tel: (20) 621-2223. Fax: (20) 627-5245. US & Canada Bookings (Renaissance Hotels) 1-800-468-3571. Super saver rates from 285 NLG per double room per night (B.P.). Year round rack rates from 350 NLG per double room per night (E.P.). All major credit cards accepted.*

Situated within steps of the Leidseplein, the newly renovated 8 story Renaissance Hotel offers 432 large and extremely comfortable rooms and suites, each with air conditioning, private bathrooms, electronic trouser press, mini-bar, and modern furnishings. The hotel is a favorite among medium sized groups and conventions due to the fact that it offers a good restaurant, two bars, a disco, available parking, an optional health club, sauna, steam bath, 24 hour room service, safe deposit boxes, a convention center with meeting rooms, and a good staff. There are also several dozen fully equipped apartments nearby for those who are staying longer and desire more home style accommodations.

**AMERICAN HOTEL,** *Leidsekade 97. Tel: (20) 624-5322. Fax: (20) 625-3236. US & Canada Bookings (Inter-Continental) 1-800-327-0200. Special Package rates from 325 NLG per double room per night (E.P.). Year round rack rates from 475 NLG per double room per night (E.P.). All major credit cards accepted.*

With its prominent location in the exciting Leidseplein square, this turn of the century 4 star art nouveau hotel is one of the most requested places to stay in all of Amsterdam. The American offers 188 art deco-style rooms and suites that all have nice private bathrooms, remote control satellite television with pay per view movies, direct dial telephones, mini-bar, hair dryer, comfortable furnishings, and views out onto the bustling city streets. Facilities here include the amazingly beautiful Brasserie Americain restaurant, a nice lounge, a private water taxi stop, express laundry and dry cleaning, room service, a newsstand, boutiques, business meeting rooms, health club, available child care, and nearby parking. A good choice for those who want to be near all the action and attractions of town.

**GRAND HOTEL KRASNAPOLSKY,** *Dam 9. Tel: (20) 621-2223. Fax: (20) 627-5245. US & Canada Bookings (SRS Hotels) 1-800-223-5652. Special Package rates from 370 NLG per double room per night (E.P.). Year round rack rates from 485 NLG per double room per night (E.P.). All major credit cards accepted.*

Located in the heart of downtown Amsterdam's Dam square, this 5 star old world hotel has recently undergone a massive renovation project that has made it even more deluxe. There are 292 rooms in various categories offering private bathrooms, nice furnishings, remote control satellite television, mini-bar, and sound proof windows overlooking either the Royal Palace or one of several side streets. The hotel also has a brand new fully equipped health club, indoor parking, 24 hour room service, plenty of business meeting rooms, opulent public lounges, several restaurants and bars, boutiques, daily afternoon tea, and a great Sunday brunch. Favored by large groups and conventions, the location here is ideal, and the service is relatively good for such a large establishment.

### Moderate

**THE JOLLY CARLTON HOTEL,** *Vijzelstraat 4. Tel: (20) 622-2266. Fax: (20) 626-6183. US & Canada Bookings (Jolly Hotels) 1-800-221-2626 or (212) 213-1468. Special package rates from NLG 290.00 per double room per night (B.P.). Year round rack rates from NLG 395.00 per double room per night (E.P.). All major credit cards accepted.*

As soon as I walked into the lobby of this modern 4 star city center hotel, I knew I was in for a remarkable experience. Located just across the street from the dramatic Munt Tower and its adjacent year round floating flower market, the Jolly Carlton is even more comfortable and well situated than some of Amsterdam's very expensive 5 star properties. From the moment you pass through the doors and into the hotel's peaceful marble-lined lobby, the extremely polite multilingual staff here go to great lengths to make sure that you really feel at home.

There are 219 spacious and sun-drenched air conditioned rooms and suites (many with wonderful terraces) that each have large marble and tile private bathrooms with heated towel racks, fine custom designed furnishings, wall to wall carpeting, huge double glazed soundproofed windows, tastefully selected designer fabrics, remote control satellite color television with optional movie channels, a well stocked mini-bar, electric trouser press, an executive style desk, a selection of Italian soaps and shampoos, and direct dial telephones that can accept portable computer modem outputs.

There's also an outstanding gourmet Italian restaurant, a terraced cafe and lounge, all day room service, expertly designed business meeting and conference rooms, secure underground parking garage, special dedicated non-smoking guest rooms, express laundry and dry cleaning, and countless fine boutiques and entertainment venues just feet away from the Carlton's front door. With a dedicated staff of extremely professional workers from all over the world, all you have to do is ask for something and it magically arrives just moments later. The Jolly Carlton Hotel represents a great value for the money in the moderate price range, and receives one of my highest recommendations for downtown hotels in Amsterdam.

**HOTEL AMBASSADE**, *Herengracht 335. Tel: (20) 626-2333. Fax: (20) 624-5321. Year round rack rates from 275 NLG per double room per night (B.P.). All major credit cards accepted.*

I first found out about the Ambassade when the manager of a competing property told me he was jealous of this amazingly beautiful and refined little 3 star hotel. The Ambassade is housed in several 17th century canal houses that have been combined to create a unique hotel with some of the most charming rooms and public spaces found in Amsterdam. Located on one of the city's most famous canals, this is really a great place for those looking for a deluxe bed and breakfast inn with full hotel services and a great staff.

The hotel offers over 50 superbly decorated double rooms that all have private bathrooms, color television, direct dial telephone, mini-safe, and windows that in most cases look out onto the water. There are also spectacular antique lined lounges, a nice breakfast room, 24 hour room service, nearby parking, laundry and dry cleaning services, and plenty of character in general. Ask to look at a few different rooms before you pick the one that's right for you.

**THE PARK HOTEL,** *Stadhouderskade 25. Tel: (20) 671-7474. Fax: (20) 664-9455. US & Canada Bookings (UTELL) 1-800-44-UTELL. Special package rates from 292 NLG per double room per night (B.P.). Year round rack rates from 325 NLG per double room per night (E.P.). All major credit cards accepted.*

Celebrating its 100th anniversary this year, the inviting 4 star Park Hotel is a great choice for groups and individuals looking for affordably priced accommodations in central Amsterdam. Perfectly located just a few steps away from the most important downtown sights and attractions including the Rijksmuseum and the Leidseplein, this medium-sized full service property has an unusually friendly and inviting ambiance. Considering its unbeatable location, spacious well maintained accommodations, surprisingly relaxed and inviting atmosphere, and range of facilities, the Park Hotel represents one of the better values for the money in the moderate price range

All of the Park Hotel's 187 large rooms and split level suites offer fully equipped private bathrooms, remote control satellite television with pay per view movies, am-fm clock radios, direct dial telephones with voice mail, complimentary coffee and tea set ups, electronic trouser press, comfortable furnishings, individually controlled heating systems, and wonderful views over the city or small terraces overlooking the canals.

Facilities include a good restaurant featuring hearty international cuisine priced well below what you might expect, a rather cozy cafe and bar, several extremely relaxing English country-style lounge areas laden with fine furnishings and plush sofas, secure underground car parking, same day laundry and dry cleaning service, safe deposit or mini-safe lockers, a full range of well appointed business meeting and conference rooms, free morning newspapers, designer boutiques, and 24 hour porter service. The atmosphere here is casual and friendly with a good mixture of international guests that often get acquainted with each other during their stay. The hotel's multilingual staff is always a pleasure to deal with and will be more than happy to help you plan a walk through town or even arrange special excursions.

**GOLDEN TULIP BARBIZON PALACE,** *Prins Hendrikkade 59. Tel: (20) 556-4564. Fax: (20) 624-3353. US & Canada Bookings (Golden Tulip) 1-800-344-1212. Special Package rates from 249.50 NLG per double room per night (E.P.). Year round rack rates from 390 NLG per double room per night (E.P.). All major credit cards accepted.*

Located just across the street from Amsterdam's downtown Centraal Station, this stunningly beautiful 5 star full service hotel was created from a series of antique residences that were connected together. With its year round clientele of groups and individual travelers, this nice and surprisingly friendly deluxe hotel is well worth the price. On my last visit here, the front desk staff hand drew me a map of the lesser known sights in the old part of town, and then spent over half an hour giving me tips on when the quietest time was to visit each museum and attraction they suggested.

There are 263 nicely decorated rooms and suites, each with private bathrooms, air conditioning, mini-bar, direct dial telephones, remote control satellite televisions with movie channels, extremely comfortable furnishings, and even several duplex rooms with antique oak beams. Facilities available on location include several restaurants, two bars, a health club, an excursion desk, available car rentals, safe deposit boxes, laundry and dry cleaning services, available child care, boutiques, excellent business meeting and conference rooms, room service, outdoor parking, an adjacent congress center, a nearby boat dock, and a really nice staff. Highly recommended for those who desire a central location and a high level of service in the moderate price range. Ask about their special low season and weekend rates.

**CANAL HOUSE HOTEL,** *Keizersgracht 148. Tel: (20) 622-5182. Fax: (20) 624-1317. Year round rack rates from NLG 210 NLG per double room per night (C.P.). Most major credit cards accepted.*

This little bed and breakfast inn is situated on a major downtown canal in a pair of converted 17th century homes. The rooms here are all rather different in both size and price from one another, but all feature private bathrooms, plenty of antiques, direct dial telephones, comfortable furnishings, and either canal or garden views. This is a quiet place that has minimal facilities such as a breakfast room, an old world bar, a peaceful courtyard garden, and no television.

**ASCOT HOTEL,** *Damrack 95. Tel: (20) 626-0066. Fax: (20) 627-0982. US & Canada Bookings (Swissôtels) 1-800-637-9477. Special weekend rates from 270 NLG per double room per night (B.P.). Year round rack rates from 450 NLG per double room per night (E.P.). All major credit cards accepted.*

I was very impressed when I checked into my lovely room in this friendly modern 4 star hotel, just a few steps away from the Dam square. The Ascot offers 110 rather nicely decorated rooms air conditioned rooms that all have large private marble bathrooms, nice modern furnishings, remote control satellite television with movie channels, direct dial telephones, mini-bar, am-fm clock radio, and views out onto the center of the city. Facilities include nearby parking, 24 hour room service, express laundry and dry cleaning, a nice Swiss restaurant, a relaxing bar, a nearby health club, car rental kiosks, available secretarial services, excursion desk, business meeting rooms, nearby parking and two special executive floors with larger rooms that have complimentary coffee and tea makers as well as mini-safes. This hotel is a favorite of visiting businessmen who want great service at good prices in the heart of the city.

**HOLIDAY INN CROWNE PLAZA CITY CENTER**, *Nieuwezijds Voorburgwal 5. Tel: (20) 620-0500. Fax: (20) 620-1173. US & Canada Bookings (Holiday Inn) 1-800-465-4329. Special Package rates from 220 NLG per double room per night (E.P.). Year round rack rates from 495 NLG per double room per night (E.P.). All major credit cards accepted.*

Located in the heart of the city center, this surprisingly nice and modern 5 star low rise hotel is a great bargain if you can book one of their "Great Rate" prices available throughout the year. There are 270 large and comfortable air conditioned rooms and suites that all offer private bathrooms, remote control satellite television with movie channels, mini-bar, electric trouser press, coffee and tea making facilities, hair dryers and either interior or exterior view sound proofed windows. Facilities include an indoor swimming pool, whirlpool, health club, sauna, solarium, a restaurant, bar, business meeting rooms, indoor parking, and a car rental and excursion desk. The service here is well above average, and you can walk to almost every sight in the downtown district within a few minutes.

**THE MERIDIEN APOLLO HOTEL**, *Apollolaan 2. Tel: (20) 673-5922. Fax: (20) 570-5744. US & Canada Bookings (Meridien Hotels) 1-800-543-4300. Special Weekend rates from NLG 240 NLG per double room per night (B.P.). Year round rack rates from NLG 395 NLG per double room per night (E.P.). All major credit cards accepted.*

The medium sized modern 4 star Meridien Apollo is situated along-side the wide waterways of the south Amsterdam's Zuid section. Known primarily as a favored selection for budget-conscious international businessmen attending conferences at the nearby RAI convention center and World Trade Center, this rather pleasant full service property is also well worth the consideration of leisure travelers, especially when its great weekend rates are available.

There are 228 rooms and suites offering private bathrooms with hair dryers and heated towel racks, electric trouser press, remote control satellite television with pay per view movies, large executive style desks, complimentary coffee and tea making facilities, am-fm clock radio, comfortable furnishings, mini-bar, direct dial telephones, and large windows with either water or city views. Also available are free parking areas, a casual brasserie, a formal restaurant, express laundry and dry cleaning, an adjacent private marina, a newsstand and gift shop, 24 hour room service, available safe deposit boxes, a beauty salon, a complete business support center, business meeting rooms, and a superb executive board room. If you are in town for business or want to be a few minutes ride away from the excitement of downtown Amsterdam, the Meridien Apollo is a good choice.

**AMSTERDAM WIECHMAN HOTEL,** *Prinsengracht 328. Tel: (20) 626-3321. Fax: (20) 626-8962. Year round rack rates from 230 NLG per double room per night (C.P.). Cash Only - No credit cards accepted.*

This is a cute 3 star hotel located inside of three old canal houses in a quiet part of the city. The hotel offers 38 spacious rooms with private bathrooms, comfortable hardwood furnishings, wall to wall carpeting, telephones, and in some cases great views. The dramatic lounge, breakfast room, and reception areas are complete with fine tapestries and parquet flooring.

### Inexpensive

**THE BRIDGE HOTEL,** *Amstel 107. Tel: (20) 623-7068. Fax: (20) 624-1565. Low season rack rates from 100 NLG per double room per night (C.P.). High season rack rates from 150 NLG per double room per night (C.P.). All major credit cards accepted.*

Situated on downtown Amsterdam's picturesque Amstel River near the Waterlooplein and the Magere Brug (Skinny) bridge, this cute little 3 star hotel is a real gem. The Bridge has 27 spacious and sun-drenched single and double rooms that all feature spotless modern private bathrooms, simple but rather comfortable hard wood furnishings, individually controlled heaters, hair dryer, small desks, direct dial telephones, plenty of closet space, and if you spend a bit more money you can have a great view out over the river. The ambiance here shows a touch or romance and relaxation that I am used to finding only in much more expensive hotels. The folks working here treat their guests incredibly well, and they proved to me that tastefully designed accommodations with personalized European hospitality can be affordable. I highly suggest The Bridge Hotel for all those on tight budgets who still want a great place to stay with a perfect location.

**TULIP INN-DAM SQUARE,** *Gravenstraat 14. Tel: (20) 623-3716. Fax: (20) 638-1156. US & Canada Bookings (Golden Tulip) 1-800-344-1212. Year round rack rates from 160 NLG per double room per night (C.P.). All major credit cards accepted.*

Housed in a former distillery just steps away from Dam square, the 3 star Tulip Inn is one of the city's best bargains. All of this charming little hotel's 33 rooms have private bathrooms, modern furnishings, direct dial telephones, complimentary coffee and tea facilities, remote control satellite televisions with movie channels, and either interior or exterior views. Although the facilities are rather limited, it is near everything you would want to see, and the people working here are among the friendliest and most helpful I have encountered in a hotel in this price range. For these prices, the Tulip Inn at Dam Square is a great choice for those on somewhat tight budgets.

**RHO HOTEL,** *Nes 11. Tel: (20) 620-7371. Fax: (20) 620-7826. Year round rack rates from 195 NLG per double room per night (B.P.). Special weekend rates from 160 NLG per double room per night (B.P.). All major credit cards accepted.*

This unusual hotel is located in a converted theater complete with an original deco interior. The Rho is now a nice 100+ room 3 star hotel in the heart of the theater district near the Dam square. All of the rooms feature private bathrooms, mini-bar, modern furnishings, direct dial telephones, nice art work, and either interior or exterior views. This is a good value for the money, especially considering the price includes breakfast buffet.

**HOTEL HESTIA,** *Roemer Visscherstraat 7. Tel: (20) 618-0801. Fax: (20) 685-1382. Year round rack rates from 160.00 NLG per double room per night (C.P.). Most major credit cards accepted.*

Located just a couple of blocks away from the Leidseplein on a safe and quiet residential street, this friendly little family-owned 3 star hotel is a really good choice for this price range. The Hestia offers 18 modern rooms with private bathrooms, simple modern furnishings, direct dial telephones, mini-bar, color television, and large windows overlooking the city. Facilities include a nice new breakfast room, nearby parking, and a nice staff.

**AMSTERDAM HOUSE BOATS AND APARTMENTS,** *Amstel 176a. Tel: (20) 626-2577. Fax: (20) 626-2987. Year round rack rates from 150 NLG per apartment per night (E.P.). Some major credit cards accepted.*

If you are staying in the city for a week or more and want to stay in your own private apartment or houseboat, this is a good place to check out. The owners rent out dozens of apartments and self-contained houseboats that may contain everything from full kitchens to saunas and pianos. All units come with maid service, and can be outfitted according to your needs.

**AMSTEL BOTEL,** *Oosterdokskade 2. Tel: (20) 626-4247. Fax: (20) 639-1952. Year round rack rates from NLG 140 NLG per double room per night (E.P.). Most major credit cards accepted.*

Permanently docked on a waterway within view of the Centraal Station, this 4 story floating boat/hotel is definitely an unusual selection. This modern white boat offers 176 little single and double cabins with private bathrooms, direct dial telephones, color satellite television, and basic furnishings. While far from deluxe and not all that comfortable, many people enjoy the experience of staying here.

**HOTEL VAN HAALEN,** *Prinsengracht 520. Tel: (20) 626-4334. Fax: None. Year round rack rates from 115 NLG per double room per night (C.P.). Cash Only - No credit cards accepted.*

Situated on one of the city's famous canals, this basic 1 star hotel offers about two dozen single and double rooms with either shared or private bathrooms, telephone, and basic furnishings. The homey public areas and breakfast room are full of unusual antiques, and it is only a couple of minutes walk away from the Rijksmuseum. Nothing fancy, but well worth the money for this location.

### Cheap

**HOTEL INTERNATIONAL**, *Warmeosstraat 1. Tel: (20) 624-5520. Fax: (20) 624-4501. Year round rack rates from 80 NLG per double room per night (E.P.). Cash Only - No credit cards accepted.*

Located above a charming bar and café of the same name on the city's oldest street, the Hotel International is a special little inn that makes you feel that you have gone back through the centuries. This basic, rather clean, and well situated budget property has 10 small but comfortable rooms with either shared or private bathrooms that have simple pine wood furnishings, exposed brick walls, wood beam ceilings, modern wash basins, and in some cases great views out onto the historic part of the city. There are no real facilities to speak of, but the café below has great lunches, and the neighborhood is rather amusing. This is a good selection for those looking for an inexpensive private room in a central location.

**NJHC-VONDELPARK HOSTEL**, *Zanpad 5. Tel: (20) 683-1744. Fax: (20) 616-6591. US & Canada Bookings (Hostelling International) 1-613-237-7884. Year round rack rates from 27.50 NLG per person in a dormitory per night (C.P.). Year round rack rates from 80 NLG per double private room per night (C.P.). Cash Only - No credit cards accepted.*

This was one of the first city center hostels that really impressed me with its value for the money and amazing location. After a recently completed renovation and the addition of a new modern annex, this ever-popular hostel is quite a nice place to stay. The accommodations come in several varieties ranging from totally private single and double rooms with their own private bathrooms and courtyard views, to large size dormitories with well over a dozen bunk beds and shared bathrooms. The private rooms are much more comfortable than I had ever expected, and with the new addition of electronic mini-safes, even the dorms are a great value.

While a continental breakfast is included, lunch and dinner are quite good and cost half the price of a regular restaurant. This hostel is just two blocks away from the Leidseplein and faces right onto the Vondelpark. The minimal regulations here include the need for a Hostelling International membership card (available on the premises) as well as a 2:00am curfew and an afternoon lockout, but for these prices it is well worth the effort to book this place well in advance!

**HOTEL KING**, *Leidsekade 86. Tel: (20) 624-9603. Fax: (20) 620-7277. Year round rack rates from 85 NLG per double room per night (E.P.). Cash Only - No credit cards accepted.*

This is a basic and simple 1 star budget hotel in a 17th century canal house just off the Leidseplein. The hotel offers 25 single and double rooms with basic but clean and comfortable interiors, and shared bathrooms. No facilities to speak of, but a good safe place to overnight near everything.

**ARENA BUDGET HOTEL**, *'s-Gravesandestraat 51. Tel: (20) 694-7444. Fax: (20) 663-2649. Year round rack rates from 25 NLG per person in a dormitory per night (E.P.). Year round rack rates from 90 NLG per double private room per night (E.P.). Cash Only - No credit cards accepted.*

Located on a small street near the southeastern edge Amsterdam, Arena is a low budget hotel, concert venue, dance club, cultural enter, hip café, and restaurant all wrapped up into one. Built in an old orphanage and an adjacent church, this bizarre establishment offers its young and casual guests rooms in both large co-ed and single sex dormitories with up to 80 bunk beds (some partitioned in sub sections for 8 persons), as well as much more private 2 through 8 bed rooms with private bathrooms. While far from deluxe, the accommodations are comfortable, there is no curfew, and the entertainment and inexpensive dining facilities here are among the most enjoyable in town. If you spend the time to look around, the older wings of this structure are filled with fine frescoes and antique hand-carved grand staircases.

**HANS BRINKER**, *Kerkstraat 136. Tel: (20) 622-0687. Fax: (20) 638-2060. Year round rack rates from 39.50 NLG per person in a dormitory per night (C.P.). Year round rack rates from 120 NLG per double private room per night (C.P.). Cash Only - No credit cards accepted.*

This student and backpackers budget hotel near the Leidseplein prides itself on having "No Parking, No Bellboys, No Air Conditioning, No Bidet, No Sauna, No VIP Rooms, No Mini-bars, No Escort Girls, No Swimming Pool, No Room Service, and No Hole in Your Pocket." What it does have is a series of 500 beds in small dormitories and a scattering of private rooms, all with shared bathrooms and basic services. There is no curfew, and there is a bar and disco.

**HOTEL KABUL**, *Warmoesstraat 38. Tel: (20) 623-7158. Fax: (20) 620-0869. Year round rack rates from 32 NLG per person in a dormitory per night (C.P.). Year round rack rates from 92 NLG per double private room per night (C.P.). Cash Only - No credit cards accepted.*

This budget backpacker and student hotel in the oldest part of downtown has several basic and simply furnished private rooms for between 1 and 16 people each. Although not as nice or friendly as the establishments listed just above, it is a reasonably good choice for the money. Make sure to use a safe to lock up your belongings while you are away! There is a good bar with live music on weekends, an inexpensive restaurant, and no curfew.

## WHERE TO EAT

*Very Expensive*

**RESTAURANT EXCELSIOR**, *Hotel de L'Europe, Nieuwe Doelenstraat 2. Tel: (20) 623-4836. All major credit cards accepted.*

Located on a river-view section of the sophisticated Hotel De L'Europe, this elegantly decorated French restaurant serves what is perhaps the finest gourmet cuisine in all of Amsterdam. Internationally acclaimed chef Jean Jacques Menanteau has created superb menus that offer such impressive selections as hearty Lobster bisque for 22.50 NLG, game consommé with wild mushrooms at 17.50 NLG, smoked Scottish salmon for 38.50 NLG, Sevruga caviar at 88.50 NLG, goose liver pate for 47.50 NLG, fresh lobster salad at 50 NLG, fillet of turbot in black truffle sauce for 75 NLG, roasted pheasant with endives at 47.50 NLG, partridge served with sauerkraut for 75 NLG, filet of sole meuniere at 65 NLG, hare with wild mushrooms for 48.50 NLG, and much, much more.

The ambiance here is rather formal, with settings made from the highest quality silver and bone china. Favored by Dutch bank executives and political leaders, this formal restaurant has a tranquil and serious atmosphere, with guests often opting for the 3 to 5 course gourmet lunch and dinner menus that cost from 62.50 NLG to 165 NLG per person that come complete with a selection of vintage wines from their massive cellars. Ask for a riverview table when you make your necessary reservations, dress to the max, and you will be sure to have a fantastic two hour gastronomic experience.

**LA RIVE**, *Amstel Hotel, Professor Tulpplein 1, Tel: (20) 622-6060. All major credit cards accepted.*

It is rather fitting that the city's finest 5 star hotel should also be home to a fantastic formal French restaurant. La Rive's lavish formal dining room features an extensive menu designed by executive chef Robert Kranenborg that may include cream of pheasant soup with chestnuts and vegetables at 32.50 NLG, langoustino ravioli with truffle sauce for 45 NLG, sautéed lobster with cucumber mango salad at 95 NLG, charcoal grilled scallops for 47.50 NLG, fried sweetbread with snails and truffle at 57.50 NLG, fried sole with Jamaican peppers and grape sauce for 47.50 NLG, roasted wild duck with sour berries at 45 NLG, rib eye steak with Madeira wine and truffle sauce for 70 NLG, fillet of roasted venison with pickles and raisins at 65 NLG, caramelized apples in a puff pastry for 27.50 NLG, warm chocolate cake with better sweet chocolate sorbet at 27.50 NLG, and a wonderful assortment of the world finest wines. Reservations are essential here, and men must wear a jacket and tie.

**RESTAURANT SAZANKA,** *Hotel Okura, Ferdinand Bolstraat 333, Tel: (20) 678-7111. All major credit cards accepted.*

This Teppan-Yaki style grill room serves Amsterdam's best cooked to order gourmet Japanese cuisine. They offer several all-inclusive menus that range from 90 NLG to 165 NLG per person and include streak, poultry, and seafood items grilled at a large hot table in front of you such as Kushiyaki chicken, Scottish sirloin with garlic, Dutch shrimp, fillet of Turbot, jumbo shellfish combinations with lobster and scallops, salmon steaks, thin sliced sirloin roll, sea bass filets, and more. All menus are served with a salad topped with ginger sauce, perfectly cooked rice, fried rice, miso soup, tempura, stir fried vegetables, exotic sorbets, and other delicious side dishes.

The chefs are all from Japan, and they do not get into the Benihana type knife throwing routines. Even the wine list has been well thought out, and contains many bottles from around the world. Many of the same Japanese businessmen and well-dressed couples come here week after week, so you know you are in for a great meal. There is no strict dress code. Reservations are a good idea but are not always necessary.

*Expensive*
**RESTAURANT HALVEMAAN**, *Van Leijenberghlaan 320, Tel: (20) 644-0348. All major credit cards accepted.*

This superb gourmet restaurant is well worth the effort to get to, via a 15 minute ride away from the city center in the Buitenveldert district. Situated in a modern two story water-front structure on the edge of a peaceful park, Restaurant Halvemaan is the creation of famous local chef John Halvemaan who is among the most creative cooks in Holland. Their dinner menu changes rather frequently, but tends to feature 3, 4, and 5 course gastronomic arrangements that are priced from 80 NLG per person and up, as well as several a la carte items. Lunches are somewhat less dressy events and cost around 65 NLG a person.

Since they only have space for around 55 patrons, reserve early in order to get a table (note: it's open on weekdays only). Select from amazingly prepared specialties such as steamed bouillon of quail with goose liver and shitake mushrooms, lentil soup with duck confit, scallops and langoustinos with assorted seasonings, rib-eye steak tartar, rack of lamb with basil mousse, duck breast with green cabbage, pigeon with navy beans in a port wine sauce, fried lobster with tomato confit and garlic mousse, poached pears, caramelized bread and butter pudding, creme brulee with grapefruit, and an outstanding optional wine list. Dress fairly well. This is one of Amsterdam's finest culinary experiences!

**RESTAURANT D'VIJFF VLIEGHEN**, *Spuistraat 294, Tel: (20) 624-8369. All major credit cards accepted.*

This truly great Dutch restaurant in the city center is housed in a series of 17th century mansions. The name of this famous establishment translates to "The 5 Flies," and its kitchen creates new Dutch-style cuisine that is both delicious and beautifully presented. Using a carefully selected assortment of fresh market ingredients, the a la carte menu usually features such mouth-watering dishes as cream of potato and beet root soup for 12 NLG, confit of quail at 22.50 NLG, white bean soup with smoked bacon for 22.50 NLG, game consommé with smoke dried beef at 12 NLG, rabbit fillet in aspic with shallot for 19.50 NLG, terrine of shellfish with oyster sauce at 20.50 NLG, smoked eel tartare with sauerkraut for 27.50 NLG, wild duck breast with coriander salad at 23.50 NLG, pan fried sole for 46 NLG, grilled turbot with ratatouille at 47.50 NLG, lamb chops baked in a pastry filled with herbed mustard for 45.50 NLG and venison in red wine sauce and vegetables at 42.50 NLG.

Desserts include poached pear in marsala and vanilla for 11.50 NLG, warm French toast with marzipan ice cream at 15 NLG, and caramel walnut parfait with a creamy dark beer sauce for 17.50 NLG. They also have vegetarian menus, seasonal special menus, and hundreds of local and imported apéritifs and liqueurs to compliment your meal. The ambiance here is semi-formal yet relaxed, with a great staff that will help you choose the day's best offerings. This is a must for all visitors to Amsterdam that can afford one great Dutch meal, and reservations are required on most nights.

**BRASSERIE AMERICAIN**, *American Hotel, Leidsekade 97, Tel (20) 624-5322. All major credit cards accepted.*

Built in 1902 from a design by W. Kromhout, this Art Nouveau Brasserie and cafe looks directly out onto the Leidseplein square and has become one of the city's most famous meeting points. This Art Deco café is decorated with marble floors, huge plants, period oil paintings based on Shakespeare's *A Mid-Summer Night's Dream*, stained glass windows, and vintage Jugendstil lamps.

A favorite of the older and more sophisticated set, their menu features innovative selections such as marinated yellow fin tuna with mushroom compote at 17.50 NLG, sweetbreads with smoked shitake mushrooms for 13.50 NLG, home made bread filled with shrimp and snails at 16.50 NLG, smoked Scottish salmon with scrambled eggs and truffles for 19.50 NLG, Irish entrecote with shallots at 38.50 NLG, grilled North Sea flounder with balsamic vinegar sauce for 53 NLG, tournedos of rabbit with asparagus and hazelnut sauce at 32.50 NLG, swordfish with rosemary and tomatoes for 29.50 NLG, scrag of calf braised in bay leaves at 29.50 NLG, lamb with lentil biscuit served with roti sauce and cloves for 38.50 NLG, Grilled jumbo shrimp and mullet with spinach and coconut at 35.50 NLG, and great desserts and flavored coffees such as their famed meringue of macadamia nuts with chocolate mousse and passion fruit coulis at 13.50 NLG.

They also have a great lunch menu and a fine Sunday brunch with live jazz music for 49.50 NLG a head.

**RESTAURANTE CARUSO,** *Jolly Carlton Hotel, Vijzelstraat 4. Tel: (20) 622-2266. All major credit cards accepted.*

Situated just off of the floating flower market near thc Munt Tower, this is one of the only authentic gourmet Italian restaurants in the city. The chefs here are all from Italy, and so are many of the freshly flown-in ingredients. The menu is large and varied enough to suit almost anybody and includes such mouth-watering dishes as cream of artichoke soup with bacon at 11 NLG, Genovese style minestrone soup for 11 NLG, Italian cured ham with fresh mozzarella at 19 NLG, carpaccio of Angus beef for 24 NLG, eggplant and zucchini parmigiana at 19 NLG, grilled tuna on compote of red onion for 23 NLG, breaded prawns with basil and tomato at 24 NLG, tagliolini pasta with king crab for 24 NLG, bass ravioli with lobster sauce at 23 NLG, grilled turkey for 34 NLG, lobster fra diavolo with pasta at 54 NLG, roasted breast of duck with wine sauce for 42 NLG, veal parmigiana at 44 NLG, lamb chops with rosemary for 39 NLG, and a wonderful array of fantastic wines, cheeses, and desserts. Suits are requested but not mandatory, and reservations are a good idea if possible.

### *Moderate*

**RESTAURANT SELECTA**, *Vizelstraat 26. Tel (20) 624-8894. All major credit cards accepted.*

This outstanding Indonesian restaurant near the Muntplein offers a stunning array of freshly prepared and exotically spiced dishes. You can relax and unwind in a tranquil setting complete with authentic Indonesian art and music, and can even people-watch through their huge picture windows. There is an a la carte as well as a fixed price menu here, but I strongly suggest you try the typical Rijsttafel (rice table) menus that cost between 29.75 NLG and 56 NLG per person and include several meat, fish, poultry, or vegetarian dishes that will delight you.

Among my favorite selections are the Indonesian chicken soup, assorted pickled vegetables, prawn crackers, tepid vegetables with peanut sauce, lamb sate, beef in spicy gravy, skewers of grilled pork, vegetables in coconut sauce, saffron rice, spring rolls, roast pork in sweet and sour sauce, and the prawns in chili sauce. All items can be made as spicy or mild as you prefer, and the friendly staff speak English rather well. I really love this place, and I highly recommend it to all visitors!

**THEATER-CAFE BLINCKER**, *St. Barberenstraat 9. Tel: (20) 627-1928. Most major credit cards accepted.*

Convieniently located near the city's theater row off of the street called Nes, this delightful ultra-modern two floor brasserie is the most popular eating spot for the somewhat chic pre- and post-theater crowd.

Inside their checkerboard style interior, patrons can choose from a variety of well-prepared and presented international specialties such as soup of the day at 5.50 NLG, salad with smoked chicken for 16 NLG, pasta of the day at 18.50 NLG, pasta panne for 9 NLG, fresh pate at 9 NLG, warm pastrami for 10 NLG, cannelloni stuffed with cheese and meat at 18.50 NLG, shrimp with pasta and blue cheese sauce for 24 NLG, cheese fondue at 21 NLG, rib eye steak for 26 NLG, and tiramisu for 10 NLG.

**MANCHURIAN RESTAURANT**, *Korte Leidspoorstraat 10. Tel: (20) 623-1330. All major credit cards accepted.*

After searching the entire Leidseplein area for a good restaurant, this in among my favorite exotic choices. This Chinese/Indonesian restaurant just steps away from all the bars and clubs offers a great selection of Asian dishes that can be prepared as spicy or soft as you prefer. Among my personal favorites here are the rice table combination dinners that are priced between 49.75 NLG and 79 NLG per person, depending on what items are selected. Included in these combinations are the following items that can also be ordered a la carte: prawn won ton soup at 9.50 NLG, Indonesian chicken soup with curry and bean sprouts for 8.50 NLG, Peking hot and sour soup at 9.75 NLG, assorted dim sum for 24 NLG, Vegetarian fortune with seaweed and vegetables at 12.50 NLG, steamed lobsters for 29.50 NLG, crispy beef at 23 NLG, chicken with nuts at 18.75 NLG, and more!

**THE GURU OF INDIA**, *Lance Leidsedwarsstraat 56. Tel: (20) 624-6966. Visa cards accepted.*

I was surprised that this semi-fancy Indian restaurant near the Leidseplein was as delicious at it turned out to be. The Guru's large menu offers many of the specialties that one would expect from a fine Indian restaurant, including dal soup for 6 NLG, mulligatawany soup at 7.50 NLG, butterflied prawns for 21.50 NLG, chicken chat at 7.50 NLG, tandoori steak kebob for 12.50 NLG, assorted samosas at 7.50 NLG, Kashmiri chicken with garlic for 29.50 NLG, tandoori lamb chops at 32 NLG, prawns in curry sauce for 39.50 NLG, lamb vindaloo at 26 NLG, vegetarian alu mater for 14.50 NLG, and plenty of puffy breads and strange drink combinations to please your palate. There is no dress code to speak of, and the service is rather polite and professional.

### Inexpensive

**RESTAURANTE SATURNINO**, *Reguliers Dwarsstraat 5. Tel: (20) 639-0102. All major credit cards accepted.*

This is undoubtedly the best value in fine Italian food that Amsterdam has to offer (and they stay open until at least 1:00am). Located on an odd little street just a block or so from the Munt tower, this home-style regional restaurant is staffed by real Italians that really know how to make great pastas and main courses at affordable prices. My last meal here was so good that I could hardly believe how low the bill was! Their extensive menu includes huge portions of delicious mixed salads at 6 NLG, green salads for 5 NLG, Gorgonzola cheese salads at 15 NLG, fusilli in tomato sauce for 10 NLG, lasagna vegetarian style at 15 NLG, risotto Milanese for 15 NLG, spaghetti with clam sauce at 16 NLG, pasta with 3 sauces for 20 NLG, chicken with chilies at 22 NLG, fried calamari for 19 NLG, grilled shrimp at 28 NLG, grilled tuna for 29.50 NLG, entrecote with capers at 24.00, and a large assortment of superb pizzas starting at just 10 NLG each.

**MR. COCOS**, *Thorbeckeplein 8. Tel: (Unlisted). Cash Only - No credit cards accepted.*

If you are in the mood for a lively restaurant and pick-up bar that serves huge portions of standard American style food, make sure to check out this place. Their logo reads "lousy food and warm beer", but neither is true. After sitting down at the simple wooden tables and benches below all sorts of curiosities left by former guests, a menu is presented to you that includes French onion soup for 6.75 NLG, chili con carne at 9.75 NLG, garlic shrimp for 12.50 NLG, tuna melts at 9.75 NLG, BLT's for 9.50 NLG, fillet of fish sandwiches at 9.75 NLG, garlic bread for 4 NLG, house salads at 4.75 NLG, pepper steak for 19.75 NLG, chicken sate at 18.50 NLG, potato skins with your choice of toppings for 9.75 NLG, fish and chips at 18.75 NLG, and the house specialty of all you can eat ribs or chicken at just 21.75 NLG. Bring your jeans and Tee shirts and wait until the drinking crowd rolls in for some real fun.

**DE BALIE**, *Kleine-Gartmanplantsoen 10. Tel: (20) 624-3821. Cash only - No credit cards accepted.*

This casual bar and cafe around the corner from the Leidseplein caters to a crowd of locals involved in theater and the arts. Here you can enjoy small meals, appetizers, and snacks at good prices like their tuna sandwiches for 5.50 NLG, warm brie cheese sandwiches at 5 NLG, the city's best BLT's for 5.75 NLG, goat cheese salads at 10 NLG, home made soup of the day for 7 NLG and after 5pm the menu also features additional items such as calamari a la Romana at 6.50 NLG, tortellini with marscarpone cheese and lemon sauce for 11 NLG, and a wonderful mixed salad with mustard dressing at 7 NLG.

**PUCCINI TRATTORIA E CAFE**, *Staalstraat 21. Tel: (20) 626-5474. Cash only - No credit cards accepted.*

Puccini is a marvelous bakery and an adjacent cafe that serves the casually dressed lunch crowd from the nearby city hall and opera house. Besides having the absolute best desserts anywhere in this city, they also have a limited lunch and late afternoon menu that lists gorgonzola cheese sandwiches at 5 NLG, peppered salami sandwiches for 4.50 NLG, goat cheese sandwiches at 5 NLG, tuna salad sandwiches for 5.75 NLG, fresh soup of the day at 5.50 NLG, fruit salad with yogurt for 6 NLG, a giant mixed salad with grilled chicken at 15.50, and slices of their famed apple or chocolate cakes for 4.50 NLG and up. A great place to kill your diet in one shot, and well worth the effort to find.

**CAFE INTERNATIONAL,** *Warmoestraat 1. Tel: (20) 624-5520. Cash only - No credit cards accepted.*

This cozy brown cafe style pub at the base of the city's oldest street is a great place to enjoy a simple lunch featuring an assortment of home-made soups, salads, sandwiches, and light meals. The young and friendly crowd of tourists and locals sit for hours drinking ice cold beer and talking with each other while listening to great music, especially during their free Sunday afternoon jazz concerts. Expect to pay about 16.50 NLG per head for a filling three course lunch with a beer, and dress any way you feel comfortable.

**DELICIOUS TRAITEUR,** *Heisteeg 8. Tel: (20) 622-4850. Cash only - No credit cards accepted.*

This great little takeout and catering establishment is the perfect place to grab a few containers of gourmet salads, main courses, and cheeses before heading out for a sunny afternoon picnic. The shop features over three dozen varieties of warm and cold dishes sold by the kilogram and usually stocks freshly made selections such as Turkish spinach soup, Creole crab soup, Italian pasta salad, assorted quiches, lasagna with or without meat, Lebanese lamb curry, meat loaf with parma ham and pesto, Japanese teriyaki with miso, veal parmigiana, several special vegetarian dishes, and a wide array of delicious home made desserts. My last take out lunch here cost about 19.75 NLG per person and was as good as many of the much more expensive above mentioned restaurants!

**EETCAFE PICO (DELLA MUNDO),** *Nieuwmarkt 3. Tel: (20) 627-4919. Cash only - No credit cards accepted.*

Tucked away in a small storefront overlooking the Waag castle in the Nieuwemarkt square, this impressive little Italian inspired restaurant is a real gem. Inside its large cafe and tiny back dining room you can listen to classical music and choose from a menu that includes sandwiches with ham and mozzarella and pesto for 7.50 NLG, old local cheese and Italian salami sandwiches at 6 NLG, warmed goat cheese on French bread for 7.50 NLG, mixed salads at 7.50 NLG, balsamic salad with gorgonzola and mozzarella cheese for 15.50 NLG, Tomato soup with cheese at 7.50 NLG, eggplant parmigana at 19.50 NLG, lasagna with spinach and ham for 21.50 NLG, tiramisu for 7.50 NLG, and plenty of other desserts and flavored coffees.

A nice simple place to unwind and enjoy fresh food at reasonable prices. No dress code to speak of, and a nice staff to help you choose.

### Cheap

**MENSA ACADEMICA (ATRIUM)**, *Oudezijds Voorburgwal 237, Tel: (20) 525-3999. Cash only - No credit cards accepted.*

This student cafeteria of the University of Amsterdam, built in a modern atrium between two historic buildings, often serves as many budget-minded tourists as it does hungry students. Open from noon until 2:00pm and again from 5:00pm until 7:00pm daily, their limited menu changes daily, but commonly offered dishes include lasagna, hamburgers, roasted chicken, grilled fillet of hake, pasta with alfredo sauce, and there is always a vegetarian choice. Prices for a full meal with salad and a side dish cost just 5 NLG for students from this school, or 7.50 NLG for visitors. Skip the coffee; it is the only tasteless thing they serve here!

**NEW YORK PIZZA**, *several locations, including: Damstraat 24, Tel: (20) 422-2123. Cash only - No credit cards accepted.*

These folks really did their research in New York City style pizza by the slice before choosing their name. This establishment (and their others scattered throughout the city at Spui 2, Reguliersbreestraat 17, and Leidsestraat 23) offers really good pizza by the slice starting at 3.75 NLG and by the pie starting at 26.25 NLG, and unlike most other Dutch pizza firms they only use 100% real mozzarella cheese. For a bit more money you can request toppings such as pepperoni, mushroom, ham, pineapple, tuna, broccoli, spinach, tandori chicken, or a vegetarian combo. The crust is light and crispy, and they will be glad to add salads, soft drinks, cappuccino, and great Movenpic ice cream to your order. Ask them about their delivery service directly to your hotel room!

## SEEING THE SIGHTS

The following are a series of short walking tours that will help guide you through the city's downtown districts and their most popular attractions. While I have tried to make these tour segments connect to each other in a logical way, not all visitors to this city will have enough time, or the desire, to do everything I have listed. Also note that the approximate times given for each tour's duration are subject to significant change, depending on how intensively you wish to explore each listed sight.

My suggestion is to decide what you are in the mood to see, and choose the appropriate tour(s) to fill up that specific day. There are also dozens of less important museums, attractions, commercial districts, and monuments that may be found in other sections of this chapter. These are my personal recommendations of the best things to see and do in Amsterdam, but perhaps you too will find a few others of your own. Good luck – I know you'll enjoy your adventure in one of Europe's most enchanting capital cities!

## TOUR 1

• *From the* **Centraal Station** *to the* **Dam.**

• *Approximate duration (by foot) is about 3.5 hours, including museum, monument, and boutique visits.*

### Around the Station

The most logical place to begin your exploration is over by the front of the **Centraal Station** rail passenger terminal. Built by PJH Cuypers and Al van Geldt during the 1880's, this Neo-Renaissance red brick structure rests at the northernmost edge of the city's downtown (**Centrum**) district. Although merchant ships no longer offload their freight at the port side docks that lined the station's back end, Centraal Station is still used by over one hundred thousand rail commuters each day on their way to work, school, or sightseeing trips. The most notable features of the station's highly decorated main facade are the twin towers that contain an original clock and a functioning wind direction locator, and a relief of the peoples of the world paying homage with their products to the maiden, the symbol of Amsterdam's patroness.

Just in front of the station is the strange little **Stationsplein** square that becomes packed with young street performers and backpackers during the warmer months. The square is surrounded by dozens of well-indicated stops for an assortment of city buses and trams that can take you near almost any point in Amsterdam. As you walk through to the other side of the Stationsplein, you will soon see a few small modern buildings that contain a VVV municipal tourist information office, the NZH-GVB public transportation information and ticket center, and a couple of kiosks selling tickets for canal cruises and other excursions.

### TOURIST INFORMATION OFFICES

*Take the time at this point to walk inside both the **VVV** and **NZH-GVB** information offices at the edge of this open plaza. The VVV offers an assortment of both free and inexpensive tourist brochures, sightseeing excursion pamphlets, cultural agendas, bicycle path listings, and detailed city street maps. The NZH-GVB information office can sell tickets and give you fold-out maps off all public transportation routes in and around Amsterdam, as well as sell you more complete schedules for the buses, trams, trains, and night buses that service the city and its suburbs. Some of these documents and services may be hard to find elsewhere, and will be extremely helpful during your stay!*

**Down the Damrak**

From the station front square, carefully cross a bridge above the small Open Haven Front waterway (paying special attention not to get run over by passing trams coming from all directions). Continue straight along the **Damrak**, a wide avenue that now continues straight ahead towards the heart of town. This first block of the Damrak is mainly lined on the right hand side by a series of fast food restaurants, overpriced tourist cafes, currency exchange bureaus, and tacky souvenir shops. The left hand side of this section of the Damrak is bordered by water front piers that are home to several more canal cruise excursion kiosks.

If you stay on the right side of the avenue, the first odd little attraction of note to see is the **Venustempel Sexmuseum** at building #18. This bizarre little museum of sex and eroticism is a good place for adults to get some background into Amsterdam's world famous reputation for liberated sexual practices. Inside you will find several floors full of glass enclosed exhibition cases containing ancient Chinese erotic art, antique erotic etchings, television monitors showing vintage porno films, bondage apparel, hard and soft core photographs of every imaginable sex position, and assorted adult toys. *The museum is open daily from 10:00am until 11:30pm and costs 3.75 NLG per person to enter.*

As you continue further along the Damrak you can now cross over to the left side of the street and walk up another long block or so until reaching the large rectangular **Beurs van Berlage**, the former stock exchange and its square tower, at building #277. Designed by famed Dutch modern architect Hendrik Petrus Berlage and completed in 1903, this structure is now mostly used as a venue for special cultural events, theater performances, and classical music concerts.

The simple brick exterior is not all that impressive, but if you walk to the main entrance on the adjacent Beursplein square you can take a self-guided tour. Inside there are impressive meeting halls embellished with dramatic friezes, decorative brick walls, fine stained glass windows, exposed beam ceilings, ornate tapestries, interesting statuary, beautiful steel and iron fixtures, and bold arch topped columns. The tall tower is also open for those who want a great photo opportunity from a panoramic viewing platform. *The complex is usually open (when a special event is not taking place!) Tuesday through Sunday from 10:00am until 4:00pm and costs 6 NLG per person to enter.*

**Around the Dam Square**

A short walk farther along the Damrak will lead you straight into the lively **Dam** square. This exact spot has been Amsterdam's main central square since the 13th century, when the building of a large dam allowed a major merchant port on the Amstel river to be located here. The river has since been diverted elsewhere through the city, and the ports have also been moved, but the Dam is still surrounded by a number of great sights and monumental structures that all demand your attention. In the center of the Dam square is a 22 meter (72.6 foot) tall obelisk known as the **Nationaal Monument** with two roaring lions at the base. Created by John Raedecker as a monument to Holland's fallen soldiers in World War II, buried nearby are jars containing the soil of all of Holland's regions and East Indian colonies. This rather modern statue has been less than favorably reviewed by most locals since it was first unveiled in 1956, and is now the meeting point for groups of separated tourists and mating pigeons throughout the year.

The most important attraction along the Dam is the wonderfully opulent quadrilateral **Koninklijk Paleis** (Royal Palace), on the right side of the square (now divided in half by a major intersection) as you enter it from the Damrak. This Classical style sandstone building was constructed begun in 1648 from a design by Jacob van Campen to serve as a replacement for the town hall that had previously burnt down on the same site. In order to ensure that the building would never sink or sag due to the sandy consistency of the ground below, well over 13,000 wooden piles were sunk under the foundation.

Later transformed into a royal palace in 1808 for Louis Bonaparte after he was crowned as the King of Holland, the interior was then filled to the brim with opulent period furnishings that can still be seen to this day. Once inside the palace visitors should make sure to visit the giant first floor Burgelzaal (Citizen's Hall) with its powerful fresco, fine chandeliers, magnificent statue of Atlas by Artus Quellien, and maps of the eastern and western hemispheres carved into the massive marble floor. Also worthy of note are the **Vierschaar** (Hall of Justice), and a few other small side courts and halls that have all magnificently adorned with sculptures and antique art. *The palace is usually (but not always) open daily between June and August from 12:30pm until 5:00pm, and from Tuesday through Thursday between September and May from 1:00pm until 4:00pm. The entrance fee is currently 5 NLG per person.*

Just across the street from the palace's north facade on Mozes en Aaronstraat is the 14th century late Gothic **Nieuwe Kerk** (New Church). It was in this house of worship that all Dutch kings and queens have been crowned since 1815. Although destroyed by fires and then renovated several times throughout the centuries, at one time this was the city's most important Protestant church, but has since been converted into a venue for traveling art exhibits and other special events. If you happen to enter during one of the several scheduled temporary exhibitions, make sure to get a glimpse at the church's 17th century carved wooden pulpit, massive brass choir screen, magnificent pipe organ, gilded ceilings, and the highly decorated stone tomb of Admiral Michiel de Ruyter. Since the church is no longer open on a set schedule, inquire at any VVV office in town for entrance details and exhibition schedules.

From the front of the church, you can also take a right turn and walk a block or so away from the Dam square along Mozes en Aaronstraat until running into the Neo-Gothic former **Postkantoor** (Post Office Building). Built in 1890 by C. P. Peters to house the city's main post office, this bold spire-topped building was converted a handful of years ago into the so-called **Magna Plaza** shopping center. Inside the building's lavish interior set amid dozens of arch-topped columns you will find several floors packed with dozens of trendy clothing boutiques, bustling record stores, consumer electronics shops, art galleries, and café-restaurants. The center is open daily throughout the year during normal retail business hours and costs nothing to enter.

---

### AMSTERDAM'S MAJOR MUSEUMS

*Allard Pierson Museum, Oude Turftmarkt 127, Tel: (20) 525-2556*

*Amstelkring Museum, Oudezijds Voorburgwal 40, Tel: (20) 624-6604*

*Amsterdams Historisch Museum, Kalverstraaat 92, Tel: (20) 523-1822*

*Anne Frank Huis, Prinsengracht 263, Tel: (20) 556-7100*

*Bijbels Museum, Herengracht 366, Tel: (20) 624-2436*

*Nederlands Filmmuseum, Vondelpark 3, Tel: (20) 589-1400*

*Van Gogh Museum, Pauus Potterstraat 7, Tel: (20) 570-5200*

*Joods Historisch Museum, Joans D.aniel Maijerplein 2, Tel: (20) 626-9945*

*Museum van Loon, Keizersgracht 672, Tel: (20) 624-5255*

*Open Haven Museum, KNSM Laan 311, Tel: (20) 620-5522*

*Museum Het Rembrandthuis, Joordenbreestraat 4, Tel: (20) 624-9486*

*Rijksmuseum, Stadhouderskade 42, Tel: (20) 673-2121*

*Nederlands Scheepvaartmuseum, Kattenburgerplein 1, Tel: (20) 523-2222*

*Stedelijk Museum, Paulus Potterstraat 13, Tel: (20) 573-2911*

*Theatermuseum, Herengracht 168, Tel: (20) 623-5104*

*Tropenmuseum, Linnaeusstraat 2, Tel: (20) 568-8215*

*Willet Holthuysen Museum, Herengracht 605, Tel: (20) 523-1870*

---

After window shopping at the mall, return to the edge of the Dam and several more sights will soon come into view. On the right side of the square at building #30 is a branch of the London and Paris-based **Madame Tussaud Scenerama** wax museum. If you have not already been to one of these tourist traps, it's almost worth the time to see wax castings, multimedia presentations, and other silly exhibits about famous personalities and events in Amsterdam's history and possible future. *The museum is open daily from 10:00am until at least 5:30pm and costs 17.50 NLG per person to enter.*

The last sight directly on the Dam worth noting is the luxurious **De Bijenkorf** department store at building #1, diagonally across the square from the wax museum. Here you can stock up on everything from the latest French perfumes to moderately priced designer clothing, furniture, and home electronics. This is the largest store of its kind in the city, and is open year round Monday through Saturday during normal retail business hours.

### TOUR 2
• *From the **Dam** square to the **Rembrandtplein**.*
• *Approximate duration (by foot) is about 4 hours, including museum, monument, boutique, and side street visits.*

### Along the Kalverstraat
From the towering monument in the Dam square, walk through the square past the front entrance to the wax museum and turn left down the amusing **Kalverstraat**, Amsterdam's most active retail shopping street. As you walk along this pedestrian-only lane (where cattle markets were held during the 15th century), you will notice hundreds of stores selling consumer goods at fairly reasonable prices.

A few short blocks up on the right hand side, at building #92, you will find an old archway cut through a narrow facade. The arch itself is topped by a copy of relief that dates back to 1581 featuring eight orphans followed by a request for donations, and above that is a coat of arms featuring with three X's topped by a royal crown. This highly decorated entranceway leads into an inner courtyard that cuts into the **Amsterdams Historisch Museum** (Amsterdam Historical Museum). Housed in a series of restored 16th century convent buildings that were later converted into the city's main orphanage, this fine collection of historical art and exhibits is a great place to step back into Amsterdam's past.

After walking through the first courtyard (now bordered on the right by a popular restaurant), continue on past a second larger courtyard and look for the main entrance of the museum. Once inside the museum complex, make sure to ask for an informational brochure in English as you purchase your tickets. From the ticket desk you are lead past a small gift shop and past 21 different rooms on several floors that all depict various stages of the city's development from the 13th through the 20th century. For those interested, I suggest first following the signs leading to the "Filmzolder" chapel ceiling theater on the 3rd floor to view a brief free

film presentation (subtitled in English) entitled *Getting to Know the Amsterdams Historisch Museum*.
Once you have sat through the film, return back down to the first floor and start exploring the exhibitions. From the first floor until the attic, exhibits relate to the city's expansion and population growth (Room 1), Early development and architecture (Room 2), Maritime trade, 14th and 15th century industries, the miracle of 1345 turns the city into a center of pilgrimage (Room 3), 16th century growth, the wave of immigrants, religious and political unrest, and economic crisis (Room 4), Dutch merchants sail the seven seas (Room 5), Amsterdam's great fire of 1652 and the rebuilding of the city (Room 6), International trade increases but the Republic loses its dominance in the 18th century (Room 7), Rapid industrial growth (Room 8), Master Flemish artists (Room 9), Religious suppression and later tolerance (Room 10), The city's many churches (Room 11), Power, money, and political corruption in the 18th century (Room 12), 18th century art (Room 13), Family life in the big city (Room 14), Civic planning (Room 15), The Velvet Revolution and the proclamation of the Republic (Room 16), Temporary exhibitions relating to the 20th century (Rooms 17 & 18), The museum's library of rare books (Room 19), Crafts from the 17th and 18th centuries (Room 20), A collection of Archaeological relics (Room 21).

Upon returning to the ground floor, stop off at the Regent's Chamber where the orphanage's governors once met. This room's 17th century ceiling frescoes, sculptures, furnishings, and portraits are all worth a good look. Another attraction here is the Van Speyk room where this famous Dutch naval hero had once lived when he was an orphan. *The museum is open Monday through Friday from 10:00am until 5:00pm, Saturday and Sunday from 11:00am until 5:00pm, and costs 7.50 NLG per person to enter.*

Once you have departed the history museum, there is one final attraction to visit before leaving the complex. If you head back past the end of the large inner courtyard and turn right, you can enter the **Schuttersgalerij** (Civic Guard Gallery). This atrium-style gallery and passageway is lined on both sides by a stunning series of 16th-17th century portraits of the Civic Guard marksmen who defended the city. *The glass enclosed gallery is open during the same hours as the history museum, and costs nothing to enter.*

**Towards the Begijnhof Square**
After walking through to the other end of the gallery, pass through the exit and immediately turn right, walk a few steps, and then head down the staircase on your left-hand side that leads into the tranquil **Begijnhof** square. Almost entirely hidden from casual visitors, this quaint little neighborhood surrounding a nice park dates back to the 14th century

when it became occupied by the houses of a Roman Catholic sisterhood of widows and spinsters (known as *Begijntjes*) that worked as charity workers. Although no more Begijntjes still exist, the Begijnhof is still populated solely by elderly females, and men are not allowed on the property after its gates are all locked at 10:00pm. Due to the destruction by fire of the original wooden residences that once stood here, most of the brick structures along the square only date back to the 17th century.

The large **Engelse Kerk** church in the heart of the square was built in 1419 as a Roman Catholic house of worship for these women, but was later converted into a Presbyterian church. The building can be visited during posted mass hours to see its medieval tower, the graves of several Begijntes, and a selection of plaques and panels by the famous artist Piet Mondrian.

Other sights in the Begijnhof include the 17th century **Joannes en Ursula Kerk** at buildings #29 and #30 that became a secret chapel for the religious women after Catholic services had been officially banned in Amsterdam. A few doors down at building #34 is the wood facade of the **Het Houten Huis**. Built in 1477 (before the city had forbidden the construction of timber houses), this is Amsterdam's oldest standing residence and is adorned on its side by a series of antique gable stones.

**Towards the Muntplein Square**

After walking past the Begijnhof's famous wooden house, take a few more steps towards the back edge of the square, walk through the arch, and follow a small set of stairs leading out onto a wide street named Spui. This street is surrounded by popular grand cafes and is the sight of a major year round open air used book market on Fridays, and is also the location for a summertime Sunday art fair. Bear to the left on Spui and follow it for a few blocks or so until you can turn right onto Kalverstraat. Follow this street for a couple of more blocks until it ends.

At the end of Kalverstraat you are led directly into a bustling plaza known as the **Muntplein**. Once the location of a 15th century public sheep market, this square has since become dominated by the great **Munttoren** (Mint Tower). Built in the 17th century atop a fire ravaged gateway in the city's medieval walls, this unique monument boasts a wonderful spire topped clock tower designed by Hendrick de Keyser. A half century later, a carillon can still be heard ringing through the city streets. The tower's name comes from the time when occupying French troops moved the municipal mint here for a short time. The ground floor of the adjoining structure now is home to the **Holland Gallery de Munt B.V.**, where an assortment of handicrafts and Delft tiles are sold.

### On to the Rembrantsplein

Carefully cross the main avenue directly in front of the tower and continue straight along the **Reguliersbreestraat**. Packed on both sides by several fast food joints, sex shops, and pinball machine arcades, this street is also home to Amsterdam's most popular cinema. The Art Deco **Tuschinski Theater** has been delighting local audiences since it first opened its doors in 1921. Although the days of live performances are over, the building still packs in the crowds daily for selection of first run blockbuster movies in the main hall and five other small theaters upstairs. Every inch of the lobby and theaters' interior is covered by exotic marble and hardwoods, spectacular carpets, period frescoes, and one of a kind lighting fixtures. General admission tickets for normal screenings are the same price here as they would be at a regular movie theater, but semi-private balcony boxes can be rented for a small surcharge of around 20 NLG a person. On my last visit here I even noticed a rather well dressed young couple enjoying a romantic adventure in one of these special sections as they were being served champagne!

On special occasions silent films are shown here that are accompanied by live music played on the oldest Wurlitzer organ in Holland. Also note that many movies get interrupted by a half hour intermission. during which time a café-bar serves drinks and refreshments. For those not interested in watching a movie, the building's interior can be toured a few mornings each week during the summer for about 5 NLG per person. Check with the front ticket office for exact schedules and details.

---

### TAKE A RELAXING COFFEE BREAK ON REMBRANDTPLEIN

*Facing the Rembrandtplein there are two unusual places to enjoy a refreshing coffee or mixed drink while taking a short break at the end of this tour. The wonderfully relaxed **Café de Kroon** at building #17 has a glass-enclosed top floor square-view terrace adjacent to the main hall that is decorated with plush sitting areas, antique medical instruments, collections of strange stuffed lizards, giant insects, massive chandeliers, and other curiosities. Drink prices here are reasonable, and the clients are a good mix of locals and foreigners.*

*Across the plaza at building #26 is the remarkable **Café Schiller**, where every wall and sitting booth is filled with Art Deco statues and paintings. The prices here are a bit high, and the ambiance is somewhat less inviting, but it is still worth the effort to pop inside for a few minutes.*

---

At the end of this street you will find yourself entering the action-packed **Rembrandtplein**. Back in the 19th century this large square was the home to a public butter market, but is now known primarily as one of

Amsterdam's main nightlife centers. After about 7:00pm there are thousands of tourists and locals who walk through this square on their way to dozens of bars, discos, and cafés that face onto the central park with its 19th century statue of Rembrandt.

## TOUR 3
• *From the* **Rembrandtplein** *square to the* **Leidseplein.**
• *Approximate duration (by foot) is about 2.5 hours, including flower market, boutique, café, and side street visits.*

### Towards the Bloemenmarkt
Walk back down to the beginning of the Rembrandtplein to return towards the Muntplein. For a change of scenery, I suggest departing this square via a somewhat different route than you had taken to get here during the previous tour. This time follow **Reguliersdwarsstraat**, a strange little street that runs past the rear of Tuschinski Theater. Along this short route there are several bars, discos, restaurants, and designer boutiques that tend to attract a flamboyant gay clientele. Also along the way there is a small entrance on the right that leads to **Rik's Bioscope**. This small cinema becomes packed with students almost every night because of its policy of screening major second run films at the unbelievably low ticket price of just 2.50 NLG per person. When you reach the intersection of Vijzelstraat, turn to the right and follow it for a block or so until you are within sight of the Munttoren tower.

Make a sharp left turn and walk along Single, a small lane passing along this side of the canal. A few paces later you will pass directly in front of the floating waterside kiosks that are home to Amsterdam's fragrant **Bloemenmarkt** (Flower Market). This sight was once full of moored boats belonging to suburban gardeners that sailed along the Amstel river to bring their goods to market. These days the old boats have all been replaced with a full block of adjoining anchored barges that sell a variety of flowers, tulip bulbs, orchids, plants, and shrubs. The market is open throughout the year every Monday through Saturday until about 5:30pm or so. The shops that face onto the market are mostly tourist traps, but you can still find a few good cafes and lunch restaurants around here. Be advised that pickpockets are known to operate in this area, so be extra careful.

### On to the Leidseplein
At the end of the flower market, turn left onto the main thoroughfare known as **Leidsestraat** that cuts farther into the city as it becomes yet another principal shopping zone. As you cross over the next three canals, you will find some of the city's better value clothing boutiques, perfume

shops, exchange kiosks, dozens of ethnic restaurants, and a VVV tourist information kiosk. One of the most important department stores in Amsterdam, **Metz & Co.**, is located at this street's intersection with the Keizersgracht. Built in the late 19th century, this dramatic structure was designed by J. van de Looy to contain the offices of the New York Life insurance company but was later converted into a chic six floor temple of fashion and expensive household furnishings. Still frequented by the city's wealthier residents and visitors, the building's top floor has a wonderful café and restaurant with some of the best panoramic views of downtown Amsterdam.

The street then leads into the center of the infamous **Leidseplein**, known throughout the world as a great place to party. The square is surrounded by countless bars, theaters, restaurants, and nightclubs that fill to capacity, especially on weekend nights. After about 10:30pm, thousands of people from around the world walk (or in some cases, crawl) between the drinking establishments and exotic restaurants located on the square and its intersecting side streets. Each venue attracts a totally different crowd that may be either relaxed casual singles under 25, Armani suited yuppies, middle aged divorcees, pot smoking tourists in leather jackets, and every possible variation in between. When the weather is warm enough the square is lined by outdoor tables from the adjacent cafés that attract sidewalk artists and roaming bands of street performers. Due to the high volume of people that end up here, the Leidseplein is a great place to catch one of the city's many buses, trams, and taxis, even quite late into the night.

The Leidseplein is dominated by two large structures that line the right side of the central plaza. The first of these is the Neo-Renaissance **Stadsschouwburg** civic theater at building #26. Designed in the late 19th century by Al van Gendt and Jan Springer, this red brick structure hosts an assortment of live plays, ballets, modern dance recitals, and concerts throughout the year. In the far corner of this structure's facade is the **Uitburo** cultural information center, open during normal retail hours and offering free brochures and schedules for almost every music, dance, and theater performance given that month in the city.

Directly across a small lane from the theater is the tower-topped facade of the **American Hotel**. Built in 1902 from a design by W. Kromhout, this Art Nouveau hotel is best known for its expensive Brasserie Americain restaurant and cafe that looks directly out onto the square. This Art Deco café is decorated with marble floors, huge plants, period oil paintings based on Shakespeare's *A Mid-Summer Night's Dream*, stained glass windows, and vintage Jugendstil lamps. A favorite of the older and more sophisticated set, this is a memorable place to enjoy a meal or drink while watching the crowds roll by.

**The Leidseplein's Interesting Side Streets**

Not all of the action takes place directly on the Leidseplein itself, so the following is a brief circle (well, really a rectangular) tour around a few intersecting side streets that are also worth a quick look. After exiting the American Hotel, return back to the Stadschouwburg theater and cross over onto the other side of the square. Turn to the right so that you pass in front of the **Bulldog Palace**, one of Amsterdam's largest "smoking" coffee shops, and when you reach the Grand Café Heineken Hoek at the corner you will turn left onto the **Kleine-Gartman Plantsoen**. On left side of this street there are several more bars, grand cafés, and a modern multiplex cinema called the **Pathe City Cinema** where you can see several almost current hit movies, many of which are shown in English.

Just across the way is **De Balie** cultural center at building #10. The complex is known for its fine schedule of often obscure independent films and lecture series, and also contains a surprisingly affordable café and casual restaurant that are frequented by intellectuals engaging in lively discussions. At about this point the road splits in two, as it becomes divided by a small park complete with bronze sculptures of overgrown lizards. Keep to the left side of the street and walk about half a block more before turning to the left onto the Leidsekruisstraat. Located just behind the Leidseplein, this narrow lane is inundated with plenty of small nightspots that attract a fair amount of young single locals. Follow this street for a block until bearing left onto the Korte Leidsedwarstraat, where restaurants with foods from every continent can be enjoyed. Walk along this small lane as it cuts back through the edge of Leidsseplein square and continue for one more block before reaching the canal. Don't cross the canal, but instead turn left, walk a half block to the next corner, and turn left again onto the Lijnbaangracht.

A small metal footbridge half way down on the right hand side of this block and just across from the district's new main police station leads to **De Melkweg** (The Milky Way), at building #234. This converted dairy factory is now one of Amsterdam's foremost multiple floor entertainment complex, and boasts two medium-sized live concert halls, a performance art and theater venue, a modern art & photo gallery, a smoking coffee shop, a restaurant and café, and a cinema showing cult films and imported documentaries.

This is a great place for those under 35 or so to spend hours drifting back and forth between several simultaneous entertainment events. *The Milkweg is open most nights from about 8pm until at least 3am. Admission varies between 7.50 NLG and 20 NLG per person depending on exactly what events are scheduled that night, plus an additional 4 NLG for a mandatory temporary membership card to enter the complex.*

**WILD TIMES AT THE MELLWEG!**

*The first time I visited the **Melkweg** was 12 years ago, when I spent the evening here watching a Fellini film, seeing a Ramones concert, viewing a truly unique version of the dance of the Seven Veils (complete with 2 snakes!), and debated international economic policies with a group of lesbian skinhead anarchists. The only problem was that I ordered a piece of delicious chocolate cake at the café that turned out to be loaded with cannabis. I don't remember what happened for the next eight or so hours, but I think I had a great time!*

*Complete schedules for the Milkweg's various rock concerts, jazz bands, live performances, and movie screenings can be found well in advance via their internet web sight, at **http://www.knoware.nl/melkweg/melkweg.htm***

After passing the Milkweg, continue along the same block until it leads back to the Leidseplein. This will give you an idea of what else there is to do during the evening in this part of town.

### TOUR 4
· *From the **Leidseplein** to the **Museumplein** and the **Spiegelkwartier**.*
· *Approximate duration (by foot) is at least 7 hours, including, museum, antique shop, art gallery, designer boutique, café, and side street visits.*

### Across the Canal towards Vondelpark
From the center of the Leidseplein, walk up for a block or so until turning left onto the Kleine-Gartman Plantsoen. Stay on the right side of the street and walk about half a block before turning right on a small lane called the Hirsch Passage. The passage leads directly into a shopping and office complex that surrounds the tranquil **Max Euweplein square**.

If you walk through to the far end of the plaza you will soon come a pretty little canal bordered by a few waterfront cafés with outdoor terraces and the stops for several excursion boats. This plaza is also home to the modern **Holland Casino-Amsterdam** and its Lido dinner theater. Here you can play poker, roulette, black jack, slot machines, and other major games of chance. *The casino is open daily throughout the year from 1:30pm until 2:00am, and costs around 6 NLG per person to enter.*

From the front entrance of the casino complex, there is a small bridge leading directly over to the other side of the canal. Follow this bridge and then cross the street and turn left onto the Stadhouderskade. A block or so down this road on the right side is a gated entranceway that leads into **Vondelpark**, one of Amsterdam's largest green spaces. Named after its statue of famous poet Joost van den Vondel, this massive 100 acre public park first opened in 1865. After several expansion projects, Vondelpark now features jogging paths, tennis courts, a bandstand for free summer concerts, a youth hostel, countless species of plant-life, and a wide variety of both wild and domesticated animals. All of the streets that face the perimeter of the park are full of elegant private mansions. *The park is open daily from sunrise to sunset, and costs nothing to enter.*

### FREE ENTRY TO HOLLAND CASINO!

*I would like to point out a few helpful hints about visiting the Holland Casino. The house rules here make it obligatory for those entering to be above 18 years old, wear proper attire (no ripped jeans or sneakers), and present a valid passport upon arrival. One way to get into the casino for free is to visit any major hotel in town and ask the front desk for a voucher that will let you enter the casino for free, as long as you follow the above rules. These vouchers cost the hotels nothing, and the front desk staff will usually be glad to give you a few just by asking them politely.*

**Into the Heart of the Museumplein**

After a peaceful stroll through the park and its gardens, return to the main gateway on the Stadhouderskade and turn right to follow it down about a half block and bear slightly to the right onto Hobermastraat. At the next corner make a right turn down the exclusive **Pieter Cornelisz (P.C.) Hoofstraat**, an exclusive lane packed with the city's most chic designer boutiques and cafés. This is where the other half shop, and it is typical to find Porsche, Ferrari, and Mercedes convertibles double parked while their owners are squeezing beautifully wrapped gift boxes into their car's tiny trunks.

After walking a few blocks down P.C. Hoofstraat, turn left down Van Baerlestraat, yet another good place to windowshop for expensive gifts and designer clothing. A short walk further down this street will lead you past the front facade of the **Concertgebouw**. Built in 1888 from plans by Al van Gendt, this Neo-Renaissance concert hall is best known for having amazing acoustics and hosting symphonic concerts. At this point turn around to backtrack one long block up Van Baerlestraat and this time turn to the right when you reach Paulus Potterstraat, the heart of the great **Museumplein** park and museum center.

**The Stedelijk Museum**

Directly on your right side is the **Stedelijk Museum** located at building #13, Amsterdam's most important showcase for modern art. This Neo-Renaissance building was built in 1895 from plans drawn up by A.W. Weissman, and has a facade decorated with statues of notable Dutch artists. Inside you will find that the museum completely changes its offerings every 3-4 months. This is due to the fact that the Stedelijk has become known as the city's main venue for temporary exhibitions of modern works (mostly on loan from other famous museums) focusing on a specific era or theme. While most of these special events are well worth the effort to see, it would be impossible for me to explain or predict what exactly will be there at the time you wish to visit.

Even the works shown from the museum's own permanent collection change all the time, but usually consists of a limited selection of drawings and paintings by such artists as **Picasso, Monet, Cezanne, Matisse, Mondrian, Chagall, Appel, Calder, Jones, Warhol**, and others. There are also several other small rooms that may show video presentations or display fine examples of sculpture, photography, and unique furnishings. *The museum is open daily from 11:00am until 5:00pm and costs 11 NLG per person to enter.*

### The Van Gogh Museum

Just next door to the Stedelijk Museum on the same street is the great **Van Gogh Museum** at building #7. Built for the Vincent van Gogh Foundation in the 1970's from plans designed by Gerrit Rietveld, this modern structure houses the world's largest permanent collection of works by **Vincent van Gogh** (1853-1890). Inside you will find three floors filled with over 200 paintings and 500 drawings by this Dutch master artist, as well as 700 of his personal letters, a series of Japanese prints he once owned (and in some cases imitated), and a selection of original works by other famed European artists including **Monet, Toulouse-Lautrec, Pissarro, Gauguin** and **Redon**.

Upon entering the building, I suggest paying a small surcharge to use the museum's excellent multilingual Audio Tour CD-Rom system. This small computer audio system will enable visitors to access historical background and expert commentary about both the artist and many of his works. After walking up one floor you will find countless paintings showcased in sequential order. Among the many highlights of his first important works while still living in Nuenen are the unsigned *Peasant Cemetery* showing the crumbling church of Nuenen, and the *Potato Eaters* depicting a family of poor potato farmers sitting around a table topped while drinking coffee and eating a dish of potatoes they recently had pulled from their farm, and the dark *Studies of Peasant Women* series.

Further into the exhibit you will pass by works from the time he lived with his brother in Paris and began to change his style towards those used by the impressionists he met by using much brighter colors. The most famous of these paintings include *A View of Paris, Le Grande Jatte Bridge*, and *Self Portrait with a Straw Hat*. From here you will be led past the paintings he created while living in Arles, France along with Gauguin for

## THE BRIEF LIFE OF VINCENT VAN GOGH

*Vincent van Gogh* was born on March 30, 1853, in the southern Holland town of Zundert. His father, a Protestant pastor, soon decided that he and his younger brother Theo would be trained for a future career in the arts trade as their uncle had already successfully done. Vincent worked for various art dealers in Holland, England, and France for several years before deciding that he should become a minister. After dropping out of the religious school he was attending, and finding it impossible to secure work as a lay preacher in nearby Belgium, he made up his mind to become a serious painter. Since he had no real income, Vincent started receiving financial support from his brother Theo, now working for a major art dealer in Paris, who continued to support Vincent throughout the artist's life. After practicing his drawing skills he moved back in with his parents in their new home in the village of Nuenen for a couple of years and started painting on a regular basis. It was during this period that van Gogh created a series of dark stiff paintings based local peasant life. He then moved to Antwerp to further practice his art for about another half a year.

In 1886, Vincent moved to Paris to live in the apartment of his brother Theo, during which time he was introduced to impressionist artists such as Gauguin, Bernard, and Toulouse-Lautrec. Their influence made a dramatic impact on Vincent, who soon changed his own style and started to brighten up the imagery on his canvases. By 1888 he had moved into a rented house in the city of Arles in the south of France to seek constant sunshine and brilliant colored scenery to help inspire his art. For a while, Gauguin joined him here during what was to be Vincent's most fruitful period.

At the end of 1888, the artist cut off part of his ear and was hospitalized in Arles for several months. Realizing that his mental condition was fragile, he committed himself for one year to an asylum in the French town of Saint-Remy. He painted several of his most disturbing, expressionistic, and well known works while institutionalized, and later left for the town of Auvers-sur-Oise near Paris to live with his doctor. Even though he was able to relax a little and painted over 75 works, Vincent was constantly depressed. Van Gogh continued to suffer, and ultimately shot himself in the chest. He died July 29, 1890. Throughout his life, Vincent sent many paintings to his younger brother Theo to be sold in the galleries of Paris, but none were ever actually purchased before Theo died some six months later.

a short while. Some of the most notable works shown here from this period are the *Sunflowers* series, *Drawbridge*, the *Yellow House at Arles*, *The Street*, *Zouave* and *Bedroom at Arles*. Now the exhibit focuses its attention on the final years of van Gogh's later, troubled life, mostly spent in hospitals. The pieces of this final era, such as *Crows in the Wheat Fields,* are full of bizarre colors and frenzied violent interpretations that perhaps give some indications as to Vincent van Gogh's mental instability and deepening depression.

On the next floor up is what The Van Gogh Study Collection. This collection is comprised of a rotating selection of his drawings and lithographic works that are too fragile to be on permanent display. There are also a couple of dozen Japanese woodblock prints that Vincent and Theo had once collected, as well as a selection of works by **Gauguin**, **Toulouse-Lautrec**, **Monet**, **Pissarro**, and **Redon** from the Van Gogh Foundation's private collection. The uppermost floor is set aside for temporary exhibitions of other notable artists. *The museum is open daily from 10am until 5pm, and admission costs 12.50 NLG per person (plus an optional 7 NLG per person for the Audio Tour).*

**The Rijksmuseum**

After leaving the Van Gogh museum, turn right back onto Paulus Potterstraat and make the first right turn onto Hobbermastraat, and the next possible left onto Museumstraat. This main avenue leads directly to the palatial Neo-Gothic **Rijksmuseum** and its amazing collections of art from around the globe. This is Holland's largest museum and was built in 1885 by P.J.H. Cuypers. It now contains over 200 rooms filled to the brim with examples from its massive permanent collection of over one million pieces of 15th through 17th century paintings, sculpture, prints, drawings, applied arts, Deftware, fine bone china, glassware, gold and silver jewelry, furniture, model ships, antique weapons, and Asian art.

Since it is quite possible to spend days on end exploring this fantastic museum, I have decided to concentrate on the highlights of the most important sections. A multilingual Audio Tour CD-Rom system can be rented here for a small surcharge, and I suggest you take one to fill in many more details about what you are about to see. After ascending a flight of stairs you will reach the top of the museum's main entrance, containing huge church-like stained glass windows, and a few more modern wall hangings, depicting the arts of painting, sculpture, and architecture. From here, pass the Audio Tour rental table and take a right turn to begin your visit.

In the first several galleries, from room #201 through room #208, you can stroll past dozens of fine **15th and 16th century** religious paintings, including *The Tree of Jessie* by Jan Mostaert (1475-1555) detailing Christ's ancestral family tree going as far back as Jessie; the *Seven Panels of Alkmaar's Kerk* by the Master of Alkmaar depicting the seven acts of charity; *Salome and the Head of John the Baptist* by Jacob Cornelisz van Oostsanen (1470-1533) with Salome delivering a plate with St. John's head on it; *River Landscape* by Joos de Momper (1564-1635) that takes you through a wild boar hunt near a charming river; and *The Fall of Man* by Cornelis van Haarlem (1562-1638) of Adam & Eve about to munch on an apple.

In room #207 through room #236, the focus of attention switches to **17th century** Flemish paintings from the masters. Among the many important works here are four small great landscape paintings named *Winter, Spring, Summer, & Fall* by Adriaen van de Venne (1589-1662) representing people enjoying each of the four seasons; *Winter Landscape* by Hendrick Avercamp (1585-1634) showing ice skaters enjoying a winter's day; *Still Life with Turkey Pie* by Pieter Claesz (1597-1660) depicting a large turkey pie dinner; *The Merry Drinker* by Frans Hals (1581-1666) a world famous rendering of a blasted old cross-eyed man; *Self Portrait* by Rembrandt (1606-1669) with a glimpse into the way this 22 year old saw himself; *Samson & Delilah* by Jan Lievens (1607-1674) a dramatic scene from this Biblical tale; *The Interior of the Mariakerk* by Pieter Saenredam (1597-1665) that really makes you feel that you are inside church.

Other great works of art in this section include *Still Life with Peacocks* by Rembrandt (1606-1669), showing two dead peacocks; *The Feast of St. Nicholas* by Jan Steen (1626-1679) portraying the unique Dutch gift giving celebrations still held on December 5th; *The Windmill at Wijk bij Duurstede* by Jacob van Ruisdael (1629-1682) which is perhaps the most important landscape painting of the 17th century; *The Kitchen Maid* by Johannes Vermeer (1632-1675) that uses shadows and light to almost magically illuminate a maid doing her chores; *The Painter's Studio* by Adriaen van Ostade (1610-1685) detailing a struggling artist working with his various apprentices; *The Love Letter* by Johannes Vermeer (1632-1675) depicting a women receiving a love letter; *The Night Watch* by Rembrandt (1606-1669), a famous portrait showing the civic guards defending Amsterdam; and *The Stamping Officials* by Rembrandt (1606-1669) in which guild officials can be seen inspecting fabric.

For those who have the time, a vast assortment of **additional exhibits** can be found in various parts of the museum. There are examples of other 18th and 19th century paintings from European masters, a special room with thousands of prints and drawings from major artists dating back over the last 350 years, a special restricted art research area known as the Study Collections, an impressive selection of antique Asian arts and crafts, tree-lined sculpture gardens, and a less than exciting Dutch History area with old naval documents, model ships, and relics taken from shipwrecks.

For more spice, I suggest viewing the museum's great collection of sculpture and decorative arts. This section fills several rooms on all three floors of the building and includes Medieval sculptures, rare European furnishings, 17th century Delftware, 18th century Meissen porcelain, hand crafted 16th century Italian jewelry, antique doll houses, Flemish tapestries, engraved stemware, and plenty of other unique 16th through 20th century objects de art.

*The museum is open daily from 10:00am until 5:00pm and costs 12.50 NLG per person (plus an optional 7.50 NLG per person for the "Audio Tour").*

### The Spiegelkwartier

Depart the Rijksmuseum via the tunnel-like passageway that divides the building's ground floor and leads back towards the adjacent canal. Cross the canal and continue straight along Spiegelgracht for a couple of blocks until it reaches the heart of the charming **Spiegelkwartier** art gallery and antique shop district. This little neighborhood is Amsterdam's finest area for viewing high quality antiques, jewelry, paintings, Delftware, and various expensive little objets d'art. A handful of streets such as the Keizersgracht, Kerkstraat, and Prinsengracht all intersect with this small district and also have several fine galleries to visit.

### SPIEGELKWARTIER'S ART & ANTIQUE SHOPS

*These are among my favorite art and antique shops in the Spiegelkwartier district:*

**Jan Roelofs Antiquairs** *(antique furnishings), Spiegelgracht, 5*

**Boekhandel Lankamp & Brinkman** *(art books & collectibles), Spiegelgracht , 19*

**L.J. Mennink Antiekverkopers** *(antiques scientific instruments), Spiegelgracht, 21*

**Mládez** *(painted antique furnishings), Nieuwe Spiegelstraat, 9*

**Peter Korf de Gidts** *(antique glass & Delftware), Nieuwe Spiegelstraat, 28*

**Amsterdam Antiques Gallery** *(several shops), Nieuwe Spiegelstraat, 34*

**Roel de Slegte** *(antique jewelry & clocks), Nieuwe Spiegelstraat, 37 Eduard Kramer*

**Jan Jansen** *(antique ceramics & pocket watches), Nieuwe Spiegelstraat, 64*

**Toth Ikonen** *(Russian religious icons), Nieuwe Spiegelstraat, 68*

**Dick Meijer** *(Egyptian, Roman, an Pre-Columbian art), Keizersgracht, 539*

**T & L Nelis** *(antique medical instruments), Keizersgracht, 541*

**Paul Rutten** *(Eastern and African art), Keizersgracht, 574*

**W.C.P. Zwiep** *(primitive art), Kerkstraat, 93*

**Couzijn Simon** *(antique toys & dolls), Prinsengracht, 578*

**TOUR 5**
• *From the* **Centraal Station** *to the* **Nieuwmarkt** *via the* **Red Light District**.
• *Approximate duration (by foot) is at about 3 hours, including, museum, church, boutique, café, and side street visits.*

**Towards Amsterdam's Oldest Neighborhood**
From the front of the Centraal Station, walk through the Stationsplein and over the bridge crossing over the small Open Haven Front waterway. At the end of the bridge carefully cross over Prins Hendrikkade and turn left. The first major sight you will pass by will be the Neo-Baroque **Sint Nicolaaskerk** at building #73. This Roman Catholic church and its huge towers were built in 1887 from plans by A.C. Bleys and is dedicated to the Saint Nicholas, the patron saint of sailors. You can enter the church to its fine stained glass windows, coffered ceilings, and perhaps even listen to a sermon (conducted in Spanish on Sunday afternoons). *The church is open daily throughout the year during posted mass hours and costs nothing to enter.*
After exiting the church, turn left and backtrack a half a block or so before turning left onto a tiny old lane called Sint Olofspoort. This lane widens out in a few paces and continue straight ahead as it merges with and changes its name to the **Warmoesstraat**, the oldest street in all of Amsterdam. Centuries ago this was a busy lane where sailors would take their leave and often pick up prostitutes before heading back out on the open sea. This intriguing lane leads past an odd assortment of restaurants, cheap hotels, "smoking" coffee shops, gay discos, sex shops, and radical boutiques. Although the street may feel a bit seedy, it is rather safe during the day due to the fact that a police precinct is also located here.
About the only specific attraction here is the **Geels & Co. B.V. Koffie en Theemuseum** (Coffee and Tea Shop & Museum) at building #67 where you can get some insight into the history and roasting methods of Amsterdam's oldest and most famous purveyor of coffee beans and tea leaves, and perhaps even buy a kilo of one of their great blends. *The museum is open on most Tuesdays, Fridays, and Saturdays from 2:00pm until 5:00pm and is free to enter.*
After leaving the museum, turn left on a small lane called the Enge Kerksteeg and walk for a few steps until it merges into the **Oudekerksplein** square. This small plaza is dominated by the Gothic **Oude Kerk** (Old Church), Amsterdam's oldest standing church. This impressive structure was built as a Roman Catholic church way back in 1306 and it soon grew into a basilica adorned with a dazzling array of religious period art and sculpture. During the Alteration of 1578, the Calvinists changed this into a Protestant house of worship, and either destroyed or removed almost all of its irreplaceable works of art in the process. Somehow a series of original decorative pillars, 15th and 16th century wall and ceiling paint-

ings, and 17th century stained glass windows managed to survive the Alteration somewhat intact. Well worth noting are the 18th century wooden pipe organ, Medieval choir stalls, the bell tower and carillon, and the tombs of Rembrandt's wife Saskia and some of the commanders of the 17th century Dutch naval fleet. *The church may be visited November through February on Fridays, Saturdays, and Sundays from 1:00pm until 5:00pm, March through October on Monday through Saturday from 11:00am until 5:00pm and Sunday from 1:00pm until 5:00pm, and costs 5 NLG per person to enter.*

After leaving the church, walk along the Oude Kerksplein until it merges with the canal-front Oudezijds Voorburgwal where you will make a left turn. About two blocks up on the left hand side of this street at building #40 is the **Museum Amstelkring**. Built as three adjoining canal houses in 1663 by local merchant Jan Hartman, these structures seemed to be quite typical from the outside. What makes them different is that their attics conceal a clandestine church that once was used by many of the neighborhood's Catholics who were had to hide their religious practices from public view after the Alteration of 1578. Several of these hidden houses of worship were scattered throughout the city, but this is the only one that has been completely preserved in its original state. Since 1888, this has become the sight of a wonderful museum. Before even getting to the narrow wooden church upstairs, you should first tour all of the exhibits in this beautifully decorated canal house.

After entering via the ground floor (originally a retail shop) you will continue past a marble corridor and head up the stairs to the *Sael* (reception salon). This symmetrical room is one of the finest examples of 17th century Dutch Classicist style interior design and contains a magnificent carved wooden ceiling, marble flooring, period furnishings, and two spiral mantelpiece columns topped by a fine painting. Then you head upstairs to the canal-view *De Bovenkamer* (living room) with its exposed beams and fantastic 300 year old hand painted armoire by Hans Franz. A small stairway then goes past the humble chaplain's room. Another curved staircase now ascends to the **Ons' Lieve Heer op Solder** (Our Lord in the Attic) church. The church dates back to 1663, but most of the interior was replaced in 1735 during renovations. Make sure to get a good look at the church's main altar, with its painting called *The Baptism of Christ* by Jacob de Wit, the revolving rosewood tabernacle, and the two silver angel statues in front of the fake marble columns. From here the tour leads up a staircase near the organ and up onto the first gallery where a series of priests' portraits are on display.

Further along the tour you can view several more rooms filled with a huge collection of religious art and liturgical items including paintings, prints, prayer books, tapestries, silver chalices, and a monstrance. As you descend back down towards the exit, be sure not to miss the 17th and 19th century kitchen rooms and the library. *The museum and its hidden church are open year round from Monday through Saturday from 10:00am until 5:00pm and Sunday from 1:00pm until 5:00pm and costs 5 NLG to enter.*

### Through the Red Light District

After leaving the museum, bear right to follow Oudezijds Voorburgwal and make a left at the next corner onto the Lange Niezel. Follow this small lane as it crosses over two small canals and then make a right turn onto the **Oudezijds Achterburgwal**, the main drag of Amsterdam's infamous **Red Light District**. This is where thousands of (mostly male) visitors spend hours walking up and down the side streets staring at 18 to 25 year old prostitutes who sit in small red curbside windows wearing only their bras and panties (or even less sometimes). These girls come from all over the world to tend to dozens of walk-in clients each day. There are also several peep show and live sex act clubs, like the famed **Casa Rosso** at building #37 of this street.

---

### AMSTERDAM'S INFAMOUS RED LIGHT DISTRICT

*Known all over the world for its hundreds of young prostitutes that sit in front of curbside windows bordered by red light bulbs, the **Red Light District** is one of the top tourist attractions in Amsterdam. This is certainly an interesting zone to visit during daylight hours, but real business takes place here and you should be advised what not to do.*

*While prostitution has essentially been tolerated by the government since the 14th century, many of the girls working in this end of the sex trade are either heroin addicts or virtual slaves from former iron curtain and third world nations, with almost no chance of finding a normal job back where they come from. Do not attempt to photograph these women, and don't even think about creating a scene while in this area. I am not condoning the practice, but if you intend to look for companionship around here, check with the people over at the **Prostitution Information Center** on Enge Kerksteeg #3 and buy a copy of Mariska Majoor's "Pleasure Guide" pamphlet for 3.25 NLG. Her booklet is a good place to find out about avoiding sexually transmitted diseases, where the better brothels are located, and what these services usually cost.*

*Every side street that intersects with the Oudezijds Achterburgwal tends to become a night-time hang out for lots of bizarre people including pickpockets, drunken skinheads, hard-up junkies, car radio thieves, and ethnic gang members selling poor quality hard drugs to tourists. Even though there are some undercover police around, never walk alone through this area (or for that matter any dark street in Amsterdam!) alone after the sunset.*

Continue along the Oudezijds Achterburgwal for a few blocks more until passing the **Hash Marihuana Hemp Museum** on the right side of the street at building #148. There are various exhibits on the history of cannabis, medical uses for marijuana byproducts, high-tech pot growing equipment, smoking gear, and clothing made from hemp. *This small museum is open daily from 11:00am until 10:00pm and costs 5 NLG per person to enter.*

## Along the Nieuwmarkt

Once you have departed the museum, cross over the canal and make a left turn to head back down the opposite side of Oudezijds Achterburgwal. After about half a dozen small intersections, turn right onto Bloedstraat and follow it until it ends at the **Nieuwmarkt**. Once the sight of public executions, this huge square is surrounded by several 17th century homes with unusual street side retail establishments. The central plaza fills up during a series of spectacular outdoor events that take place here including the New Year's Eve fireworks & bonfires, a year round organic produce and cheese market on Saturday, as well as a Sunday antiques market held during the summer only.

In the heart of the square is the castle-like **Waag** (Weigh House) that was built in the 15th century as a fortified gate house through the city's encircling defensive walls. The structure was first converted into a weigh house and tax inspection station before being renovated in 1619 to house the several trade guilds for those working in the arts and sciences. One such guild of surgeons used the Waag as a classroom to perform autopsies on freshly executed prisoners so that students could learn about human anatomy. Artists were also known to attend these sessions in order to better depict the human body in their work, including Rembrandt who came here in 1656 to paint his two *Anatomy Lesson* canvases. *The Waag is no longer open to the public.*

There are several interesting shops, taverns, and restaurants to check out along the sides of the Nieuwmarkt. A good place to begin is over at the **Brouwhuis Maximillaan** at building #8. This popular pub and restaurant was built on the site of a former monastery's brewery and now functions as a great micro-brewery. Visitors can stroll around the main floor and gulp down a few of their blonde, dark, or wheat beers while looking at the polished copper fermentation tanks. While guided tours are conducted for groups only, the helpful staff will usually explain a little about the beer making process to normal patrons for free.

Almost next door is the quaint **Jacob Hooy & Co.** pharmacy at building #10. This functioning apothecary dates back to 1743 and still has an original set of spice jars, antique measuring devises, and hand painted cabinet that once stored medicinal herbs. Over at building #34 is the **Café**

**'t Loosje**, a small traditional neighborhood Brown Café with an interior featuring antique hand-painted tile murals and plenty of amusing locals.

## TOUR 6

• *From the* **Nieuwmarkt** *to the* **Muntplein** *via* **Waterlooplein** *and the University.*

• *Approximate duration (by foot) is at about 5 hours, including, museum, church, boutique, café, flea market, book market, city hall, and side street visits.*

### Near the Nieuwmarkt

From the far edge of Nieumarkt sqaure, walk down the main canal front street called **Kloveniersburgwal**. On the left side of the street you can take a peek at the **Trippenhuis** at building #29. Built in 1662 from plans by Justus Vingboons for armament merchants L. and H. Trip, this huge mansion is actually two adjoining structures that were once separated from each other on the inside. Among the unusual features of its Classical facade are the mortar shaped chimneys and 8 dramatic columns. In 1817, these houses were converted into the State Museum of Painting, but has been closed to the public since 1885 when its collections were moved into the Rijksmuseum.

Continue along the same side of the canal for a couple of blocks until you are able to turn left down Zaandstraat. A block or so up the street intersects with the Zuiderkerkhof as it passes the Renaissance **Zuiderkerk** (South Church), Amsterdam's first Protestant church. Built in 1611 from plans by Hendrick de Keyser, the most impressive feature of this building is its magnificent spire that contains a clock and a carillon. The church is now as an office building for municipal offices, but sometimes can be toured in the summertime. *Check with the front office staff or any VVV office for the current admission price and hours.*

Walk along the church's adjacent courtyard until passing under the old archway, crossing to the opposite side of the street, and turning right onto the Sint Antonies Breestraat. At the next corner you will find a small square known as the **Sint Antoniessluis plaza**, with benches overlooking the point where two canals diverting the Amstel river have been separated by one of 16 remaining locks. The 17th century black wooden house that can be found tilting above the canal is a former **Slugswacht** (lock keepers house). This charming old canal house has been converted into a rather laid-back bar called **Le Petit Café de Slugswacht** where you can get a great Belgian beer or a strong coffee while staring out from the windows on the top floor to get a great view over the nearby sights.

One of the most noticeable monuments that can be seen from the benches or café at the canal-side Sint Antoniessluis plaza is the **Montelbaans Toren** tower. Located a few blocks behind the lock keepers house, the base of this structure is all that remains from a medieval gate-house through the city walls. In 1606, it was converted into an octagonal clock tower from plans drawn up by Hendrick de Keyser. These days the tower is home to the offices of the city's water department, and cannot be visited by the general public, so it is best to enjoy the view from here!

### Rembrandt's Home & Studio

From the café, cross the street and turn left as it changes it name to the Jodenbreesraat. A few steps from the corner you will find the **Het Rembrandthuis Museum** at building #4. This stately three story canal house was bought by the famous artist Rembrandt and his rich wife Saskia in 1639, for the then hefty sum of 13,000 NLG. It was here for the next 19 years he would live and work on some of his most famous works.

The ground floor was where the Rembrandt family lived and received guests. Now the works that are displayed on this level consist of a large portion of the 200-plus Rembrandt etchings that the museum owns, an etching press, as well as an assortment of 17th century furnishings that came from other houses of the same age. None of the paintings found in the museum were painted by Rembrandt, but are instead examples of works by his contemporaries, teachers, and even a few of his better students. The next floor up was a small mezzanine which you can't enter, but another small set of stairs continues to what was once the location of the artist's studio. Here he worked, gave lessons, and spent most of the daylight hours in the process of creating his art. His studio had a set of large split picture windows with inspiring views out over the St. Antoniessluis that not only let in plenty of sunlight, but also ventilated the whole floor. Even more of Rembrandt's fine biblical, nude, self-portrait, landscape, and portrait etchings can be found here, all tagged with informative bilingual descriptions.

There is also a cabinet room adjoining the studio where paints and brushes were stored. Make a point to stop over by the museum's tiny gift corner where they sell reasonably priced high quality reproductions of exhibited Rembrandt etchings printed on hand-made parchment; these are an excellent gift idea. *The museum is open year round from Monday through Saturday from 10:00am until 5:00pm, Sunday from 1:00pm until 5:00pm, and costs 7.50 NLG per person to enter.*

### The City Hall & Opera House

From the museum, turn right to continue along the Jodenbreestraat and after a half a block you will make a right turn on the café-lined Houtkoperstwarsstraat until the next corner. At this point you will find yourself in the center of the **Waterlooplein square**. This is the location of a great daily antique and second hand clothing flea market that spurs out

## THE LIFE AND TIMES OF REMBRANDT

*Rembrandt Harmensz van Rijn was born on July 15, 1606, in the nearby Dutch town of Leiden. At age 7, his father (a wealthy miller) sent young Rembrandt to the town's Latin school before becoming a full time student at Leiden University. While at school, Rembrandt became the pupil of Jacob van Swanenburg, a painter who was well known for his renderings of Hell. A few years later this now talented young artist moved to Amsterdam to attend roughly six months of lessons under the supervision of historical artist Pieter Lastman, who was known for paintings inspired by biblical stories, myths, and history. In 1624, Rembrandt returned to Leiden to open his own studio and began to develop his own style of historical painting, creating dramatic scenes full of tension provoked by his careful use of light. He also experimented with drawings and etchings that focused primarily on studies of vagrants, nudes, and self portraits. During his seven years of work in Leiden, his reputation as an independent master artist began to emerge, with such works as Self Portrait and Tobias & Anna With a Kid, (both now in the Rijksmuseum), as well as Beggar with a Wooden Leg (exhibited in the Het Rembranthuis Museum).*

*After moving back to Amsterdam in 1631 to further his career, he began to acquire several wealthy patrons. A few years later he married Saskia van Uylenburgh, the niece of an art dealer who owned a house where Rembrandt had lived for a while. In 1639, the couple moved into the house that now contains the Het Rembrandhuis Museum and converted its upper floor into a studio where the artist could better paint, etch, draw, and even give lessons on the side. While they had four children, only their son Titus, born in 1641, survived into adulthood. In 1642, Saskia died soon after Rembrandt began his most famous work The Night Watch (found in the Rijksmuseum). Seven years later the artist fell in love with his housekeeper, Hendrickje Stoffels, and they had a daughter, Corneilia.*

*Among his many fine paintings from this period in his life is the amazing Portrait of Jan Six (displayed at the Six Collection). During the next several years, Rembrandt's financial situation grew increasingly worse, and he ad to declare bankruptcy in 1666. After selling his home and most of his paintings, Rembrandt moved into another apartment with his family on the Rozengracht. To regain some of their lost fortune, the artist painted new works that were then sold by his wife and son who had begun working as art dealers. In 1663, his lover Hendrickje died, followed by son Titus in 1668. On October 4, 1669, Rembrandt himself died and was buried in Amsterdam's Westerkerk.*

for a couple of blocks in several directions, especially on Saturdays when it attracts twice as many vendors.

The large ultra-modern structure on the opposite side of the square is Amsterdam's **Stadhuis** (City Hall) complex. Built in 1988 from plans by Wilhelm Holzbauer, this is the site of hundreds of little offices staffed by municipal employees, and contains a few interesting attractions and venues. Enter the city hall via the nearby automatic sliding glass door entrance and walk straight along the inner atrium style passage. Near a cross-section mural of the nation from east to west you will find a set of three glass tubes, marked as the **Normaal Amsterdams Peil** (Amsterdam Ordnance Datum). This device marks high and low water tides, the zero water level standard for Europe, and demonstrates the levels attained during the 1953 floods in northern Holland.

At this point, you will then bear left to go deeper into the complex until you pass next to the **Muziektheater** (Opera House). This 1,650 seat venue is used to host many if the city's best ballet and classical music performances. *The Stadhuis complex is open weekdays from 8:00am until at least 11:00pm, and weekends from 10:00am until at least 11:00pm, and costs nothing to enter (there is a separate admission charge for Muzietheater events).*

**Around the Waterlooplein**

Now retrace your steps back out of the building and onto the Waterlooplein square and turn right. At the next corner on the left hand side is the **Mozes en Aaronkerk** (Moses and Aaron Church), at building #205. Built in 1841 from plans by T Sluys, the church's facade features a gable stone of Moses and Aaron. The building is now off limits to the general public, unless a special event has been scheduled. From the front of the church, continue a few paces until reaching the corner and carefully cross through the M.R. Visserplein plaza and its major traffic circle.

On the other side of the plaza and slighly to the left is the Classical **Portuguese Synagoge** (Synagogue) at building #3. This gigantic house of worship was built by Elias Bouman in 1675 for the Sephardic community living in this district, the former Jewish quarter of Amsterdam. Having lived in Portugal until the horrors of the Spanish Inquisition began to take hold in their neighborhoods, many Jews moved here and were allowed to both practice their religion openly and become rather prosperous merchants. You can walk inside the synagogue to view its beautiful interior that boasts a fine vaulted ceiling, huge columns, antique menorahs (religious candle sticks), and copper chandeliers. *The synagogue is open year round from Sunday through Friday from 10:00am until 3:00pm and is free to enter.*

After exiting the synagogue, turn left to follow this edge of the plaza around for a block or so before reaching the Nieuwe Amstelstraat and its adjacent Jonas Daniel Meijerplein on your left. This square is home to the **Joods Historisch Museum** (Jewish Historical Museum) at building #2. Thoroughly restored a decade ago, the museum is actually a complex of four adjoining 17th and 18th century synagogues that now showcase exhibitions on the history of the Jews in Holland.

Walk around the original **Grote Synagoge** (Great Synagogue) of 1671, with its Hebraic prayer scrolls and marble galleries. In the **Nieuwe Synagoge** (New Synagogue) of 1752 there is a wonderful 18th century wooden ark topped by the Ten Commandments in Hebrew, and a collection of religious silver and art. *The museum is open daily year round from 11:00am until 5:00pm and costs 7 NLG per person to enter.*

### Towards the University

After exiting the museum, continue to head down Nieuwe Amstelstraat. About a block or so later this street ends, and you will turn right onto Amstel to follow along the waterfront side of the Stadhuis and Muziektheater complex. After rounding the corner, the street name changes to Zwanenburgwal and then you will find a small bridge that crosses over to the other side of the canal. Walk across the bridge and continue straight ahead on onto **Stallstraat**.

This small lane was formerly where samples of fabrics were inspected by quality control officials working for the cloth guild in the 17th and 18th centuries. This activity has been wonderfully depicted in Rembrandt's famous painting of *The Stamping Officials* in the Rijksmuseum. Nowadays this delightful pedestrian-only lane is lined with boutiques selling music books, artist supplies, hand crafted furnishings, and exotic silver jewelry. Here you will also find a few great little ethnic restaurants and cafés, including the incomparable **Puccini Café** at building #21, serving some of the best home-made pies and cakes found anywhere in Holland!

Continue along the same lane, and after crossing two more canals, turn right onto the far side of Kloveniersburgwal. About half a block up on the left side of this street is an 18th century gateway known as the **Oudemanhuispoort** (Old Mans' House Gateway). Walk through this doorway and past several used book vendors into a lively inner courtyard garden, surrounded by old lecture halls and classroom buildings belonging to the downtown campus of the **Universiteit van Amsterdam** (The University of Amsterdam). Cut all the way through the university's courtyard garden, then turn right onto the canal-front Oudezijds Achterburgwal. At the next corner, make a right turn onto Grimburgwal as it crosses the canal. On the right side of this corner, there is a lovely 17th century building known locally as the **Huis op de Drie Grachten** (House on the Three Canals) that has windows overlooking all three canals that intersect here.

## The Archaeology Museum

Continue along Grimburgwal for a few short blocks as it passes by additional university buildings, art galleries, jewelers, and book shops. At about the third corner, turn left onto the bridge that crosses over the canal and leads into the **Oude Turftmarkt**. A few steps after the bridge, you will find the **Allard Pierson Museum** at building #127. This is the archaeological museum run by the University of Amsterdam, with a fine collection of important relics from around the world. You can see mummies, musical instruments, wine jars, vases, statuettes, weapons, funerary vases, oil flasks, glass ware, and carvings that date back through the early Egyptian, Greek, Cypriot, Roman, and Coptic civilizations. They even have a computer that translates your name into hieroglyphics. *The museum is open year round Tuesday through Friday from 10:00am until 5:00pm, Weekends from 1:00pm until 5:00pm, and costs 5 NLG per person to enter.*

## Heading for the Muntplein

From the museum, turn left and keep walking down the Oude Turfmarkt until making a right turn onto Nieuwe Dolenstraat. Now cross the nearby bridge over Amstel river, and soon you will be directly in front of the **Muntplein** and its tower.

## TOUR 7

• *From the* **Muntplein** *to the* **Dam** *square via a zig-zag main canal route.*
• *Approximate duration (by foot) is at about 4.5 hours, including, museum, private art collection, canal house, café, and drawbridge visits.*

## Along the Amstel River

Depart the Muntplein and turn right on Amstel to follow it alongside the riverbank. After several blocks the street curves sharply to the right and passes by the first of three bridges, known as the **Blauwbrug** (Blue Bridge). This beautiful iron and stone bridge was built in 1883 to replace a former 17th century blue painted wooden span that once crossed the river at this point. This newer and more structurally solid version is adorned by unusual carvings of maritime themes and a set of decorative old lighting fixtures.

After passing the stone bridge, continue along the right side of Amstel and in about a block and a half or so you will pass in front of the **Six Collection** at building #218. This private house belongs to Baron Six, a direct descendant of former mayor Jan Six who filled his 17th century canal house will priceless period paintings and decorative art. Among the most important paintings in this private collection are works by **Thomas de Keyser** (1596-1667), **Frans Hals** (1580-1666), **Albert Cuyp** (1620-1691), and two famous portraits of Six family members by their friend

**Rembrandt** (1606-1669). There are also various antique furnishings, silver, and porcelain that are well worth seeing.

Before getting all excited about visiting this mansion, I must let you know that it is strictly off-limits to the general public, unless you have made advance arrangements with the Rijksmuseum's information offices and you have presented your passport. *The collection can be viewed during various weekday mornings, only with advance permission from the Rijksmueum, and costs nothing.*

After exiting the art collection, continue heading down Amstel for another couple of blocks until reaching the second of the bridges that span this section of the river. The narrow wood and iron **Magere Brug** (Skinny Bridge) is Amsterdam's most famous and photographed drawbridge. Built in the late 1960's on the site of a former 17th century bridge, the Magere Brug still opens and closes for the continuous barge and houseboat traffic traveling along the Amstel river until just after sunset. At night it is spectacularly illuminated and can be seen from several blocks away. One block past the Skinny Bridge, turn left down the quiet Prinsengracht.

## ALONG THE THREE MAIN CANALS

*The first real development of this area began in 1613, after civil planner Hendrick Staets was hired to greatly expand the area of downtown Amsterdam. He achieved this objective by digging three new curved canals, lined on either side by tranquil residential streets, to surround what were then the boundaries of the city center. The first of these new canals to be completed was the* **Herengracht** *(Gentlemen's Canal), where the richest and most influential merchants built elegant double canal houses and decorated them with ornate gables and sculptured moldings. Soon after, two more canals were excavated and called the* **Keizersracht** *(Emperor's Canal) and the* **Prinsengracht** *(Prince's Canal). Although not quite as prestigious, they too became lined with other beautiful homes. When all of the construction was completed, the whole area featured hundreds of fine gabled houses with decorative cornices and wall plaques.*

*Today, most of the original canal houses are worth millions of dollars and have been bought up as investment properties or exclusive office buildings, but some families do still live here. There are also a limited number of moored antique wooden houseboats that have been granted permits to moor themselves along the waterways. The best thing to do while visiting this area is to pay attention to the facades of each building you pass, and keep an eye out for unique decorative and structural features.*

**Along the Prinsengracht**

As you walk along the tranquil canal front **Prinsengracht** (Prince's Canal), all of the structures are rather beautiful. The first real attraction here is the **Amstelveld** park on the far right hand corner of this street's second block. The park itself is usually filled with parents enjoying some free time with their young children. On the edge of the park is the **Amstelkerk** (Amstel Church). Built in 1668 from plans by Daniel Stalpaert, this wooden church was later renovated in the Neo-Gothic style by the mid-19th century, and again converted to house private offices as well as the delightful little **Kort Café**.

Several blocks further along the same side of the canal is the Renaissance **Westerkerk** (Western Church) at building #281. Built in 1631 by plans from Hendrick de Keyser, this beautiful Protestant church has a massive spire (the tallest in the city) that is adorned by a clock, a carillon, and a golden crown symbolizing Emperor Maximilian of Austria. Those with strong legs should try and make the steep walk to the tower's viewing platform to have a great panoramic photo opportunity. Inside there is little of note besides a fine 17th century organ with panels painted by Gerard de Lairesse (1641-1721). This is also where you'll find the tombs of Rembrandt and his son Titus. *The church and its tower are open from April through September on Monday to Saturday from 10:00am until 4:00pm, and the spire costs 4 NLG per person to visit.*

 A few doors further down the next block is **Anne Frankhuis** (Anne Frank House) at building #263. This museum is located in the 17th century canal house where two Jewish families who were in the spice business (The Franks and the Van Daans) hid from the occupying Nazis from July 1942 until August 1944. For a little over two years, the families were confined to a set of secret rooms hidden by a revolving bookcase, but were later betrayed by a Dutch Nazi sympathizer, arrested by the Gestapo, and sent off to concentration camps. During much of her time in hiding, the teenage Anne Frank kept an inspiring diary of her experiences and inner thoughts, which was published by her father in 1947 – the only member of the two families that survived the death camps. *The Diary of Anne Frank* has since sold more than 12,500,000 copies around the world, and the house continues to attract an average of over 1,500 visitors a day.

Upon entering the house you will be shown a short video presentation, and then can walk through the secret bookcase doorway to see the simple upstairs rooms where Anne and her family once lived. There are also several exhibits detailing the atrocities of life under the Nazis, and more recent racist and anti-Semitic events in Europe. The house gets packed within a half hour of its opening, so get here early! *The museum is open year round on Monday through Saturday from 9:00am until 5:00pm, Sunday from 10:00am until 5:00pm, and costs 7 NLG per person to enter.*

A few blocks further up the opposite side of the street is the **Noorderkerk** (Northern Church) built in 1623 by plans from Hendrick de Keyser. Designed in the shape of a Greek cross, the church is now closed to the public so that a major renovation can be completed. Surrounding the church is the tree-lined **Noordenmarkt** (The Northern Market). This normally quiet square becomes packed during the Monday morning flea market and Saturday live bird, handicraft, and organic produce market. From here, walk a couple of blocks down until the street ends at Brouwersgracht, where you will turn right, walk to the next corner, and bear right along the Keizersgracht.

**Along the Keizersgracht**

After turning onto the left hand side of the **Keizersgracht** (the Emperor's Canal), walk straight for a couple of blocks. The first specific sight you will pass is the **Huis met de Hoofden** (House of Heads) at building #123. This lovely early 17th century brick canal house has an impressive facade decorated with the sculpted heads of six Roman gods. While the building may not be open to the general public, it is still well worth taking a close look at.

Another handful of blocks along the opposite side of the street is the **Felix Meritis Society** at building #324. Built in 1778 by plans from Jacob Husley, the four bold columns rising up from the main entrance portal make this one of the city's most distinctive Neo-Classical structures. The Felix Meritis Society, a group of rich merchants whose goal was to advance the arts and sciences, originally had the interior fitted with a concert hall, reading rooms, and scientific research laboratories. After many years, the society once again occupies this address and now has made it into one of the best venues to view special theatrical events that are scheduled throughout the year.

The last real attraction along this street, just a couple of blocks further up, is the **Museum van Loon** at building #672. Built in 1672 from plans by Adriaan Dortsman, this charming mansion was first home to local artist Ferdinand Bol before eventually ending up in the hands of the ultra-rich Van Loon family. The Van Loons filled almost every room with their own collection of 16th through 18th century family portraits, antique furnishings, tapestries, frescoes by Jacob de Wit (1695-1754), and sculptures. Visitors can wander around the house to see the art collection and various delightfully furnished rooms before stopping off at the adjacent rose garden. *The museum is open Mondays from 10:00am until 5:00pm and Sunday from 1:00pm until 5:00pm, and costs 5 NLG per person to enter.*

From the museum, continue along the same street until it ends at Amstel. Here you will turn left, walk up until the next corner, and again turn left onto the far side of the Herengracht.

**Along the Herengracht**

Since the **Herengracht** (Gentleman's Canal) was the first of the three new canals completed, this was where the largest and most opulent of the new 17th century canal houses were built. About half a block up along the right hand side is the **Museum Willet-Holthuysen** at building #605. This spectacular 17th century canal house once belonged to Abraham Willet, a wealthy art collector who amassed a huge assortment of fine oil paintings, silver decorative pieces, antique oriental vases, and opulent furnishings. While in the mansion you can stroll among 10 of the most beautifully decorated rooms you could ever imagine, each filled from top to bottom with this once private collection. Make sure to get a glimpse of the museum's garden before you leave. *The museum is open daily throughout the year from 11:00am until 5:00pm and costs 5 NLG per person to enter.*

From the museum, continue along the same side of the street for a few blocks until reaching the intersection of the Vizelstraat. For the next two blocks along both sides of the Herengracht there are a series of wonderfully designed and decorated canal houses that make up the area known as the **Bocht (Golden Bend)**. These have been among the most prestigious addresses in town since it became the new home to Amsterdam's richest and most powerful residents after this canal was completed. Almost all the structures along this stretch of the Herengracht have been bought up by banks and multinational corporations.

A short walk along this little sector will take visitors past some of the best examples of 17th through 19th century Classical canal house architecture. Most of the buildings cannot be visited by the general public, but their exteriors still display the fantastic statues, allegorical scenes, and sandstone facades that are unique to this small wealthy neighborhood. Among the landmarks most worthy of extra attention here is building #475 that was built vy Daniel Marot and Jacob Husley in 1730, and the **Kattenkabinet** (Gallery of Cats) at building #497, where during specially marked exhibits you can walk inside to view its gallery of cat paintings and statues. Another couple of blocks up (although not technically still past of the Golden Bend), you should also get a good look at the awesome facades of buildings #380 through #388.

Further along the Herengracht, you will soon come to the **Bijbels Museum** (Bibles Museum) at building #366. These 17th century canal houses were built from plans by Philip Vingboons in 1662 and feature massive gables and decorative stone carvings. Two of these houses have been converted into a museum that now contains rare bibles, scale models of biblical sights, archaeological findings from the Middle East, and several rooms filled with various thematic exhibits. *The museum is open year round from Monday through Saturday from 10:00am until 5:00pm, Sundays from 1:00pm until 5:00pm, and costs 3 NLG per person to enter.*

## AMSTERDAM'S CANAL HOUSES

*Most of the 16th through 18th century canal houses in this city share some common structural and decorative features. Since taxes on buildings in Amsterdam were calculated on the width of each structure's facade, many of these structures were built as narrowly as possible. This created a series of typical floor plans that were thin but rather long.*

*The gables on top of canal houses usually adorn an attic from which a long wooden hoisting beam can be seen protruding. This beam was necessary to winch furnishings and other merchandise up from the street and into the top floors. By now you may also have noticed that many of these building's facades seem to be leaning towards the pavement. This is not a matter of foundation slippage, but rather a method to accomplish two important tasks. First, this tilting helped to assure that rain water would run off the roofs and drip onto the street instead of coming into contact with the porous bricks or sandstone of the front wall. It also decreased the chance of bulky materials banging into the fragile facade and its windows as they were being lifted up towards the attics.*

*Among the less functional features commonly found in these structures are the decorative moldings and statuary that adorned the gables or cornices of the roofs. The richer the owners, the more opulent the decorations. There are even many fine examples of hand-carved wall plaques that were used to point out the name or occupation of those living inside a specific house, because address numbers simply did not exist back then. Other elements that may be seen on some of these structures include old wooden shutters, exposed steel structural beam anchors, and spies (little angled mirrors that would allow upper floor tenants to see who was at the front door before letting them in).*

From the museum, continue walking down the street until reaching the **Theatermuseum** (Museum of Theater) at building #168. This museum of the Netherlands Theater Institute is filled with costumes, props, scripts, stage plans, posters, books, and miniature set designs relating to live plays. The collection is exhibited in two adjacent houses that are in and of themselves rather spectacular.

One of them was built from plans by Philip Vingboons in 1638 and features frescoes by Jacob de Wit (1695-1754), scrolled stucco moldings, fine marble flooring, and a grand staircase. The adjoining house where the museum's library is kept was built from plans by Hendrick de Keyser in 1617 and has a brick facade with an unusually sculpted gable. *The museum is open year round from Tuesday through Friday from 11:00am until 5:00pm, Saturday from 1:00pm until 5:00pm, and costs 5 NLG per person to enter.*

**Back to the Dam Square**

After exiting the museum, continue along the Herengracht and turn right at the next corner onto Leliegracht. Cross over the canal and walk straight ahead for several blocks (as the street name changes first to the Oude Leliestraat and then to Molsteeg). At the end of the road, turn right onto Nieuwezijds Voorburgwal and, at the next corner, turn left onto Mozes en Aaronstraat that will lead you directly into the Dam square to end this tour.

**TOUR 8**
• From the **Heineken Brouwerij** *brewery to the* **Albert Cuypmarkt** *street market.*
• *Approximate duration (by foot) is at about 2.5 hours, including brewery tour and outdoor market visits.*

One of Amsterdam's most popular and entertaining attractions is a visit and tour through the **Heineken Beer** brewery off of the Wetering Plantsoen square on Stadhouderskade #78. After arriving to pick up your tickets before they sell out by 10:00am or so, visitors will be led through this massive brick building where this leading brand of Dutch beer was produced until 1988. Heineken is no longer made in Amsterdam, but this former brewery is now a museum hosting tours for those interested in seeing how beer is made.

Inside you will find exhibits on the history of beer, equipment used in the brewing and bottling process, and examples of Dray horses and the wooden beer wagons that they once hauled through the streets of town. When the tour is over, visitors over 18 years old are allowed to drink themselves silly with plenty of free Heineken beer. *The brewery is open Monday through Friday year round with guided tours at 9:30am, 11:00am, and additional tours in the high season at 1:00pm and 2:30pm, the fee is 2 NLG per person.*

Once you have had enough brew, exit the brewery and turn left onto Stadhouderskade and at the first corner turn left again to head down Ferdinand Bolstraat. This street leads into the southern section of the city, and after several blocks, turn left onto the Albert Cuypstraat. This street is the home to the amusing **Albert Cuypmarkt**, Amsterdam's largest outdoor market. Here you can find hundreds of kiosks offering fresh cheese, cold cuts, meats, fish, bread, desserts, fruits, vegetables, affordable jewelry, cheap clothing, leather jackets, Tee shirts, shoes, sun glasses, and cassettes. This is a great place to spend a few hours shopping for bargains while people-watching, and is well worth the effort to visit. *The outdoor market is open year round on Monday through Saturday from 10:00am until 4:15pm and costs nothing to visit.*

## GUIDED SIGHTSEEING TOURS
### Bicycle Tours

While traffic sometimes comes to a screeching halt in the downtown area, bicycles are a great way to see the sights. There are a few companies that offer excellent three hour or so bike tours through the more interesting areas of the city. Their English speaking guides will discuss the history of the sights that you'll pass, including the Anne Frank House, Rijksmuseum, Vondelpark, Magere brug, Het Rembrandthuis, the Red Light district, and the university area, to name a few.

Some of these rides depart daily at 9:30am and 1:00pm, while others leave only on Saturday afternoons at around 5:00pm, and cost about 32 NLG a person including the bike rental. Just keep in mind that you will usually not enter any of the attractions, and that these often are canceled due to bad weather and low demand.

The following establishments run this type of excursion.

• **Yellow Bike Tours**, *Nieuwezijds Kolk 29, Tel: (20) 620-6940*
• **Amsterdam Travel & Tours**, *Dam square, Tel: (20) 627-6236*
• **Cycle Tours Holland**, *Keizersgracht 181, Tel: (20) 627-4098*

### Boat Tours

A wide variety of local companies offer 75 minute guided tours of the city via **motorized canal boats**. While these excursions (narrated by either a multilingual guide or a tape recording) do not stop to let you get on and off during the ride, this is a fun way to get a good glimpse of Amsterdam on your first day. The boats themselves have either glass-enclosed or open air seating areas and can accommodate about 50 people comfortably, even during the winter when they are heated.

The route these boats take through the canals usually pass by the Munttoren, Zuiderkerk, Blaubrug, St. Nicolaaskerk, Oude kerk, Artis Zoo, Anne Frank huis, Magere Brug, Rembrandthuis, Dam Sqaure, Rijksmueum, and Centraal Station. Departures are scheduled just about every half hour between 10:00am and at least 5:30pm daily throughout the year.

Most of these companies have their landings either in front of Centraal Station, at the piers along side the Damrak, or near the Rijksmuseum. The current prices average about 14 NLG per adult and 8 NLG per child. These same organizations also offer a series of longer boat rides on specific high season dates including 90 minute lunch cruises, two hour candle light wine and cheese cruises, and two and a half hour dinner cruises that cost between 40 NLG and 145 NLG a head.

The following is a list of companies that you can call or visit for tickets and exact schedules for these boat rides, or you may stop in at any VVV tourist information offices for additional information.

• **Holland International**, *Prins Hendrikkade 33a, Tel: (20) 622-7788*
• **Meyer's Rondavaarten**, *Damrak pier 4, Tel: (20) 623-4208*
• **Rederij Noord-Zuid**, *Stadhouderskade 25, Tel: (20) 679-1370*
• **Rederij Amsterdam**, *Nicolaas Witsenkade 1a, Tel: (20) 626-5636*
• **Rederij Lovers**, *Prinshendrikkade 76, Tel: (20) 622-2181*
• **Rederij P. Kooy**, *Rokin 125, Tel: (20) 623-4186*
• **Rederij Plas**, *Damrak pier 3, Tel: (20) 624-5406*

## Bus Tours

A few major tour operators can see you tickets for their two or three hour guided sightseeing bus tours, usually offered in English, through the streets of Amsterdam. These tours offer a good basic introduction to the main sights of town, and may even allow you to get off the bus and walk around a few major attractions for 10 minutes each. Some companies offer one departure daily in the early afternoon, while other companies have both one daily departure in the morning and another in the afternoon. If you reserve a day in advance, the buses that tend to depart from around the Dam square or Centraal Station areas may even be able to pick you up and drop you off in front of one of several major hotels for no additional cost.

Typical itineraries for the two hour excursion will include visits to Dam Square, the Red Light district, the Portuguese Synagogue, an old windmill, nearby canals, and a diamond polishing factory. The longer (and much better) 3 hour tour may also include stops at the Anne Frank huis and the Rijksmuseum. Prices range from 25 NLG to 42.50 NLG per adult with half price for children under 13, and in many cases a free canal boat excursion will also be included in the price.

For specific schedules, reservations, prices, and features, contact one of the companies listed below or visit any Amsterdam VVV tourist office.
• **Holland Key Tours**, *Dam 19, Tel: (20) 624-7304*
• **Holland International**, *Damrak 90, Tel: (20) 625-3035*
• **NZH Travel Excursions**, *Prins Hendrikkade 48, Tel: (20) 639-0391*
• **Lindbergh Excursions**, *Damrak 26, Tel: (20) 622-2766*
• **Best of Holland**, *Damrak 34, Tel: (20) 623-1539*

## Horse-Drawn Carriage Rides

Horse-drawn carriages can be hired year round for about 15 NLG per person per half hour. These can be found at major plazas around the city, such as the Dam square and near the Leidseplein.

For more details, please contact the following company or the VVV tourist office.
• **Karos**, *Hogehilweg 14, Tel: (20) 697-7869*

## Walking Tours

If you want to be in a fun group designed to show you the most famous districts of town, these are the best bet. A few companies will take you on a two to three hour hike through the old canal side lanes and brown cafés with a short stop in the Red Light district. These usually run on weekend mornings, afternoons, or evenings, and cost between 15-30 NLG per person.

In the unique case of Camille's Pleasure Tours, on Thursday through Sunday at either 1:30pm, 3:30pm, or 8:00pm you will be guided on a 90 minute walk through the exciting and strange lanes of the Red Light district in total safety. During her 15-20 NLG excursion, you find out more about the history and current status of the world's oldest profession. Some of these hikes will also include stops inside an erotic museum, old cafés, several unusual boutiques, and perhaps the Amstelkring museum and its hidden church. Most of these walking tours are only available between April and September.

Call one of the following companies for more information and reservations.
- **Camille's Pleasure Tours**, *Reggestraat 26, Tel: (20) 694-9597*
- **Amsterdam Travel & Tours**, *Dam square, Tel: (20) 627-6236*
- **Yellow Bike Tours**, *Nieuwezijds Kolk 29, Tel: (20) 620-6940*

## NIGHTLIFE & ENTERTAINMENT

### Cinemas
- **Alfa**, *Klein-Gartmanplantsoen 4, Tel: (20) 627-8806*
- **Alhambra**, *Weteringschans 134, Tel: (20) 623-3192*
- **Bellevue Cinerama**, *Marnixstraat 400, Tel: (20) 623-4876*
- **Calypso**, *Marnixstraat 402, Tel: (20) 626-6227*
- **Cinecenter**, *Lijnbaansgracht 236, Tel: (20) 623-6615*
- **City**, *Kleine-Gartmanplantsoen 13, Tel: (20) 623-4579*
- **Kriterion**, *Roeterstraat 170, Tel: (20) 623-1708*
- **The Movies**, *Haarlemmerdijk 3, Tel: (20) 624-5790*
- **Rik's Bioscoop**, *Rehuliersbreestraat 33, Tel: (20) 624-3639*
- **Tuschinski**, *Reguliersbreestraat 28, Tel: (20) 626-2633*

### Discos & Dance Clubs

Most of the following clubs reserve the right to refuse entry to anyone who doesn't look like they belong there. This means that unless you are going to a gay club, single men that are not accompanied by a woman may occasionally be denied entrance. In general, the best nights to hit a disco are on Thursdays (Student Night), Friday, Saturday, and Sunday (Gay Night). When you enter you are expected to pass through a metal detector, pay 1 NLG to leave your jacket at the mandatory coat check, and order drinks that tend to run about double the normal price you would expect to pay in a local bar.

If you want to avoid problems returning on another busy night to a club that you like, introduce yourself as you give a 3 NLG tip to the doorman on the way out at the end of the night. These doormen are also the best sources for information about other chic discos and even some good after hours clubs.

**ROXY**, *Singel 465. Tel: (20) 620-0354.*

This converted old theater across the canal from the floating flower market is perhaps one of the best large discos for well dressed singles between the ages of 19 and 35 to dance the night away. The admission is generally around 15 NLG a head and the doormen are pretty good about letting strangers in if you arrive before 11:00pm. Once inside you will find a huge dance floor and a couple of more intimate sofa lined lounges upstairs behind the balcony. The music here is usually cutting edge house, techno, and funk. Best nights here are Thursday, Friday, and Saturday for the straight crowd, and Sunday for the gay crowd.

**SOUL KITCHEN**, *Amstelstraat 32. Tel: (20) 620-2333.*

Located a block or so past the Rembrandsplein on the way to the Waterlooplein, the Soul Kitchen is a great place to dance to rhythm and blues, soul, and funk from the 70's and 80's with a few modern tunes thrown in every now and then. The casually dressed crowd ranges from about 20 to 30 years old, and they really know how to have a good time. Getting in is not a problem as long as you fork over around 10 NLG each, but long lines start to form by 11:30pm on the better nights of Thursday through Saturday.

**ODEON**, *Singel 460. Tel: (20) 624-9711.*

This is Amsterdam's best student oriented multilevel disco. Situated a few steps away from the floating flower market, this laid back and totally casual club has no restrictive entrance policy, and everyone inside is out to have a good time. On busy nights there are up to three separate floors, each with different music that may range from 70's disco to 90's house and techno. Thursdays are the best night (but a student card from a local university may be required to enter). Fridays and Saturdays are fun too.

**SEYMORE LIKELY TOO**, *Nieuwezijds Voorburgwal 161. Tel: (20) 420-5062.*

Located fairly close to the Dam square, this intimate little dance club is one of the town's most friendly places to hang out. The music changes depending on that specific night's theme, but the disc jockeys here really know how to mix it up. Most clients are between 20 and 28 years old and dress in every imaginable style. The doormen here don't give people hassles, and the admission on the weekends is about 10 NLG per person.

**IT**, *Amstelstraat 24, Tel: (20) 625-0111.*

Just down the street from the Rembrandsplein, this bastion of gay and lesbian hard core exhibitionism is often difficult to enter, since the less than friendly doormen pick those who look as gay as possible. Once you have paid the 10 NLG or so cover charge, you can enter the giant dance floor where people wear little or nothing at all. This is one of the city's most famous clubs and the music is extremely loud and mechanized. Saturdays and Sundays are the best nights here, and rather bizarre things happen until 5am or so.

**RICHTER**, *Regulierdwarsstraat 36. Tel: (20) 626-1573.*

Located in the heart of the gay district near the Rembrandtplein, this mixed straight and gay disco gets packed on weekend nights with a well dressed crowd that loves house and techno music. The admission is about 10 NLG per person, and unless there is a long line, you should have minimal problems entering the building that has been decorated in a earthquake motif.

**MAZZO**, *Oudezijdsvoorburgwal 216. Tel: (20) 626-7500.*

This is the city's most hypnotic alternative "Rave" style dance club. Located in the heart of the Red Light district since a fire destroyed its normal home, this is a unique club favored by a young, casually dressed crowd who are often high on Ecstasy. The music is mixed by DJs from all over Europe, and the beat is intense. They are open several nights a week until 5:00am or so and charge around 12 NLG to get in.

### Multipurpose & Live Music Venues

These establishments offer live concerts on several nights a week, but in some cases will also offer a variety of other events such as dance parties, live theater performances, and special theme nights. Use the phone numbers listed below to find out what is scheduled, or ask any Amsterdam VVV tourist office for a copy of the 3.50 NLG bimonthly *What's On In Amsterdam* magazine. Several boutiques, bars, and cafes also give out free copies of the weekly *Week Agenda* and *Uitlist* entertainment schedules if you ask for them.

**MELKWEG**, *Lijnbaansgracht 234. Tel: (20) 624-1777.*

This converted daily factory turned multimedia arts and music complex is just a block behind the Leidseplein. On any given night you will find several hundred people from 18 to 30 years old several different sections of the building either dancing, catching a major rock or reggae concert, screening foreign movies, watching performance art and theater, smoking joints, eating, and getting drunk. It costs about 4 NLG to get a temporary membership card to enter, plus somewhere between 7 NLG and 20 NLG per special event. There is no restrictive door policy, and it is a great place to really see how Amsterdam hangs out all night.

**PARADISO**, *Weteringschans 6. Tel: (20) 623-7348.*

Made famous by a recent Rolling Stones live concert video shot here, this giant old building a couple of blocks from the Leidseplein is both a live music and dance club venue, depending on what hour you arrive. Major North American and European rock and rap bands stop here during their world tours. There is also a smaller upstairs stage for lesser known groups, VIP lounges, and smaller bar areas. On nights when there is no major live act, the whole complex turns into one big dance club with a mixture of ethnic and Dutch house music lovers. Admission costs from 12.50 NLG and up, and since there have been more than a few incidents, security is serious here.

**ARENA**, *'s Gravesandestraat 51. Tel: (20) 694-7362.*

This industrial looking former city orphanage in the southeastern part of the city is one of the most unusual places to party in the city. It has two separate concert hall venues including one that has been built from a beautifully frescoed old church. Normally you can see up and coming bands from all over Europe here, and then stay until they break down the stage and host a dance club in the same hall. There is also a great inexpensive café and restaurant, and a youthful crowd that dresses in jeans and leather jackets most of the time. One ticket will usually let you check out all the events that are taking place simultaneously, and admission costs upwards of 7.50 NLG.

**BIMHUIS**, *Oude Schans 73. Tel: (20) 623-1361.*

This is the city's premier jazz club for internationally known touring bands. Located in the eastern part of town near the Montelbaans tower, the Bimhuis hosts a wide array of live jazz several night a week with ticket prices averaging around 17.50 NLG. They also schedule free workshops throughout the week for local and visiting musicians to gain stage experience and learn more about the art of playing and improvising jazz.

**PH 31**, *Prinshendriklaan 31. Tel: (20) 673-6850.*

If you are looking for a venue to see good live countercultural rock and experimental music, this is the place to go. Located near Vondelpark, this concert hall is filled with young squatters and others on the fringe of society who come here to see cheap shows from bands that are far from the mainstream. The cover is about 7.50 NLG and the drinks are cheap. They also offer a Saturday afternoon chill out with your hangover party featuring tea and cake served with live music.

**DE HEEREN VAN AEMSTEL**, *Thorbeckeplein 5. Tel: (20) 620-2173.*

Besides being a great café and bar for the 25 to 40 year old crowd, this friendly local pub just around the corner from the Rembrandtplein offers two or three live soul and jazz shows during most weeks of the year. There is usually no cover charge, you can dress any way you prefer, the concerts are excellent, and the drinks are normal price.

**DE KORTE GOLF**, *Reguliersdwarsstraat 41. Tel: (20) 626-5435.*

This tiny split level informal bar offers live rock and jazz music including weekly open mike jazz sessions on weekends. Normally there is no cover charge, and the drinks are regular price.

**AKHNATON**, *Nieuwezijds Kolk 25. Tel: (20) 624-3396.*

This multi-cultural cultural center and dance club is situated behind the Damrack near the Centraal Station. Several nights a week there are Arabic, salsa, and reggae concerts or dance parties that cost between 10 NLG and 15 NLG per person to attend. The crowd is casual, ethnic, and fairly young.

**BOURBON STREET**, *Leidesekruisstraat 8. Tel: (20) 623-3440.*

This live jazz cabaret behind the Leidseplein offers live music from local and visiting groups almost every night of the week. Sometimes the cover is around 7.50 NLG and other times it is free, but the place is lots of fun.

---

## "SMOKING" COFFEESHOPS

*These are the best and most reliable of Amsterdam's world-famous cafés, where you can purchase dozens of varieties of the world's strongest imported and domestic marijuana and hashish from a menu. Although not exactly legal, these establishments are in fact licensed to sell these products in small amounts. When you arrive all you have to do is ask for the "Weed List" and you will see what products are being sold. The typical price range is about 9 NLG to 16 NLG per gram, and there may be a minimum order of 25 NLG. Be careful about ordering any "Special" hash-laced cakes or beverages as they tend to have extremely inconsistent effects.*

*These coffeeshops give their clients a relaxing environment to meet other people while providing a nice place to smoke your purchases. While Dutch law is tolerant of the procession of small quantities of these products, do not attempt to bring any of it home, or into another European nation!*

*Some of the better known places include:*

**Tweede Kamer**, *Heisteeg 6*
**The Greenhouse**, *Waterlooplein 345*
**The Grasshopper**, *Oudebrugsteeg 16*
**Dutch Flowers**, *Singel 387*
**Sensi Café**, *Oude Dolenstraat 20*
**The Bulldog Palace**, *Leideseplein 13*
**The Doors**, *Spuistraat 46*
**Cum Laude**, *Langebrugsteeg 7a*
**Siberie**, *Brouwersgracht 11*
**Kadinsky**, *Rosmarijnsteeg 9*

## Great Bars & Grand Cafés

The following is a brief summary of some of Amsterdam's best places to mingle with local people and enjoy a good drink in a comfortable, lively ambiance. Most of these establishments are open daily until about 3:00am or so, and in many cases offer good music, drinks, meals, and perhaps even a small dance floor. I have included only those places that do not refuse anyone from entering (unless it is packed inside) and normally have no entrance fee.

**CAFÉ DE KROON**, *Rembrandplein 17. Tel: (20) 625-2011.*

This wonderfully laid-back grand café overlooking the Rembrandplein is one of my favorite places to hang out in the early evenings. The café has a large bar and an opulent central lounge that is rung by dozens of small tables with plush seats filled with people from every possible age group dressed in every imaginable way. If you look around the walls and on the bar itself you can also catch a glimpse of their strange collection of antique medical instruments, stuffed reptiles, and other turn of the century curiosities. There is also a full menu, some of the best cappuccino in town, and live piano music on some nights.

**MR. COCOS**, *Thorbeckeplein 8. Tel: 20 (Unlisted).*

Head here when you want to party with an extremely social bunch of casually dressed single 18 to 25 year old locals. Just around the corner from the Rembrandtplein, this outrageous bar (and restaurant) is packed to the gills during their two-for-one happy hours between 5:00pm and 7:00pm, and again from 10:00pm until well past 1:00am, on Thursday through Saturday nights. The music is mixed by extremely talented DJs, the drinks are super strong, and patrons are here primarily to meet new people. If you stay here long enough, chances are you won't leave alone.

**DE JAREN**, *Nieuwe Doelenstraat 20. Tel: (20) 625-5771.*

Located a few steps away from the University, this ultra-modern split level café is packed each afternoon and evening with both students and professors. Many of this inviting establishment's casually dressed patrons can be found sipping on beer, coffee, or liqueurs, either on the ground floor near the main bar and nearby rack of international newspapers, upstairs in the restaurant area, or out on the tranquil river-view terrace.

**KORSAKOFF**, *Lijnbaanstraat 161. Tel: (20) 625-7854.*

This is where the local 18 to 24 year old thrash dancing punks, skinheads, anarchists, and performance artists hang out. Situated along a canal several blocks behind the Leidseplein, this three level venue sometimes hosts live hard core concerts, but on most nights it has no doormen, no cover charge, cheap drinks, and loud music until late on Thursday through Sunday nights.

**IN DE WILDEMAN**, *Kolksteeg 3. Tel: (20) 638-2348.*

Located on a tiny lane behind Damrak, this wonderful pub offers over 75 different beers from all over the world, including well over a dozen on tap. If you want to try some great brews and talk with a mature group of mellow locals, this is a great place to visit.

**PALLADIUM**, *Kleine-Gartmanplantsoen 7. Tel: (20) Unlisted.*

Open daily from the afternoon until the early morning hours of the night, this glittery café/restaurant/bar is the place to see and be seen by the well dressed yuppie crowd. They play good dance music and get packed with well dressed 25 to 40 year olds that try and pick each other up.

**BROUWERIJ 'T IJ**, *Funenkade 7. Tel: (20) 622-8325.*

Located below southeastern Amsterdam's Molen De Gooyer, one of the city's only remaining windmills, this down to earth micro-brewery serves a wide array of its own reasonably priced pilsners and darker seasonal beers. The crowd here is local middle class workers that know how to throw back mug after mug of some of the freshest and best tasting beer found anywhere in the city.

### Brown Cafés

These are traditional wood-paneled neighborhood pubs with an old world ambiance that are scattered throughout the city and serve a good variety beer, *jenever* (a traditional Dutch gin), and mixed drinks in an intimate setting. Most of these brown cafés are filled with antique brass tap fixtures, old wooden tables, and friendly locals who sit around and talk about life.

Unique to Holland, these relaxing drinking establishments often play old Dutch folk songs and serve light snacks such as cheese platters and sandwiches. They're open from lunch time until about 1:00am.

Below is a listing of my favorite centrally located brown cafés in alphabetical order, but you may very well find a few more good ones one your own:

• **Amstel Taveerne**, *Amstel 54, Tel: (20) 623-4254*
• **'t Doktertje**, *Rozenboomsteeg 4, Tel: (20) 626-4427*
• **Eijlders**, *Korte Leidsedwarsstraat 47, Tel: (20) 624-2704*
• **Café de Eland**, *Prinsengracht 296, Tel: (20) 623-7654*
• **Frascati**, *Nes 59, Tel: (20) 624-1324*
• **Haarlemsch Koffiehuis**, *Prins Hendrikkade 36, Tel: (20) 624-8098*
• **Café Heuvel**, *Prinsengracht 568, Tel: (20) 622-6354*
• **'t Hok**, *Lange Leidsedwarsstraat 134, Tel: (20) 624-3133*
• **Hoppe**, *Spui 20, Tel: (20) 623-7849*
• **Café International**, *Warmoesstraat 1, Tel: (20) 624-5520*
• **De Kleine Karseboom**, *Nieuwendijk 51, Tel: (20) 624-9251*

- **Kempinski**, *Leidseplein 14, Tel: (20) 623-8361*
- **'t Koggeschip**, *Singel 43, Tel: (20) 639-0018*
- **Het Bruine Paard**, *Prinsengracht 44, Tel: (20) 622-8538*
- **Petit Café de Slugswacht**, *Sint Antoniessluis, (20) 623-7861*
- **De Prins**, *Prinsengracht 124, Tel: (20) 624-9382*
- **De Leydsche Poort**, *Leidseplein 11, Tel: (20) 624-3454*
- **Het Molenpad**, *Prinsengracht 653, Tel: (20) 625-9680*
- **'t Smalle**, *Egelantiersgracht 12, Tel: (20) 623-9617*
- **De Zwart**, *Spuistraat 334, Tel: (20) 624-6511*

**Theaters & Concert Halls**
- **Brakke Grond**, *Nes 45, Tel: (20) 624-0394*
- **Beurs van Berlage**, *Damrak 243, Tel: (20) 627-0466*
- **Carre Theater**, *Amstel 115, Tel: (20) 622-5225*
- **Concertgebouw**, *Concertgebouwplein 2, Tel: (20) 671-8345*
- **De Balie**, *Kleine-Gartmanplantsoen 10, Tel: (20) 623-2904*
- **Engelenbak**, *Nes 71, Tel: (20) 626-3644*
- **Felix Meritis**, *Keizersgracht 324, Tel: (20) 623-1311*
- **Frascati**, *Nes 63, Tel: (20) 623-5723*
- **Muziektheater**, *Asmtel 3, Tel: (20) 625-5455*
- **Stadsschouwburg**, *Leidseplein 26, Tel: (20) 624-2311*

## SHOPPING
**Art & Antique Auctions**
- **Chrisite's**, *Corn Schuystraat 57, Tel: (20) 575-5255*
- **Sotheby's**, *Rokin 102, Tel: (20) 627-5656*

**Diamonds**
  The following offer diamonds for sale and factory tours:
- **Coster Diamonds**, *Paulus Pottersraat 6, Tel: (20) 676-2222*
- **Gassan Diamonds**, *Nieuwe Uilenburgerstraat 175, Tel: (20) 622-5333*
- **Stoeltie Diamonds**, *Wagenstraat 17, Tel: (20) 62-7601*
- **Van Moppes Diamonds**, *Albert Cuypstraat 2, Tel: (20) 676- 1242*

**Major Markets**
- **Albert Cuypstraat Outdoor Produce and Clothing Market**, *Albert Cuypstraat.* Year round from Monday through Saturday from 9am until 4:30pm.
- **Antiekmarkt de Looier Indoor Antique Market**, *Elandsgracht 109.* Year round from Saturday through Thursday from 9am until at least 5pm.
- **Artmarkt Outdoor Arts Market**, *Spui.* Sundays from 10am until 6pm April through November Only.

· **Artmarkt Outdoor Arts Market**, *Thorbeckeplein.* Sundays from 11am until 6pm April through December Only.
· **Bookmarkt Outdoor Used Book Market**, *Spui.* Year round on Fridays from 10am until 6pm.
· **Bloemenmarkt Outdoor Floating Flower Market**, *Singel.* Year round from Monday through Saturday from 10am until 5pm.
· **Boerenmarkt Outdoor Farmers Market**, *Noordermarkt.* Year round on Saturdays from 9am until at least 3pm
· **Nieuwmarket Outdoor Antique Market**, *Nieuwmarkt.* Sundays from 10am until 4pm May through September Only..
· **Nieuwmarket Outdoor Farmers Market**, *Nieuwmarkt.* Year round on Saturdays from 10am until 3pm.
· **Waterlooplein Outdoor Flea Market**, *Waterlooplein.* Year round from Monday threough Saturday from 9am until 5pm.

## SPORTS & RECREATION
### Bicycle Rentals
· **Mac Bike**, *Marnixstraat 20, Tel: (20) 626-6964*
· **St. Nicolaas Rent a Bike**, *St. Nicolaasstraat 16, Tel: (20) 623-9715*
· **Holland Rent a Bike**, *Damrak 247, Tel: (20) 622-3207*
· **Bulldog Rent a Bike**, *Oudezijds Voorburgwal 126, Tel: (20) 624-8248*
· **Damstraat Rent a Bike**, *Damstraat 24, Tel: (20) 625-5029*
· **Mountainbike Truus**, *Leidsekruisstraat 23, Tel: (20) 638-9481*
· **Koenders Take a Bike**, *Centraal Station, Tel: (20) 624-8391*

### Boat, Canoe, & Pedal Boat Rentals
· **Aan de Wind**, *Mauritskade 1, Tel: (20) 692-9124*
· **Canal Bike**, *Weteringschans 24, Tel: (20) 626-5574*

### Botanical Gardens
· **Hortus Botanicus**, *Plantage Middelaan 2, Tel: (20) 625-8411*

### Bowling
· **Knijn Bowling**, *Scheldeplein 3, Tel: (20) 664-2211*

### Casinos
· **Holland Casino Amsterdam**, *Max Euweplein 62, Tel: (20) 620-1006*

### Golf Clubs
· **Olympus Open Golf Club**, *Abcouderstraatweg 46, Tel: (20) 645-7431*
· **Waterland Golfbaan**, *Buikslotermeerdk 141, Tel: (20) 636-1010*

**Health Clubs & Fitness Centers**
- **Fitness Aerobic Center Jansen**, *Rokin 111, Tel: (20) 626-9366*
- **Barbells Gym**, *Weteringdwarsstraat 3, Tel: (20) 627-3060*
- **Spafit Fitness Center**, *Leidsegracht 84, Tel: (20) 624-2512*
- **Splash Palace Fitness Center**, *Prins Hendrikkade 72, Tel: (20) 556-4899*
- **Sporting Club Leidseplein**, *Korte Leidsedwarsstraat 18, Tel: (20) 620-6631*

**Public Swimming Pools**
- **Floraparkbad**, *Sneeuwbalweg 5, Tel: (20) 636-8121*
- **Marnixbad**, *Marnixplein 5, Tel: (20) 625-4843*
- **De Mirandabad**, *De Mirandalaan 9, Tel: (20) 642-8080*
- **Sloterparkbad**, *Slotermeerlaan 2. Tel: (20) 611-4565*
- **Zuiderbad**, *Hobbemastraat 26, Tel: (20) 679-2217*

**Zoos**
- **Artis Zoo**, *Plantage Kerklaan 40, Tel: (20) 623-1836*

# EXCURSIONS FROM AMSTERDAM

Several locally-based tour operators offer tickets for a good selection of half and full day excursions, departing from Amsterdam either daily or only on specific days of the week, usually depending on the season. I have listed a few of the most popular extended excursions and the most reliable companies that run them, but almost all of these tour operators have the same tours (often on differing schedules and days). Advance reservations are usually necessary, and free transfers to and from several major Amsterdam hotels can be arranged.

Contact the companies listed below, or the Amsterdam VVV tourist office, at least a day in advance to reserve your place and to determine the exact times and days of the week for your preferred excursion, which language the tour will be narrated in, and where the nearest pick-up location for you will be on that specific day. Entrance fees to attractions are generally included, but meals and beverages are usually not included.

### Half-Day Zaanse Schans, Marken, and Volendam tour

This is a 4 1/2 hour guided bus tour that first stops at the picturesque hamlet of De Zaanse Schans to see its windmills and visit a wooden shoe maker. From there you depart for the famed traditional fishing villages of Volendam and Marken to wander around the colorful old wooden fisherman's houses, before heading off to a cheese making factory. During the summer this tour departs twice daily at about 10:00am and 2:30pm, during the winter it leaves once daily at 10:00am. The price is 38 NLG per adult or 19 NLG per child.

Operated by **Lindbergh Excursions**, *Damrak 26, Tel: (20) 622-2766.*

**Half-Day Keukenhof garden tour**

After driving south towards the town of Lisse, you will be admitted into the giant Keukenhof gardens with over 7,000,000 flowers in bloom during the season. A visit to another garden or tulip show will also be included. This excursion departs at least twice daily between late March and late May at about 9:30am and 2:30pm. The price including admission fees is 47.50 NLG per adult or 44.50 NLG per child.

Operated by **Holland International**, *Damrak 90, Tel: (20) 625-3035*

**Half-Day Zaanse Schans & Edam tour**

This is a 3 1/2 hour guided bus tour that first stops at the picturesque hamlet of De Zaanse Schans to see its windmills and visit a wooden shoe maker. From here you will be brought to the charming medieval port city of Edam. This tour departs daily at 9:30am during the summer, and on Tuesday, Thursday, Saturday, and Sunday during the winter at about 2:30pm and costs 45 NLG per adult or 22.50 NLG per child.

Operated by **Holland Key Tours**, *Dam 19, Tel: (20) 624-7304*

**Half-Day Manor House & Lake tour**

After driving southeast to the fortified town of Naarden and the lake district of Gooi, the bus will then proceed along the Vecht river as it passes by several stately manor houses. This excursion departs Sundays only throughout the year at about 9:30am and costs 45 NLG per adult or 22.50 NLG per child.

Operated by **Holland International**, *Damrak 90, Tel: (20) 625-3035*

**Full Day Den Haag, Delft, Rotterdam, & Kinderdijk tour**

Your eight hour excursion will begin with a short ride to the world's largest flower auction at Aalsmeer, then you will drive past the embassies of Den Haag until reaching the seaside at Scheveningen. From here the next stop is at a Delft pottery factory in Delft, followed by a visit to the famed 19 windmills (they function only on Saturdays from April through September) of Kinderdijk via a short ride to the sights of Rotterdam. This tour departs daily during the summer at 10:00am, and on Tuesday, Thursday, and Sunday during the winter at 10:00am, and costs 62.50 NLG per adult or 31.25 NLG per child.

Operated by **NZH Travel**, *Prins Hendrikkade 48, Tel: (20) 639-0391*

**Full Day Antwerp & Brussels tour**

This excursion leaves for the two most important cities of Belgium and stops at the market square and cathedral of Antwerp, before moving on to the royal palace, boutiques, monuments, and lace factories of central Brussels. This tour departs at 9:30am on Thursday through

Sunday during the summer, and during the winter at 10:00am on Saturdays only, and costs 59 NLG per adult or 29.50 NLG per child.
    Operated by **Best of Holland**, *Damrak 34, Tel: (20) 623-1539*

## PRACTICAL INFORMATION

**Stationplein VVV Tourist Office** - *Stationsplein, 10* - (20) 551-2512
**Leidseplein VVV Tourist Office** - *Leidseplein, 1* - (6) 340-34066
**Schiphol Airport VVV Tourist Office** - *Airport Arrivals Area* - (6) 340-34066
**Schiphol Airport General Info** - *(20) 601- 9111 or (6) 350-34050*
**Schiphol Airport V.A.T. Tax Refund Center** - *(20) 446-6720*
**Schiphol Airport Lost Luggage Claims** - *(20) 649-1433*
**Schiphol Airport Lost Property Desk** - *(20) 601-2325*
**Schiphol Airport Taxi Stand** - *(20) 653-1000*
**KLM Airlines Reservations** - *Metsustraat, 2* - *(20) 474-7747*
**Martin Air Reservations** - *(20) 601-1222*
**KLM-NZH Airport to Hotel Shuttle** - *(20) 649-5651*
**American Consulate** - *Museumplein, 19* - *(20) 664-5661*
**Amsterdam Radio Dispatched Taxis** - *(20) 677-7777*
**International Train Schedules** - *(20) 601-0541*
**Domestic Train and Bus Info** - *(6) 9292*
**GVB Municipal Transit Head Office** - *Prins Hendrikkade, 108* - *(20) 551-4911*
**GVB Municipal Transit Info Office** - *Stationplein 14, (6) 9292*
**Uit Buro Cultural Event Ticket Office** - *Leidseplein, 26* - *(20) 621-1211*
**American Express Travel Services** - *Damrak 66* - *(20) 520-7777*
**Amsterdam Chamber of Commerce** - *De Ruyterkade, 5* - *(20) 652-3660*
**Amsterdam City Hall** - *Stadhuis-Amstel, 1*- *(20) 552-9111*
**Amsterdam Main Post Office** - *Singel, 250* - *(20) 556-3311*
**Amsterdam Police Headquarters** - *Elandsgracht, 117* - *(20) 559-9111*
**Amsterdam Traffic and Parking Police** - *(20) 553-0300*
**Amsterdam Medical Center** - *Meibergdreef, 9* - *(20) 566-9111*
**Emergency Medical Referral** - *(6) 350-32042*
**Emergency Hotline** - *06-11*

# 14. ROTTERDAM

The modern city of **Rotterdam**, population 589,678, has the largest port of any city in the world. Since its reconstruction at the end of the Second World War, it has become a center for modern architecture and a constantly evolving showcase for new concepts in 20th century urban development. While many Dutch people complain that since the city had its heart bombed out it is not so impressive, I disagree.

There are well over a dozen fine museums, hundreds of great boutiques, waterview cafés, excellent restaurants and nightlife, and a population of hard working middle class residents that are among the most friendly in any major Dutch city. Of course, there are still some big city problems, such as hard drugs coming in from the nearby ports, and some instances of petty crime, but this is a great place to spend a couple of days wandering around on your own.

Almost all the sights and attractions are well within walking distance from each other, and with careful observation you can find charming little districts that are well worth exploring. As is the case in all big cities in Holland, if you intend to bring a car with you I suggest parking it during your entire stay and using the public transportation system, taxis, or your feet to get around.

Make sure that you include a visit via water taxi to the **Hotel New York** for a sunset drink, and make the effort to check out the **Oudehaven** and **Delfshaven** historical harbors while here. Rotterdam is also a good location from which to enjoy day trips to nearby towns via bicycle, rental car, excursion boat, bus and train.

## ROTTERDAM'S HISTORY

In the late 13th century, the area that is today known as Rotterdam was little more than a fishing and farming village of traditional huts located near the base of a dam on the Rotte river. Soon the first in a series of man-made waterways that lead out towards the sea was excavated, and by 1340 Rotterdam became a charted city. Once the city had expanded its

**HISTORIC DELFSHAVEN DISTRICT, ROTTERDAM**

series of canals and waterways, it soon became one of Holland's major commercial routes to the Rhine river. After the Spanish fleet pillaged the city in 1572, it was redeveloped, and soon became the second largest port in the country.

As the 19th century approached, local businessmen began plans to develop additional harbors and residential areas in the southern part of the city just across the Maas river from the downtown core. Complicated dredging projects and the construction of even larger artificial waterways allowed for huge docks to be created. These allowed for an ever increasing number of ships to carry cargo transported here from the nearby inland railways, and take these products to points along and beyond the North Sea. As the shipping companies grew richer and employed thousands of local laborers in their trade, the city's economy grew and it soon became one of the largest cities in Holland. By 1936, Rotterdam's unique man-made harbor had become the biggest in the world.

On May 14, 1940, the Nazi's made a surprise air raid on the city and destroyed almost all of the original city center. Even more damage was suffered by Rotterdam when it was later bombed by allied air forces in 1943, and then had its harbors decimated by the retreating Germans in 1944. With its historical downtown zone literally in pieces, and over 25,000 homes and businesses devastated by bombs and fires, a massive reconstruction project was badly needed at the end of the war. This task was rapidly accomplished with the creation of the new Botlek port in 1953, followed by the construction of a huge state-of-the-art **Europoort** shipping area 24 kilometers (15 miles) west of the city in 1968. The residential and commercial areas of town were also quickly rebuilt with modern (and often uninspiring) cement and glass complexes springing up all over the place.

While almost all of the beautiful old brick structures that once dominated the city are gone, many of the new residential and commercial developments have been designed using innovative techniques pioneered by Europe's leading architects.

## ORIENTATION

Rotterdam is located in the south central section of the **Zuid-Holland** province. It lies 59 kilometers (37 miles) south-southwest of the capital city of Amsterdam, and 26 kilometers (16 miles) southeast of Den Haag.

## ARRIVALS & DEPARTURES

### By Air

**Rotterdam Airport** services a limited selection of private, charter, and some European commuter flights. Located about 9 kilometers (6 miles) northwest of the city center off of Route A-13, this airport is not normally used by visitors coming from North America. It is much more likely that American and Canadian visitors flying to this city will arrive here via land links from the much larger **Schiphol Airport** near Amsterdam, about 49 kilometers (30 miles) to the north.

### By Bus

Many of the bus lines between Rotterdam and other parts of Holland, as well as the rest of Europe, tend to stop at either the **Centraal Station** train depot on the north end of downtown, or the **Zuidplein** depot on the south edge of town. Be sure to call in advance to find out exactly where and when your bus comes in. Connections between this station and any other point in Amsterdam can generally be made by the adjacent public bus, tram, or metro stations for 3 NLG per person each way, or via taxi for roughly 9.75 NLG or so depending on where you are going.

### By Car

Downtown street-side parking spots are impossible to find.

From **Amsterdam**, the easiest way to get to Rotterdam is to follow **A-10** ring road around until connecting onto the **A-4** south for about 47 kilometers (29 miles), then exit onto the **A-13** south for about 13 kilometers (8 miles), and finally merging into the **E-19** ring road east until finding the "Centrum" exit some 13 kilometers later.

From **Den Haag** you should take the **A-12** west for some 8 kilometers (5 miles) before exiting onto the **A-4** south for about 4 kilometers (2.5

miles), then follow the **A-13** south for about 13 kilometers (8 miles), and finally merge into the **E-19** ring road east until finding the "Centrum" exit some 13 kilometers later.

**By Train**

Rotterdam is linked to almost any other point in Holland and Europe by an exhaustive series of rail lines. There are a few different rail stations, each with its own series of daily arrivals and departures. Those arriving here directly from Schiphol Airport in Amsterdam can also take advantage of frequent rail service linking these destinations. The best location for service to and from downtown Rotterdam is via the large **Centraal Station** train depot at the north edge of the city's downtown section. Connections between this station and any other point in Amsterdam can generally be made by the adjacent public bus, tram, or metro stations, for about 3 NLG per person each way, or via taxi for roughly 9.75 NLG or so.

Use the train information phone numbers listed in the *Practical Information* section at the end of this chapter to reconfirm, in advance, the exact time and station for your destination.

## GETTING AROUND TOWN

**By Public Transportation**

The city of Rotterdam's **RET** (Rotterdamse Electrische Tram) municipal transit authority offers a vast array of public transportation methods to get you safely and easily around town. There are a couple of metro lines, dozens of bus and tram lines, and 13 night buses to choose from. Almost all of these vehicles stop at one point in front of Centraal Station. Just keep in mind that buses can be entered via the front door, while most trams and all metros have several entry doors you can use.

The normal hours of operation for most of the system is from about 6:30am until roughly 12:15am. After that your only choices are the more expensive and less frequent Friday and Saturday-only night buses that run from Centraal Station and various major stops through the city between 1:00am and at least 3:00am. All of these systems utilize the same types of tickets and passes.

If you buy your tickets or passes in advance from an RET municipal transit office, the VVV tourist office, a metro station, post office, or one of many tobacco shops, you will save a lot of money. Special discounted unlimited local use **Dagkaart Travelcard** Rotterdam public transportation passes can be obtained for use here by paying 12 NLG for one day, 18 NLG for two days, and 24 NLG for three days. Night buses cost 5 NLG per person and do not accept any other type of tickets. They also accept **Nationale Strippen Kaarts**, strip tickets that allow one or more people to each use two blank strips per zone of local travel.

To get free copies of the extremely useful RET public transit system maps entitled *De Lijnen,* just pop into the VVV offices listed in the *Practical Information* section at the end of this chapter.

## By Taxi

There are hundreds of licensed taxis roaming the streets and major passenger arrival points of the city during all hours of the day and night. Drivers are quite honest in comparison to those currently found most other European or North American cities. To find a taxi, either hail an unoccupied cab driving by with its "Taxi" roof light illuminated, go to one of the dozens of obvious taxi stands throughout the city, or call *(10) 462-6060* for a radio response pick-up on demand. The main taxi ranks are located at the Stationsplein, Eendrachtsplein, and in front of the Blaak metro station. During rainy days, festivals, trade fairs, or weekday morning and evening rush hours (8am until 10am and 6pm until 8pm) there may be a short wait until you get lucky.

Taxi meters charge at about the rate of 3 NLG per kilometer, so this works out to somewhere around 8.50 NLG to 13.50 NLG per ride (not per person) between most downtown locations depending on exact distance and traffic conditions.

## By Water Taxi

If the weather is nice, you may wish to reach the unique **Holland-Amerika Lijn** building (now the **Hotel New York**) over by the newly developed **Kop Van Zuid** peninsula of southern Rotterdam by water taxi. These small craft run on a set schedule from the marina near the Museum Voor Volkenkunde and from the docks behind the maritime museum, and charge about 7 NLG per person round trip for the 8 minute boat ride. Check with the boat's skipper about what time the last water taxi returns to the mainland (usually around midnight). Also keep in mind that these boats do not operate when the winds are strong or the fog is heavy.

## WHERE TO STAY - IN ROTTERDAM

In addition to the hotels listed immediately below in this section, I've also listed three hotels in the next section just outside of Rotterdam for those of you who don't wish to stay in the city.

### *Expensive*

**PARK HOTEL ROTTERDAM,** *Westersingel 70. Tel: (10) 436-3611. Fax: (10) 436-4212. US & Canada Bookings (UTELL) 1-800-44-UTELL. Year round rack rates from 305 NLG per double room per night (E.P.). All major credit cards accepted.*

After staying in almost every hotel in Rotterdam, this fantastic 4 star deluxe property easily gets my highest recommendation. Situated only a two minute walk away from the Museumpark and the Binnenwegplein in the heart of the downtown business and shopping district, the Park Hotel is a stunning example of modern architecture. There are 189 beautifully decorated rooms and luxurious suites located in both a peaceful garden-side wing dating back to 1922, and the more modern towers that were added recently. All of the accommodations come complete with private bathrooms, remote control satellite television, optional in-room movies, mini-bar, am-fm clock radio, extremely comfortable bedding, direct dial telephones with computer modem jacks, an executive style desk, as well as superb city views, powerful air conditioners, and mini-safes in most rooms.

The facilities are the best in town, and include opulent public lounges and sitting areas, **The Empress** gourmet French restaurant, a wonderful bar, free private parking, a fully equipped heath club, a sauna, free use of an internet and computer work station, a full range of business meeting and conference rooms, 24 hour room service, express laundry and dry cleaning, a tranquil inner courtyard and garden, optional massages, private dining rooms, available child care, and a fantastic staff that will be sure to remember your name. For those with a little extra money to spend, reserve one of the extraordinary deluxe corner rooms on the upper floors of the hotel's glittering silver tower. The Park Hotel is a great place to stay while visiting the city for business or pleasure, and is certainly the best hotel in Rotterdam! Make sure to ask about the hotel's great special summer and weekend rates.

**ROTTERDAM HILTON**, *Weena 10. Tel: (10) 414-4044. Fax: (10) 411-8884. US & Canada Bookings (Hilton Hotels) 1-800-445-8667. Special package rates from 198 NLG per double room per night (E.P.). Year round rack rates from 445 NLG per double room per night (E.P.). All major credit cards accepted.*

The Hilton hotel is exactly what you would expect an American-style business and conference hotel to look and feel like. Located in the busiest part of the city (near the Centraal Station), this giant 5 star hotel has 253 air conditioned rooms and suites that all have private bathrooms, color cable television, direct dial telephones, plush furnishings, sound proofed windows, mini-bar, wall to wall carpeting, and am-fm clock radios.

Services and facilities here include a full complement of business meeting rooms and secretarial services, an indoor garage with valet parking, 24 hour room service, express laundry and dry cleaning, non-smoking rooms, a newsstand, boutiques, a beauty salon, a good restaurant, a lounge, and a disco. Service here is good, and the clientele are almost all in town on some type of business.

*Moderate*

**HOTEL NEW YORK,** *Koninginnenhoofd 1. Tel: (10) 439-0500. Fax: (10) 484-2701. Year round rack rates from 180 NLG per double room per night (E.P.). Most major credit cards accepted.*

This new hotel is actually located on the waterfront of the Kop van Zuid peninsula in the southern part of the city. Converted from the opulent turn of the century Art Nouveau style headquarters of the Holland America cruise ship line, this unusual hotel is best reached by water taxi via the harbor areas of Leuvehaven and Veerhaven. There are 72 uniquely shaped and decorated rooms (and suites) with a variety of memorable views, all with modern private bathrooms, a bizarre selection of seemingly second har·' furnishings, direct dial telephones, remote control satellite televisions, huge picture windows, heating systems, and superb harbor and city views. There are also two dramatic towers that contain a small private museum as well as a truly unforgettable deluxe room with a view that is well worth the small surcharge.

The complex also boasts a great affordable restaurant (packed on weekends), an oyster bar, a tea salon, a cute gift shop, free parking, old world style business meeting rooms, 24 hour room service, a winter garden, boutiques, a nearby waterside park, several original executive offices full of fine wooden panels and carpets, and more. If you are looking for a romantic escape from the hectic city, this is certainly an interesting place to go!

**HOTEL INNTEL,** *Leuvehaven 80. Tel: (10) 413-4139. Fax: (10) 413-3222. US & Canada Bookings (UTELL) 1-800-44-UTELL. Special Package rates from 178 NLG per double room per night (E.P.). Year round rack rates from 260 NLG per double room per night (E.P.). All major credit cards accepted.*

This modern, full service 4 star hotel is located directly on one of Rotterdam's most active waterways, just a few blocks away from the heart of the city. The Inntel features 150 city and water-view double rooms that all feature complete private bathrooms, satellite remote control color television with optional movie channels, mini-bar, direct dial telephone, ample closet space, double glazed soundproofed windows, individually controlled heating systems, hair dryers, and nice solid furnishings.

Guests here are a good mix of international businessmen and travelers looking for comfortable and affordable accommodations within easy walking distance to all the major attractions and commercial sectors of town. The hotel features the waterside **Le Papillion Restaurant** with fantastic full American buffet breakfasts (the best in this city!), as well as moderately priced al la carte lunch and dinner menus, the cozy Waterway lounge serving cocktails and great coffee, a glass-enclosed penthouse health club with complimentary use of the sauna and heated swimming pool, a work out room, sun tan machine, solarium, free covered parking, an adjacent IMAX movie theater, available business meeting and convention/reception rooms, car rental and sightseeing desk, and a major metro station just across from the main entrance. This is a good choice for those who want to be near downtown, but still enjoy a waterfront location.

**HOLIDAY INN ROTTERDAM**, *Schouwburgplein 1. Tel: (10) 433-3800. Fax: (10) 414-5482. US & Canada Bookings (Holiday Inn) 1-800-465-4329. Special weekend rates from 185 NLG per double room per night (B.P.). Year round rack rates from 325 NLG per double room per night (E.P.). All major credit cards accepted.*

The 4 star Holiday Inn Rotterdam is a nice place to stay. This towering executive class property is located a couple of blocks away from the Centraal Station and just a two minute walk to the Lijnbaan shopping area. All of the hotel's 100 rooms have private bathrooms, remote control satellite television, am-fm clock radio, mini-bar, direct dial telephone, and comfortable furnishings. Among the many facilities are a good restaurant, a bar, several business meeting rooms, boutiques, 24 hour room service, and nearby parking. This is an especially good deal if you can book one of their special package or weekend rate deals.

**SAVOY HOTEL**, *Hoogstraat 81. Tel: (10) 413-9280. Fax: (10) 404-5712. US & Canada Bookings (Supranational) 1-800-441-1414. Special package rates from 175 NLG per double room per night (E.P.). Year round rack rates from 245 NLG per double room per night (E.P.). All major credit cards accepted.*

This modern 3 star hotel near Coolsingel in the middle of the downtown core is a good value for the money. The Savoy offers some 95 medium-sized rooms with private bathrooms, remote control satellite television, executive desks, direct dial telephones, soundproof windows, and nice furnishings. The hotel also has a restaurant and bar, adjacent parking, and a good location.

### Inexpensive

**HOTEL EMMA**, *Nieuwe Binnenweg 6. Tel: (10) 436-5533. Fax: (10) 436-7658. Year round rack rates from 150 NLG per double room per night (C.P.). Most major credit cards accepted.*

This cute little family-owned and operated hotel on one of the best shopping streets in the center of the city is a great choice for those looking to save some money. The 3 star Hotel Emma offers 26 simple but rather comfortable medium-sized rooms that all have private bathrooms, color television, direct dial telephone, heating systems, nice hardwood furnishings, wall to wall carpeting, mini-bar, sound proofed windows, and either interior or city street views. There is also nearby parking, a rooftop terrace, reading room, a complimentary continental breakfast, and one of the friendliest staffs in the city.

**HOTEL MARIA BAAN,** *Rouchenstraat 345. Tel: (10) 477-0555. Fax: (10) 476-9450. Year round rack rates from 95 NLG per double room per night (E.P.). Most major credit cards accepted.*

While far from fancy, this small family owned 2 star hotel not far from Delfshaven offers 22 rooms with either private or shared bathrooms, color television, am-fm clock radio, heating systems, simple but comfortable furnishings, and direct dial telephone.

*Cheap*
**NJHC-ROTTERDAM CITY HOSTEL,** *Rochussenstraat 107. Tel: (10) 436-5763. Fax: (10) 436-5569. US & Canada Bookings (Hostelling International) 1-613-237-7884. Year round rack rates from 27.50 NLG per person in a dormitory per night (C.P.). Cash Only - No credit cards accepted.*

This popular city center hostel near the Binnenwegplein is a nice place to stay for those looking for safe and friendly accommodations at bargain basement prices. The rooms here are actually a series of small and medium-sized dormitories with 8 or more bunk beds, individual lockers, semi-private bathrooms and courtyard views. There is also a great bar and lounge area complete with board games and tourist information, a complimentary continental breakfast, a courtyard garden, bicycle storage area, electronic baggage lockers, a great young staff, and an inexpensive restaurant.

The minimal regulations here include the need for a Hostelling International membership card (available on the premises) as well as a 2:00am curfew and an afternoon lockout, but a key for the front door can be obtained so that you can arrive after the curfew and still enter the building. Popular with student groups, university students, European backpackers, and small families, at these prices it is well worth the effort to book this place well in advance!

## WHERE TO STAY - NEAR ROTTERDAM
*Expensive*
**DE ARENDSHOEVE HOTEL,** *Molenlaan 14, Bergambacht. Tel: (182) 351-000. Fax: (182) 351-155. US & Canada Bookings (Relais & Chateaux) 1-212-856-0115. Year round rack rates from 265 NLG per double room per night (E.P.). Special Gourmet Packages from 655 NLG per double room per night (M.A.P.). All major credit cards accepted.*

This beautiful new deluxe Relais & Chateaux hotel is located about an 18 minute drive northeast of Rotterdam. Situated in the charming canal-lined village of **Bergambacht**, near several interesting museums, the De Arendshoeve Hotel has become a favored place for those who expect the finest accommodations, services, facilities, and cuisine available in this part of Holland. All of the 27 spacious, sun-drenched rooms and suites have been uniquely decorated with exquisite taste and contain giant tile bathrooms, remote control satellite television, individually controlled heating systems, beautiful hardwood furnishings, selections of nice art prints, fresh flowers, high quality amenities, a fully loaded mini-bar, plenty of closet space, multiple direct dial telephones, electric trouser press, executive desks, dual alarm am-fm clock radio, mini-safe, hair dryer, and multiple windows looking out onto the adjacent windmill and nearby village.

Besides offering several acres of extremely well-manicured grounds, the hotel also features 24 hour room service, a beauty salon and spa, sauna, whirlpool bath, a magnificent indoor heated swimming pool, the cozy Scarlatti lounge, available massage therapy, several business meeting and reception rooms with complete audio/visual rental services, pretty canal-side gardens, and impressive public spaces decorated with stunning antiques, stained glass, and vintage ceramic murals.

The hotel's highly acclaimed **Restaurant Puccini** is open for lunch and dinner with a menu offering creatively prepared and remarkably presented gourmet cuisine and rare wines with a definite Italian flair. If you're looking for exciting activities in the area while staying here, the friendly professional staff at reception will be glad to arrange a round of golf, day trips to many nearby sights, or even an entertaining night of live theater. Highly Recommended as an oasis of tranquillity and comfort!

*Moderate*
**GOLDEN TULIP BARBIZON CAPELLE**, *Barbizionlaan 2, Capelle. Tel: (10) 456-4455. Fax: (10) 456-7858. US & Canada Bookings (Golden Tulip) 1-800-344-1212. Special weekend rates from 175 NLG per double room per night (E.P.). Year round rack rates from 275 NLG per double room per night (E.P.). All major credit cards accepted.*

This excellent 4 star hotel is located just a 10 minute drive away from downtown Rotterdam in the eastern suburban business district of **Capelle**. The property boasts 101 large and well designed rooms that all offer deluxe private bathrooms, sound proofed windows, remote control satellite television with optional movie channels, mini-bar, electric trouser press, direct dial telephones, extremely comfortable furnishings, wonderful large beds, and nice art work.

Facilities include free outdoor parking, 24 hour room service, complimentary morning newspapers and fruit baskets, a full service restaurant, an English style pub, express laundry and dry cleaning, plenty of business meeting rooms and conference areas, a nice terrace, and a great staff. If you have a car and want to be near but not directly in Rotterdam, this is a good choice for this price range.

*Inexpensive*
**HOTEL IBIS VLAARDINGEN,** *Westlandseweg 270, Vlaardingen. Tel: (10) 460-2050. Fax: (10) 460-4059. US & Canada Bookings (Sofitel) 1-800-763-4835. Special weekend rates from 75 NLG per double room per night (E.P.). Year round rack rates from 99 NLG per double room per night (E.P.). All major credit cards accepted.*

Located in **Vlaardingen**, about a 14 minute drive west from Rotterdam, this new modern 2 star hotel is a good choice for those with cars who want to spend as little money as possible for nice accommodations. The modern French-owned Ibis has 90 medium-sized modern rooms with private bathrooms, direct dial telephones, remote control television, am-fm clock radio, and simple but comfortable furnishings. There is free outdoor parking, a restaurant, a bar, business meeting rooms, and a coffee shop. This is perhaps the best choice for suburban hotel rooms in this price range.

## WHERE TO EAT
*Very Expensive*
**RESTAURANT PARKHUEVEL,** *Heuvellaan 21. Tel: (10) 436-0766. All major credit cards accepted.*

Master chef Cees Helder has created a fantastically luxurious and formal Michelin rated 2 star dining establishment, in a very pretty setting at the edge of the Maas river alongside a beautiful park. Here several dozen exceedingly well dressed patrons (many reserve a table far in advance!) will find an outstanding menu that features the finest gastronomic delights from around Europe, served in a classical French style with rich creamy sauces. Since their menu changes rather often, you might want to call them to see what is currently offered, but expect to spend a minimum of 105 NLG per person before adding wine to the bill. An excellent choice for the most demanding visitors that are looking for the finest cuisine in all of Rotterdam. Highly recommended!

*Expensive*
**RESTAURANT HARMONIE,** *Westersingel. 95. Tel: (10) 436-3610. All major credit cards accepted.*

With its tranquil old world wooden interior, this favorite haunt of local businessmen serves up a great menu of seasonally changing international specialties. On one my last visit, the menu featured tomato beef consommé at 13 NLG, a house special soufflé with green beans for 19.50 NLG, petits fours with shrimp at 28 NLG, grilled fresh fish of the day with lemon butter for 36.00 NG, filet of turbot truffle butter at 42 NLG, a daily vegetarian plate for 32.50 NLG, melon salad with marscarpone cheese mousse at 12 NLG, and special 3, 4, and 5 course gourmet menus from 52.50 NLG to 77.50 NLG per person.

**RESTAURANT DE CASTELLANE**, *Corner of Witt de Withstraat and Eendrachtsweg. Tel: (10) 414-1159. All major credit cards accepted.* This rather fancy and semi-formal gourmet restaurant near Museumpark has a fantastic menu of internationally inspired seasonal specialties. The last time I ate here, their superb menu included creamed bean and mussel salad with a curry vinaigrette at 17.50 NLG, light fish soup with scampi ravioli for 12.50 NLG, beef bouillon with mushroom mousse at 12.50 NLG, pate sautéed with leek in a shrimp bouillon for 32.50 NLG, Scottish salmon with shitake mushrooms at 44.50 NLG, stuffed rabbit with pistou for 39.50 NLG, tournedos of beef at 47.50 NLG, and a great selection of homemade pastries starting at 9.75 NLG each.

**OCEAN PARADISE CHINESE RESTAURANT**, *Parkhaven 21. Tel: (10) 436-1750. All major credit cards accepted.* This fancy looking but rather casual Chinese restaurant is built on a floating barge that is permanently moored in front of the Euromast tower. Besides offering great city and river views, this rather good restaurant offers a gigantic menu with over a hundred classic items such as shark fin soup at 4.50 NLG, won ton soup for 6.75 NLG, egg rolls at 5.50 NLG, fried rice noodles with pork at 22.50 NLG, stuffed eggplant with oyster sauce for 24.75 NLG, Chinese vegetables with garlic sauce at 18.50 NLG, roast suckling pig for 38 NLG, chicken with lemon sauce at 25.50 NLG, spicy spare ribs for 29.75 NLG, kung pao shrimp at 49.75 NLG, scallops with ginger and scallions for 49.75 NLG, and Peking duck at 47.50 NLG.

*Moderate*

**RESTAURANT ZINC**, *Calandstraat 12. Tel: (10) 436-6579. Cash only - No credit cards accepted.* Located around the corner from the charming Veerhaven harbor, this unique establishment serves up what may be the finest affordable gourmet cuisine in all of the city. Designed with a minimum of luxury and space, the interior of this amazing establishment seems to be based on an artist's studio, and is lined by crates of fresh seasonal vegetables, bare light bulbs, undecorated wooden tables, and a bustling open kitchen where Rob Basis practices his superior skills of culinary creation. Every night there is a totally different 3 or 4 course menu priced at around 50 NLG per person that will utilize a small selection of the day's freshest meat, poultry, and seafood specials. After your order is taken by the friendly staff here, the chef (usually standing just a few feet away) whips up an incredible main course that is both innovative and simply outstanding.

Since only about two dozen of Rotterdam's most fortunate residents (dressed in everything from jeans to Chanel outfits) can fit inside during their two evening sittings, reservations are almost always a must. Check this place out, and let me know if you can find a better meal at even double the price anywhere in the region! Highly recommended as the most memorable little restaurant in Rotterdam.

**CAFÉ LOOS**, *Westplein 1. Tel: (10) 411-7723. Most major credit cards Accepted.*

Located just off the Veerhaven harbor near the Museum Voor Volkenkunde, this delightfully casual grand café and bistro has a superb menu that features a fine selection of delicious dishes such as consommé with gnocchi for 8.50 NLG, salad with grilled scallops at 22.50 NLG, salmon in a creamy beer sauce for 26.50 NLG, Chinese vegetables with goat cheese at 12.50 NLG, assorted oysters starting at 18.50 NLG per dozen, a vegetarian daily special for 25.50 NLG, grilled tuna with percorino cheese sauce at 36 NLG, lasagna with meat for 19.75 NLG. At lunch the menu also features tomato soup with basil for 6 NLG, club sandwiches at 8 NLG, crab salad for 7.50 NLG, Maltese salads at 10.50 NLG, omelets starting at 12.75 NLG, quiche for 8.50 NLG, grilled rib eye steak at 25 NLG, lasagna with lamb meat and gorgonzola for 16 NLG, and much more. A great place to enjoy a good meal at reasonable prices!

**RESTAURANT NEW YORK**, *Koninginnenhoofd 1. Tel: (10) 439-0500. Most major credit cards accepted.*

This giant restaurant in the historic Holland-Amerika Lijn cruise ship terminal and office building across the water from the heart of the city offers giant lunch and dinner menus that have many surprises. Among the best items prepared by their team of skillful chefs are the farmer's soup at 5.50 NLG, veloute of mushrooms for 7.50 NLG, salad with warm goat cheese at 11.50 NLG, lamb salad for 14 NLG, mozzarella cheese with fresh basil and tomato at 12.50 NLG, shrimp cocktail for 13 NLG, deep fried sardines with lemon at 8.50 NLG, half lobster with cream sauce for 28.50 NLG, ragout of sweetbread in a puff pastry at 17 NLG, wild rabbit with green cabbage for 28 NLG, fricassee of scampi and chicken at 27 NLG, breast of duck in orange sauce for 25 NLG, fried trout in lemon butter at 22.50 NLG, omelet with fresh herbs for 7.50 NLG, quiche with leek and Roquefort cheese at 7.50 NLG, tiramisu for 8.50 NLG and honey cake soufflé at 8 NLG. This innovative menu has something to please everyone, and the ambiance alone is well worth the water taxi ride across the river to get here. Highly recommended, especially during sunny afternoons!

**MILLER'S RESTAURANT**, *Voorhaven 3, Delfshaven. Tel: (10) 477-5181. All major credit cards accepted.*

If you have just spent several hours strolling along the historic streets of Delfshaven, you deserve to treat yourself to a fine meal in one of this area's best intimate restaurants. Both floors of this old canal house now are home to a nice intimate restaurant featuring antique exposed beams and brickwork, candle topped tables, original artwork, and large picture windows facing the harbor.

Their menu features crab soup at 8.50 NLG, goat cheese salad with parma ham for 16.50 NLG, salad with home-made marinated salad at 14.50 NLG, a seafood stew with scallops for 18 NLG, lamb with shitake mushrooms at 33 NLG, grilled swordfish with garlic for 29.50 NLG, filet of red snapper in saffron sauce at 33 NLG, entrecote for 34.50 NLG, mocha tarts at 8.50 NLG, and plenty of fine wines and aperitifs by the glass. A nice little place to have a casual seafood lunch or dinner.

**HET HEERENHUYS DE HEUVEL**, *Baden Powelllaan 12. Tel: (10) 436-4249. Most major credit cards Accepted.*

Located in the beautiful park alongside the Euromast, this former 18th century manor house has been beautifully transformed into a great casual restaurant and café with one of the city's best outdoor terraces. You can enjoy either simple snacks at the café or more sophisticated full course meals in their adjacent opulent dining areas.

Menus include pasta with basil and smoked chicken at 11.50 NLG, goat cheese with chutney for 14.50 NLG, fresh grilled tuna filet at 33.50 NLG, a unique sesame seed topped lasagna at 32.50 NLG, grilled entrecote with pistachio butter for 39.50 NLG, vegetable tarts at 23 NLG, ricotta pudding with apricots for 13.50 NLG, and many more innovative dishes.

Their café has the best coffee in town and serves up affordable sandwiches, salads, and hearty pastas from about 6 NLG to 13.50 NLG each that are made with plenty of care. A great place to sit back and enjoy wonderful food in a really relaxed environment, especially at their outdoor park-side tables in the summertime. Advance reservations for indoor dining is strongly recommended.

### Inexpensive
**WESTER PAVILJOEN**, *Mathenesserlaan 155. Tel: (10) 436-2645. Cash only - No credit cards accepted.*

This casual yet chic café and restaurant on the corner of the Nieuwe Binnenweg has an open kitchen that prepares some of the tastiest lunches and dinners in this price range. Their extensive menu features winter salad with hazelnuts and blue cheese for 9 NLG, Caesar salad at 12.50 NLG, French onion soup for 5.50 NLG, club sandwiches at 8 NLG, roast beef sandwiches for 5.50 NLG, vegetarian daily special at 14.50 NLG, grilled beef steak for 20.50 NLG, a daily fish special at 17.50 NLG, oven baked chicken fillet with pesto for 17 NLG, grilled lamb chops with mint at 22.50 NLG, and a great selection of desserts, local and imported beers, and all sorts of wines by the bottle or carafe.

**CAFÉ BRASSERIE DUDOK**, *Meent 88. Tel: (10) 433-3102. All major credit cards accepted.*

This trendy ultra-modern café, bakery, and restaurant is a wonderful place to sit back and enjoy a great meal in extremely comfortable setting, and is open from the early morning hours through the late evening. Among the best items on their giant menu are French onion soup for 6.75 NLG, half melon with port sauce at 9.75 NLG, nicoise salads for 12.50 NLG, Greek salad at 12.75 NLG, gazpacho for 5.50 NLG, pasta with seasonal vegetables at 13 NLG, calamari with Cajun sauce for 9.75 NLG, assorted club sandwiches at 11.25 NLG, broccoli quiche for 8.75 NLG, burger plates at 6.75 NLG, vegetarian couscous for 15 NLG, mixed grill at 27 NLG, roast beef sandwiches for 6.50 NLG, and slices of the one-of-a-kind apple pie at 4.75 NLG.

**RESTAURANT DA SILVIO**, *Scheepstimmermanslaan 15. Tel: (10) 436-4478. All major credit cards accepted.*

The charming Mr. Da Silvio of southern Italy has recently opened this small little gem of an Italian pasta and pizza restaurant, just a few blocks up from the Veerhaven. Inside you will find seating for about 44 lucky patrons that can have a tough time deciding which of the home-made specialties is better than the others.

Choice specialties include fish soup at 10 NLG, cream of tomato soup for 6.50 NLG, over a dozen assorted pizzas starting at 10.50 NLG each, salmon carpaccio for 16 NLG, mixed salads at 4.50 NLG, lasagna for 16 NLG, cannelloni with spinach at 15 NLG, tagliatelle with cream sauce at 17.50 NLG, calamari for 22.50 NLG, and a vast selection of daily meat and fish specials starting at under 25 NLG. A great place to enjoy a truly affordable pasta lunch or a more upscale complete dinner.

**SORGH & HOOP**, *Nieuwe Binnenweg 9. Tel: (10) 436-2996. Cash only - No credit cards accepted.*

When you're in the mood for a spicy exotic meal, head over to this four floor Surinam-style restaurant just off the Binnenwegplein. Full of local students and office workers that know really good (and reasonably priced) food when they see it, Sorgh & Hoop offers a great big meals and fresh fruit cocktails that can be found no where else.

The four page menu includes fresh mango of the day at 3.50 NLG, vegetarian egg rolls for 5.50 NLG, marinated chicken sate at 7.50 NLG, cassava soup for 6.50 NLG, huge bowls of peanut soup with chicken and rice at 13.50 NLG, Javanese salads for 6.50 NLG, lamb curry at 10.50 NLG, complete roti meals with curried chicken for 21.50 NLG, fish specials starting at 19.50 NLG, and several dozen Surinam and Indonesian dishes that I could not even begin to translate starting at around 24 NLG each.

*Cheap*

**MESSINA PIZZERIA**, *Boompjes 388. Tel: (10) 433-3055. Cash only - no credit cards accepted.*

While far from fancy, this simple little Italian restaurant near the Imax theater offers a great selection of traditional cuisine prepared by a fun loving group of Italians that have moved to Rotterdam. Their menu includes assorted pizzas from 12.50 NLG and up, mozzarella cheese and tomato salad at 13.50 NLG, mixed salads for 7 NLG, tuna salad at 9 NLG, shrimp cocktail at 12.50 NLG, melon and prosciutto ham for 14.50 NLG, lasagna at 14.50 NLG, pasta with 4 cheeses for 15.50 NLG, spaghetti carbonara at 14.50 NLG, tortellini with gorgonzola sauce for 15.50 NLG, ravioli with pesto at 15 NLG, fried calamari for 22.50 NLG, chicken cacciatora at 14.50 NLG, and a nice tiramisu for 6.50 NLG. They will be even be glad to deliver these items directly to your downtown hotel room free of charge until 10:00pm.

**MAD MIC'S BREAKAWAY CAFÉ**, *Plaza Shopping Center on Weena. Tel; (10) 233-0922. Cash only - No credit cards accepted.*

This American-style bar and restaurant is the "Friday's" of Rotterdam. This place gets crowded after 5:00pm with the after work office crowd, and stays often much later with a young and rather hungry crowd of mostly singles. Their basic but hearty offerings include nachos for 11.50 NLG, Caesar salad at 8.50 NLG, Waldorf salad for 8.75 NLG, Buffalo wings at 12.75 NLG, chili burgers from 15.50 NLG, rack of ribs at 18.50 NLG, tuna sandwiches for 7.75 NLG, hot dogs at 4.75 NLG, and soup of the day for 5.50 NLG.

## SEEING THE SIGHTS

**TOUR 1**

• *From* **Centraal Station** *to the* **Oudehaven** *harbor and the* **Binnenwegplein***.*
• *Approximate duration (by foot) is about 6.5 hours, including museum, park, church, harbor, architectural monument, café, boutique, and side street visits.*

**Through the Downtown Shopping District**

After leaving through the front doors of the **Centraal Station**, keep walking straight ahead through the **Stationsplein** plaza with its bus, tram, and taxi stands. At the end of the square, cross the street and then turn left onto a wide avenue known as the Weena. Just off the corner you will find a well marked entrance leading into the modern **Plaza** shopping center complex. After walking into the mall you will pass along a food court, several boutiques, and the **Holland Casino**. On the far side of the shopping center an exit will take you back outside onto the Karel Doormanstraat, where you will turn to the right.

About a later block you will turn left onto the Kruiskade, and then make the first right turn onto the **Lijnbaan**. Designed by Jacob Bakema in the 1950's to become one of downtown's most active pedestrian-only shopping lanes, here you will find hundreds of low to medium-priced retail shops and boutiques that always seem to have sales.

About a block further up the Lijnbaan, take a left turn onto the **Stadhuisplein**. This unusually narrow plaza is home to several popular bars, pubs, and cafés that put up outdoor tables when the weather gets nice. At the far side of this plaza, there is a bronze statue of four local residents that signifies the strength that they needed to rebuild Rotterdam into a major city after it was almost totally destroyed in World War II.

### Along the Coolsingel

The square then terminates at the intersection of downtown's main boulevard, called the **Coolsingel**. Just at the near right hand corner you will find the main **VVV** tourist information center at building #67. This is where you can ask for directions, purchase public transportation tickets, find out about local events, and buy a great fold-out map of the city and its attractions for only 4 NLG.

From the tourist office you will carefully cross over Coolsingel and head towards the towering facade of the **Stadhuis** (City Hall) complex at building #40. Built from plans by Henry Evers in 1920, this awesome structure and its impressive bell tower is not generally open to the public. If, however, you quickly walk inside during normal weekday business hours, the guards will usually let visitors inside to gaze up at the entrance hall's magnificent double story marble rotunda that features stained glass windows and amazing brass lamps and railings. Just next to the city hall is the beautiful **Postkantoor** (Main Post Office), at building #42, that was built in the same period and boasts fine hand-painted and cofferred ceilings.

### Towards the Sint Laurenskerk Church

From the post office, continue down the Coolsingel until reaching the next corner where you will turn left onto a shopping street called Meent. While there are many nice shops and boutiques along Meent, the most impressive attraction is without doubt the **Café Brasserie Dudok** bar and restaurant at building #88. Designed by a famed local architect named Dudok, this ultra modern hang out for all kinds of locals was originally a bank building. Make sure to get a slice of their adjacent bakery's amazing apple pie before leaving the building. About another block down, the street crosses over a bridge and then you will bear right onto Oppert.

At the end of this lane you will find yourself entering the Grote Kerkplein. The massive late Gothic style church that can dominates this square is the 15th century **Sint Laurenskerk** church. Although badly damaged during the Nazi air bombing raids of Rotterdam on May 14th of 1940, the church was fully restored just after the war and contains several fine features including 3 amazing organs, vaulted wooden beam ceilings, stained glass windows, brass chandeliers, copper choirs screens, and thematic bronze entrance doors by Italian sculptor Giacomo Manzu.

Normally there are also special exhibits of modern sculpture and paintings, as well as black and white photographs of the devastation of the city during the war. *The church can be visited for free from 10:00am until 4:00pm from Tuesday through Saturday year round, and during the scheduled biweekly Sunday masses.*

### The Outdoor Market and the Oudehaven

After exiting the church, follow the adjacent Wijde Kerkstraat a few steps until making a left turn onto the Hoogstraat. From here this street leads directly into the **Markt** square along the **Binnenrotte**, the site of Rotterdam's gigantic Tuesday and Saturday **Outdoor Market**. This is one of the country's largest outdoor flea markets. You can stock up on everything from fresh cheese and produce to cheap clothing and sunglasses. The market is plenty of fun to visit any time of the year.

Surrounding the same huge market square there are several bizarre modern buildings that are all worth taking a good look at from this vantage point. Among my favorites are the seven story **Centrale Bibliotheek** public library directly in front of you, the towering pyramid topped **"Pencil Building"** next to it, and the UFO-shaped steel and glass **metro station** about a block away on the right. From this corner, bear right towards the strange looking metro station and just after passing the **Blaaktower** (also known locally as the "Pencil Building"), take a left turn on a small lane marked as the Prominade Overblaak. This lane leads up into the truly weird **Kijk-Kubus** cube house apartments. Built in 1956 from plans by architect Piet Blom, these world-famous experimental (and quite surrealistic) cube shaped four floor miniature houses are raised up off the ground by a series of concrete pillars and have a strange slant to them.

This is a good place to see how this city has become famous for unique urban planning and development schemes, and these cube houses are unique in the world. *A model cube apartment at unit #70 can be visited daily from 11:00am until 5:00pm, Friday through Saturday only in January and February, for a charge of 3.50 NLG per person.*

After walking through the model unit, walk through towards the back of the complex and you will soon find a terrace overlooking the **Oudehaven** (Old Harbor) area. This is the oldest remaining harbor in the city and has been lovingly reconstructed to show what it was like back in the 15th century. Surrounded by both modern and antique structures, the harbor front is lined by dozens of small cafés and restaurants that come to life in the warm months. A special open air museum type of exhibition, called the **Openlucht Binnenvaart Museum**, displays a wide variety of old wooden sailing ships for the public to view daily for free. As you descend the stairs to the harbor area, you can walk around the pier side terraces and can enjoy a refreshing drink or snack. After relaxing around the old ships for a while, follow Gelderskade along as it proceeds along the right side of the harbor and passes next to the towering white facade of the famed **Het Witte Huis** (White House) office building. Built in 1898 from plans by Willem Molenbroek, when completed it became Europe's tallest skyscraper and was fortunately spared by the bombing raids of 1940.

**Towards the Spido Dock**

Now continue along the Gelderskade until it reaches the riverside Maasboulevard, where you will take a sharp right turn. Soon the street name changes to Boompjes and after a few rather long blocks it comes to a bridge that crosses over the bottom of the Leuvehaven harbor. On the near side of this bridge is the departure point for the **Spido** harbor excursion boats that depart from the adjacent pier on an assortment of excursions throughout the year (see the *Guided Sightseeing Tours, By Boat* later in this section for more details).

Just after crossing the bridge, turn to the right and a few steps ahead on the side of the Leuvehaven harbor is the **Imax** theater. The Imax theater centers around a 360 degree domed movie screen where you can see screenings of special high tech and three dimensional films of nature, space, and exotic locations. These movies are accompanied by awesome digital soundtracks that blast out from a sound system with well over 20,000 watts. *The Imax theater presents short films year round from Tuesday through Sunday and costs 15 NLG per person to enter.*

**Towards the Leuvehaven Harbor area**

From the Imax theater you will walk up the street that follows alongside the **Leuvehaven** harbor for a couple of blocks while you happen upon the **Walk of Fame**, Rotterdam's answer to Hollywood's famed Walk of the Stars. Soon you will pass by buildings and piers that make up the **Maritiem Buitenmuseum** (Maritime Boat Museum) at Leuvehaven #50, where you can stroll alongside several old ships, cranes, grain elevators, anchors, and steam engines. This is a nice place to wander through when the weather is nice. During the warm months they also schedule a series of inexpensive boat excursions along the Maas river area. *The boat museum is open around the year, Monday through Friday from 10:00am until 4:00pm, Saturdays and Sundays from 12 noon until 4:00pm, and is free to enter.*

After popping by at the boat museum, keep walking up the side of the harbor for another half block until you reach a modern triangular structure at the near right corner that is home to the **Maritiem Museum Prins Hendrik**. Built in 1986 from plans by W.G. Quist, this maritime museum offers an array of exhibits detailing the life and times of voyages by sea. Inside there are old maps, scale models of sailing vessels, antique navigational instruments, and relics from the days when the harbor was developing into a major center of trade. Moored in the Leuvehaven harbor just behind the museum is a fully restored 19th century Dutch ironclad warship, called the *De Buffel* that can be visited to see a series of elegant cabins. *The museum is open year round from Tuesday through Saturday from 10:00am until 5:00pm, Sundays from 11:00am until 5:00pm, and admission is 6 NLG per person.*

From the maritime museum, make a right turn onto a wide avenue called Blaak. After about a block or so you will again turn right onto Posthoornstraat, which will lead you into the **Wijnhaven** harbor. Here, at Wijnhaven #20a, is the ultra-modern **Ships from Distant Lands Museum**. Once inside this floating museum, visitors can enjoy several large exhibits of antique and reproduction sailing vessels from around the globe. *The ship museum is open year round from Tuesday through Friday from 10:00am until 4:00pm, Saturday and Sunday from 12 noon until 5:00pm, and costs 5 NLG per person to enter.*

After leaving the ship museum, take the Poosthornstraat back to Blaak and cross the street before turning to the left. A block or so later you will turn right onto the Korte Hoogstraat. At building #31 of this street is the **Historisch Museum Het Schielandshuis** history museum. Housed inside a palatial restored 17th century white stone mansion designed by Jacob Lois, the museum contains a permanent collection dedicated to showcasing the culture and art of Rotterdam before the war.

There are four floors full of period furnishings, silver and gold works, traditional clothing, antique ceramic murals, and dozens of 17th through 19th century paintings that relate the history of the city. Among the highlights are the portraits of executives from the offices of the Dutch East India Company and several drawings by Atlas van Stolk. There are also seasonal temporary exhibitions that focus on specific elements of life here in the old days. *The history museum is open year round from Tuesday through Saturday from 10:00am until 5:00pm, Sundays from 11:00am until 5:00pm, and admission is 6 NLG per person.*

**Towards the Binnenwegplein Shopping District**
Once you have toured the history museum, retrace your steps back down to Blaak and turn right. At the next major intersection is the Churchillplein plaza. Now cross directly over to the other side of the plaza,

bear to the right, and walk up **Coolsingel**, the main boulevard cutting through the city's downtown core. After a couple of short blocks you can turn left onto the **Binnenwegplein**.

## THE BINNENWEGPLEIN - ROTTERDAM'S HOT SPOT!

*The **Binnenwegplein** is the city's most famous and enjoyable pedestrian-only shopping square. Lined by hundreds of department stores, fast food joints, boutiques, and bars, here you will get a good idea of how many of the local residents spend much of their free time during all hours of the day and night. Keep walking along the street for a few blocks until you can turn left at the first opportunity. After a few short blocks, the Binnenwegplein merges first into the **Oude Binnenweg**, and then into the **Nieuwe Binnenweg**, as they cut through the entire western side of Rotterdam. There are countless unusual designer boutiques, furniture stores, book shops, cafés, restaurants, nightclubs, striptease shows, "smoking" coffee shops, and pubs all along this thoroughfare.*

*Stroll along the first 10 blocks or so of these streets, but don't think about venturing beyond 'S Gravendijk street after dark, as petty crimes have been known to occur in frequently in those outlying districts. Check the restaurant and nightlife sections of this chapter for more information about several great (and totally safe) places to go around here.*

### TOUR 2
• *From the **Binnenwegplein** through **Museum Park**, and onward to **Delfshaven**.*
• *Approximate duration (by foot) is about 7 hours, including museum, park, harbor, café, boutique, gallery, church, windmill, and side street visits.*

### Towards the Witte de Withstraat
From the lower base of the Binnenwegplein, walk a few blocks up before turning left onto the Karel Doormanstraat. At the next intersection, the street name changes to the Hartmansstraat, and in one more block you will turn right onto **Witte de Withstraat**.

Among the highlights of this five block long street are the **Centrum van Hedenaagse Kunst Witte de With** (Witte de With Center for Contemporary Art) at building #50, where seasonal exhibits and lectures on the visual arts are held during various times of the year. *When exhibits are scheduled, the arts center is open Tuesday through Sunday from 11:00am until 6:00pm and they usually cost about 2.50 NLG per person to attend.* Across the street and up the block is the **Nederlands Foto Instituut** (Dutch Photography Institute) at building #63, where a wide variety of temporary exhibits of master photographers from around the globe. *When exhibits* *are scheduled, the photo institute is open Tuesday through Sunday from 11:00am until 6:00pm and they usually cost about 2.50 NLG per person to enter.*

## THE SOHO OF ROTTERDAM

*Witte de Withstraat is one of the city's most entertaining streets to visit day or night. Similar in ambiance to New York's bohemian Soho and Greenwich Village districts, here there are dozens of galleries, museums, theaters, rare book shops, and restaurants that draw an eclectic mix of local artists and entertainers. At night, over a dozen bars and clubs on this street and its intersecting lanes tend to fill up with every possible type of party animal. There are also restaurants in every price range, including a few that stay open way past midnight. This is a great area for art lovers to wander around, and even late at night it is usually rather safe due to the nearby police station.*

### Through the Museumpark

The Witte de Withstraat ends its intersection with the Eendrachtsweg and the street then changes name to become Mathenesserlaan. A short distance later on your left hand side will be an entrance to the **Museumpark**, a park that contains four major museums and art exhibition spaces. The first and most important building that you will pass while in the park and museum complex is called the **Museum Boymans-van Beuningen** art museum at Museumpark #18. Known primarily for its amazing array of 14th through 20th century masterpieces, this museum is loaded to the brim with fantastic works by some of the world's most famous artists.

Named after two local art connoisseurs that donated their private collections to the city, this is without a doubt the most impressive art museum in Rotterdam. Although the permanent collection is frequently rotated to make room for various temporary exhibits, the building is divided into the following four separate sections.

The museum's fantastic **Old Masters** section usually features such works as *The Tower of Babel* by Pieter Brueghel, *Three Marys at the Open Sepulcher* by Jan and Hubert van Eyck, *The Vagabond* by Hieronymus Bosch, *Portrait of Titus* by Rembrandt, the *Achilles* series by Rubens, and assorted paintings by others such as Titian, Frans Hals, Pieter Aertsen, Hans Memling, Pieter Saenredam, Gerrit Dou, and Jan van Scorel.

Over at the **Modern Art** section, there are several well-known paintings and sculptures, including *Impressions of Africa* by Salvador Dali, *The Red Model* by Rene Magritte, *Self Portrait with a Pen* by Carel Willink, *Mother and Child* by C.J. Constant, and hundreds of other remarkable pieces by Van Gogh, Richard Serra, Monet, Sisley, Pissaro, Max Ernst, Kandinsky, Giorgio de Chirico, and Mondrian.

During your walk through the **Prints and Drawings** department, you will find a large amount of perfectly preserved 16th through 20th century prints, drawings, and etchings, like *Two Feet* by Albrecht Durer, *Cambodian Dancers* by Rodin, *Recumbent Lion* by Rembrandt, and other selections from Leonardo da Vinci, Goya, Manet, Cezanne, and Picasso.

The **Applied Art and Design** areas feature an unusual assortment of fine furnishings, glassware, earthenware, modern decorative art, grandfather clocks, industrial design, and works in precious metals. All around the building there are inner courtyards lined with statuary, limited access research libraries, study rooms, lecture halls, and rooms used for special events and temporary exhibits. For those who wish to buy art books and postcards, there is also a great museum shop. *The art museum is open year round from Tuesday through Sunday from 10:00am until 5:00pm and costs 7.50 NLG per person to enter, plus additional charges for their fine temporary exhibits.*

Across the street from the art museum is the **Nederlands Architectuurinstituut** (Dutch Institute of Architecture) at Museumpark #25. Located in a rather modern building designed by Jo Coenen, this museum and center of learning (known locally as the **N.A.I.**) has four exhibition rooms filled with illustrations of Dutch and international architecture. A specialized library and research center can also be visited, and lecture series are often hosted by world famous experts in the fields of urban development, landscape, and interior design. *The architecture institute is open around the year on Tuesday through Sunday from 10:00am until 5:00pm and costs 7.50 NLG per person to enter.*

Further into the park a road leads past several green areas and then heads for the **Kunsthal Rotterdam** exhibition building at Westzeedijk #341. This is the sight of major seasonal touring art shows and since the exhibitions change so often an exact description of its current events and contents is not possible. Check with the VVV tourist office or the ticket counter to see what exactly is going on here during your visit. *The art exhibition building is open during assorted special events throughout most of the year on Tuesday through Sunday from 10:00am until 5:00pm and costs 7.50 NLG per person to enter.*

Also on this side of the park is the **Natuurmuseum Rotterdam** natural history museum at Westzeedijk #345. This small museum features exhibits about the nature and environment of Holland. While far from exciting, it is a good place for those interested in seeing stuffed birds, unusual mammals, and a few excavated bones from prehistoric creatures. *The natural history museum is open year round on Tuesday through Sunday from 10:00am until 5:00pm and costs 3 NLG per person to enter.*

**Around the Scheepvaartkwartier & the Veerhaven harbor**

Depart the Museumpark via the exit alongside the Kunsthal and then turn left onto Westzeedijk. After walking a few blocks make a right turn onto Scheepstimmer Maanslaan. About 2 blocks down this street you will make a left turn down Westerstraat and follow it until it ends at the river front. Now turn right onto Willemskade and soon you will reach the **Museum Voor Volkenkunde** ethnology museum at building #25. This is one of the city's best little museums and features great multimedia shows, photographs, art, and artifacts from all over the world. Although they always have rather interesting temporary exhibits, you can expect to find displays musical instruments, tribal masks, folk art, religious symbols, weapons, and other objects reflecting the ways of life in far off lands. *The ethnology museum is open throughout the year on Tuesday through Sunday from 10:00am until 5:00pm and costs 7.50 NLG a head to enter.*

After exiting the ethnology museum, turn right and walk to the end of this street and bear right onto Veerkade to follow the waterfront along the side of the charming little **Veerhaven** harbor. This is the center of the picturesque **Scheepvaartkwartier** warehouse district that was spared from the ravages of Nazi bombs. The harbor itself is now home to the permanent mooring of a several old wooden sailing ships that once plied European waters. At the edge of the harbor is an exclusive private men's club, and the dock next to it is the point of departures and arrivals for the Water Taxi boats that head for the Hotel New York in the strange looking Holland America Line building across the river.

---

**BY WATER TAXI TO THE HOTEL NEW YORK**

*This harbor-side quay is the sight of the Water Taxi boats that go across the Nieuwe Maas river and disembark at the **Hotel New York**. Housed in the art deco former **Holland Amerika Lijn** headquarters on the Wilhelmina pier of the **Kop Van Zuid** peninsula, this strange establishment is one of the most delightful (and least known) attractions in town. Once the site of transcontinental passenger ship terminals, this whole area has been slated for massive urban development programs and recreation zones. The 7 NLG round trip fare per person for a very scenic 8 minute ride on a small boat across the river is well worth the money, especially at around sunset when you can sit in the hotel's extraordinary café and restaurant. Normal operating hours for the water taxis are about every half hour or so in both directions between 9am and 12 midnight daily.*

---

Follow along the top edge of the harbor as the street name changes to the Westerplein and then merges into the **Parklaan**. At building #14 of this street is the **Professor Van der Poel Museum** (Dutch finance and taxation museum). Inside this building you will find a varied assortment of exhibits relating to modern and historic methods of tax collection. There are displays of old coins, weapons, tax documents, Egyptian-era Papyrus tax audit scrolls, old prints and paintings relating to tax collection and gin smugglers, and even several items taken from pirates. *The finance museum is open year round on Tuesday through Sunday from 11:00am until 5:00pm and is free to visit.*

About a half block up, Parklaan will then lead you directly into the **Park de Huevel** (also known as the Park Zochers) recreation area with many little ponds, bicycle paths, and walking trails. There are even a few romantic restaurants and a large disco scattered around the park. Walk through this romantic park towards the giant **Euromast**. This modern telecommunications tower was originally built in 1960 from plans by local architect H. Maaskant.

Ten years after the concrete and steel tower was completed, a Swiss firm was hired to add on the so-called Space Tower observation deck that made this the tallest structure in the Netherlands at a height of 185 meters (611 feet). Visitors can take a high speed elevator to a great panoramic viewing area and a restaurant. *The Euromast is open daily year round from 10:00am until 5:00pm during the winter and 7:00pm during the summer, and the admission price with an elevator ride costs 14.50 NLG per person.*

Just in front of the tower is a floating Chinese restaurant, and next to it are a series of piers and docks that are the sight of several boat excursion rides, such as the **Flying Dutchman** hydrofoil that departs only during the warmer months. For more details about excursion boats and hydrofoil rides, see *Guided Sightseeing Tours* later in this chapter.

**Towards Historic Delfshaven**

From the Euromast turn right onto the canal front Parkhaven, and follow it until you can turn left to cross over the Parkhavenbrug draw-bridge. After crossing the bridge, walk straight along the right hand side of Westzeedijk for about two long blocks until turning right onto a small lane called the Pieter de Hoochweg. About a block and a half later you will then turn left onto the wide Willem Buytewechstraat and keep walking along this small avenue until crossing over the Achterhavenbrug draw-bridge. At the other side of the bridge, the street name changes to the Havenstraat; take a left turn at the second corner onto the quaint little Voorstraat and head into the historic **Delfshaven** district.

The first notable sight on the quayside **Voorstraat** is the shuttered 17th century waterfront **Zakkendragershuisje** (Grain Sack Carriers Guild House) at building #13. Once the offices of local porters that offloaded sacks of grain from the moored ships that docked along the **Voorhaven** canal and harbor behind this structure, the building has since been converted into a tin foundry with an interesting tin shop. *The former guild* *house and its foundry can be visited for free year round on Tuesday through Friday from 10:15am until 5:00pm, Saturdays and Sundays from 11:00am until 4:30pm.*

---

### CHIC DELFSHAVEN!

*The Delfshaven was originally a separate port village with a quay where the Dutch Pilgrims departed Holland on their way to America in 1620. The village later prospered as a port area serving the needs of the Dutch East India Company and several smaller Delft-based shipping companies. By 1886, this area was swallowed up by Rotterdam and has recently become a rather chic residential area filled with expensive yuppie condos and upscale retail businesses that thrive on the tourist trade. Since it was not of any real strategic significance, it was spared from the destruction of World War II bombing raids and has been developed into a major tourist attraction. Many of the 17th through 19th century warehouses and former distilleries along this area have recently been converted into delightful boutiques, art and crafts galleries, seafood restaurants, and trendy cafés. While this tour will only cover the highlights of the Delfshaven district, you should take at least three hours to wander around its little side streets and piers.*

---

A few steps further, this charming street lined with plenty of fine gabled canal houses changes its name to the **Aelbrechtskolk**. On the left hand side of the lane at building #20 you will find a cute 16th century pinnacle topped chapel known as the **Oude Pilgrim Kerk** (Old Pilgrim Fathers Church) at building #20. Open for public viewing throughout the day, this was the house of worship that was used by Pilgrims before they sailed for the New World in 1620 and eventually founded their settlement in Massachusetts.

From here the street name once again changes to the **Voorhaven**, where you find several fine shops including an amusing **Antieke Clokken** antique clock store and restoration center at building #4. Then you will pass a couple of interesting houseboat restaurants before reaching the **De Dubbelde Palmboom** (Double Palm Tree) museum at building #12. This converted five story 19th century warehouse now exhibits antiques, crafts, photographs, scale models, and other relics that depict the ways of life and commerce along the river from the middle ages to the present time. Up in the attic there is a great inexpensive café with fine views out on the harbor. *The museum is open throughout the year (although it has recently been known to shut down for renovations during the low seasons) on Tuesday through Saturday from 10:00am and 5:00pm, Sundays from 1:00pm and 5:00pm, and costs 6 NLG per person to enter.*

At the end of this street you can take a peek at the old **Molen de Distilleerketel** windmill that was used to grind grain for the local distilleries. From the windmill, retrace your steps back down the street until turning left to cross over the first wooden bridge that spans this narrow harbor. From here you can cross over either of the two charming bridges that lead on to the other side of the Voorhaven harbor. Make the effort to stroll around the harbor's special open air museum of sorts called the **Openlucht Binnenvaart Museum**. *This exhibit displays a wide variety of old wooden sailing ships for the public to view daily for free here.*

This side of the harbor is lined with dozens of antique shops, galleries, restaurants, cafés, and bars that become busy only in the warmer months. Among the highlights here is the **Museum Andries de Potter** ceramics museum at building #19, and several converted distilleries that now contain good eating establishments.

## GUIDED SIGHTSEEING TOURS
### By Boat

A few local companies offer guided tours of the city's harbor and nearby suburbs via hydrofoil, ferry, and steamboat cruises. While these excursions (narrated by either a multilingual guide or a tape recording) do not stop to let you get on and off during the ride, this fun way to get a glimpse of Rotterdam's waterfront and famous harbor while here. The boats themselves have either glass-enclosed or open air seating areas and can accommodate well over 250 people comfortably, even during the winter when they are heated.

**The Flying Dutchman** company offers two different hydrofoil sightseeing cruises during the high season. Their excursion **FD 804** is a 45 minute trip through the **Botlek**, the world's largest harbor area. It runs every hour on the half hour from 11:30am until 4:30pm on Wednesdays through Sundays between June 14th and September 17th. During the somewhat slower seasons between April 19th and June 11th as well as between September 20th until October 29th it departs every hour on the half hour from 11:30am until 4:30pm on Wednesday, Thursday, and Sunday only. The price is 14.50 NLG per person, and the boats leave from the Parkhaven docks in front of the Euromast tower.

Their other scheduled excursion, **FD 805**, travels along the river for 90 minutes as it passes alongside the nearby coastal communities of Dordrecht, Rhoon, Spijkenisse, and Hoogvliet before heading back to Rotterdam via the Botlek area and the world's largest harbor. The price is 34.50 NLG per person including a sandwich lunch and departs on Saturdays only at 11:30am from June 17th until September 16th, and also leaves from the Parkhaven dock in front of the Euromast tower.

For complete schedule and reservation details, contact either the VVV tourist office, or Flying Dutchman directly at *Tel: (10) 436-1222*.

**Holland International's** year round **Spido** ferry harbor excursions offer 75 minute sightseeing trips around the city's port daily on a year round basis for 12.50 NLG per person. The same company has a series of half day, full day, and candlelit dinner and dancing cruises that depart on various days and times during the high season schedule and cost between 21 NLG and 97.50 NLG per person depending on the exact trip you wish to take. These trips almost all leave from the Spido boat dock on the Leuvehaven harbor near the Imax theater.

For exact schedules and specific information about what is available during you stay in Rotterdam, contact either the VVV tourist office, or call Spido directly at *Tel: (10) 413-5400*.

**By Foot**

A group of knowledgeable native residents have started a company called **Walks through Rotterdam**, and now run a series of guided walking tours (in English and Dutch) through various areas of the city including the old harbors, modern architectural structures, galleries, boutiques, parks, artistic monuments, unique neighborhoods, and quaint side streets. They list three different tours at 9:30am, 12:15pm, and 3:00pm that all leave from the Engels brasserie at Stationsplein #45 (adjacent to Centraal Station) and continue for about 140 minutes.

These trips are given daily except for Thursday for a limit of 15 individuals, and reservations should be booked by calling *Tel: (10) 404-8339* from 6pm until 8pm at least one day in advance. The current fee for each participant is 15 NLG and includes a half hour break.

## NIGHTLIFE & ENTERTAINMENT
### Bars, Pubs, & Grand Cafés
**CAFÉ LOOS**, *Westplein 1. Tel: (10) 411-7723.*

For those looking for a relaxing and sophisticated grand café that also serves fine food, check out this hot spot near the Veerhaven harbor. The Café Loos has a split level bar and restaurant sections where you can listen to fine jazz and soft rock music and meet plenty of the city's more affluent 25 to 35 year olds.

**ROTOWN**, *Nieuwe Binnenweg 19. Tel: (10) 436-2669.*

Rotown is a busy bohemian-style bar that hosts occasional live concerts. Located steps away from the Binnenwegplein, the drinks here are both cheap and strong, and people are usually under 25 and into black leather jackets and hard core rock and roll. There are plenty of tables to sit down and people-watch, as well as a long bar where you will end up talking to people you have never met.

**HOTEL NEW YORK**, *Koninginnehofd 1. Tel: (10) 439-0525.*

This spectacular Art Nouveau grand café and oyster bar in the former Holland-Amerika Lijn building is perhaps the most memorable place to enjoy an early evening cocktail. Located just an eight minute ride by water taxi across the river from downtown, the Hotel's bar is a wonderful place to bring someone special!

**CLUB DE POEL**, *Eendrachtsweg 28. Tel: (10) Unlisted.*

It would be hard to imagine a more welcoming place to spend a few hours than this unusual three floor bar, smoking coffeeshop, café, and billiard hall. Located steps away from the Witt de Withstraat, the club plays great music and attracts a good mix of single 20 to 25 year olds. The ambiance is casual and friendly. Make sure to climb up the stairs to hang out on all three levels. A great place for those looking to meet nice locals!

**JAZZCAFE DIZZY**, *'S Gravendijkwal 127. Tel: (10) 477-3014.*

Dizzy is a fun and intimate jazz club and tapas bar near the Nieuwe Binnenweg that offers a wide array of free and inexpensive live jazz concerts several days a week. Even when there is no live music, their sound system plays great classic and international jazz tunes for its young and mellow crowd.

**LE VAGABOND**, *Nieuwe Binnenweg 99. Tel: (10) Unlisted.*

If you want to meet the typical 20 to 30 year old crowd of neighborhood locals, this simple pub is a great spot. The drinks are strong and cheap, and the discussions range from philosophy to the benefits of remaining permanently unemployed with full benefits. A good place to start off a long night of drinking.

**BAJA BEACH CLUB**, *Karel Doormanstraat 6. Tel: (10) Unlisted.*

Popular with both locals and visitors, this famous local night spot features scantily dressed male and female bartenders (mostly models) that get up on the bar and start dancing between serving rounds of drinks. This is definitely a serious pick-up spot for the 18 to 35 year old single crowd, but most people here are trying to get their paws on the staff, mostly imported from America. The music here ranges from Madonna to George Michael, and the ambiance is truly tasteless yet fun! Get here before 11:45pm or you may have problems entering.

**BIG BEN**, *Stadhuisplein. Tel: (10) Unlisted.*

This huge but welcoming English-style pub is the sight of some of Rotterdam's best action for single people, especially when the weather gets warm and the outdoor tables are packed. In any case, on weekend nights there is a friendly crowd of local and commuting students and young adults that are here to meet people and perhaps find someone to spend the night with! They play great music from the 60's to the 90's, and the rather strong drinks here are a real bargain.

**SENSI CAFÉ**, *Neuwe Binnenweg 181. Tel: (10) 436-4765.*

The Sensi Café is the best "smoking" coffee shop in the city, and also offers occasional free rock and reggae concerts as well as other stoned out special events. Everyone at this place gets totally blasted out of their minds, and usually start here before heading off to other nearby drinking establishments afterwards.

### Discos & Dance Clubs

Most of the discos and dance clubs in Rotterdam are much less difficult and cheaper to enter than their counterparts in Amsterdam. In fact, the average admission price here is just 10 NLG (and even free in some places) and the doormen generally do not refuse entry to anyone. The best nights to hit a disco here are usually on Thursdays (Student Night), Fridays, Saturdays, and holidays. When you enter you may be expected to pass through a metal detector, pay 1 NLG to leave your jacket at the mandatory coat check, and order drinks that tend to run about double the normal price you would expect to pay in a local bar. Closing times range from 3:00am until 5:00am, depending on the night and the specific event scheduled.

**DANSE SALON**, *Maasboulevard 300. Tel: (10) 414-4393*

The Dance Salon is currently Rotterdam's hottest dance club, and gets totally packed with over 1,000 provocatively dressed clubbies on Thursday through Saturday nights until the wee hours of the morning. Located in the basement of a river-front building a few blocks away from the Oudehaven, expect to pay around 10 NLG to get in, and dress as well as possible. The music is a mixture of house and techno.

**PARKZEIST**, *Park Zochers. Tel: (10) 436-3558*

This old mansion style brick building in the park behind the Euromast is one of the city's most active discos. Packed to the gills on weekend nights after 11:15pm or so, the Parkzeist has a mixed crowd of university aged locals dressed in every imaginable way. The music here changes depending on who the DJ is that night, but it is a good place to hang out and dance for a while.

**LEVEL**, *Eendrachtsweg 27. Tel: (10) Unlisted.*

This medium-sized disco just of the Witte de Withstraat offers low cover charges and a serious crowd that really knows how to hit the dance floor. The music is super fast house and techno each night, and it is open until rather late in the evening.

### Multipurpose & Live Music Venues

These establishments offer live concerts several nights a week, but in some cases will also offer a variety of other events such as dance parties, live theater performances, and special theme nights. Use the phone numbers listed below to find out what is scheduled, or ask at any local record store or at the Rotterdam VVV tourist office for a free copy of the *M Magazijn* monthly entertainment magazine.

**NIGHTTOWN**, *West Kruiskade 28. Tel: (10) 436-1210*

This large multilevel dance club commonly hosts live rock concerts by independent and major label bands from all over the world. Typically frequented by local students dressed in jeans, the doormen here are fairly good about letting you in. There is a cover charge than can cost around 12.50 NLG or so, and to enter on Thursdays you must hold a local university card.

**PODIUM PLAN C**, *Slepersvest 1. Tel: (10) 412-4352*

Located alongside the Oudehaven and under the Kijk-Kubus cube house complex, this multi-purpose disco/live music venue/theater/café offers a wide variety of rock, jazz, and blues concerts on Wednesday through Saturday nights, as well as disco dancing on Sunday night. On most nights there is little or no entry fee, and the typically casual 20 to 30 year old patrons are much more laid-back than the over zealous security staff.

## PRACTICAL INFORMATION

**Main VVV Tourist Office** - *Coolsingel 67* - *(10) 402-3200*
**Rotterdam Radio Dispatched Taxis** - *(10) 462-6060*
**International Train Schedules** - *(10) 411-7100*
**Domestic Train and Bus Info** - *(6) 9292*
**RET Municipal Transit Head Office** - *Kleiweg 244* - *(10) 447-5591*
**American Express Travel Services** - *Meent 92* - *(10) 433-0300*
**Rotterdam Chamber of Commerce** - *Beursplein 37* - *(10) 405-7777*
**Rotterdam City Hall** - *Stadhuis-Coolsingel 40* - *(10) 417-9111*
**Rotterdam Main Post Office** - *Coolsingel,42* - *(10) 454-2221*
**Rotterdam Police Headquarters** - *Haagse Veer 23* - *(10) 424-2911*
**Police Emergencies** - *(10) 414-1414*
**Medical Emergencies** - *(10) 411-5504*
**Emergency Hotline** - *06-11*

# 15. DEN HAAG - THE HAGUE

The diplomatic town of **Den Haag** – The Hague – seat of the Dutch government, is one of the calmest and most elegant cosmopolitan centers in all of Holland. Home to several members of the royal family including the Queen, The Hague is a safe and enchanting destination to spend at least a few days in while you walk along small lanes that lead to fantastic mansions, palaces, museums, restaurants, and boutiques.

You may see thousands of suited professionals walking to and from their offices in the wide array of governmental, political, and banking concerns, but this is not as conservative of a town as you may first think. In fact, as soon as their work is done, most residents shed their suits and ties before heading out (in various states of undress) to the nearby beaches of **Schevenginen**, or instead gather in a wide variety of local pubs when the weather is a bit colder.

Hundreds of great sights and attractions are well within walking distance from each other, and there are dozens of well preserved residential and commercial districts that are all well worth wandering around. Make sure that during your stay you explore the **Denneweg** and **Noordeinde** shopping streets, the **Binnenhof** parliamentary complex, the amazing **Mauritshuis** museum, the 16th century **De Grote of St. Jacobskerk** church, the impressive old world **Hotel Des Indes**, the **Passage** shopping arcade, the **Plaats** and **Plein** squares, and the nearby beaches.

## DEN HAAG'S HISTORY

The history of Den Haag dates back to the year 1247, when Count William II was declared King of the Romans by the Pope. He soon decided to expand a rural country lodge built by his father (Count Floris IV) into a castle that would become the Binnenhof, the official residence of the Counts of Holland. By the mid-15th century, one small village sprang up around the castle walls, while another grew around the Grote Kerk church and the old city hall. Soon these villages merged into one large town known as Den Haag, and the combined area became the official capital of the government. For close to 200 years this new village expanded in both population and slow but steady economic prosperity. As the late 17th century approached, wealthy diplomats and noblemen constructed dozens of palatial mansions near the castle and helped to increase the town's status as a major center of political power and decision making.

After Napoleon took over the republic in 1806, his brother Louis Bonaparte moved the capital to Amsterdam. Once French control of the county ended, the House of Orange returned from exile to crown William I as the King of the Netherlands in 1814. The king almost immediately brought the seat of the government back to Den Haag, although Amsterdam still retained its designation as the nation's capital.

The town once again prospered, and was to become the site of several important peace conferences, international tribunals, and other major diplomatic meetings. Since industry was never a large part of the local economy, Den Haag also developed a reputation as a center for international business and banking, an industry that in one way or another still supports a large number of local residents. While never actually acquiring the status of a chartered city, this so-called "Largest Village in Europe" is still the home to the royal family.

## THE NORTH SEA JAZZ FESTIVAL

*While Den Haag is the sight of many special events and festivals around the year, it has become well known for hosting the spectacular **North Sea Jazz Festival**. Held each year at the city's huge **Nederlands Congresgebouw** in mid-July, this event is the kick-off point for the European concert tours of many of the world's finest jazz and fusion bands. The weeks preceding the festival are also marked by several surprise concerts that allow the participating musicians to practice their sets in small clubs around town before performing at this and other festivals. If you intend to visit the area during this great event, make sure to book your hotel reservations far in advance!*

## ORIENTATION

Den Haag (also known both as **'s-Gravenhage**) is located just off the coast along the western edge of the **Zuid-Holland** province of the Netherlands, and has a population of 448,356. It lies 57 kilometers (35 miles) southwest of the capital city of Amsterdam, and 26 kilometers (16 miles) northwest of Rotterdam.

## ARRIVALS & DEPARTURES

### By Air

Almost all visitors flying to this city will arrive here via land links from the much larger **Schiphol Airport** near Amsterdam, about 48 kilometers (30 miles) to the northeast.

### By Bus

Many of the bus lines between Den Haag and other parts of Holland as well as the rest of Europe tend to stop at the depot just behind the **Centraal Station** train depot on the eastern edge of downtown. Make sure to call in advance to find out exactly where and when your bus comes in (for phone numbers, see *Practical Information* section at the end of this chapter). Connections between this station and any other point in Den Haag can generally be made by the adjacent public bus or tram stops for 3 NLG per person each way, or via taxi for roughly 13.75 NLG or so, depending on where you are going.

### By Car

Downtown street-side parking spots are reasonably hard to find.

From **Amsterdam**, the easiest way to get to Den Haag is to take the **A-10** ring road around until connecting to the **A-4** south for about 43 kilometers (27 miles) before exiting onto the **A-12** west for about 8 kilometers (5 miles) until finding the "Centrum" exit.

From **Rotterdam** you should take the **E-19** ring road west until connecting to **A-13** north for some 13 kilometers (8 miles), then exit onto the **A-4** north for about 4 kilometers (2.5 miles), then follow the **A-12** west for about 8 kilometers (5 miles) until finding the "Centrum" exit.

The HTM local transit authority also offers a special reduced rate **StrandExpres Combikaart** park and ride program. This new system allows visitors driving into the city for a summertime day trip to the beaches at Scheveningen to use the parking lot at Centraal Station and take the tram to and from the beach, all for just 11 NLG per carload. For specific details, contact the HTM at *(70) 342-9292 or (70) 384-8586*, or just pop into one of their kiosks at the local train stations.

### By Train

Den Haag is linked to almost every other point in Holland and Europe by several major rail lines. There are two different rail stations, each with its own series of daily arrivals and departures. Those arriving here directly from Schiphol Airport can also take advantage of frequent rail service linking these destinations, sometimes via a mandatory change of train at the suburban Den Haag **HS** (Holland Spoor) rail station.

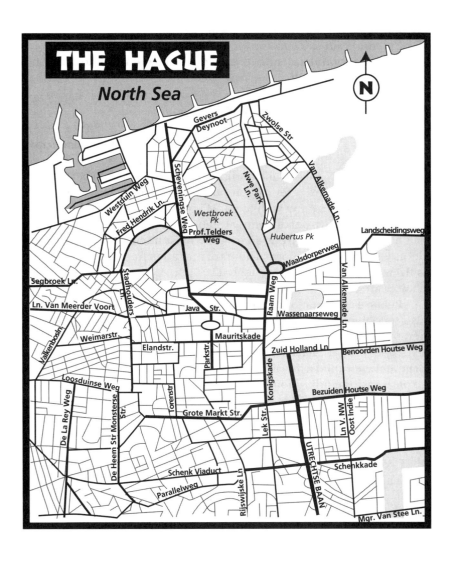

The best location for service to and from downtown Den Haag is via the large **Centraal Station** train depot at the eastern edge of the city's downtown section. Connections between this station and any other point in Den Haag can generally be made by the adjacent public bus and tram stops for around 3 NLG per person each way, or via taxi for roughly 13.75 NLG or so depending on where you are going.

Use the train information phone numbers listed in the *Practical Information* section at the end of this chapter to reconfirm, in advance, the exact time and station that you may need.

## GETTING AROUND TOWN

### The Public Transportation System

Den Haag's **HTM** (Haagsche Tramweg-Maatschappij) municipal transit authority offers a vast array of public transportation methods to get you safely and easily around town, and all the way to both Scheveningen and Delft. There are a few dozen bus and tram lines to choose from depending on where you wish to go. Many of these vehicles stop at one point or another in front of Centraal Station. Just keep in mind that buses can be entered via the front door, while most trams have several entry doors you can use. The normal hours of operation for most of the system is from about 6:30am until roughly 11:30pm. After this time, your only choices are either to walk, or to take a taxi.

Public transportation accepts **Nationale Strippen Kaarts**. There are also special local **Travelcards** that offer unlimited travel on the busses and trams, priced at 15.25 NLG for two days, and 17.75 NLG for three days, and 3.75 for each additional day up to a total of nine days. Rides to Scheveningen and Delft will require passing through more than 1 zone, so please ask the driver how many strips to validate. To get free copies of the extremely useful HTM public transit system maps entitled *Lijnennet Kaart*, just pop into the VVV office *(Koningin Julianaplein 30, Tel: (6) 340-35051)* or the HTM office *(Wagenstraat 35, Tel: (70) 342-9292 )*.

### By Taxi

There are over a hundred licensed taxis roaming the streets and major passenger arrival points of the city during all hours of the day and night. Drivers here are frequently dressed in suits and own or operate expensive Mercedes and Renault sedans and station wagons, and carry cellular phones in order to better serve the demanding diplomatic and banking industry clientele that they have built up over the years. These typically multilingual taxi drivers are extremely honest, and can tell you more than a few great stories. To find a taxi, either hail down an unoccupied cab driving by with its "Taxi" roof light illuminated, go to one of the dozens of obvious taxi stands throughout the city, or call *(70) 364-2828* for a radio response pick-up on demand.

The main taxi ranks are located at the Buitenhof, the Centraal Station, Holland Spoor Station, and in front of the Hotel des Indes. During rainy days, festivals, trade fairs, or weekday morning and evening rush hours (8am until 10am and 6pm until 8pm) there may be a short wait until you get lucky. Taxi meters charge at about the rate of 3.75 NLG per kilometer, so this works out to somewhere around 10.50 NLG to 15.50 NLG per ride (not per person) between most downtown locations depending on exact distance and traffic conditions. Over 20% of the city's taxis now accept major credit cards for fare payments!

## WHERE TO STAY

*Very Expensive*

**INTER-CONTINENTAL HOTEL DES INDES**, *Lange Voorhout 54. Tel: (70) 363-2932. Fax: (70) 345-1721. US & Canada Bookings (Inter-Continental) 1-800-327-0200. Special weekend rates from 320 NLG per double room per night (B.P.). Year round rack rates from 505 NLG per double room per night (E.P.). All major credit cards accepted.*

If you are looking for the most prestigious and historic accommodations in all of Den Haag, Inter-Continental's deluxe 5 star Hotel des Indes fits the bill. Located just across the street from the Paleis Lange Voorhout and steps away from the famed Denneweg shopping street, this is one of Holland's most luxurious city center properties. As soon as you walk through the front doors and step inside the opulent two story grand salon, you can't help but feel like you are the guest of the Baron that originally lived in this former mansion. The beautiful public spaces here are filled with exotic hardwoods, imported marbles, fine wrought-iron grillwork, hand cut crystal chandeliers, plush antique furnishings, and magnificent works of art.

The hotel offers 76 large classically styled rooms and suites that all contain deluxe private bathrooms, remote control satellite television, mini-bar, direct dial telephone, mini-safe, electric trouser press, extremely comfortable period furnishings, and large windows with either interior or historic street views. The hotel also offers a posh afternoon tea (especially interesting on Sundays), a fine gourmet restaurant, one of the most elaborate bars I have ever seen, business meeting rooms, express laundry and dry cleaning, a valet, full concierge service, secured parking, room service, a serious ballroom, and a top notch staff. The ambiance here is private, formal, and unusually tranquil, with a guest list that will leave most people totally awestruck. If only the best will satisfy you, this is definitely the place to stay while in The Hague!

**HOTEL KURHAUS**, *Gevers Deynootplein 30, Scheveningen. Tel: (70) 416-2636. Fax: (70) 416-2646. US & Canada Bookings (SRS Hotels) 1-800-223-5652. Special weekend rates from 380 NLG per double room per night (B.P.). Year round rack rates from 440 NLG per double room per night (E.P.). All major credit cards accepted.*

After spending a couple of nights in a superb beach view room at this wonderful luxury hotel, I never wanted to leave! The dramatic Hotel Kurhaus is one of Scheveningen's most famous landmarks, and remains the center of this suburb's social seen. This fabulous 5 star sea-front hotel started life in the late 19th century and has since hosted countless members of royalty, heads of state, movie stars, and upscale travelers from around the world. Besides having direct access to a long sandy beach, the hotel is also famous for its awesome two story fresco-topped grand hall (Kurzaal), where local residents casually mingle with guests over drinks and stunningly laid-out luncheons on days when live orchestral concerts are not in progress.

There are 241 regal rooms and suites fully equipped with large private bathrooms, remote control satellite television with movie channels, direct dial telephones, mini-bar, electric trouser press, mini-bar, fine art work, extremely comfortable bedding, and huge windows with terrific ocean views in many cases. The facilities here include the excellent **Kandinsky** gourmet restaurant, a seaside terrace restaurant, a private beach area, available water sports gear, in house concert series, an adjacent branch of the Holland Casino, private parking, nearby tennis and golf, plenty of business meeting and conference rooms, boutiques, an adjacent shopping center, and some of the friendliest staff members in town. This is one of my favorite hotels in the Netherlands, and I highly recommend it to anyone in search of a few nights of supreme luxury and comfort.

### Expensive

**CARLTON AMBASSADOR HOTEL**, *Sophialaan 2. Tel: (70) 363-0363. Fax: (70) 360-0535. US & Canada Bookings (UTELL), 1-800-44-UTELL. Special weekend rates from 193 NLG per double room per night (E.P.). Year round rack rates from 365 NLG per double room per night (E.P.). All major credit cards accepted.*

It would be hard to imagine finding a more comfortable deluxe hotel right in the heart of Den Haag's Mesdag-quarter, the exclusive downtown embassy row section. Newly reopened after a comprehensive renovation, this great 4 star hotel has an ambiance that reminds me of a peaceful country inn. All of the hotel's 80 fantastic rooms and suites have been redesigned in either English Tudor or Dutch Traditional styles, and include beautiful hand-painted hardwood furnishings, stylish deluxe private bathrooms with heated towel racks and shower massage, huge picture windows that open out onto the gardens of adjacent embassies, executive sized desks with fax/modem and extra telephone ports, electronic mini-safe, fully loaded mini-bar, complimentary coffee and tea, remote control color satellite television with optional in-room movies, and some of the most soothing guest rooms I have seen in any major city.

The hotel offers a good restaurant, business meeting rooms, fireside lounges, an extensive room service menu, free morning newspapers in the language of your choice, and some the city's friendliest staff. Although not as famous or expensive as the 5 star properties in Den Haag, the fact is that the Carlton Ambassador is now one of the most requested hotels for visiting diplomats, banking executives, and deluxe travelers from around the globe. Highly Recommended!

**SOFITEL DEN HAAG**, *Koningin Julianaplein 35. Tel: (70) 381-4901. Fax: (70) 382-5927. US & Canada Bookings (Sofitel) 1-800-763-4835. Year round rack rates from 340 NLG per double room per night (E.P.). Most major credit cards accepted.*

Located just steps away from the city's Centraal Station, this modern 4 star hotel is a good choice for those that are in town for business. There are 144 medium-sized air conditioned rooms that all feature private marble bathrooms, remote control cable television, mini-bar, direct dial telephone, great bedding, and simple but tasteful furnishings. The hotel also has nearby parking, a nice bar, a good restaurant, an adjacent shopping center, business meeting rooms, a car rental desk and travel agency, and a nice staff.

### Moderate

**PARK HOTEL**, *Molenstraat 53. Tel: (70) 362-4371. Fax: (70) 361-4525. Special weekend rates from 155 NLG per double room per night (C.P.). Year round rack rates from 265 NLG per double room per night (C.P.). Most major credit cards accepted.*

The Park Hotel is definitely the best choice for those visiting the wonderful city of Den Haag who are looking for extremely comfortable downtown accommodations at affordable prices. Located in the charming old town section of the Centrum district, just a couple of blocks away from the Royal Noordeinde Palace and Gardens, this extremely welcoming 4 star full service hotel combines a blend of excellent facilities with an unusually high level of personalized service. The hotel also has the added benefit of being within easy walking distance to almost every major sight and attraction in town.

Each of the 114 perfectly maintained rooms and suites feature huge marble bathrooms with hair dryers, independently controlled heating systems, remote control satellite television with optional movie channels, electric trouser press, direct dial telephone, am-fm clock radios, the most

comfortable beds in town, richly finished hardwood furnishings including executive desks, plenty of closet space, artistic lithographs, and in
most cases have great views out on to quaint centuries-old lanes filled with
boutiques and restaurants.

Facilities include secure indoor parking, dual elevator service to all
floors, a Mudejar-style grand staircase, a peaceful dining room serving a
superb complimentary continental breakfast buffet, business meeting
and private reception rooms, glass display cases filled with unusual art and
antiques for sale, a relaxing main lobby bar, plush sofa-lined lounges, and
a staff that will help you plan the perfect excursion or self-guided walking
tour while at the same time making sure you never want to stay in any
other hotel in Den Haag. The Park Hotel offers both travelers and
businessmen one of Holland's best accommodation values for the money.
Don't forget to ask about their fantastic weekend rates, available in
limited quantities during much of the year.

**CARLTON BEACH HOTEL,** *Gevers Deynootweg 201 (Scheveningen).
Tel; (70) 354-1414. Fax; (70) 352-0020. US & Canada Bookings (UTELL),
1-800-44-UTELL. Special weekend rates from 195 NLG per double room per
night (E.P.).Year round rack rates from 275 NLG per double room per night
(E.P.). All major credit cards accepted.*

Located just above the beach and seaside cafes of beautiful
Scheveningen, this modern yet attractive seven story resort hotel is a great
place to stay while in town! The Carlton Beach features 185 nicely
designed sea-view rooms, suites, and family rooms that all have nice
private bathrooms, large balconies, extremely comfortable furnishings,
mini-bar, direct dial telephone, am-fm clock radio, satellite television, and
lots of sunlight. Facilities here include a complete array of business
meeting rooms, adjacent parking spaces, a nice restaurant and breakfast
room, an extremely friendly staff, available excursions by bus, complimentary Holland Casino entry vouchers, available child care services,
direct access to a picture perfect beach, an indoor pool, a health club, and
much more.

**GOLDEN TULIP HOTEL CORONA,** *Buitenhof 39. Tel: (70) 363-
7930. Fax: (70) 361-5785. US & Canada Bookings (Golden Tulip) 1-800-344-
1212. Year round rack rates from 285 NLG per double room per night (E.P.). All
major credit cards accepted.*

The cute little Hotel Corona is situated in the middle of the city's most
famous square, a stone's throw away from some of the most important
landmarks, restaurants, museums, and shops in central Den Haag. This
3 star property has just 26 nicely decorated rooms and suites with private
bathrooms, satellite television, am-fm clock radio, mini-bar, and nice
interior or plaza view windows. Facilities here include an outdoor café, a
fine French restaurant, a nice terrace bistro, a lounge, a private garage,

and a good staff that works hard to keep guests returning year after year. This is a great place to stay, and is well worth consideration.

**NOVOTEL DEN HAAG CENTRE**, *Hofweg 5. Tel: (70) 364-8846. Fax: (70) 356-2889. US & Canada Bookings (Sofitel) 1-800-763-4835. Year round rack rates from 210 NLG per double room per night (E.P.). Most major credit cards accepted.*

This modern 4 star hotel inside downtown's Passage shopping arcade offers a good location for visitors to this area. The hotel has 106 modern and well designed rooms that all have private bathrooms, direct dial telephones, remote control satellite television with pay per view movies, mini-bar, Passage or street side view windows, and nice simple furnishings. There is nearby parking, a full service bar and restaurant, a pleasant lobby area, business meeting rooms, 24 hour room service, express laundry and dry cleaning, wheelchair accessible rooms, and an adjacent tram stop.

**HOTEL ATLANTAZEE**, *Seinpostduin 24 (Scheveningen). Tel; (70) 352-3500. Fax; (70) 352-2683. Year round rack rates from 165 NLG per double room per night (E.P.). Most major credit cards accepted.*

This unassuming modern six floor hotel is situated about a two minute walk to the beach. Inside there are 44 simply furnished double rooms with nice sea or city view windows, private shower-only bathroom, clock radio, direct dial telephone, and good bedding. Nothing fancy, but a good value in this price range!

### Inexpensive

**HOTEL 'T CENTRUM**, *Veenkade 6. Tel: (70) 346-3657. Year round rack rates from 110 NLG per double room per night (C.P.). Cash only- no credit cards accepted.*

This simple family owned 2 star city center hotel near the Noordeinde Palace is one of the best budget choices in the downtown area. The hotel has 10 rooms with either private or shared bathrooms, televisions, heating systems, basic furnishings, and not much else. They can also rent out studio apartments throughout town for those who want self-catering facilities. Nothing special, but for Den Haag this is a good price.

## WHERE TO EAT

### Moderate

**LE HARICOT VERT**, *Molenstraat 9. Tel: (70) 365-2278. Cash only - No credit cards accepted.*

Master chef Herman van Overdam and his wife Thecla have created this romantic little gourmet restaurant on a historic street in the heart of Den Haag. You will be led to one of several tables surrounded by antique cooking utensils, stained glass windows, and hardwood paneling. The dress code is casual, and they always play great jazz music. Besides offering the dinner items listed below, the restaurant has a superb lunch menu (at less than half the price for many of the same items listed below), as well as an incredible 5:00pm until 6:30pm early bird dinner menu featuring a specially selected multiple course Dutch menu for just 12.50 NLG (the best bargain in town!). Most of the faithful clientele here don't even ask to see the huge menu, they just tell Mr. Van Overdam to bring something special.

Just to give you an idea of what you might expect to see on the weekly a la carte menu, they may offer Thecla's fish soup at 15 NLG, onion soup with melted cheese for 8.50 NLG, goat cheese salad at 15 NLG, melon with ham and port wine for 15 NLG, escargots at 12.50 NLG, omelets from 18.50 NLG, fresh tuna steak with capers for 35 NLG, shrimp scampi at 38.50 NLG, rack of lamb for 38.50 NLG, grilled T-bone steak at 48.50 NLG, mixed fish and seafood pan at 39.50 NLG, and some of the tastiest desserts found anywhere in the country. This is an excellent choice; call for a lunch or early bird dinner reservation.

**LES OMBRELLAS**, *Hooistraat 4. Tel: (70) 365-8789. Most major credit cards accepted.*

This cute restaurant near one of the city's few remaining downtown canals offers an intimate setting for a nice meal. The spacious bright interior is adorned by umbrellas above the candle-lit tables. Their delicious menu features mainly fish and seafood items including shallot soup with creme de casis at 9.50 NLG, lobster bisque with shrimp and lobster ravioli for 17.50 NLG, fried mussels with tomato garlic sauce at 12.50 NLG, Dover sole for 48.50 NLG, oysters from Zeeland at 19.50 NLG, marinated raw salmon with mustard dill sauce for 18.50 NLG, stuffed crab at 22.50 NLG, terrine of fish and seafood for 14.50 NLG, mango parfait with fig sauce at 14.50 NLG, rum and raison ice cream with coconut at 10 NLG, and much more!

**RESTAURANT LE CHANTERELLE,** *Keizerstraat 348 (Scheveningen). Tel: (70) 354-3598. All major credit cards accepted.*

Located on one of Scheveningen's most charming shopping streets, this beautifully decorated little gourmet restaurant is among the best in the area. You can order superb dishes from a seasonally changing menu that may includ huge salads at 14 NLG, crepes with smoked trout mousse for 14 NLG, escargot at 19 NLG, veal consommé with herbs for 8.50 NLG, fresh salmon with saffron sauce at 35 NLG, tournedos of veal in Provencale sauce for 40, assorted cheese plates starting at 14 NLG, and a fantastic array of mouth-watering sorbets and other desserts from 13.50 NLG each. A really nice place to have a long relaxing dinner.

## Inexpensive

**TWEEDUIZENDVIJF**, *Denneweg 7. Tel: (70) 364-4094. Cash only - No credit cards accepted.*

This great local pub and restaurant offers a good selection of various, inexpensive home-made items throughout the day and early evening. Their menu includes warm baguettes with cheese and Spanish ham for 4.75 NLG, pizza style sandwiches at 6.26 NLG, tomato soup with basil and melted camembert cheese for 5.25 NLG, Spanish omelets at 6.25 NLG, vegetarian soup for 5 NLG, French onion soup at 5.75 NLG, curried chicken at 9.75 NLG, Indian style lamb for 9.75 NLG, tuna sandwiches at 5.25 NLG, salmon and salad sandwiches for 7.50 NLG, and the best cappuccino and ice cold beer in town!

**LUNCHROOM CHOICE**, *Keizerstraat 158 (Scheveningen). Tel: (70) 350-1222. Cash only- No credit cards accepted.*

This cute little lunch counter and restaurant is open from 10am until about 8pm and features some of the best inexpensive home cooked meals in town. Their simple menu includes hearty portions of ham and cheese tosties for 3 NLG, vegetable soup at 4 NLG, bratworst for 10.95 NLG, apple waffles at 2 NLG, beef steak for 12.95 NLG, salmon salad sandwiches at 4 NLG, curried chicken salad for 4 NLG, and a host a daily specials. While far from fancy, this cozy establishment is a much better place to have a lunch or an early dinner than many of the expensive seaside restaurants in town!

**CASABLANCA**, *Kettingstraat 23. Tel: (70) 365-1000. Cash only - No credit cards accepted.*

Casablanca is about the best "Shoarma" fast food restaurant in town. Open until at least 1:00am, this is the place that people go to munch out while running from one bar to another. Their menu includes roasted lamb sandwiches for 7 NLG, half roasted chicken at 9 NLG, meat kebobs at 16 NLG, Arabic pizza from 3.50 NLG, lamb cous cous at 13.50 NLG, and plenty of other sandwiches and Middle Eastern specialties.

## Cheap

**NEW YORK PIZZA**, *Gevers Deynootweg 666, Scheveningen. Tel: (70) 358-6806. Cash only - No credit cards accepted.*

This establishment offers really good pizza by the slice starting at 3.75 NLG and by the pie starting at 26.25 NLG, and unlike most other Dutch pizza firms they only use 100% real mozzarella cheese. For a bit more money you can request toppings such as pepperoni, mushroom, ham, pineapple, tuna, broccoli, spinach, tandoori chicken, or a vegetarian combo. The crust is light and crispy, and they will be glad to add salads, soft drinks, cappuccino, and great Movenpic ice cream to your order. Ask them about their delivery service directly to your hotel room!

## SEEING THE SIGHTS
### TOUR 1
• *From* **Centraal Station** *to the* **Grote Kerk.**
• *Approximate duration (by foot) is at least 5 hours, including museum, gallery, church, café, boutique, and side street visits.*

### Towards the Plein Sqaure

After arriving at **Centraal Station**, your first stop in Den Haag should be at the city's main **VVV** tourist information office. Located just steps away from the station and its adjacent Babylon shopping center on a small square called the **Koningin Julianiaplein**, this is a great place to pick up copies of inexpensive walking maps and free informative brochures.

From the VVV office, walk straight through to the far end the large parking lot and make a right turn onto Rijnstraat for a few steps before turning left onto the wide avenue called the Bezuidenhoutseweg. Keep walking straight as this street changes it name to the Herengracht and leads directly into the historic heart of the city. After passing a couple of blocks lined by several nice old buildings containing government offices, movie theaters, and small discos, the street starts to curve sharply to the left. At this point do not follow the curve, but rather cross the street and continue walking essentially straight ahead on the smaller lane directly in front of you that is known as the Korte Poten. Lined on both sides by a series of fine silversmith's shops and brown cafés, a block or two down the street changes its name to the Lange Poten.

Just to your right hand side will be a large square known simply as the **Plein**. This charming downtown plaza is home to many outdoor cafes and street performers during the warmer months, and centers around a large 19th century statue of Prince William I of Orange by sculpter Louis Royer. During late December, there is also a fantastic Christmas market here with hundreds of vendors selling crafts and home-made seasonal baked goods while being serenaded by local choirs. The tree-lined square was originally a vegetable garden, but has since been paved (a massive municipal parking lot lies just below) and is now surrounded by a series of beautiful governmental buildings that for the most part are not open for inspection to the general public.

Among the highlights here at the Louis XIV-styled former **Government Official's Residence** building at Plein #24, built in 1741 from plans by I. De Moucheron and now home to the nation's Offices for Visual Arts. Across the square at Plein #2 is the gabled Neo-Renaissance styled former **Department of Justice** building that was built in 1876 from plans by C.H. Peters and is currently being used by the CDA political party.

## On to the Binnenhof

After wandering around the square, continue up the Lange Poten for another block or so until bearing right onto the wide avenue called the Hofweg. A few steps later off to the left side at building #5 is the famed **Passage** glass-covered indoor shopping arcade. Built in 1882 and enlarged in 1925, this beautiful passageway is lined by a string of designer boutiques and is unique in Holland. Several windows from the suites and guest rooms of the adjacent 4 star Novotel hotel face directly down onto the upscale shops. As you walk through the arcade, turn right at the first fork to wander down its older Neo-Renaissance styled wing and then exit the building.

After exiting the Passage, turn right onto Gravenstraat and in a few steps you will find yourself at the edge of the dramatic **Buitenhof** square, a former forecourt of the palace that has stood here since the middle ages. Nowadays the square is home to several impressive shops including the exclusive (and equally expensive) **Maison de Bonneterie** department store. Built in 1913 from plans by A. Jacot, this elegant store is where Queen Beatrix still does much of here shopping! I strongly suggest walking through the first few floors of this establishment to view its fine hand-made chandeliers, glass dome, and even peek at a few price tags that will certainly put you into instant shock. There is also a surprisingly inexpensive lunch restaurant here that is quite the social gathering point for the wives of wealthy local diplomats and bankers. The square also is home to several other shops, hotels, and restaurants that face onto an antique equestrian statue of King William II.

From the far end of the plaza near the statue, walk across the street and pass beneath the archway that leads into the **Binnenhof** complex. This massive courtyard plaza is filled with several distinguished parliamentary and governmental buildings that are centered around the spectacular turrets of the Gothic **Ridderzaal** (Knight's Hall), a medieval castle originally built in the 13th century for Count Floris V. The castle is mostly used for official state visits and the opening ceremonies of parliament presided over by the queen each year in late September.

Also along the courtyard are several other parliamentary buildings, including the 17th century Louis XIV-style **Treveszaal** (Truce Hall), the 17th century **Eerste Kamer** (Upper House of the States General) with its baroque interior and fine wooden ceilings, as well as the 18th century **Tweede Kamer** (Lower House of the States General) that was originally a Louis XVI-style ballroom. Visitors may go to the castle's side entrance at #8a to watch a multimedia presentation about the history and inner workings of the Dutch government, and then be guided for 30 minutes or so in small groups around the Knight's Hall and at least one of the States General buildings to view their ornate interiors. I advise you to call the tour desk, *Tel: (70) 364-6144,* or stop by at least a day in advance to book a space on these tours as they tend to sell out often. *Tours of the castle and parliament buildings are offered year round (when state visits are not scheduled) between Monday and Saturday from 10:00am until 3:45pm and cost 5.50 NLG per person.*

## The Mauritshuis

After leaving the castle, walk towards the back of the parliamentary complex and walk through the 17th century **Grenadierspoort** (Grenadier's Gateway). Just after passing through this archway with its royal crest of a red lion and a crown, on your left hand side you will find a stately looking Dutch classical Baroque building surrounded by a black iron gate. If you make the next left turn to follow the building's facade onto the tiny Korte Vijverberg you can find the main entrance to the **Koninklijk Kabinet van Schilderijen Mauritshuis** (The Mauritshuis Royal Cabinet of Paintings). Constructed by Pieter Post in 1634 from plans drawn up by Jacob van Campen, the Mauritshuis museum started its life as a mansion for Count Johan Maurits van Nassau-Siegen, the former governor of Brazil. After a devastating fire in the early 18th century, the mansion's interior was fully renovated, and soon it was converted to house a fantastic royal picture gallery of immense importance.

Recently restored, this small but delightful three story museum is among the finest art museums in all of Holland, and is one of the city's top attractions. Although the works are constantly rotated, I have compiled a short sampling of some of the best highlights of the permanent collections. The ground floor of the museum contains rare paintings by various 15th through 17th century Dutch and Flemish masters, such as *Portrait of a Man* by Hans Memling, *Adam and Eve in Paradise* by Reubens, *Portrait of Cornelis Schellinger* by Pieter Pietersz, *The Silversmith* by Antonio Moro, and a few nice landscapes by Van Dijck, Adriaen Brouwer, Jan Bruegel, Metsys, Jordeans, and Van der Weyden.

Upstairs on the first floor you can usually find several masterpieces of Dutch painters from the Golden Age, including *Anatomy Lesson of Dr. Tulp* and *Two Negroes* as well as 14 others by Rembrandt, *View of Delft Girl with a Turban* by Vermeer, *The Young Bull* by Paulus Potter, *The Way You Hear It is The Way You Sing It* by Jan Steen, *Head of a Child* by Frans Hals, *The Goldfinch* by Carel Fabritius, *The Louse Hunt* by Gerard ter Borch, and several ore from artists including Ruysdael, Gerrit Dou, Avercamp, and van Ostedes. The museum also contains a private research library, a nice gift shop, a cafeteria, and a special study center for the arts. *The museum is open throughout the year between Tuesday and Saturday from 10:00am until 5:00pm, Sundays from 11:00am until 5:00pm, and admission costs 10 NLG per person.*

**Nearby Museums & Galleries**

Once you have exited the Mauritshuis, turn left onto the **Korte Vijverberg**, a small 17th century lane with several regal townhouses, including the one at #3 that houses the queen's cabinet. On the right side of the street at building #7 you can enter the **Haags Historisch Museum** (The Hague Historical Museum). Situated in the former 17th century Dutch Classical style Civil Guard barracks, this history museum presents exhibitions devoted to Den Haag's development from the 14th through he 20th century. Included inside are fine antique furnishings, old prints and paintings, regular and 3-D photographs, silver pieces, doll houses, scale models, antique maps, fine porcelain, and even a computer that tests your knowledge on local street names. *The history museum is open year round between Tuesday and Friday from 11:00am until 5:00pm, Saturdays and Sundays from 12noon until 5:00pm, and admission costs 8.50 NLG a head.*

After a short visit to the history museum, continue to the next corner where you will turn left onto the Lange Vijverberg as it passes alongside the charming **Hofvijver** reflecting pond and gardens alongside the parliament complex. At building #14 of this wide street you will find the entrance to the **Bredius Museum** of 17th century art. Located inside a wonderfully restored 18th century patrician mansion, this small but impressive museum contains the once private collections of Dr. Abraham Bredius, an art connoisseur and director of the nearby Mauritshuis museum from 1889 to 1909.

After his death, the city inherited over 150 works by famous artists such as Rembrandt, Jan Steen, Adriaen van Ostade, Albert Cuyp, Van de Nerr, and others. There are also several fine paintings and drawings by lesser known artists, as well as an assortment of well preserved antique furnishings and ceramics. *The art collection is open year round between Tuesday and Sunday from 12noon until 5:00pm, and costs 6 NLG per person.*

Continue along the same street until you reach the next intersection with the street called Buitenhof, where you will cross the street and walk into the **Plaats** square. This lively plaza is centered around a statue of Johan de Witt. As soon as you enter the square, turn left and walk beneath the royal crest-topped archway of the 14th century **Gevangenpoort** (Prisoner's Gate) at building #33. Once a gateway to the Knight's Hall, it has been used throughout the centuries as a prison. The gate house now contains the tiny **Rijksmuseum Gevangenpoort** museum. You can see a small exhibition of medieval implements used for torturing such former inmates as Cornelis de Witt, the former republican leader of Den Haag who was tortured here before being lynched by an angry mob of local residents in 1672. *The torture museum is open year round for scheduled tours between Monday and Friday from 11:00am until 5:00pm, Sundays from 1:00pm until 5:00pm, and admission costs 5 NLG a head.*

A few steps away from the prison is the **Schilderijengalerij Prins Willem V** (Painting Gallery of Prince William V) at building #35. This former 18th century inn was converted by Prince William V, then the alderman of Den Haag, to hold his private gallery of Dutch Golden Age masterpieces before many of them were eventually relocated to the Mauritshuis. This is the country's oldest museum and still contains more than 120 paintings from the royal collection are crammed next to each other along every square inch of wall space in just one long hall. You can see works here by Paulus Potter, Jan Steen, Wouwermans, Frans van Mieris, Bloemaert, Gerad ter Borch, and Willem van de Velde. *The gallery is open year round between Tuesday and Sunday from 11:00am until 4:00pm, and costs 2.50 NLG per person to enter.*

**Towards the De Grote of St. Jacobskerk**

From the gallery continue along the same street until turning right to head back through the Buitenhof square. Walk to the rear of the square and head straight down Gravenstraat. After a block or so you can keep your eyes open on the right hand side for the facade of the **'t Goude Hooft Café** (The Golden Head Café). Although this famous inn has stood on this spot since 1423, the structure that you now see here was completely rebuilt in 1938 and contains one of Den Haag's most fun bar-restaurant. At this point keep walking straight as the street merges into the Dagelikse Groenmarkt. On the right hand side of the this street is the 16th century Renaissance-style **Oude Stadhuis** (Old City Hall) building. This dramatic structure is surmounted by a fantastic bell tower, and several interesting old sculptures and inscriptions adorn the facade.

After few steps further up the next block, the street name changes to the **Riviervismarkt**, where you will find the Gothic 16th century **De Grote of St. Jacobskerk**. This church was fully restored several years ago and is mostly used to host special events, such as corporate dinners. During the summer it is open to the public, and you can view its reconstructed hexagonal spire, a finely carved pulpit, an unusual gabled nave, truly amazing original stained glass windows, a fine carillon with 51 different bells, and the tombs of prominent local residents and military figures. *The church is open only during July and August between Monday and Saturday from 11:00am until 4:00pm, and admission is 5 NLG per person.*

---

## DEN HAAG'S OUTDOOR FOOD MARKET

*The plaza directly in front of the Grote Kerk is the site of Den Haag's best fresh produce, bread, and cheese market. Held on every Wednesday from 11:00am until about 6:00pm, the market is a great place to try local delicacies that can be found nowhere else.*

## TOUR 2

• *From the Grote Kerk to the Denneweg.*
• *Approximate duration (by foot) is about 4 hours, including museum, gallery, palace, park, garden, café, boutique, and side street visits.*

### Around the Noordeinde Palace

From the front of the Grote Kerk, head back down the Dagelikse Groenmarkt and a half a block or so after passing the old city hall you will bear left onto the **Hoogstraat**. This is one of the city's best shopping streets and is lined on both sides with hundreds of expensive designer clothing shops, antique stores, art galleries, and jewelers. After a couple of blocks the street name changes to **Noordeinde**, and you will soon see a large antique equestrian statue of Prince William I of Orange. Just opposite the statue at building #68 is the fabulous **Noordiende Paleis** royal palace. This Dutch Classical Baroque style building started out as a regal 16th century mansion, but was greatly expanded and redesigned in 1640 from plans by Jacob van Campen and Pieter Post. These days it is home to the offices of Queen Beatrix, who spends many of here days inside these walls. While the palace cannot be visited owing to security reasons, a good look through the blue and gold railings and onto the forecourt will give you some idea of how lavish this seemingly understated structure really is.

After getting a good look at the palace, continue along Noordeinde for a few paces before bearing to your right through a small square and onto the Paleisstraat. The peaceful little square that stands between the royal palace and Gothic Hall is home to a lively outdoor **stamp and coin market** every Wednesday from 11:00am until 4:00pm.

At building #3 of this street is the **Gothic Hall**, an English Gothic-style palace built in 1840 from plans drawn up by King William II himself. The king had been so impressed with the structures he saw in England while studying at Oxford that he commissioned a series of Gothic buildings to be built around Den Haag. This structure is currently not open to the public. From here the street curves a bit and at the next corner you will bear right onto Oranjestraat, and then after a block or so turn right onto Parkstraat. At building #65 of this lane you will see the Neo-Gothic **Sint Jacobuskerk** church. Constructed in 1875 from plans by P.J.H. Cuypers, the church and its towering spire are unfortunately closed to the general public.

### Along the Lange Voorhout

After walking down Parkstraat a few blocks, turn left onto the **Lange Voorhout**, a wide linden tree-lined avenue that is home to some of the most expensive mansions and prestigious offices in town. On the left hand side of the avenue you will notice the former 15th century **Kloosterkerk** church and monastery with the towering gables at building #2, as well as several banks and embassies housed in 15th through 17th century mansions with fine gables. On the opposite side of the street you will see a couple of art galleries flanked by the early 19th century **Diligentia** theater and classical music hall at building #5, and the famed **Pulchri** society of artists headquarters at building #15.

After a rather long block, the street runs straight into a delightful tree-lined plaza area. The most famous attraction along this plaza is the rococo **Paleis Lange Voorhout** palace and museum, built in 1760 from plans by P de Swart for a government official. The building was purchased by the royal family as a small royal residence in 1845. These days the palace is now home to some of Europe's most important temporary museum exhibits that normally feature a retrospective of a single artist's most important works. Among the recent exhibits here was the spectacular Vermeer collections that saw tickets selling out months in advance. *The palace museum is open (during special exhibits) year round from Tuesday through Sunday from 11:00am until 5:00pm and costs at least 10 NLG per person depending on the event.*

From your position facing the front of the palace, turn left and walk a half block to the next corner where you will find the amazingly ornate **Hotel des Indes**. This luxurious 5 star hotel started life back in the mid-19th century when it was built by A. Roodenburg as the mansion for Baron van Brienen, a notorious nobleman that loved to throw lavish parties in his huge frescoed ballroom. The mansion was later converted into a hotel complete with antiques from the "Indes" (Indonesia) and has become the home away from home for many world leaders and movie stars, as well as hosting a Sunday afternoon tea that is the social gathering point for the rich widows of men who made their fortunes in Indonesia. A walk through the inner rotunda will give you a good idea of what life was like for the rich and famous in the good old days.

### Along and Around the Denneweg

Now exit the hotel and turn left onto the Vos in Tuinstraat. After a couple of tiny blocks turn right onto Hooistraat and then make the next left turn onto **Hooikade**. This small lane with its unique 18th century houses is directly in front of one of the only canals remaining in the downtown sector, and is also the sight of a lovely cast-iron bridge that dates back to 1866.

At the next corner, turn left onto Spekstraat and a block later turn right to now find yourself on the boutique and restaurant-lined **Denneweg**, perhaps the most famous street in town. During the middle ages this was the principal road leading to the nearby beach areas, and is still surrounded on both sides by various 18th and 19th century townhouse facades with their original stone, wood, and cast-iron elements. As you continue along this fine street, make sure to stop off at the great **Tweeduizendvijf** (2005 Café) at building #7 for some of the best cappuccinos (and ice cold beer) found in Den Haag. This is a truly special establishment in the city and even features great sandwiches and three internet linked computers for those that want to keep in touch electronically with home or the office.

After relaxing at the laid-back café for a while, continue along the Denneweg to window shop at the dozens of fine boutiques.

## TOUR 3
• *Assorted **Downtown** Attractions.*
• *Approximate duration (by tram and bus) will vary.*

These are just a few of the many other interesting sights around the outskirts of central Den Haag that are best reached from downtown via taxi, bus, or tram.

The **Vredespaleis** (Peace Palace) at Carneigieplein #2 is an enchanting castle-like building that is home to the United Nation's International Court of Justice, as well as the Court of Arbitration and The Hague's Academy of International Law. Built in 1904 with a donation of some $1.5 million from American millionaire Andrew Carnegie, the peace palace features many hand-crafted traditional furnishings and architectural elements contributed from nations all over the world, including a towering Swiss clock, wrought-iron gates from Germany, English stained glass windows, statuary from America, and massive Belgian entrance doors. Visitors may call *Tel: (70) 346-9680* to reserve a spot in one of a few daily guided tours of the palace and its adjacent gardens. Public transportation to the palace includes trams #7 and #8 as well as buses #4 and #14. *The palace is open to visitors (when the court is not in session) year round Monday through Friday from 10:00am until 12 noon and again from 2:00pm until 4:00pm, and the entrance fee is 5 NLG per person.*

The **Haags Gemeentemuseum** (Hague Municipal Museum) at Stadhouderslaan #41 is Den Haag's largest museum complex and was built in 1935 from plans by H.P. Berlage. The museum includes various wings that display exhibits on 19th and 20th century modern art and sculpture, rare prints, industrial design, antique musical instruments, handicrafts, Delftware, ancient earthen and glassware, jewelry, and a newly added Dutch costume section. Among the highlights are the **Hague School** pieces, assorted works by Monet, Van Gogh, Kandinsky, and Constant, as well as the abstract paintings by Piet Mondriaan, and the drawings of Karel Appel of the famous Cobra Group. Public transportation to the art museum includes trams #8 and #10 as well as buses #4, #14,

#65, #68 and #88. *The modern art museum is open year round from Tuesday through Sunday from 11:00am until 5:00pm, and admission is 8 NLG per head.*

The **Miniatuurstaad Madurodam** (City in Miniature) at Haringkade #175 is a scale model of a fairy tale Dutch city based on reproductions of the country's most famous landmarks, and is fun for the whole family. First opened in 1952, the model city is built to a 1:25 scale and a two mile long path will lead visitors past countless palaces, canal houses, windmills, gardens, ports, an airport, a railroad, and even a nude beach. Each evening after sunset the tiny streets, parks, and buildings are lit up by thousands of miniature lights. Public transportation options to this attraction include trams #1 and #9 as well as buses #22 and #65. *The Madurodam is open daily from 9:00am until 10:00pm during the summer, and 9:00am until 4:00pm during all other times of the year, and costs 19.50 NLG per person.*

The **Panorama Mesdag** at Zeestraat #65 contains Europe's largest circular canvas that was painted by famed local marine artist Hendrik Willem Mesdag in 1880. The museum showcases this 18,000 square foot painting of typical life in the nearby seaside village of Scheveningen, as well as many of the artist's (and his wife Sina's) fine drawings and paintings. Public transportation to the panorama museum includes trams #7 and #8 as well as buses #4, #5, #13, and #22. *The panorama museum is throughout the year from Monday through Saturday from 10:00am until 5:00pm, Sundays from 12noon until 5:00pm, and costs 5 NLG per person to enter.*

## EXCURSION TO SCHEVENINGEN
• *Off to the beaches at **Scheveningen**.*
• *Approximate duration (by tram and foot) is about 4 hours, including beach, pier, museum, park, garden, café, boutique, and side street visits.*

### The Beach Town of Scheveningen
**Scheveningen** is a popular seaside resort about 4.5 kilometers (3 miles) west of downtown Den Haag. You can get here via a scenic 12 minute ride along tram lines #1, #7, or #9 that run daily in both directions from 7:00am until well past midnight.

While this area has been the sight of several small fishing hamlets since the 12th century, it was not until the early 19th century that Scheveningen began to attract tourists to its sandy beaches. In 1818, local resident Jacob Pronk opened the community's first bathing house that eventually grew into the Hotel Kurhaus. Soon many more hotels and seafood restaurants were constructed to deal with the large influx of sun worshippers who flocked here from all over Holland. These days this suburb of Den Haag has been developed to its maximum potential as a major center for sports, shopping, entertainment, and recreation. There are several pavilions along the beach where you can rent beach chairs and water sports gear, take showers, change your cloths, find public bathrooms, and grab a cool drink. The ocean's water quality here is usually quite good, and there are some lifeguards on duty during the peak season.

## SPORTS & RECREATION AT SCHEVENINGEN

*Since this area is so popular with sun worshipping tourists from all over Europe, plenty of sporting and leisure activities are offered by local companies. I have included the following list of organizations that provide fun things to do when you have had enough of the beach scene.*

*For more information, contact these establishments, or local the VVV tourist office at Tel: (70) 350-0500.*

**Cat Sailing, Windsurfing, and Watersports Center,** Strandweg, Tel: (70) 358-5149

**Scheveningen Bowling Alley,** Gevers Deynootweg 990, Tel: (70) 354-6262

**Rederij Groen Deep Sea Fishing,** Dr. Lelykade 1, Tel: (70) 355-3588

**Zeesportvisserij Fortuna Fishing Boats,** Dr. Lelykade 2, Tel: (70) 355-5461

**Manege Le Cavelier Equestrian Center,** Alkmaarsestraat 20, Tel: (70) 355-0016

**Stal Wittebrug Horse Riding,** Badhuisweg 245, Tel: (70) 354-0523

**Mets Tennisbanen Tennis Center,** Berkenbosck Blokstraat 20, Tel: (70) 355-9849

**Minerva Boat Excursions,** Dr. Lelykade, Tel: (70) 351-4262

**Midgetgolf Westbroekpark Minigolf,** Kapelweg 35, Tel: (70) 355-4721

**Around the Seaside**

To begin your tour, get off any of the above-mentioned tram lines at the "Kurhaus" stop. From here, cross over to the left side of Gevers Deynootweg and walk a few steps until reaching the new **Palace Promenade** shopping center, open daily and housing several nice boutiques. After taking a quick peek inside the mall, continue along the Gevers Deynootweg for about a block until reaching the VVV tourist office at building #1134. Here you can pick up all sorts of great maps and brochures, and there is even a 24 hour tourist information computer for those arriving after business hours. After visiting the tourist office, continue along the same street for a few steps until making a left turn at the next corner and heading in the direction of the sea.

At the end of this small lane, turn right and merge onto the elevated **Zeekant** avenue, the location of many seaview condos and hotels. Follow the Zeekant until it ends a block later near a pair of towering monoliths, turn left, walk a few steps down, and bear left again to now intersect with the **Strandweg** (also known as the "Boulevard"),home to countless restaurants, bars with open air terraces, and gift shops. The entire right side of the Strandweg is lined by dozens of small water-front beach clubs that rent lounge chairs and sun umbrellas during the summer.

A short distance ahead off the the right hand side of this busy boardwalk style walkway, jutting straight out into the North Sea, is the **Van der Valk** pier. This concrete pier was originally made of wood, but it had to be completely rebuilt after being seriously damaged by a fire and then demolished by the Nazis in 1943. Extending over 375 meters (1,238 feet) out above the sea on a platform supported by 180 pylons, this is one of the major attractions in town. There are several carnival style amusement kiosks, restaurants, coin operated telescopes, and souvenir shops along the pier, as well as a 45 meter (148 foot) tall panoramic observation deck. *The pier is open daily around the year from 9am until 11:00pm with no admission charge.*

**STRANDWEG PROMENADE AT SCHEVENINGEN**

From the entrance gate of the pier, turn right to continue to walk along the beach-front **Strandweg** promenade. About a block or so later on the left side of the walkway you will pass the facade of the wonderful **Hotel Kurhaus**. First constructed on the sight of the city's bathing house in 1885 from plans by J. Henkenhaff and F. Ebert, this is the most important landmark in town. Visitors to Scheveningen should not miss wandering around the hotel's public Kurzaal (grand hall), painted with fine frescoes and offering a lovely setting for a drink or meal. The grand hall is also the sight of a fantastic classical music concert series. Walk through the hotel's grand hall and walk down a set of stairs to pass by the front desk and exit through the hotel's main (non-seaview) entrance.

After leaving the hotel, bear right onto the small lane just in front, and a half a block up on the right hand side you will find a set of stairs. Head up the stairs, walk straight into a small square, and bear left down a wide unnamed pedestrian lane. About a block or so later on the right side, you will find a set of stairs leading down to the entrance of the **Sea Life Centre**. This modern aquarium attraction boasts a small glass walled underwater tunnel in the sea where visitors can view marine life such as sharks, sting rays, eels, star fish, shrimp, and hundreds of different fish in surroundings close to their natural environment. *The aquarium is open daily year round from 10:00am until 6:00pm (until 9:00pm during the summer), and costs 13.50 NLG to enter.*

### Towards the Old Part of Town

From the aquarium, return to the charming café-lined square just in front of the Kurhaus hotel, walk through it, and then bear right onto the Gevers Deynootweg. On the left side of this main drag you will find the massive **Movie World** multiplex cinema, and just across from it is the sparkling new home of the town's **Holland Casino**. A couple of blocks later you can take a right turn onto Hartveltstraat to see the **Museum Beelden Aan Zee** art museum that contains a private collection of sculptures. *This art museum is open year round from Tuesday through Sunday from 11:00am until 5:00pm and costs 6 NLG per person to enter.*

After exiting the museum, continue along the Gevers Deynootweg and a couple of blocks later curves sharply to the left and then merges into the Jurriaan Kokstraat. Follow this street for a few blocks until you can turn right onto the **Keizerstraat**, the main street of the old city center. Full of interesting 18th and 19th century gabled townhouses that now contain boutiques and pubs, the most interesting sight along this quaint commercial street is the **Oude Kerk** (old church) at building #8. This 16th century Gothic church contains a beautiful 18th century organ, an ornate pulpit, and fine choir stalls.

### Down towards the Harbor

After looking inside the church, keep walking down the Keizerstraat until reaching the **Vissersmomument** (Fisherman's Monument) near the sea. This is a towering sculpture of a fisherman's wife dressed in traditional costume. These days some 200 or so older women can still be seen along this area dressed in such a manner. From the statue, turn left to follow along the sea-front Zeekant and you will soon pass the 19th century **Gedenknaald** obelisk and the 36 meter (119 foot) tall **Vuurtoren** lighthouse. After passing the lighthouse, keep walking until you reach the end of the sea wall. Take the stairway down and turn left onto the **Vissershavenweg** as it passes the **DeHaven** harbor. Follow this street for a couple of blocks and turn right onto the **Dr. Lelykade**. This is the departure area for several daily (summertime only!) boat excursions in the North Sea that cost around 10 NLG for a 45 minute ride, and about 45 NLG for a half day cruise. For more specific pricing, schedule, and other information, contact the VVV tourist office.

At building #39 of this street is the **Zee Museum** (sea museum). Located in an old fish auction house, this marine biology museum features over 25,000 specimens of shellfish, coral, and other marine life. *The museum is open year round Monday through Saturday from 10:00am until 5:00pm, Sundays from 1:00pm until 5:00pm, and costs 4 NLG per person to enter.*

After visiting the harbor, it is time to return to the beach and enjoy an incredible seafood lunch or dinner, and perhaps take a swim, or take advantage of one of the many leisure and sporting activities offered in Scheveningen.

## NIGHTLIFE & ENTERTAINMENT
### Bars, Discos, & Grand Cafés
**SOCIETEIT DE PYPELA**, *Noordeinde 16a. Tel: (70) 364-4197.*

Although rather difficult to find due to its somewhat hidden entrance in a small alleyway, this after-hours club is my favorite club. Open Wednesday through Saturday from Midnight until at least 5am, this is where the real party animals hang out. The drinks are reasonably priced, there is no dress code or cover charge, the friendly doorman will never give you problems, and their DJ plays great funk, soul, blues, and rock. If you want to meet friendly local people and have a hell of a time, this is the place to go!

**DE SWARTE RUITER**, *Grote Markt. Tel: (70) Unlisted.*

This popular bar is a good place to hang out with the locals. You'll find a huge selection of domestic and imported beer, stiff mixed drinks, and a real rock and roll ambiance.

**DE TIJD**, *Kettingstraat 12. Tel: (70) 364-4490.*

Housed in a former theater, the Tijd is the Den Haag's best disco for young adults. The music here is rather loud and tends to be a combination of funk, house, and techo. The dress code is casual but neat, and the best nights to show up are on Thursday (student night), Friday, and Saturday.

**EXPOSURE**, *Westduinweg 232 (Scheveningen). Tel: (70) 354-3356.*
This is the wildest disco in the area and tends to attract scantily dressed singles that are looking for some action. The place gets totally packed by 12:45am, and the doorman can get picky, so arrive before midnight (especially on weekends) to avoid problems. The cover charge runs about 10 NLG and the extremely hot and erotically inspired music pumps until the early morning hours.
**DE PAAP**, *Pappstraat 32. Tel: (70) 365-2002.*
If you are looking for a good bar with live rock music several nights a week, de Paap is a good choice. The crowd here dresses in jeans and leather jackets and tend to be 20 to 30 year olds into alternative music.

## PRACTICAL INFORMATION
**Main VVV Tourist Office** - *Koningin Julianaplein 30 - (6) 340-35051*
**Scheveningen VVV Tourist Office** - *Gevers Deynootweg 1134 - (70) 350-0500*
**Visitor's & Convention Bureau** - *Nassaulaan 25 - (70) 361-8813*
**Den Haag Radio Dispatched Taxis** - *(70) 364-2828*
**Domestic Train and Bus Info** - *(6) 9292*
**HTM Municipal Transit Head Office** - *Wagenstraat 35 - (70) 342-9292*
**American Express Travel Services** - *Venestraat 20 - (70) 370-1100*
**Den Haag Main Post Office** - *Waldorpstraat 15 - (70) 384-5845*
**American Embassy** - *Lange Voorhout 102 - (70) 310-9209*
**Canadian Embassy** - *Sophialaan 7 - (70) 361-4111*
**Police Headquarters** - *Burg. Patijnlaan 35, (70) 310-4911*
**Medical Emergencies** - *(70) 346-9669 or (70) 345-5300*
**Emergency Hotline** - *06-11*

# 16. DELFT

**Delft** is one of the most delightful small cities in Holland to take in the sights: picturesque inner city walks past beautiful old canal houses and countless historic monuments. Known around the world for its centuries-old tradition of hand-crafting fine hand made **Delftware** blue and white porcelains, this wonderful small city was also the birthplace and home of respected Golden Age artist **Johannes Vermeer**. While over 15% of the local population is comprised of university students, the town still has a life and ambiance of its own.

There are over 60 bridges spanning the various romantic canals of Delft. As you stroll along some of them, you'll walk past many of the fine structures, plazas, and tranquil side streets now famous throughout Europe. Highlights here include visits to the popular café-lined **Markt** square with its bold **Nieuwe Kerk** and **Stadhuis** buildings, shopping in some of the region's best antique shops, enjoyable lunches on canal-side terraces, bargaining with the merchants for unusual objects found at fun outdoor markets, quick stops inside as many as half a dozen great little museums, a tranquil canal boat cruise through the heart of the old town, and a visit to a **Delftware** factory before trying one of the city's many fine restaurants and night spots.

Delft is especially enjoyable during the much less crowded low season months, and is well worth the effort to get to from nearby cities such as Den Haag, Amsterdam, and Rotterdam.

## DELFT'S HISTORY

The city grew from its routes as an old agricultural settlement near the sight of the Oude Kerk in the middle ages. By 1100, a canal was dug around the small hamlet, and sometime after a series of defensive walls (now all but destroyed) began to encircle the growing village. It was granted its first town charter in 1246.

With the opening of a major canal to the Mass river and a new harbor located at nearby Delfshaven (now part of Rotterdam), Delft became a rather prosperous center for exports of locally produced cloth, carpet, and beer. The disastrous fire of 1536 and the devastation of the black plague in 1537 ravaged the town's population.

Prosperity returned to Delft in the late 16th century, when Prince William of Orange moved to a local convent as he led Holland's battle against the occupying Spanish forces. The prestige of having the founding father of Holland living in their town certainly helped to support the economy and bring in thousands of new merchants, skilled craftsmen, and government workers. After the prince was assassinated in his home during 1584, his family still kept close links with Delft and the community somehow eventually managed to get things moving in a positive direction. In 1645, an explosion of stored gunpowder kegs in the town's arsenal destroyed much of the old part of town and killed scores of people, including artist Carel Fabritius.

As the Golden Age took shape, Delft became an important part of the Dutch East and West India Companies' business dealings, including the importation of ceramics and porcelain from China. Some 32 factories and small local workshops began to imitate and then refine the Chinese style of earthenware and soon became famous for producing the blue and white Delftware than can still be found in better boutiques throughout the world. Hundreds of fine canal houses, gabled warehouses, and factories quickly sprung up along the quaint waterways through the now thriving city. At about the same time, several artists from the area such as Pieter de Hoogh, Jan Steen, William van Aelst, and Johannes Vermeer made the so-called **Delft School** of painting one of Europe's most famous.

Unfortunately a major decline, sparked by a series of wars and growing trade competition, had begun to greatly affect the economy of Delft by the start of the 18th century. The factories were almost all gone, the harbor ceased to function as it once did, and most of the city's residents could no longer find gainful employment. With the help of King William II, Delft was rewarded as the new home of the campus of the **Royal Academy of Civil Engineers** (now absorbed into the **Technical University of Delft** with over 14,000 students) and other major educational institutions that brought the city back on its feet. Industry returned, and to this day Delft has maintained its position as a major center for manufacturing, high technology, and old world craftsmanship.

## ORIENTATION

Delft is situated in the west central section of the Netherland's **Zuid-Holland** province, with a population of 91, 941. It lies 56 kilometers (35 miles) south-southwest of the capital city of Amsterdam, 21 kilometers (13 miles) northwest of Rotterdam, and only about eight kilometers (5 miles) south-southeast of neighboring Den Haag.

## ARRIVALS & DEPARTURES

### By Air

Almost all visitors reaching this city by airplane will arrive here via land links from the large **Schiphol Airport** near Amsterdam 44 kilometers (27 miles) to the north-northeast.

### By Bus

Many of the bus lines between Delft and other parts of Holland tend to stop at the depot just in front of the **Station Delft** train depot on the southwest edge of downtown. Make sure to call in advance to find out exactly where and when your bus comes in. Connections between this station and any other point in Delft can generally be made by the adjacent public bus stops for about 3 NLG per person each way, or via taxi for roughly 11.50 NLG or so depending on where you are going.

### By Car

Downtown street-side parking spots are not easy to find.

From **Amsterdam**, the easiest way to get to Rotterdam is to follow **A-10** ring road around until connecting onto the **A-4** south for about 47 kilometers (29 miles), then exit onto the **A-13** south for about 5 kilometers (3 miles) until finding the "Centrum" exit.

From **Rotterdam** you should take the **E-19** ring road west until connecting to **A-13** north for some 9 kilometers (6 miles), then exiting at the "Centrum" exit.

From **Den Haag** you should take the **A-12** west for some 8 kilometers (5miles) before exiting onto the **A-4** south for about 4 kilometers (2.5 miles), then follow the **A-13** south for about 5 kilometers (3 miles), and finally exiting at the "Centrum" exit.

### By Train

Delft is linked to almost any other point in Holland and Europe by several major rail lines. This city has two different rail stations, each with its own series of daily arrivals and departures. The large **Station Delft** train depot at the southwest edge of the city's downtown section is the major point of mass transport arrivals.

Connections between this station and any other point in Delft can generally be made by foot, or by using the adjacent ZWN public bus and HTM public tram stops for around 3 NLG per person each way, by **Treintaxi** for 6.00 NLG per person, or via taxi for roughly 13.50 NLG or so depending on where you are going. Call the train information phone numbers listed in the *Practical Information* section at the end of this chapter to reconfirm, in advance, the exact time and station you may need.

## GETTING AROUND TOWN

**By Public Transportation**

While almost any sight within Delft is well within walking distance from any point downtown, the region's **HTM** transit authority also offers a selection of public tram lines to get you safely and easily around town (as well as directly to and from neighboring Den Haag and Scheveningen), while their **ZWN** bus company also has many additional routes in and around town. They accept **Nationale Strippen Kaarts**. Almost all of these buses and trams stop at one point or another in front of the Station Delft. The normal hours of operation for most of the system is from about 6:00am until roughly 11:45pm. After that your only choices are either to walk, or to take a taxi. Locations outside of downtown Delft such as Den Haag or the nearby beaches at Scheveningen will take you through more than one zone, so you must ask the driver how many blank strips are required. To get free copies of the extremely useful *Vervoer in Delft* public transit system maps, or the HTM's *Lijnennetkaart Haaglanden* Delft and Den Haag transit systems, just pop into the VVV, HTM, or ZWN offices listed in the *Practical Information* section at the end of this chapter.

**By Taxi**

There are almost a hundred licensed taxis roaming the streets and major passenger arrival points of the city during all hours of the day and night. Drivers here have new Renault, Mercedes, and Opel 4 door sedans with enough trunk space to hold a few pieces of luggage. Drivers are polite, honest, and typically multilingual. To find a taxi, either hail an unoccupied cab driving by with its "Taxi" roof light illuminated, go to one of the obvious taxi stands throughout the city, or have the nearest hotel or restaurant call for a radio response pick-up on demand.

The main taxi ranks are located at the Station Delft, the Delft Zuid Station, and near the Markt square. Taxis here are metered and charge somewhere between 13.50 NLG to 17.50 NLG per ride (not per person) between most downtown locations depending on exact distance and traffic conditions. A limited number of the city's taxi's now accept major credit cards for fare payments.

## WHERE TO STAY

*Expensive*

**DELFT MUSEUMHOTEL & RESIDENCE,** *Oude Delft 189. Tel; (15) 214-0930. Fax; (15) 214-0935. US & Canada Bookings (Best Western). 1-800-528-1234. Year round rack rates from 235 NLG per double room per night (E.P.). All major credit cards accepted.*

Located on the city's most famous canal-front street, this unusual superior first class hotel is comprised of eleven different 17th through

20th century buildings. The hotel has 50 nicely decorated rooms and suites, each with large modern private bathrooms, comfortable bedding, remote control satellite television, am-fm clock radio, large windows, direct dial telephones, electric trouser press, interior or side street views, and both mini-bars. Facilities include a bar, a restaurant, business meeting rooms, nearby public parking, room service, express laundry and dry cleaning, safe deposit boxes, and a helpful staff.

*Moderate*
**HOTEL LEEUWENBRUG**, *Koornmarkt 16. Tel: (15) 214-7741. Fax: (15) 215-9759. Year round rack rates from 158 NLG per double room per night (B.P.). All major credit cards accepted.*

This is certainly my favorite hotel in the whole city! Situated in a pair of beautifully converted canal-front patrician houses, this delightful 3 star (it deserves 4) city center hotel is one of the country's most welcoming properties. There are 38 spacious and uniquely decorated canal and courtyard view rooms with private bathroom, direct dial telephone, wall to wall carpeting, remote control satellite television, antique furnishings, fine art work, and plenty of charm. Facilities here include a good restaurant, one of the prettiest lounge and lobby areas found anywhere, nearby parking, business meeting rooms, the best complimentary buffet breakfast in Delft, an excellent friendly staff, and a great courtyard garden. For these rates the Leeuwenbrug is certainly a bargain, especially if you get one of their fabulous rooms with French or stained glass windows looking out over the quiet canal. Highly recommended as the most relaxing place to stay in town!

**HOTEL DE KOK**, *Houttuinen 15. Tel; (15) 212-2125. Fax; (15) 212-2125. Year round rack rates from 135 NLG per double room per night (C.P.). All major credit cards accepted.*

This nice 3 star family-owned and operated hotel near the Station Delft is a nice place to stay. Established back in 1852, the Hotel de Kok feels more like an inn. There are 14 large and well-designed rooms with modern private bathrooms, remote control satellite television, direct dial telephone with computer modem ports, am-fm clock radio, hair dryers, and a mini-bar. There are also charming public sitting rooms and a fantastic garden front terrace. The service here is personalized, and the property has a warm and tranquil ambiance.

**HOTEL DE KOOPHANDEL**, *Beestenmarkt 26. Tel; (15) 214-302. Fax; (15) 212-0674. Year round rack rates from 145 NLG per double room per night (C.P.). All major credit cards accepted.*

Located in a charming square lined by outdoor cafés and good pubs, this small 3 star hotel is also worth consideration. There are 10 medium-sized rooms with private bathroom, color television, powerful heating systems, simple but cozy furniture, and either interior or exterior views. Facilities include a ralaxing bar and restaurant, nearby parking, and a polite front desk staff.

### Inexpensive
'T RAEDTHUYS, *Markt 38. Tel; (15) 212-5115. Fax; (15) 213-6069. Year round rack rates from 90 NLG per double room per night (C.P.). All major credit cards accepted.*

This is a simple and inexpensive inn, located just above a busy restaurant in the heart of the city's historic Markt square. The inn offers about 10 single and double rooms with private bathroom, basic furnishings, and minimal services.

## WHERE TO EAT
### Very Expensive
DE ZWETHHEUL, *Rotterdamseweg 480. Tel: (10) 470-4166. All major credit cards accepted.*

Situated in the southern part of the city, this extremely elegant dining establishment owned by Cees Wiltschut is perhaps the finest gourmet restaurant in the whole region. The De Zwethheul is housed in a remarkable converted old river-front farmhouse that now boasts a bright modern interior and a beautiful outdoor terrace. This is the place to go when you want to dress well and be treated to amazing French cuisine and wines.

The menu changes often, but usually includes such items as smoked Scottish salmon terrine with crab salad at 36 NLG, mixed salad with scallops and truffles for 42.50 NLG, soup of creamed white bans with calf's cheeks at 18.50 NLG, consommé with profiteroles for 17.50 NLG, ravioli of Norwegian lobster and free range chicken at 32.50 NLG, sautéed codfish with frog leg fritters for 39.50 NLG, grilled filet of sole with foies gras and a truffle coriander sauce at 65 NLG, crispy sweetbreads in a cream of morel sauce for 52.50 NLG, sautéed rib-eye steak with truffles at 49 NLG, and plenty of delicious desserts including chocolate tart with sweet pears and whisky for 22.50 NLG and walnut tarts with home made walnut ice cream and hazelnuts at 18.50 NLG.

My suggestion would be to try one of their fabulous multiple course selected menus that start from 55 NLG at lunch, and 75 NLG at dinner, and ask the talented sommelier about his best wine choice for your meal. Highly recommended as the best restaurant in Delft. You'll most likely need to make advance reservations.

*Expensive*

**RESTAURANT L'ORAGE**, *Oude Delft 111. Tel: (15) 212-3629. All major credit cards accepted.*

L'Orage is an exceptionally good gourmet French restaurant that has a casual but elegant ambiance. A series of several small tables dot the intimate dining room and fire side lounge, and provide a perfect setting for a delicious meal form a seasonal menu that includes carpaccio of beef, salads with camembert cheese, lobster bisque, grilled ham with radishes and champagne butter sauce, grilled rib-eye steaks with warm oysters and asparagus, tuna in a soya-sesame dressing, filet of Australian beef in wine sauce, superb desserts, and much more.

The chef has recently received an award for being the best "Lady Chef" in Holland. There is no strict dress code here, and their multiple course lunch menus start from 38.00 NLG per person, dinner from 69.00 NLG , and daily evening specials at 52.00 NLG a head.

**RESTAURANT DE KLIKSPAAN**, *Koornmarkt 85. Tel: (15) 214-1562. Most major credit cards accepted.*

This sophisticated 45 seat restaurant in the heart of historic downtown Delft is another good choice. The sensuous period style dining room boasts a menu offering shrimp cocktails for 22.50 NLG, crab cocktail at 24.50 NLG, smoked salmon for 24.50 NLG, house salad at 16.50 NLG, cream of mustard soup for 14.50 NLG, lobster bisque at 15.50 NLG, Roquefort salad for 15.50 NLG, oysters from Zeeland at 27.50 NLG, carpaccio of tuna for 17.50 NLG, beef entrecote at 42.50 NLG, scampis with pasta for 19.50 NLG, bilinis of salmon at 24.50 NLG, Chinese style shrimp for 47.50 NLG, rib-eye steaks at 44.50, and several good desserts.

*Moderate*

**LA BAMBA**, *Koornmarkt 93. Tel: (15) 214-4021. All major credit cards accepted.*

When you're in the mood for a nice juicy grilled steak, check out this strange little Argentinean restaurant in the heart of town. Even though the fake cow hide seats put me off at first, the food was rather good and reasonably priced. Here you can enjoy melon cocktail with port wine at 8.50 NLG, clear vegetable soup for 6.00 NLG, South American goulash at 6.50 NLG, salad with olives and salmon for 9.50 NLG, shrimp cocktail at 12.75 NLG, fresh grilled corn on the cob for 6.50 NLG, grilled Argentinean sausages at 9.50 NLG, meat patties for 9.00 NLG, jumbo shrimp with garlic at 14.50 NLG, Argentinean rump steak for 17.50 NLG, salmon filet with spicy lemon sauce at 28.50 NLG, and of course their famous Argentinean sirloin steak with pepper for 22.75 NLG.

**RHODOS**, *Wijnhaven 11. Tel: (15) 214-2609. All major credit cards accepted.*

I was pleasantly surprised during my last visit to find this great relaxed Greek restaurant in the city center. The large menu here included spinach pies at 8.50 NLG, warm feta cheese and tomato salad for 13 NLG, mousaaka at 10 NLG, lamb cutlets for 24.00 NLG, giros at 19.50 NLG, souvlaki for 19.50 NLG, mixed grill at 23.50 NLG, a vegetarian special for 23.50 NLG, and grilled salmon with wine sauce at 29.50 NLG.

*Inexpensive*

**STADSPANNEKOECKHUYS**, *Oude Delft 113. Tel: (15) 213-0193. Most major credit cards accepted.*

This conveniently located pancake house and outdoor café offers over 5 dozen varieties of wonderful home-made pancakes starting from 11.75 NLG that are filled with everything from fresh fruits to meat and cheeses. While far from fancy, this is a great place to enjoy affordable food at good prices.

**KLEYWEG'S STADS KOFFYHUIS**, *Oude Delft 133. Tel: (15) 212-4625. Cash Only - No credit cards accepted.*

With its pleasant view out over the canal, this well known café and lunchroom features several dozen different types of coffee, as well as huge pancakes and the best sandwiches in town. Frequent winner of the "Most Delicious Sandwich in Holland" award. Expect to spend about 14.75 NLG a person for a great lunch either inside or on their outdoor terrace.

## SEEING THE SIGHTS
• *From the **Station Delft** through the town and back to the **Delft Station**.*
• *Approximate duration (by foot) is about 5.5 hours, including museum, gallery, church, café, boutique, and side street visits.*

### From Station Delft to Oude Langendijk

After leaving the bustling **Station Delft**, walk through the Stationsplein and then carefully cross over and immediately make a left turn onto the major avenue known as the Westvest. After a few short blocks, bear right onto the cute canal front, boutique-lined street called the Binnenwatersloot. At the end of this small block make a left turn onto Oude Delft and walk a few steps before turning right to cross directly over a small bridge over another canal. At the other side of the bridge continue walking straight along the Peperstraat.

At the end of this street you will come to a dead end at yet another canal, where you should turn left onto Wynhaven and after a quarter of a block you will now bear right across a small bridge above the canal and then continue straight ahead along the **Oude Langendijk**.

## Around the charming Markt Square

After strolling a couple of blocks down the Oude Langendijk, turn left into the gigantic **Markt** square. Packed with an assortment of monumental buildings, souvenir shops, and outdoor cafés, this lively plaza has been the center of daily life in Delft for several centuries. The first stop in the plaza should be over by the VVV tourist information center at building #83 where you can pick up all sorts of specialty maps, walking tours, and brochures about the city sights for about 5 NLG each.

After departing the tourist office, make a right turn to head straight for the tower-topped archway leading into the wonderful **Nieuwe Kerk** (New Church). This is a magnificent Gothic 14th century basilica built shortly after the legendary sighting of the holy virgin by a beggar at the market in 1351, and almost totally rebuilt after damage sustained in the great fire of 1536. Inside this massive (but rather empty) house of worship you can see the amazing black and white tomb of assassinated Prince William of Orange designed by Hendrick de Keyser and decorated with bronze sculptures (and an adjacent memorial to the prince's pet dog), the tombs of over 40 members of the Dutch royal family, fantastic brass chandeliers, a huge early 19th century organ with over 3,000 pipes made by J. Batz and Co. of Utrecht, fine stained glass windows, and plenty of old tombstones.

---

### THE OUTDOOR MARKETS OF DELFT

*The **Markt square** has always been the sight of major local markets, and still continues this tradition with the **Thursday Outdoor General Market**. Held every Thursday from 9:00am until 5:00pm, this bustling market takes over much of the square with stalls selling cheese, fruits, vegetables, clothing, fabrics, antiques, and jewelry.*

*Additional outdoor markets can be found throughout the city, including the year round **Thursday Outdoor Flower Market** close to here along the canal front Hippolytusbuurt near the Oude Kerk from 9:00am until 5:00pm; the year round **Saturday Outdoor General Market** held on the Brabantse Turftmarkt square from 8:30am until 5:00pm; the summertime only **Saturday Outdoor Flea Market** along the canal front Voldersgracht from 9:00am until 5:00pm between April 13 and September 28; and the summertime only **Saturday Outdoor Art Market** on the Heilige Geestkerkhof next to the Oude Kerk from 8:30am until 5:00pm between April 6 and September 14.*

---

For those with strong legs, I suggest taking the optional 379 step walk up to the viewing platform of the 19th century tower designed by PJH Cuypers that rises up over 108 meters (356 feet) and contains a 17th century carillon made by Francois Hemony that was moved here from the nearby old town hall after it burnt had burned down. *The New Church is open 9:00am until 6:00pm daily from April 1 until October 31, and 11:00am until 4:00pm daily from November 1 until March 31. Admission to both here and the Oude Kerk is via a combination ticket priced at 4 NLG per person, the tower costs an additional 2.50 NLG per person to access by foot.*

From Nieuwe Kerk, walk straight through the plaza and head for the impressive Renaissance style facade of the **Stadhuis** (Town Hall). This fine structure was built from plans by Hendrick de Keyser in 1618 around a Gothic 13th century tower that remained after an earlier version of the town hall on this site was destroyed by a fire in 1616. The city hall is no longer open to the general public.

From your position in the Markt square facing the front of the Stadhuis, follow the right side of the building to the edge of the square and make a right turn out of the plaza. At the next corner you will intersect with a street called the **Voldersgracht**. At building #1, just in front of you with the horned cattle sculptures sticking out from the facade, is the Dutch Classical-style 17th century **Vleeshal**, a former meat market designed by Hendrik Sweaf that is now used by one on of the town's many student associations. The interior of the old meat market is not open to the general public.

While facing the front of the meat market, make a left turn down the Voldersgracht (also called the Camaretten at this point) where you will soon see the city's **De Visbanken**, a wholesale fish market that has been located here since 1342 and is still in use to this day.

### The Canals & Side Streets of Delft

A few steps later, turn left onto a canal-front street called the Wynhaven and follow this boutique and restaurant-lined road for a few blocks as the street name changes to the **Koornmarkt**. Over by the right hand side at building #67 is the entrance to the **Museum Paul Tetar van Elven**. This is the restored 18th century canal house of local painter Paul Tetar van Elven (1823-1856) and features a somewhat interesting assortment of many of his works as well as period furnishings, antiques, and the artist's private art collections. *The art museum is open 1:00pm until 5:00pm from Tuesday through Sunday between April 14 and October 19 only, and costs 3.50 NLG to enter.*

Continue walking along the Koornmarkt with its fantastic gabled canal houses. Cross the next bridge over the canal, and keep walking up the left side of the Koornmarkt. Over at building #12 is the 19th century **Synagoge** (Synagogue) with its bold ionic temple facade marked with the Hebrew year 5622. This synagogue is normally open for free (non-intrusive please) public visits during normal Saturday Jewish worship services, as well as during specially scheduled concert events.

Keep walking along the same street until once again crossing over the next bridge, this time to continue along the right side of the canal. The street name now changes to the Korte Geer and follow it until the street ends at building #1, where you'll find the unusual **Legermuseum & Armamentarium** (The Royal Netherlands Army Museum). Housed inside a striking 17th century arsenal, built to replace the one that tragically exploded and practically flattened the town in 1645, this armory now exhibits a great collection of weapons, uniforms, maps, utensils, suits of armor, portraits, scale models, and other objects pertaining to the royal and military history of the Netherlands from prehistoric times up through the middle ages and onto to the present day. *The army museum is open 10:00am until 5:00pm Tuesday through Saturday and 1:00pm until 5:00pm on Sundays and holidays with an entrance fee of 4.50 NLG per person.*

After departing the armory, retrace your steps back down the Korte Geer for about half a block and then turn right to first cross over to the other side of the canal. Then immediately turn right onto the final block on the left side of the canal, now renamed Lange Geer, and follow the street until the next intersection where you will bear right across a larger double arched bridge. At the far side of the span turn sharply to the right to walk along the canal-front **Oude Delft**, one of the city's most famous lanes. While the entire street is packed with dramatic historic structures, the first important sight to be viewed along here is the **Oostindisch Huis** located at building #39. This beautiful 17th century patrician house was the former area headquarters of the Dutch East India Company, and if you walk through the gateway you can see a fine inner courtyard. *While the interior of the building is not open to the general public, its courtyard is free to visit from sunrise to sunset daily.*

Keep walking along the picturesque Oude Delft for another block or so until passing by the front of the early 15th century **Sint Barbara Klooster** (Saint Barbara's Cloister) at building #55. This former cloister was later used as a city orphanage and has now become a student association building. The cloister cannot be entered by the general public. From the cloister, keep walking straight until you are able to cross a bridge and walk along the right hand side of the Oude Delft until reaching the **Sint Hippolytuskapel**, an impressive Gothic 14th century chapel at building #119. The chapel can now only be visited during posted mass hours and special events.

After another block and a half of passing several other well preserved 16th century canal house and historic municipal buildings, you will finally come to the awesome 13th–16th century Gothic **Oude Kerk** (Old Church), with its unmistakable leaning bell tower. Inside you will find a wonderful 16th century hand-carved pulpit with dramatically painted panels, beautiful stained glass windows by Joep Nicolas, the tombs of several notable

17th century Dutch figures such as Johannes Vermeer and naval admiral Piet Hein, and a fine pipe organ that is often played during the day. Just so you know, the tower is not open to the public and has been leaning at the same angle since it was first (incorrectly) built. *The old church is open 9:00am until 6:00pm daily from April 1 until October 31, and 11:00am until 4:00pm daily from November 1 until March 31. Admission to both here and the Nieuwe Kerk is via a combination ticket priced at 4.00 NLG per person.*

After leaving the church, cross the nearby bridge above the canal and turn right to follow the left side of Oude Delft for a few steps. Here you will find an impressive archway that leads into the peaceful chestnut tree-lined **St. Agathaplein square**. Walk through the gateway and turn right to enter the **Stedlijk Museum het Prinsenhof** at building #1. This Gothic structure was formerly the 15th century Convent of St. Agatha, and in 1572 was converted for use by Prince William of Orange and his family as their principal residence. This is where the prince was shot dead in 1584 by Balthasar Gerards, an agent of the Spanish crown.

Inside, you can not only view the bullet holes that still mark the spot of the assassination, but also stroll past several of the old convent's rooms that have been converted into a nice art museum. There are plenty of paintings by notable 16th through 17th century Dutch masters, a huge collection of Delftware, a rotating display of modern art, antique tapestries, and rare silver pieces. The museum is also well known for its temporary exhibits of Golden Age art. A few steps away from the convent is the **Volkenkundig Museum Nasantara** (Nusantara Ethnological Museum) at building #4. This structure was formerly a school for civil servants assigned to posts in the Dutch East Indies and now displays Indonesian art, artifacts, jewelry, religious items, weapons, and garments. *These museums are both open 10:00am until 5:00pm from Tuesday through Saturday and 1:00pm until 5:00pm on Sundays and holidays. A combined admission ticket is 6 NLG per person and includes also includes entrance fees for the nearby Lambert van Meerten museum.*

Now exit the square through the same archway that you entered from, and turn left back to once again walk along the Oude Delft. About half a block up on the left side of the street is the entrance to the **Museum Lambert van Meerten** at building #199. This ornate 19th century canal house was the residence of rich local industrialist Lambert van Meerten and contains a unique exhibition of items from his personal collection of Delftware, period furniture, oil paintings, and architectural relics. *The museum is open 10:00am until 5:00pm from Tuesday through Saturday and 1:00pm until 5:00pm on Sundays and holidays. Admission here is included with the ticket price of the above two museums.*

After departing this museum, turn left to continue walking on the Oude Delft until bearing left on the next corner onto the street marked

Bagijnhof. On this quaint side street you will find a small 14th century brick gateway leading towards the entrance to the **Bagijnhof** almshouse, as well as the Baroque 18th century **Oud-Katholoieke Kerk** (Old Catholic Church). *The almshouse courtyard is open daily for free from sunrise to sunset, while the church's fantastic interior can be visited for free only during scheduled masses and services.*

Continue walking along this small street until bearing right onto the wide Phoenixstraat. A block or later you can't help but notice the 17th century **Molen de Roos windmill**. The windmill was once used to grind flour and is now home to a gallery of 18th century art, as well as a pet shop. Now turn around and follow the Phoenixstraat as it merges into the Westvest and leads directly back to the Station Delft to end your tour.

---

### VISIT A DELFTWARE FACTORY!

*Of all the 32 Delftware factories that once dotted the city during the Golden Age, only one or two remain producing these collectable items to this day. The **Koninklijke Porceleyne Fles** factory has been hand-crafting the highest quality blue and white (as well as polychrome, pijnacker, and black) Delftware sine 1653. Their manufacturing center at the south edge of the city on Rotterdamseweg #196 can be visited by the general public for 3.50 NLG a person, Monday through Saturday from 9:00am until 5:00pm and on Sundays.*

*Inside you can view a special multi-lingual multimedia presentation about the history and production of these pieces, as well as view a large number of rare antique Delftware items, watch artisans demonstrate their hand-painting skills, relax in a peaceful inner courtyard, enjoy a snack at their moderately priced lunchroom, and even purchase some of their newly created works.*

*To get here by bus, take bus #63 or #129 from Station Delft towards the Technical University, ask the driver to let you off near factory, and walk three or so minutes to the entrance.*

---

### GUIDED SIGHTSEEING TOURS

There are several special guided trips offered by foot and river boat to the sights in and around Delft. The following is a brief listing of the most popular trips. For a complete listing, contact the VVV tourist information office.

### By Boat

The **Rondvaart Delft** company *(with ticket and information offices at the Koornmarkt 113, tel: (15) 212-6385)* operates a 45 minute canal cruise of small glass-topped canal boats. The cruises pass by most of the major sights and attractions in the heart of the city, departs every half hour between 10:00am and 6:00pm daily, and cost 8 NLG a person. This firm also rents out 4-person pedal boats for just 15 NLG per hour at the same location.

**By Foot**
The best way to see the city is by following an expert local guide who is fluent in English and can take you to the places only an expert would know about. Private guides can be hired for those willing to pay upwards of 195 NLG for four hours, but there's a much less expensive alternative. The **Delft VVV tourist office** has organized city walking tours for individuals who want to join a small group of other English speaking visitors as they are led by a talented guide.

These trips all leave from front of the VVV headquarters in the Markt square at 10:30am on Wednesdays between April 1 and September 1. The fee for this 90 minute walking tour is only 7.50 NLG per person. Stop by the VVV tourist information center or call them at *Tel: (43) 212-6100* for reservations and specific details.

---

### SPECIALIZED WALKING TOURS

*Another good way to be guided through the city of Delft on your own schedule is to pop by the VVV headquarters on the Markt square and purchase one of several of their special interest walking tour pamphlets in English. Among the most interesting is the blue colored 47 page "Delft" booklet at 3 NLG and the 16 page "On the Heels of Johannes Vermeer" walking tour at 5 NLG. For more details, stop in at the VVV-Delft offices during normal retail hours.*

---

## NIGHTLIFE & ENTERTAINMENT
**Bars, Discos, & Grand Cafés**
**LOCUS PUBLICUS**, *Brabantse Turftmarkt 67. Tel: (15) 213-4632.*
A great place to hang out with the younger locals and students while enjoying one of over 200 different beers on tap and in bottles. They also serve up pretty goood snacks and lunches at fair market price.
**CARROUSEL**, *Oude Delft 5. Tel: (15) Unlisted.*
Of all the bars and cafés in town, this charming old world style brown café near the Royal Army Museum is the most unique. Inside you will find plenty of interesting older locals sipping strong drinks amidst antiques and curiosities.
**GRAND CAFE CENTRAL**, *Wyjnhaven 6. Tel: (15) 212-3442.*
This combination grand café/restaurant/coffee shop/bar rests at the edge of a busy canal in the middle of the old town. Here you can sit back and listen to soft music while reading a complimentary newspaper and watching Delft's residents walk past the huge picture windows.

**ELAND**, *Burgwal 45. Tel: (15) 214-5022.*

Eland, located near the Nieuwe Kerk, is one of the city's largest discos and live music venues, and is known for hosting a wide array of rock concerts, hip hop dance nights, and all sorts of special events. Thre's no real dress code and an average cover charge of 15 NLG. Call in advance to find out what's going on here while you're in town.

**KOBUS KUCH CAFE**, *Beestenmarkt. Tel: (15) Unlisted.*

Popular with the students, this bohemian bar and outdoor café in one of the city's popular bar-lined squares is a good place to come when you want to throw on a pair of jeans and a tee shirt. Good drinks, snack foods, a fun loving crowd, and cheap prices.

## PRACTICAL INFORMATION

**Main VVV Tourist Office** - *Markt 85 - (15) 212-6100*
**Regional VVV Tourist Office** - *Nieuwe Plantage 38 - (15) 213-1942*
**Domestic Train and Bus Info** - *(6) 9292*
**HTM Municipal Transit offices** - *Wagenstraat 35 (Den Haag) - (70) 342-9292*
**ZWN Municipal Bus Company** - *Schieweg 80 - (15) 261-3311*
**Radio Dispatched Taxis** - *Bellweg 18 - (15) 262-0621*
**Emergency Hotline** - *06-11*

# 17♦ MAASTRICHT

**Maastricht** is one of the most sophisticated, peaceful, and elegant small cities in all of Europe. Due to its location in the far southeast corner of Holland, Maastricht continues to be greatly influenced by the culture and economic prosperity of neighboring Belgium and Germany (both are just a 15 minute ride away), and the residents of this captivating destination look and speak much differently than elsewhere in the country. A short walk through any of downtown's romantic and historic plazas and their adjacent side streets will reveal hundreds of well dressed residents window shopping at some of the finest designer boutiques and art galleries in Europe.

Maastricht and its dramatic neighboring communities offer many monumental castles and churches, fortunately spared the perils of destruction from war raids. Among the highlights of a trip to Maastricht are walks around the famous **Onze Lieve Vrouwe Plein** and **Markt** square, a stroll or boat ride along the banks of the **Maas** river, hikes atop the ruins of the towering fortified walls that once defended the city, a fine meal in one of Maastricht's wonderful restaurants, sipping a cold beer at an outdoor café on the **Vrithof** square, shopping on the historic **Stokstraat**, visiting a few well preserved medieval basilicas, checking out a typical outdoor market, and partying with the locals in unusual little cafés and pubs where strangers are more than welcome to join in the fun.

## MAASTRICHT'S HISTORY

Maastricht is the oldest city in the Netherlands, and has a rich and colorful history. By 50 BC, the Romans founded a small hamlet called Mosae Trajectam (the Maas River Crossing) here at the intersection of the Maas river and a major overland road. Around the year 400 AD, the first in a series of fortified walls surrounded this growing settlement. Maastricht finally grew into a major city when bishop St. Servatius moved his offices here, thus establishing Maastricht as an Episcopal see and ensuring a constant flow of pilgrims. Once the Romans had abandoned their control of the city in the 5th century, they were soon replaced by Charlemangne and his Franks. The area continued to prosper as a major center for trade until the 9th century, when another bishop decided to move the Episcopal see to the city of Liege in what is now Belgium. The local economy was devastated for the next few centuries.

A new age of prosperity came with the creation of professional guilds. In 1202, Maastricht came under the joint rule of both the Duke of Brabant and the Prince-Bishop of Liege. As the 13th century progressed, the population began to swell to over 15,000 residents. In 1229, the local leaders decided to construct a new 2.5 kilometer (1.5 mile) fortified wall around the city, but within 125 years or so the downtown had grown so much that an even larger 4.5 kilometer (2.5 mile) wall became necessary to secure the town and its people. These walls helped Maastricht to defend the city during more than 20 seiges by the Dutch, Spanish, and French armies.

In 1673, France's King Louis XIV took control of the city, and it was not until after Napoleon's defeat at Waterloo that Maastricht became part of the United Kingdom of Netherlands and Belgium. Once Belgium gained its independence from Holland in 1839, this became the southern-most city in the Netherlands. At about the same time, new industries such as crystal and glass factories were built here, and provided a huge boost to the industrial development of the region.

In 1991, the city hosted a major summit meeting of the Council of Europe, during which the historic **Treaty of Maastricht** was signed, laying the foundations for an improved European Economic Community.

---

### MAASTRICHT'S CARNIVAL

*Maastricht is the location of several terrific events during each year. Among the most popular are the **Carnival** festivities each February, with massive costume parades, dancing in the streets, and outrageous all-night parties. The entire population (as well as many visitors from all over Holland) are involved in three days of non-stop drinking binges, during which plenty of bizarre occurrences have been known to happen. If you intend to visit the area during this great event, make sure to book your hotel reservations far in advance!*

---

## ORIENTATION

Maastricht is located in the extreme southeastern corner of the country at the bottom of the **Limburg** province of the Netherlands, with a population of 123,467. It lies 178 kilometers (110 miles) south-southeast of the capital city of Amsterdam.

## ARRIVALS & DEPARTURES
### By Air
Maastricht is serviced by the **Maastricht-Aachen International Airport** located about 10 kilometers (6 miles) north of the city center off of the **A-2** highway. Visitors from major European cities may fly here directly, or connect on to one of several daily shuttle flights operated by **Air Excel** that carry passengers between this facility and Amsterdam's Schiphol Airport. Almost all North American visitors to Maastricht arrive at Amsterdam's Schiphol Airport, and tend to use either a rental car or rail service to get here from other points in Holland (the train ride through Limburg is quite beautiful).

To reach the airport, call *(43) 366-6444*.

### Buses Between the Airport & Downtown
The **Hermes** bus company runs two bus lines that each connect Maastricht-Aachen Airport to the city's Centraal Station. Local bus #61 departs from in front of the arrivals area and leaves at least twice every hour from 9am until 11:00pm daily, and costs either 11.50 NLG or 5 strips of a strippenkart. Interliner bus #420 runs much more often and only costs 6 NLG, and can drop you off at either the Centraal Station or the Markt square.

### Taxis from the Airport to Downtown
Taxis are usually dark colored diesel or natural gas powered Mercedes-Benz, Renault, or Opel 4 door sedans marked with the "Taxi" sign on their roofs. These can be found in abundant supply at well-indicated taxi stands at the airport and throughout the city's main squares and shopping zones. Keep in mind that 94% of the taxis here are medium-sized 4 door cars (although a few station wagon taxis have started to come into service). Generally, their trunks can only hold three large and perhaps a couple of carry-on bags inside as well. Unfortunately, almost no station wagon or van type taxis are available in here. The going metered rate for the 10 minute drive from Maastricht-Aachen Airport to the downtown area averages about 32 NLG per ride, not per person!

### By Bus
Many of the bus lines between Maastricht and other parts of Holland as well as the rest of Europe tend to stop at the **Busstation** depot alongside the **Centraal Station** just across the Maas river in the eastern Wyck district. Make sure to call in advance (see *Practical Information* section at the end of this chapter) to find out exactly where and when your bus comes in. Connections between this station and any other point in Maastricht can generally be made by the adjacent public bus stops for 3

NLG per person each way, or via taxi for roughly 14 NLG or so depending on where you are going.

## By Car

Downtown street-side parking spots are fairly easy to find.

From **Amsterdam**, the easiest way to get to Maastricht is to take the **A-10** ring road south until connecting to the **A-2** south for about 201 kilometers (125 miles) before finding the "Centrum" exit.

## By Train

Maastricht is linked to most other points in Holland and Europe by several major rail lines. The only location for service to and from downtown Maastricht is via the large **Centraal Station** train depot, about a 1 kilometer (.6 mile) walk across the river to east of the city center in the Wyck district. Connections between this station and any other point in Maastricht can generally be made by the adjacent public bus stops for around 3 NLG per person each way, by **Treintaxi** for 6 NLG per person, or via taxi for roughly 14 NLG or so depending on where you are going.

Use the train information phone numbers listed in the *Practical Information* section at the end of this chapter to reconfirm, in advance, the exact time and station you may need.

## GETTING AROUND TOWN

### By Public Transportation

Maastricht's **Stadsbus** municipal transit authority offers several public bus lines to get you safely and easily around town. They accept Nationale Strippen Kaarts.

Many of these vehicles stop at one point or another in front of Centraal Station. The normal hours of operation for most of these buses is from about 6:30am until roughly 11:30pm. After that your only choices are either to walk, or to take a taxi. To get free copies of the extremely useful Stadsbus public transit system map, *Openbaar Vervoer Maastricht,* just pop into their ticket offices during normal working hours.

### By Taxi

There are over a hundred licensed taxis roaming the streets and major passenger arrival points of the city during all hours of the day and night. Drivers are frequently multilingual, extremely honest, and can tell you more than a few great stories. To find a taxi, either hail an unoccupied cab driving by with its "Taxi" roof light illuminated, go to one of the dozens of obvious taxi stands throughout the city, or call *(43) 343-6000 or (43) 363-3333* for a radio response pick-up on demand. The main taxi

ranks are located at the Centraal Station, the Vrijthof, and the Markt square.

Taxi meters charge at about the rate of about 3.50 NLG per kilometer, so this works out to somewhere around 9 NLG to 12 NLG per ride (not per person) between most downtown locations depending on exact distance and traffic conditions. Many of these taxis now accept major credit cards for fare payment.

## WHERE TO STAY

*Expensive*

**GOLDEN TULIP HOTEL DERLON**, *Onze Lieve Vrouweplein 6. Tel: (43) 321-6770. Fax: (43) 325-1933. US & Canada Bookings (Golden Tulip) 1-800-344-1212. Special weekend rates from 300.00 NLG per double room per night (B.P.).Year round rack rates from 405 NLG per double room per night (E.P.). All major credit cards accepted.*

This wonderful medium-sized 4 star luxury hotel in the heart of downtown Maastricht is one of the most charming places to stay here. Located in the most impressive square of the city, this three story hotel is one of the city's best. The Derlon offers 44 large air conditioned rooms, suites, and apartments that each offer deluxe private bathrooms, remote control satellite color television, am-fm clock radio, mini-bar, wall to wall carpeting, extremely comfortable modern furnishings, nice art work, direct dial telephone, and large interior or plaza view windows. The facilities include a nice restaurant and outdoor café, a tranquil bar, valet parking, and a cellar museum full of ancient Roman artifacts. During my last visit here, I was greatly impressed by the high level of personalized service and the staff's exceedingly friendly attitude.

**HOLIDAY INN CROWNE PLAZA**, *De Ruiterij 1. Tel: (43) 350-9191. Fax: (43) 350-9193. US & Canada Bookings (Holiday Inn) 1-800-465-4329. Special weekend rates from 275 NLG per double room per night (B.P.).Year round rack rates from 375 NLG per double room per night (E.P.). All major credit cards accepted.*

This superb oasis of tranquillity and comfort is situated alongside the beautiful Maas on the Wyck side of the famous St. Servaas bridge. The Holiday Inn Crowne Plaza, one of my favorite city center hotels in all of Holland, is a deluxe modern property with 131 beautifully designed rooms, suites, and fully equipped luxury apartments, each offering huge private bathrooms, remote control satellite television, direct dial telephones, executive style desks, beautiful artwork, mini-bar, electric trouser press, mini-safe, complimentary coffee and tea set-ups, luxurious furnishings, and wonderful sun-drenched balconies with either river or historical street view in most cases.

The apartments are situated in a separate wing with its own private entrance, and many of the most demanding and famous European politicians have made these fantastic units their home away from home during E.E.C. committee meetings. The hotel boasts both French and Japanese restaurants, an outdoor river-front terrace, a nice bar, comfortable public areas, a full complement of business meeting and conference rooms with state-of-the-art audio/video gear, on-site secure outdoor parking, boutiques, available child care and secretarial services, and an international trained staff of hard working hotel industry professionals. Highly Recommended as the best choice for both business and leisure travelers that are looking for a memorable downtown hotel with a great ambiance.

### Moderate

**GUESTHOUSE DIS**, *Tafelstraat 28. Tel: (43) 321-5479. Fax: (43) 325-7026. Year round rates starting from 160 NLG per double room per night (E.P.) . All major credit cards accepted.*

This romantic little inn, located steps away from the Onze Lieve Vrouweplein on a tranquil side street full of 17th centuries townhouses, is one of the country's most unique properties. Situated just above a gallery of fine modern art, guests have their choice of six enormous, beautifully designed double rooms – featuring original exposed wooden beams, Italian leather sofas, bleached parquet floors, and a selection of tasteful modern paintings hung on the walls. All of these sun-drenched rooms have huge tile bathrooms, antique and modern designer furnishings, remote control satellite television, direct dial telephone, individually controlled heating systems, mini-bar, tables, and incredible views out over the historic side streets and private courtyard gardens of this wonderful section of the city.

For these prices, I strongly suggest calling well in advance for reservations, and don't forget to ask about their daily buffet breakfast served in a awesome 17th century Romanesque chapel, a real bargain at only 15 NLG extra per person. Highly suggested as one of the most charming and innovative small inns in Holland.

**HOTEL BERGERE**, *Stationsstraat 40. Tel: (43) 325-1651. Fax: (43) 325-5498. US & Canada Bookings (Supranational) 1-800-441-1414. Year round rack rates from 150 NLG per double room per night (E.P.). All major credit cards accepted.*

This nice medium-sized hotel is situated across the river from downtown (near the Centraal Station) in the Wyck district. The charming Bergere has several different types of tastefully designed accommodations that all have newly renovated private bathrooms, satellite television, direct dial telephone, and comfortable furnishings. Here you can also take advantage of the breakfast room and private parking. While not the most deluxe or expensive choice in town, this is still a nice place to stay near all the major sights. A good choice in this price range.

**HOTEL BEAUMONT**, *Wycker Brugstraat 2. Tel: (43) 325-4433. Fax: (43) 325-3655. Year round rack rates from 175 NLG per double room per night (E.P.). Most major credit cards accepted.*

Situated just off the main street running from the Centraal Station to the bridge leading across the river to the center of downtown, the 4 star Beaumont is a pleasant family owned and operated hotel. Here you can find 77 rooms and junior suites that all have private bathrooms, remote control satellite television, direct dial telephone, and modern furnishings. The hotel also has an excellent restaurant, a nice terrace and bar, nearby parking, and a good staff.

**GRAND HOTEL DE L'EMPEREUR**, *Stationsstraat 2. Tel: (43) 321-3838. Fax: (43) 321-6819. US & Canada Bookings (Best Weztern) 1-800-528-1234. Year round rack rates from 205 NLG per double room per night (E.P.). All major credit cards accepted.*

This nice old world style 4 star hotel is situated just across from the Centraal Station in the Wyck district of the city. There are 92 rather different standard rooms, junior suites, split level suites, apartments, and special deluxe suites that come complete with private bathrooms, satellite television, mini-safe, direct dial telephone, nice furnishings, and sound proofed windows. There is also a beautiful gourmet restaurant, a nice brasserie and bar, an indoor swimming pool, an optional sauna, indoor parking, and a full compliment of meeting rooms.

**HOTEL DU CASQUE, Helms***traat 14. Tel: (43) 321-4343. Fax: (43) 325-5155. Year round rack rates from 220 NLG per double room per night (B.P.). Most major credit cards accepted.*

Located just off the Vrijthof square in the heart of the city, this nice little hotel is popular with visitors from all over Europe. The Du Casque has 38 small but modern rooms with private bathroom, satellite television, am-fm clock radio, mini-bar, direct dial telephone, and nice but simple furnishings. There is also a steak house, a breakfast room, a small lobby area, and nearby parking.

### Inexpensive

**NJHC HOSTEL/BUDGET HOTEL DE DOUSBERG**, *Dousbergweg 4. Tel: (43) 343-4404. Fax: (43) 346-6755. US & Canada Bookings (Hostelling International) 1-613-237-7884. Year round rack rates from 28 NLG per person in a dormitory per night (C.P.). Year round rack rates from 95 NLG per double hotel style room per night (E.P.). Cash Only - No credit cards accepted.*

This is a great choice for those who are not able to afford the typically high hotel rates in the center of Maastricht. The De Dousberg is a private

hotel adjacent to a serious sporting complex, about a seven minute drive (or 15 minute bus ride via line #8) west of the city center. The hotel offers a series of nice but basic single, double, and triple rooms with private bathrooms, telephones, and television, as well as a special section of hostel rooms for up to eight people each that have semi-private bathrooms and luggage lockers.

The sports complex next door contains huge indoor and outdoor swimming pools and soccer fields that can be used for free, as well as several indoor tennis courts, a golf driving range, and a climbing wall, that are available for a small hourly surcharge. Guests of the hotel section pay a bit more for the privilege of the above-mentioned additional in-room facilities, and do not have to return by the midnight curfew imposed on the hostel section guests. Facilities also include free outdoor parking, a nearby bus stop, laundry rooms, storage lockers, conference rooms, a good cheap restaurant, an inexpensive bar, vending machines, and a nice staff. I really enjoyed my stay here, and met plenty of interesting young adults from all over the world.

## WHERE TO EAT
*Expensive*
**TOINE HERMSEN CUISINIER**, *St. Bernardusstraat 2. Tel: (43) 325-8400. All major credit cards accepted.*

This opulent and semi-formal gourmet restaurant on a historic side street in downtown Maastricht offers the finest cuisine available in town. The quaint antique building is decorated in soft French country decor, and it can comfortably seat only about 45 fortunate patrons. The menu here is French inspired with some Limburg touches, and changes often. Be prepared to dress well and spend at least 115 NLG per head for an incredible meal from chef Hermsen's acclaimed open kitchen that uses only the freshest local and imported ingredients. Ask about their incredible 4 and 5 course special menus, and make your reservations as far in advance as possible.

### Moderate
**LE VIGNERON BISTROT A VIN**, *Havenstraat 19. Tel: (43) 321-3364. All major credit cards accepted.*

This is certainly the best place in Maastricht to enjoy an excellent, yet affordable, relaxing French dinner. This welcoming little wine bar and restaurant is just around the corner from the Onze Lieve Vrouweplein and has a remarkable view out onto the Op de Therman courtyard. There are two intimate floors with about a dozen tables each, as well as a fantastic outdoor terrace. Chef Francis Bemelmans creates fine 3 and 4 course

Continental menus with a Mediterranean touch that cost either 45 NLG or 57.50 NLG respectively. There are also 18 varieties of wines by the glass, as well as an amazing list of vintage wines by the bottle with the best prices in town.

While their menu changes seasonally, the last time I visited it featured mouth watering choices such as duck pate with olives and tarragon, marinated salmon with mustard-dill sauce, beef carpaccio with pesto, mussel and oyster salad, grilled prawns, sweetbread ravioli in cream sauce, fish soup with croutons, fillet of duck in honey-thyme sauce, grilled entrecote in herbs and Bernaise dressing, fillet of lamb with balsamic vinegar, mussels in a white wine casserole, fresh black current sorbet, fresh figs with delicious pistachio ice cream in port wine sauce, and the strongest coffee in town.

**RESTAURANT 'T PLENSKE**, *Plankstraat 6. Tel: (43) 321-8456. All major credit cards accepted.*

I have been greatly impressed on several different occasions with the hearty meals offered at this modern casual restaurant in the old section of town. Their menu is much more innovative than most other restaurants in town, and tends to include fresh game and fowl from the Limburg area. You can enjoy cream of wild mushroom soup at 8.50 NLG, celery soup with game for 8.50 NLG, escargot at 17.50 NLG, fried goose liver with port wine for 30 NLG, mixed seafood with tri-color pasta at 19.50 NLG, seaweed with smoked bacon at 33 NLG, bouillabaisse for 35 NLG, smoked leg of wild boar and deer at 18.50 NLG, fried salmon in tomato fondue for 19.50 NLG, fried trout in wheat beer sauce at 30 NLG, wild boar with port wine and dates for 32 NLG, sweet and sour quail and chicken liver at 29.50 NLG, rabbit fillet in mustard wine sauce for 32 NLG, and many other exotic creations. Reservations are suggested for evenings, but are not usually needed for lunch.

**RESTAURANT BON GOUT**, *Wycker Brugstraat 17. Tel: (43) 325-0284. All major credit cards accepted.*

The first few times I shopped at this great cheese shop in the Wyck ditrict's main street, I didn't even know they had a terrific little gourmet restaurant in the back. Maastricht's best kept secret is this informal 24 seat dining room where the lunch and dinner menus concentrate on dishes prepared with aged imported cheeses. They feature several pre-selected 3 and 4 course menus ranging from 55 NLG to 85 NLG per person (not including a good selection of wines), as well several a la carte offerings that include salad with mixed salads with fresh herbs, lasagna with three different fish, warm goat cheese salad, salmon filet with Normandy cheese sauce, scallops in Champagne cheese, beef and veal with two different sauces, fillet of lamb, vegetarian pasta with wild mushrooms, duck in cheese sauce, beef cooked in wheat beer, langoustinos with caviar in

Riesling wine, fruit sorbet, chocolate mousse, baked pears with blue cheese, and much more. Advance reservations are a good idea for this fine establishment.

**IN 'T KNIJPKE**, *St. Bernardusstraat 13. Tel (43) 321-6525. Most major credit cards accepted.*

This cave-like restaurant on a small lane near the old town walls offers visitors a unique and casual ambiance in which to enjoy a nice hearty meal (until late at night) of internationally inspired favorites. The restaurant also has a tiny art film theater and café in the same building. Their small but well thought out menu features affordably priced items such as goulash for 11.50 NLG, mussels with escargot at 11 NLG, assorted cheese plates starting from 12 NLG, salad Nicoise for 13.50 NLG, frog's legs at 18.50 NLG, and several more dishes along the same lines.

### *Inexpensive*

**CAFE 'T POTHUISKE**, *Het Bat 1. Tel: (43) 321-6660. Cash only - no credit cards accepted.*

This small section of a much larger river-front restaurant just steps from the St. Servaas bridge features affordable lunch and evening snacks. The bar itself features over a dozen tasty beers on tap, as well as a good selection of inexpensive items like French onion soup for 6.50 NLG, tomato soup at 5.50 NLG, pate sandwiches for 5.50 NLG, brie cheese on a baguette at 6.50 NLG, assorted cheese plates from 12.50 NLG, tuna salad for 10.50 NLG, chili con carne at 10.50 NLG, escargots for 14.50 NLG, salad with smoked chicken at 10.50 NLG, baked mussels with garlic for 14.50 NLG, ragout of game at 17.50 NLG, fried dumplings filled with meat for 12.50 NLG, and plenty of daily specials. A nice place to sit back and soak up the old world tavern ambiance. This section of the restaurant requires no reservations and has no dress code.

**FIN BEC TRAITEUR,** *Kleine Staat 10. Tel: (43) 321-2596. Cash only - no credit cards accepted.*

This fantastic little take-out and catering establishment is the perfect place to grab a few containers of gourmet salads, main courses, and cheeses before heading out for a sunny afternoon picnic. The shop features over five dozen varieties of warm and cold dishes sold by the kilogram and usually stocks freshly made pates, imported Spanish and Italian ham, fish soup, lobster bisque, oyster soup, shrimp salad, fruit salad, mushroom and dill salad, jumbo shrimp with garlic sauce, smoked salmon, beef stroganoff, grilled chicken, duck with orange sauce, mini-pizzas, lasagna, quiches, crepes, imported aged cheeses, and a wide array of delicious home made desserts. My last take-out lunch cost about 18.50 NLG per person and was as good as many of the much more expensive above mentioned restaurants!

## SEEING THE SIGHTS

• From **Centraal Station** to the **Markt**.

• Approximate duration (by foot) is about 6 hours, including museum, Roman ruin, rampart, art gallery, church, café, boutique, and side street visits.

### Around the Wyck District

Once arriving at the Centraal Station, walk a few steps down and pop into the terminal building's VVV tourist information office to pick up a handy Maastricht street map for about 2 NLG. Now depart via the terminal's main doorway and head straight ahead up the wide Stationstraat. This charming main street cuts through the heart of the **Wyck** district of the city, and is lined on either side by well over 100 great designer boutiques, intimate restaurants, mouth-watering pastry shops, and hotels. The street also hosts an amusing **Outdoor Flea Market** each Saturday from 9:30am until 4:00pm, where you can usually find a few good deals on everything from used books to antique furnishings, as well as a Thursday afternoon **Farm Fresh Produce Market** from 2:00pm until 9:00pm.

A couple of blocks further up, the street name changes to the Wycker Brugstraat, where you should pop into a few of the 18th and 19th century townhouses that contain the area's best shops, like the **Bon Gout** cheese shop and restaurant at #17 and the incredible **Friandises** chocolate shop at #55.

### The Heart of the Old Town

The road now merges onto the Sint Servaasbrug (St. Servass bridge) that crosses over the Maas river and into the oldest parts of the city. Both sides of this river-front have great bicycle and walking paths. This awesome span dates back to the 13th century and is considered to be the oldest bridge in Holland. The piers alongside the bridge are the departure docks for several river boat excursions that are well worth considering on sunny days. For those interested, turn left just before the bridge onto the **Oeverwal**, where at building #3 you can tour the 19th century **Stadsbrouwerij de Ridder** brewery where the delicious local Wieckse Witte, Pils, and even some dark beers are brewed by the Ridder beer company. *The brewery is open to the public on Wednesday from 2:00pm until 5:00pm, if an appointment is first made with the local VVV tourist offices.*

Just after crossing the bridge, make a left turn onto the Vissersmaas. About a half block later this lane curves to the left at a small plaza where you will turn right, and then almost immediately left, to reach the **Stokstraat**. After fire repeatedly destroyed the timber structures that once stood here, rich merchant families in the 17th and 18th centuries built beautiful  homes with unique descriptive gable stones along this street. When the old fortified city walls that passed along this zone were demolished in 1867 (to make way for a major expansion of downtown), the Stokstraat turned into a slum. Since the 1960's, these buildings have been purchased by savvy local businessmen, and have been remarkably converted into dozens of expensive designer shops, jewelers, art galleries, and interior decoration boutiques. Make sure to visit building #12, where you will find the In **de Moriaan**, the narrowest pub I have ever seen!

At the right side of the street next to the above-mentioned pub, make a right turn onto a tiny lane called the Morenstraat that will then lead into the tranquil **Op de Therman** square, with several restaurants near the site where 3rd century Roman baths have been excavated. A small plaque at the back of the square lists the details and locations of these and other Roman-era structures. *The Roman Baths are open daily year round from sunrise to sunset, and is free to enter.*

### Around the Onze Lieve Vrouwe Plein

Continue straight along the same street as it cuts through the Op de Therman plaza and after a block you will make a left turn onto the Havenstraat, followed by a right turn onto the Plankstraat. Soon you will be brought into the **Onze Lieve Vrouwe Plein**, one of the city's most delightful squares. Besides being home to half a dozen good outdoor cafés and restaurants, this plaza contains several important historical landmarks. The first building that you will pass while entering the square is the Hotel Derlon. A small museum in the basement of the hotel called the **Museum Derlon** can provide visitors with an up close look at the Roman-era walls and artifacts found during a recent renovation of what has been found to be the oldest street in all of Europe. It seems that no matter where a contractor digs up a pipe in this part of town, they will soon discover even more amazing ruins! *The museum is open on Sundays only from 12noon until 4:00pm and there is no admission charge.*

Further along the same side of the square, you can't help but be drawn directly to the massive medieval sandstone Rmanesque and Gothic **Onze Lieve Vrouwebasiliek** (Basilica of Our Beloved Lady). Flanked by two fantastic medieval towers that once stood at the foot of the old town's defensive walls, this important 12th century basilica can be entered by passing through the portal leading into the Sterre der Zee chapel with its famous 15th century sculpture of Maria, and pushing open the two wooden doors on your right. Visited by at least two popes in recent history, inside the basilica you can peek at a wonderful Renaissance choir area with fine stained glass between a series of pillars capitals sculpted with biblical carvings by an Italian artist in the 12th century (a 1 NLG coin can be deposited into a box at  the left side of the altar that will light up the choir and frescoes dome for you). There are also magnificent confessional booths, a fantastically carved oak side pulpit, 17th century pipe organ, stained glass windows, extremely rare translucent alabaster stone windows, the two crypts, and the **Schatkamer** treasury that is open during the high season. *The basilica is open daily around the year from 9am until 5pm, and is free to enter. The treasury is open daily from April through September from about 12noon until 4:30pm and costs about 4 NLG to enter.*

**Further into the Old Town**

Continue through to the rear of the plaza and head straight ahead along the Koestraat as you pass by a few local bars, and a block or so later you will turn right onto the Stenenbrug. At building #1 you will find the **Bisschopsmolen** (Bishop's Mill). On most Saturdays, a charming local taxi driver unlocks the doors that lead into this 17th century mill, and grinds high grade flour for the retail bakery next door. If you happen to be in town on a Saturday, pop inside and ask him a few questions as you see the old gears at work. The mill gets its power via a waterwheel in the backyard that feeds off Belgium's Jeker river just before it merges into the Maas.

From your position facing the entrance to the mill, turn left onto Ridderstraat and walk a few paces until you find a small gateway off to the right. Walk through the gateway and head up the tiny Bisschopsmolengang until bearing to the right through the courtyard and passing the river and its water wheel. The lane now passes through the back of the courtyard and intersects with the **Achter de Oude Minderbroeders**, where you will turn left. About a block down this street on the left side you can peek through the old iron bars next to building #16 to see a series of terraces and stilted additions that are attached to a few adjacent 17th century homes. These structures just above the river once served as out houses. The street soon ends as it intersects with the St. Bernardustraat.

First turn left and walk a couple of steps to building #13 and the famous **In 't Knijpke**. This odd bar, restaurant, and art film theater is actually located in a cave and is among the stangest places I have seen in Maastricht. Now turn around and follow the other side of St. Bernardustraat up a short distance to the restored **Helpoort** (Hell's Gate), the last remaining crenallated gateway from the 13th century fortified city walls. A small riverside park surrounds the gateway and contains a special walking path called the **Stadsomwalling** that can take you along the wall ruins and some adjacent medieval bastions.

**Towards the St. Servaaskerk**

After passing through the old gateway and looking around the walls and park area, filled with cannons, bear right and follow the side of the

Helport towards a recenly added wooden garage, and turn left onto a small unmarked pathway leading towards a stone bridge. Cross the small bridge and keep following the pathway as it curves to the right and passes along a converted 17th century convent and then merges into the Begijnenstraat.

When this street ends, bear right onto the Sint Pieterstraat, walk a few steps up the left hand side of the street, and turn left on the **Lange Grachtje**. This unusual lane features more ruins of the medieval city walls that even have a pair of cave-like houses built directly into them. For a few weeks in Spring, these walls come to life with thousands of small wild flower blossoms that even find their way through the narrow slits that were originally carved into the walls to allow stones to be thrown at attacking soldiers.

At the end of this short street you are let out onto a cozy plaza where you should turn left onto the Grote Looiersstraat. After walking a couple of blocks up, look out for building #27a on the left hand side, where you will find a gateway topped by a gable stone of a rich man with his servant. The doors below the gable stone can be opened to reveal the entrance to the **Martinushof**. This small isolated series of whitewashed brick row homes around a cute inner courtyard garden were built in the 17th century, when local businessman Martinus Frencken bequeathed the bulk of his estate to create an almshouse with cottages for use by 13 elderly religious single women. Although the rules were later changed to allow two male tenants to move in, it is still a wonderfully tranquil and solemn place.

Depart this interesting inner courtyard through the same door you entered from and walk directly across the street while passing the bronze sculptures of local poet Fons Olterdissen and his pupils. Now turn left to follow the side of the De Bosquetplein square for half a block until you reach the front of the city's **Natuur Historisch Museum** (Natural History Museum), located in an old convent that contains exhibits relating to the natural history and geology of the province of Limburg. You may have to ring the bell to enter if the doors are locked. *The natural history is open Monday through Friday from 10:00am until 12:30pm and again from 1:30pm until 5:00pm, and weekends from 2:00pm until 5:00pm, and costs 3.50 NLG per person to enter.*

Retrace your steps through the square for half a block or so before turning left onto the Looiersgracht. About a block up the left side of the street you will see a statue of a donkey, and just behind the bronze is a great view out over the river and a nice bridge house. Continue up the same street as it soon merges into the Boonefantenstraat and then comes to a wide fork in the road where you will bear right onto the Tongersestraat. A few steps later turn left onto the Bouillonstraat as it passes along buildings that make up the main campus of the **Universiteit van Limburg**, with a full-time student population of over 7,500. Next bear left uphill on the Sint Servaasklooster and soon you will find a pair of dramatic churches. The smaller Gothic **Sint Janskerk** (St. John's church) dates back to the 12th century. It is mostly known for its 70 meter (240 foot) red tower, the tallest such structure in the city, that can be visited during the warmer months if you don't mind walking up 225 steps to the panoramic viewing platform.

Keep walking along the same street as you pass through a pair of double archways, and then turn right just before the end of the block to find the entrance to the larger and much more famous 10th century **Sint Servaasbasiliek** (St. Servaas Basilica) that was built upon the tomb of Saint Servaas who was the bishop of Maastricht during the 4th century. Expanded over the centuries, this basilica can be visited to see its opulent main portal complete with biblical sculptures, Holland's largest church bell in the south tower, 17th century organ, the Netherlands' only Gothic chapel, the statue of Charlemagne, a nice cloister, and the crypt of St. Servaas.

Off to the side of the cloister you will find a room marked the **Schatkamer** (Treasury Room) that features 10th through 14th century gold and silver monstrance, silk tapestries, chalices, choir stalls, ivory and jewel inlaid boxes, Roman relics, the world famous 12th century reliquary that holds the mortal remains of St. Servaas, and a huge cross supposedly made from the wood of the cross used in Jesus' crucifixion. *The basilica and its two floor treasury are both open daily around the year from 10:00am until at least 4:00pm and costs 3.50 NLG per person to enter.*

### Around the Vrijthof

From the basilica, turn right onto the Keizer Karelplein and follow it directly into the **Vrijthof**, Maastricht's largest central square. The square is lined by cafés, bars, restaurants, and theaters. During the warmer months, thousands of locals and visitors alike spend sunny afternoons sitting and socializing at the outdoor tables here. Make sure to pop into some of the more interesting establishments here, such as the richly decorated yet casual **De Struis is Ope**, a superb brown café that has been here since 1730. The cafés here are popular from the mid-afternoon until the late evening, and this area is a great place to meet fellow travelers and locals alike.

### Towards the Stadhuis & Markt Square

Now cut through this side of the square and walk down the **Grote Staat**, the city's major shopping street. Hundreds of shops in all price ranges can be found lining both sides of this wide pedestrian-only road.

The most interesting buildings here is located a couple of blocks down at the very end of the street. The **Het Dinghuis** at building #1 is home to the VVV tourist information center. Built in 1470, this superb judge's office building features an impressive gable and an original timber wall.

## MAASTRICHT'S BONNEFANTEN MUSEUM

*Recently, the superb **Bonnefanten Museum of Art and Archaeology** has moved to new quarters along the Maas river, about a 15 minute walk away from downtown. The complex is comprised of immense new brick wings and a bullet shaped metal pavilion just completed from plans by Italian designer Aldo Rossi, as well as parts of an historic structure known as the Wiebengahal. Inside you will find several worthy exhibits, including sections dedicated to Stone Age through Medieval archaeological findings, 14th through 18th century paintings by Italian and Dutch Masters such as Pieter Brueghel,, beautiful statuary, a fine collection of modern art, a large collection of prints, and locally produced earthenware and silver pieces.*

*There are also many scheduled lectures, special guided tours, art restoration workshops, a nice gift shop, and a great café. Don't even think about leaving Maastricht without spending at least a few hours here! The museum is now open to the public Tuesday through Sunday from 11:00am until 5:00pm and costs 10 NLG per person.*

At the end of the shopping road, turn left onto the Muntstraat and follow it until it merges into the enormous Markt square. This is a major point of arrival and departure for thousands of local commuters, and is rung by dozens of small restaurants and bars that are housed in well-preserved 17th century townhouses with fine gable stones. The giant building in the center of the plaza is the **Stadhuis** (City Hall) building. Constructed in 1664 from plans by Pieter Post, the towering carillon rings out with the sounds of melodies played on 43 hand-crafted bells (although it has recently stopped while they renovate the entire building). Visitors may view the magnificent entrance hall and view parts of the building's interior covered in frescoes, paintings, paneling, rich antique tapestries, and regal chambers. The city hall is *normally open from 8:30am until 12:30pm and agin from 2:00pm until 5:30pm on non holiday weekdays, and there is no entrance fee.*

The other main attraction at the square is the large **Farm Fresh Produce Market** on Wednesday and Friday mornings between 8:00am until 1:00pm. This is a great place to stock up on picnic supplies for a nice outing along the Mass river banks. The famed **Friture** Flemish (French) fried potato eatery at building #75 is always packed with lines of locals taking out huge portions of what they consider to be Maastricht's best fries (for just 4 NLG per order). Customarily ordered with a mayonnaise dressing on top (but ketchup is also available), one of these tasty treats is large enough to have as a lunch! The bars around here are for the late night crowd that show up between 1:00am and 5:00am on weekends.

**GUIDED SIGHTSEEING TOURS**
There are several special guided trips offered by foot, bus, and river boat to the sights in and around Maastricht. The following is a brief listing of the most popular trips, but for a complete listing, contact the VVV tourist information office.

**By Boat**
The following cruises are all operated by the **Rederij Stiphout** company with ticket and information offices at the *Maaspromenade 27, Tel: (43) 325-4151.*
• **Maas River Boat Cruise**. This one hour tour starts at the piers near the St. Servaas bridge and continues along the river. Departs several times daily between April 15 and September 17. The price is about 9 NLG per person.
• **Maas River and St. Pietersberg Cave Cruise**. For three hours you will glide aong the river and have a brief stop at the caves carved into the mountain of nearby Sint Pietersberg. Departures are scheduled at least three times per day between April 15 and September 10. The trip costs around 14 NLG per person.
• **Maastricht-Leige Round Trip Cruise**. This day trip includes a two and a half hour stop off at the nearby Belgian city of Liege. It departs here at 10:00am and returns at 5:30pm on Sunday, Tuesday, Wednesday, and Thursdays only between May 23 and September 3. The price is about 29 NLG per person, and reservations are required.
• **Sunday Brunch Cruise**. A two hour cruise along the river including an all you can eat warm and cold buffet lunch for 42 NLG per person. Departs at around 11:00am or so every Sunday between April 14 and December 17.

**By Bus**
There are a series of special holiday and seasonal bus tours operated by the Stadsbus municipal transit company. They schedule great guided sightseeing rides (narrated in Dutch only) through the most historic parts of town, as well as to nearby casemates and caves, for between 9 NLG and 13 NLG per person. These trips depart the Centraal Station and Vrijthof areas a few times daily during the following dates:
• Between April 8 and April 22: Monday through Saturday.
• Between July 2 and September 6: Tuesday through Saturday.
• Between October 15 and October 26: Tuesday through Saturday

For more specific information, contact the VVV or the **Stadsbus** municipal transit company with ticket and information offices at *Parallelweg 58, Tel: (43) 329-2566.*

---

### THE MAASTRICHT SELF-GUIDED "AUDIOMATE" TOUR

*Another good way to be guided through the city of Maastricht on your own schedule is to stop by the VVV headquarters on Kleine Staat #1 and rent an **Audiomate** digital audio guide system. This device (it actually looks like a cellular phone) allows visitors to punch in numbers relating to specific buildings and neighborhoods they are passing by and hear a brief description of the history and legends that corresponds to many of them. The system rents for 3.50 NLG per hour, 15 NLG for 4 hours, and 25 NLG per 8 hours, and is available in English, French, and Dutch versions. Remember to bring the unit back to the VVV offices when you have agreed to, or they will charge you for a second day! For more details, contact the VVV - Maastricht at (43) 325-2121 or pop by their offices during normal retail hours.*

---

**By Foot**

The best way to see the city is by following an expert local guide who is fluent in English and can take you to the places that only an expert would know about. Private guides can be hired for those who are willing to pay upwards of 215 NLG for four hours, but a much less expensive alternative also exists: the Maastricht VVV tourist office has organized city walking tours for individuals who want to join a small group of other English speaking visitors as they are led by a talented guide. These trips all leave from the front of the historic VVV headquarters in the Het Dinghuis building at Klein Staat #1 (just a block or so behind the Vrijthof square) at 2:00pm on specially selected seasonal dates.

The fee for either of these two different 90 minute walking tours is now only 5.25 NLG per person. The special two hour tour costs 10 NLG per person, and you can choose between a history-oriented visit around the city's remaining medieval defensive fortifications, or their Highlights of Maastricht City Walk that stops at the most famous churches, squares, side streets, and parks. Stop by the VVV tourist information centers at Kleine Staat #1 or at the Centraal Station, or call them at *Tel: (43) 321-7878* for reservations and specific details.

These are the typical dates for these trips, but they change every year depending on exactly when the Easter holidays fall on the calendar.
• Daily from March 1 through March 4
• Daily during Easter Week
• Daily during Christmas Week

• Daily from 12 October through 27 October
• Daiy from 29 June through 1 September
• Saturdays only from April 18 through June 30
• Saturdays only from 28 October through 30 November
• Sundays only from 7 January through 6 April
• Sundays only from 7 September through 11 October

## NIGHTLIFE & ENTERTAINMENT
### Bars, Pubs, & Grand Cafes
**METAMORFOOS**, *Kleine Gracht 42. Tel (43) 321-2714.*

Located near the Markt square, this bustling grand café is especially popular with the 20 to 30 year old crowd when they stay open until 5am on weekend nights. Get here before midnight and you have a good chance of meeting some fun loving locals who may even buy you a few drinks.

**JOIE DE VIVRE**, *Achter het Vleeshuis 17. Tel (43) Unlisted.*

Packed with students from the university, this rock and roll bar on a street known for drunken patrons is a great place to hang out on any night of the week. They offer a good selection of local and Belgian beers, strong mixed drinks, and never charge a cover to get in.

**FALSTAFF**, *Amorsplein 6. Tel (43) 321-7238.*

Situated a block or so behind the Vrithof, this busy pub offers a fun ambiance full of under 30 year old beer enthusiasts that flock here on weekends to sample some of the over 100 varieties of local and imported brews. A nice place to start off a long evening of bar hopping, especially when their huge open air terrace is open. Be advised that by midnight the place gets totally packed!

**IN 'T KNIJPKE**, *St. Bernardusstraat 13. Tel (43) 321-6525.*

What an unusual little place! This combination bar, café, restaurant, cheese cellar, and film house gets a real mixed crowd of all ages in the evenings, especially when they screen an important art film in their cute 84 seat theater. Patrons can sit back in their cave like basement and enjoy fine beers and drinks until 2am or so. Food is served until about 1:00am each night.

**CLINIQUE**, *Platielstraat 9. Tel (43) 325-1683.*

By day this is a great place to munch down a huge portion of spare ribs, but after 10pm or so on weekends it becomes a small dance club and bar. The night time weekend crowd ranges from 20 to 35 years old, and they really know how to drink!

### Discos, Multipurpose, & Live Music Venues
**D 'N HIEMEL**, *St. Bernardustraat. Tel (43) Unlisted.*

This unusual cave-like disco (its name translates to "In Heaven") is located just next to the 13th century Helpoort gate in the ruins of the town's medieval walls. Open on Saturday nights only, this place gets packed by midnight with a good crowd of fun loving locals who are here to dance and meet new people. Cover charge is about 10 NLG, and the drinks are strong!

**BASEMENT 5**, *Sterzaal Bredestraat 19. Tel: (43) 328-8520*
For those looking for alternative music concerts ranging from funk to punk, this concert hall on the edge of Maastricht's social circuit is about the best choice. Shows here costs an average of 10 NLG per person and feature an array of local and imported bands that are on the rise. Call in advance to find out what is scheduled during your stay.

**LOSS THEATER**, *Achter de Barakken 31a. Tel (43) 325-3933*
The Loss is a multi-purpose theater and live music venue that hosts an assortment of disco nights and rave events in between a schedule of much more serious theatrical performances. With a capacity of well over 1,000, this converted theater is the best place in town to check out special events for the 18 to 30 year old party crowd.

**BANANAS ULTRA**, *Brusselsestraat 49. Tel: (43) 325-5281*
If you haven't figured it out yet, Maastricht is not much of a disco and dance club town. This small venue in the center of downtown is about as close as it gets to a full fledged disco, and is open Wednesday through Sunday evenings from 10pm until 2am. The music changes depending on the DJ and the theme of the night, but with a relaxed door policy and a minimal cover charge, it may be worth popping inside for a while. On my last visit here, I caught some good acid, hip hop, funk, and psychedelic underground dance tunes and partied all night with some local university students.

## PRACTICAL INFORMATION

**Main VVV Tourist Office** - *Kleine Staat 1* - *(43) 325-2121*
**Centraal Station VVV Tourist Office** - *(43) 325-6270*
**Visitor's & Convention Bureau** - *Kleine Staat 1* - *(43) 328-0838*
**Maastricht City Hall** - *Markt 78* - *(43) 329-2222*
**Maastricht-Aachen Airport** - *(43) 366-6444*
**Air Exel at the Airport** - *(43) 365-0065*
**Maastricht Radio Dispatched Taxis** - *(43) 343-6000 or (43) 363-3333*
**Domestic Train and Bus Info** - *(6) 9292*
**International Train Info** - *(43) 328-1400*
**Stadsbus Transit Head Office** - *Parellelweg 58* - *(43) 329-2566*
**Emergency Hotline** - *06-11*

# 18. VALKENBURG

The popular summer-time resort town of **Valkenburg** (also known as **aan de Geul**) has been promoting itself as a major tourist destination for well over 120 years now. The seasonally popular town was once a quaint and peaceful farming village on the banks of the **Geul River**, with roots dating back to the Roman era. Nowadays, if you arrive here between late April and September, thousands of English, Belgian, and German tourists arrive each week on package tours, and fill up every narrow lane in the town's miniature Centrum.

Most of the historic relics of Valkenburg's medieval heyday now lie in ruins, but its really worth a trip inside of the many strange underground Roman quarries that have been imaginatively utilized over the centuries. Now that so many foreigners vacation here, literally dozens of amusing attractions and theme parks have sprung up within blocks of each other. Come prepared for crowds during the summer, and you'll need plenty of money.

While I certainly enjoy my visits to Valkenburg, the real fun began after I rented a bicycle and headed out on the area's amazing scenic bike routes. This entire part of southern Limburg is dotted with lush rolling hills full of grazing animals and beautiful half-timber farm houses. You can bike, drive, and hop on a bus to a handful of incredibly friendly little hamlets such as **Wittem**, **Epen**, and **Mechelen**, (each with a couple of charming inns and rustic local cafés) within a 20 kilometer (12 mile) radius of downtown Valkenburg. These settlements are pretty much as they always have been, and have preserved their peaceful and traditional ambiance. After discussing what to do in town, I'll describe some other places nearby that are well worth the effort to visit.

## ORIENTATION

Valkenburg is located in the extreme southern section of Holland's **Limburg** province, with a population of 19,347. It lies 185 kilometers (114 miles) south-southeast of the capital city of Amsterdam, and only 13 kilometers (8 miles) east-northeast of Maastricht.

## ARRIVALS & DEPARTURES
### By Air
While a major airport called the **Maastricht-Aachen International Airport** lies only 12 kilometers (7 miles) northwest of town, most visitors from North America usually fly into Amsterdam's **Schiphol Airport** and rent a car, or take the beautiful train ride here.

### By Bus
Many of the bus lines between Valkenburg and other parts of Holland usually require a change of buses at Maastricht's bus station near its Centraal Station. The local **Hermes Streekvervoer** commuter bus lines #50 and #35 both stop near the **Station Valkenburg** rail depot just a few blocks north of the Centrum, and various other points downtown. Connections between the station and any other point in Valkenburg can generally be made by the adjacent public bus stops for about 3 NLG per person each way, or via taxi for roughly 12.50 NLG or so depending on where you are going.

### By Car
Downtown street-side parking spots are fairly easy to find.
From **Amsterdam**, the best way to get to Valkenburg by car is to take the **A-10** ring road south from the city center until connecting onto the **A-2** south for about 201 kilometers (125 miles), before exiting onto route **N-590** east for about 12 kilometers (7 miles) until the Valkenburg exit.

### By Train
Valkenburg is linked to almost any other point in Holland and Europe by several major rail lines. This town's **Station Valkenburg** train depot in a castle-like building at the north side of town is the major point of mass transport arrivals. All the other service you may need can be found just a three minute walk away in the center of town. Connections between this station and any other point in Valkenburg can generally be made by foot, or by using the adjacent public bus stops for around 3 NLG per person each way, by **Treintaxi** for 6 NLG per person, or via taxi for roughly 12 NLG or so, depending on where you are going.
Use the train information phone numbers listed in the *Practical Information* section at the end of this chapter to reconfirm, in advance, the exact time and station you may need.

## GETTING AROUND TOWN
### By Public Transportation
While almost any sight within Valkenburg is well within walking distance from any point downtown, the region's **Hermes Streekvervoer**

transit company offers a selection of public bus lines to get you safely and easily around the suburbs and nearby towns. They accept **Nationale Strippen Kaarts**. Almost all of these buses stop at one point or another near the Station Valkenburg. The normal hours of operation for most of the system is from about 7:00am until roughly 10:00pm. After that your only choices are either to walk, or to take a taxi.

## By Taxi

There are a couple of dozen licensed taxis and mini-vans roaming the streets and major passenger arrival points of the city during all hours of the day and night. Drivers here have new Renault and Opel 4 door sedans, a few limousines, and even a minibus or two to allow them to drive tour groups around as well. Drivers are polite, honest, and typically multilingual. To find a taxi, either hail down an unoccupied cab driving by with its "Taxi" roof light illuminated, go to one of the obvious taxi stands throughout the city, or call *(43) 601-5555* for a radio response pick-up on demand.

The main taxi ranks are located at the Station Valkenburg, the Holland Casino, and near the Thedoor Dorrenplein square. Taxis here are metered and charge somewhere between 10.50 NLG to 14.50 NLG per ride (not per person) between most Valkenburg locations depending on exact distance. A limited number of the city's taxi's now accept major credit cards for fare payments.

## WHERE TO STAY

*Expensive*

**KASTEEL WITTEM**, *Wittemer Allee, 3, Wittem. Tel: (43) 450-1208. Fax; (43) 450-1260. US & Canada Bookings (Relais & Chateaux) 1-212-856-0115. Year round rack rates from 210 NLG per double room per night (E.P.). Special Gourmet Packages from 460 NLG per double room per night (M.A.P.) All major credit cards accepted.*

Of all the fine inns and hotels I have visited in Holland, this enchanting and surprisingly affordable hotel remains my personal favorite. Located 15 kilometers (9 miles) away from either Valkenburg or Maastricht in the peaceful hamlet of **Wittem**, this historic 12th century castle is home to a fantastic little hotel and gourmet restaurant that is truly in a class of its own. As soon as you pull into the driveway and first glimpse the castle's dramatic facade and adjacent moat, you know you're in for an unforgettable experience.

This superb Relais & Chateaux establishment offers 12 individually designed luxurious double rooms (available in both superior or deluxe categories) that all come complete with deluxe private bathrooms, extremely comfortable bedding, fine hand-crafted furnishings, color satellite television, am-fm clock radios, opulent designer fabrics, direct dial telephones, high quality hair and skin care products, and large picture windows looking out onto superb views of the nearby rolling countryside. The stunning public rooms, lounges, restaurants, private dining rooms, and awesome grand stairway are surrounded by priceless chandeliers, antiques, solid oak paneling, and Flemish paintings. Owned and personally managed by Marc and Peter Ritzen, the hotel provides an exceptionally welcoming ambiance of casual elegance. Service here is simply outstanding, with all of the friendly staff members (including the owners) working together in sharing their responsibilities as a team to ensure that you will never want to leave.

Among the many activities that you can enjoy near the hotel are horseback rides, scenic rural drives, golf courses, fresh water fishing, tennis courts, bicycle trails, invigorating hikes, wine tasting, and picnicking. Inside the castle itself is one of Holland's best continental restaurants (see complete review below in Where to Eat), where I have enjoyed some of the most remarkable meals of my life. Besides enjoying the fantastic afternoon and evening meals, make sure not to miss their superb breakfasts served daily with mouth-watering croissants, cheeses, fresh breads, and amazing home-made jams created by the Ritzen's mother. The Kasteel Wittem receives my absolute highest recommendation!

**HOTEL PRINSES JULIANA**, *Broekham 11. Tel: (43) 601-2244. Fax; (43) 601-4405. US & Canada Bookings (Relais & Chateaux) 1-212-856-0115. Year round rack rates from 215 NLG per double room per night (E.P.). Special Gourmet Packages from 430 NLG per double room per night (M.A.P.) All major credit cards accepted.*

This exclusive deluxe hotel is undoubtedly the best (and most expensive) place to stay in Valkenburg city limits. Situated just a couple of short blocks from all of the town's many sights and attractions, this extremely formal yet welcoming grand hotel has been operated by the ever-present Stevens family for more than 80 years. Still known throughout Holland as the place where the rich and famous spend their weekends, the hotel restaurant is even more formal and well respected.

This 4 star property is housed in two separate villa-style buildings just across the street from one another. Inside these stunningly large, converted old world structures, are 21 huge deluxe rooms and apartments, each with a marble covered private bathroom, exclusive designer furnishings, wall to wall carpeting, mini-bar, electric trouser press, remote control satellite television, am-fm clock radio, direct dial telephone, and in many cases wonderful views over the quaint city streets and gardens. The hotel also boasts a superb restaurant and summertime terrace, business meeting rooms, a wonderful lounge, room service, free morning newspapers in the language of your choice, and some the city's most professional staff. The Prinses Juliana is one of the most requested hotels in southern Holland for visiting diplomats, movie stars, executives, and deluxe travelers from around the world. Highly Recommended!

### Moderate

**HOTEL KASTEEL VAALSBROEK**, *Hovetstraat 3, Vaals. Tel: (43) 601-2484. Fax; (43) 601-4320. Year round rack rates from 185 NLG per double room per night (E.P.). All major credit cards accepted.*

Situated in the peaceful hamlet of Vaals, some 20 minutes away from both Valkenburg and Maastricht, this converted castle offers their guests beautiful accommodations at a reasonable price. The opulent 4 star hotel features about 50 or so deluxe rooms and large suites that all have private bathroom, antique and/or hardwood furnishings, remote control satellite television, direct dial telephone, extremely comfortable bedding, and incredible countryside views. Facilities include a great formal French restaurant, business meeting and conference rooms, plenty of scenic garden space, free parking, room service, express laundry and dry cleaning, outdoor terraces, special rooms for the physically challenged, and both indoor and outdoor swimming pools. This is a nice place to stay, as well as enjoy a fine gourmet meal!

**HOTEL HOEVE DE PLEI**, *Overgeul 1, Mechelen. Tel: (43) 455-1294. Fax: (43) 455-1495. Year round rack rates from 112 NLG per double room per night (C.P.). Most major credit cards accepted.*

This family-owned and operated converted 18th century half-timber traditional farmhouse inn rests on the banks of the Geul River near the heart of the stunningly pretty town of **Mechelen**, some 15 minutes ride away from Valkenburg. There are a series of 20 or so period style rooms that all have private or shared bathrooms, antique and/or hardwood furnishings, and great views out over the town and countryside. Facilities include a good restaurant, a fireside lounge, gardens, terraces, available child care, private parking, nearby bicycle rentals facilities, adjacent hiking paths, and a good staff. This is a great place to stay for those interested in long country drives, hikes, and bike rides, and is well worth your consideration.

**HOTEL DE KROON**, *Wilhelminastraat 8, Epen. Tel: (43) 455-1250. Fax: (43) 455-2715. Year round rack rates from 135 NLG per double room per night (C.P.). All major credit cards accepted.*

Located in the heart of the tranquil village of **Epen**, about 20 minutes away from Valkenburg, this unassuming little inn has been lovingly managed by the friendly Ensing-Ubaghs family for almost a century. You can select one of 18 nice large rooms that all feature private bathroom, remote control color television, direct dial telephone, wall-to-wall carpeting, hardwood furniture, comfortable beds, nice floral prints, and in some cases superb balconies and picturesque views out over the nearby rolling hills. Facilities at the hotel include a good regional restaurant, nearby complimentary swimming pool and tennis courts, bicycle rentals, free parking, meeting and reception rooms, and a great courtyard terrace. Well worth the price, I was quite impressed here during my last visit and would suggest this place to all visitors to the area.

**PARKHOTEL RODING**, *Neerhem 68. Tel: (43) 601-3241. Fax: (43) 601-3240. Year round rack rates from 165 NLG per double room per night (E.P.). All major credit cards accepted.*

The cute medium-sized Parkhotel Roding is housed in a nice old three story structure on the edge of town near several attractions, including the Kabelbaan cable car ride. There are 86 double and family-style triple rooms that all feature private bathrooms, satellite television, simple furnishings, am-fm clock radio, mini-bar, and nice interior or street-side windows. Facilities here include an outdoor café, a good restaurant, a nice indoor pool, room service, a lounge, gardens, available child care, private parking, business meeting rooms, and a good staff that work hard to keep families returning year after year.

### Inexpensive

**HOTEL CAFE DE LA RUINE**, *Neerhem 2. Tel: (43) 601-2992. Fax: (43) None. Low season rack rates from 75 NLG per double room per night (B.P.). High season rack rates from 115 NLG per double room per night (B.P.). Most major credit cards accepted.*

The De La Ruine is simply the best affordable hotel in the center of town. Built right alongside the 16th century Berkelpoort old town wall gateway just below the Kasteel de la Ruine castle, this adorable little hotel and restaurant offers 10 cozy antique styled double rooms (seven with private bathroom and three with shared bathroom), each with delightful period furnishings, remote control satellite color television, direct dial telephone, and lots of charm. Their country inn-style regional restaurant is quite good, and there is also nearby parking, a nice relaxing lounge, a great terrace, and a welcoming staff. Highly recommended as the best deal in downtown Valkenburg!

**HOTEL PENSION ZOMERLUST**, *Plenkerstraat 60. Tel: (43) 601-3803. Fax; (43) None. Year round rack rates from 74 NLG per double room per night (C.P.). All major credit cards accepted.*

This pension offers eight basic and simple rooms in a converted, typical old Limburg house on a street full of the town's most famous attractions. While far from deluxe, these units have shared bathrooms, reasonably comfortable furnishings, and, in some rooms, lots of sunlight.

## WHERE TO EAT

*Very Expensive*

**RESTAURANT PRINSES JULIANA**, *Broekham 11. Tel: (43) 601-2244. All major credit cards accepted.*

When you're in the mood for an elegant gourmet French meal and want to really dress up for the occasion, the Prinses Juliana is certainly the best and most serious dining room in this part of Holland. Most of the country's finest chefs have worked this famous establishment's busy kitchen, and the dishes that they have inspired over the decades can still be found on the new a la carte and prix-fixe menus. The white gloved service is extremely attentive, thus assuring my last meal here took well over three hours from soup to dessert. Affiliated with the Relais & Chateaux and Alliance Gastronomique Neerlandiase, the wine list is equally impressive and has hundreds of bottles that range in price from 25 NLG to well over 5,000 NLG each!

Among the dishes most commonly offered here are lobster bisque for 32.50 NLG, poached eggs with smoked Scottish salmon with cresson leaves and truffle cream at 39.50 NLG, marinated scallops with langoustinos in garlic for 47.50 NLG, baked goose liver with apples and soy sauce at 52.50 NLG, poached filet of sole with wild mushrooms for 57.50 NLG, grilled lobster in couscous and basil butter at 75 NLG, filet of beef in red wine sauce with wild mushrooms and noodles for 52.50 NLG, farm raised pigeon with sautéed vegetables in tarragon at 52.50 NLG, braised lamb in curry sauce covered in pastry dough for 60 NLG, and pear tarts with nougat ice cream and caramel for 22.50 NLG. An excellent place to have a quiet lunch or dinner, but bring plenty of extra cash and make reservations well in advance!

*Expensive*

**KASTEEL WITTEM**, *Wittemer Allee 3, Wittem). Tel: (43) 450-1208. All major credit cards accepted.*

Even if you're not fortunate enough to be staying in this superb inn, I strongly suggest enjoying a spectacular gourmet meal here. Situated on the ground floor of a centuries-old converted castle, both opulent dining rooms here feature fantastic weekend lunches and daily dinners that are beyond comparison. Dutch-born executive chef Marcel Bisselink has designed an innovative series of seasonal a la carte and multiple course gastronomic menus, each featuring the finest fresh ingredients blended together in perfect harmony.

Among the most delicious courses available during my last visit were perfectly marinated Scottish salmon served upon a paste of yellow peppers and anchovies for 32.50 NLG, consommé of wild game with herb puffs at 17.50 NLG, potato cream soup with shrimp and fennel for 18.50

NLG, king shrimps with pasta pesto and tomato coulis at 38.50 NLG, a magnificent poached fillet of turbot in white wine with truffles and assorted vegetables for 40 NLG, Angus rib steak in red wine and shallot sauce at 55 NLG, fillet of rabbit with mashed Brussels sprouts for 54 NLG, an amazing dish of tender lobster surrounded by saffron risotto and Chartreuse liqueur at 70 NLG, and a fine selection of regional cheeses and mouth-watering homemade desserts starting at 18.50 NLG per serving. Special gastronomic three course lunch, and four or six course evening menus, are also available which include several of the above dishes and other seasonal specials.

The restaurant's extensive wine cellars boast over 10,000 bottles of fine vintage wines from around the world. You can either select a bottle of wine from a large list, or take advantage of specially chosen selections of several different wines by the glass, designed to best to accompany your menu. The ambiance in the dining rooms is quite elegant yet relaxed, with an excellent wait staff (the only formally dressed people here) serving you on the finest Christofle silver settings and Baucher china. There is no real dress code here, and guests often socialize with each other over an after-dinner drink in the tranquil lounge. If you want to experience the finest culinary delights that Holland has to offer, this is certainly the place to go. As a member of the prestigious Alliance Gastronomique Néerlandaise, the Kasteel Wittem is highly recommended as one of the country's top restaurants.

**LE RELAIS GASTRONOMIQUE,** *Plenkerstraat 50. Tel: (43) 601-2797. Most major credit cards accepted.*

Chef Hubert Haenen runs this romantic little gourmet restaurant a couple of blocks away from the center of Valkenburg. Most of the faithful clientele here don't even ask to see the huge menu, they just tell Mr. Haenen to bring out the 150 NLG, six course surprise menu. Just to give you an idea of what you might expect to see on their seasonal prix-fixe 75 NLG per person 4 course gourmet menu, typical offerings include duck pate, fresh oysters from Zeeland, salad with smoked salad, salad with walnuts and Roquefort cheese, wild boar with truffles, smkoked salmon stuffed with shrimp, entrecote of Angus beef, filet of lam in garlic sauce, Scottish highland venison, and supreme desserts. Call well in advance for a lunch or dinner reservation.

### Moderate

**RESTAURANT EKLISIA,** *Plenkerstraat 45. Tel: (43) 601-4141. All major credit cards accepted.*

What a great find! This Greek restaurant is housed in a beautiful converted 19th century church just a couple of blocks from the center of downtown Valkenburg. Their superb moderately priced menu includes

Greek salad for 8.75 NLG, tuna salad for 9.75 NLG, sardine salad at 8.75 NLG, mixed salads for 6.75 NLG, lamb from the spit with mushroom sauce for 27.50 NLG, lamb cutlets with tasziki for 27.75 NLG, filet or grilled fresh fish at 28.50 NLG, mousaka for 21.50 NLG, and plenty of other items for those that want a break from all the French and Dutch food around town. No dress code, but reservations might be a good idea during the high season.

**RESTAURANT HERBERG DE COMMANDEUR**, *Hoofdtstraat 105, Mechelen. Tel: (43) 455-1220. Cash only - No credit cards accepted.*

This dramatic regional restaurant 20 minutes drive out of Valkenburg in the sleepy town of **Mechelen** is a real gem. Situated next to one of the town's famous 18th century water mills, this traditional old stone building and its adjacent outdoor terrace both offer hearty lunches and dinners at good prices, including assorted cheeses with home-made breads using flour ground by the old water mill at 11 NLG, tomato soup for 5.50 NLG, pate sandwiches at 6 NLG, tuna salad with anchovies for 12.50 NLG, cheese omelets at 12.50 NLG, pancakes for 9 NLG, baked fish at 18.50 NLG, pork with mushroom beer sauce for 18.50 NLG, pork filet in mushroom sauce at 21.50 NLG, grilled salmon for 25.50 NLG, and many other great dishes.

**'T MERGELHEUKSKE**, *Berkelstraat 13. Tel: (43) 601-6350. Most major credit cards accepted.*

This cute second floor restaurant above one of Valkenburg's oldest principal shopping lanes offers an intimate setting for a nice meal. Their delicious menu features Neptune salads at 22.50 NLG, goose liver pate and Dutch shrimp for 23.50 NLG, carpaccio of the house at 22.50 NLG, lambs tongue with whit cabbage salad for 22.50 NLG, shrimp ragout in pastry dough at 25 NLG, braised veal with paprika for 38.50 NLG, and plenty of great desserts starting at 12 NLG each. People here dress fairly well, but there is no strict policy.

**RESTAURANT DE MUNT**, *Muntstraat 7. Tel: (43) 601-2018. All major credit cards accepted.*

Located in the heart of downtown Valkenburg, this beautifully decorated little café and grill room is among the better affordable places to dine in this part of town. Here you can order huge portions from a seasonally changing menu that upon my last visit included melon cocktail with Port wine at 12.50 NLG, ham with melon for 19.50 NLG, shrimp cocktail at 17.50 NLG, scampi salad for 17.50 NLG, home-made fish soup at 8.50 NLG, tomato soup for 6 NLG, wiener schnitsel at 19 NLG, Hungarian goulash for 20 NLG, beef steak at 22.50 NLG, lamb cutlets in honey-thyme sauce for 35 NLG, chateaubriand in Bernaise sauce for 75 NLG, and much more. A really nice place to have a long relaxing casual dinner.

**RESTAURANT LA VENEZIA**, *W. Duysings Rijcken, Mechelen. Tel: (43) 455-2522. Most major credit cards accepted.*

This casual international restaurant with nice views offers a good menu for those who have been out burning calories all day. Their menu features tomato soup for 5.50 NLG, mushroom soup at 5.50 NLG, pancakes with apples for 8 NLG, cheese omelets at 8.50 NLG, ham and cheese for 5.50 NLG, pizza tacos at 8.50 NLG, salmon cocktail for 9.50 NLG, salad with smoked fish at 11.50 NLG, baked salmon filet for 27.50 NLG, beef steak with mushroom sauce at 22.50, entrecote in paprika for 27.50 NLG, wienerschnitzel at 19 NLG.

*Inexpensive*

**CASA PIZZERIA**, *Grotestraat 25. Tel: (43) 601-2180. Cash only - No credit cards accepted.*

This good local hangout in the center of Valkenburg has a large menu of assorted pizzas and pasta that range in price from about 11 NLG to upwards of 18.75 NLG. They also serve up complete meals of meat, chicken, veal, and fish specialties, as well as decent desserts.

**DE KOFFIEPOT**, *Grotestraat 37. Tel: (43) 601-2017. Cash only - No credit cards accepted.*

This cute little lunch restaurant and outdoor café is open from 10:00am until about 8:00pm, and features some of the best inexpensive home-cooked meals in town. Their simple menu includes hearty portions of ham and cheese toasties for 4 NLG, vegetable soup at 4.75 NLG, several types of pancakes starting at 9.50 NLG and up, tuna salad sandwiches at 6.50 NLG, curried chicken salad for 7 NLG, and a host of daily specials. While far from fancy, this cozy establishment is a fun and relaxed place to have lunch or an early dinner.

## SEEING THE SIGHTS

• *From the* **Station Valkenburg** *around the town and back.*
• *Approximate duration (by foot) is at least 8 hours, including museum, gallery, castle, cave, theme park, spa, café, boutique, and side street visits.*

### The Outskirts of Town

I suggest starting your visit to the city, no matter how you arrived, at the town's **Station Valkenburg** rail depot. The adjacent mid-19th century **Stationsgebouw** terminal building is the oldest train station still standing in Holland, and its turret and statue-topped sandstone facade looks more like a castle than a rail station.

From here, cross over to the other side of the Stationsstraat and continue walking straight downhill along a small street called the Wehryweg. After passing the sloping park in front of the modern (and often criticized) **Gemeentehuis** (New City Hall), continue along until the next corner where you will turn right onto the Geneindestraat. As you stroll by several opulent private villas, you'll pass in front of the famous Hotel & **Restaurant Prinses Juliana**, a deluxe and formal old world style inn set in two beautiful mansions on opposite sides of the street. Their respected gourmet restaurant is extremely good, and equally expensive. A couple of long blocks further along the same street, make a left turn near a pretty church to head down the Koningswinkelstraat.

Follow the Koningswinkelstraat until it forks off towards the left and keeps going down until reaching the next intersection, where you will bear left onto the **Prins Bernhardlaan**. The first attraction that you will pass on this street is the **Familiepark de Valkenier**, a small seasonal amusement park designed for the whole family. Attractions include a hall of mirrors, a haunted house, a replica Mississippi river boat, go carts, bumper cars, parachute ride, a cinema, and many other rides for people of all ages. *The amusement park is open from 10:00am until about 7:00pm daily between May and September, and costs 12.50 NLG per person.*

Just across the street is a small white bridge called the Polfermolen Brug that crosses over to the far side of the Geul River. Walk across this bridge and turn right onto the **Plenkerstraat**. A few steps along you will find the main entrance to the town's **De Leeuw Bierbrouwerij**, a great local brewery that produces much of the white and pilsner beers served in Valkenburg's many night spots and in the process making full use of its adjacent water powered mill. *The brewery is open for visits on weekdays between April and October for 3.50 NLG per person, but reservations are mandatory and tickets must be bought in advance at the VVV-Valkenburg's offices on Theodoor Dorrenplein 5, Tel: (43) 601-3364.*

After passing by the brewery, keep walking along the Plenkerstraat for a few steps until passing the modern entrance that indicates the **Romeinse Katakomben** (Roman Catacombs). Inside this former mine there are replicas of Italian catacombs that date back to the Roman era. A candlelit guided tour through the grottos lasts about 30 minutes and takes you past reproductions of tombs, sculptures, paintings, geometric stone murals, and other items placed here in 1913. *The catacombs are open daily from 10:00am and 5:00pm April through October, other time periods they open on weekends only at 2:00pm, and the entrance fee is 6 NLG per person.*

Now turn around and retrace your steps back down the Plenkersstraat, passing by the brewery, and keep walking until you reach the path on your right hand side that leads uphill to the adorable little **Openlucht Theater** (Open Air Theater), used by the community to stage plays, concerts, and other special events in the summer. Further along the same street you will also walk by the **Prehistorische Monstergrot**, a former quarry that has been converted into a small theme park complete with replica dinosaurs, simulated prehistoric landscapes, and other less than fascinating items. *The prehistoric cave is only open April through September daily from 10:00am until 6:00pm, and costs 4.50 NLG per person.*

**The Center of Town**

Keep walking along the Plenkerstraat, passing the side entrance of the **Holland Casino Valkenburg** on your left side, and after about another block and a half you will be led into the Grendelplein. This plaza is actually a major intersection located on the site of the town's former encircling defensive walls. If you look straight ahead you should be able to see a set of wall and castle ruins resting on a bluff directly above the town. Just before entering the plaza, turn sharply to the left onto the Wilhelminalaan and follow it for a half a block before passing by a small fragment of the medieval walls in a formal garden on the right hand side of the street. Next to the tower and wall is the 17th century **Kasteel Den Halder** castle that now is home to the region's VVV executives and cannot be visited by the general public.

Keep walking down this busy street, cross over a pair of bridges spanning both tributaries of the now divided Geul River, and make a right turn onto the Geneindestraat. After a quarter of a block, turn right onto the Lindenlaan, and follow it to the end making sure to stop for a moment and look out across the Geul to see the 17th century **Fransche Molen**, Holland's largest grain mill water-wheel. At the end of the street, make a left turn onto the **Passage**, a street with some of the better boutiques in town.

From here you will end up in the heart of the central **Theodoor Dorrenplein**, the main square of town. Besides being surrounded by various restaurants, bars, and outdoor cafés, the plaza centers around the 17th century **Spaans Leenhof**, a historic structure once used by officials of the King of Spain, and now home of the **VVV** tourist information center. Make sure to stop off here and pick up inexpensive walking maps, local attraction brochures, pamphlets on all the neighboring towns, and copies of the English versions of the *Wandel Kaart* hiking trail map, and at least one of their *Fietsroutes* bicycle route maps.

After exiting the VVV office, make a left turn and walk through the center of the square and continue straight as it merges into the **Grootestraat**. On the right hand side of the first block of this busiest of retail shopping and dining streets is the old **H.H. Nicolaas en Barbara Kerk** church, which is still in use after being rebuilt on this spot several times since first built in the 13th century. At building #31 of this crowded street is the **Streekmuseum**, a regional history museum housed in the **'t Oude Sjtadhoes** (former City Hall). You can view fossils, relics, antique weapons, and other objects found during the excavations of town's ruined castles, old caves, and other important structures. They also have a series of temporary exhibitions on local art, sculpture, ceramics, and/or photos. *The museum is open year round between 10:00am and 5:00pm from Tuesday through Sunday, and costs 2.50 NLG to enter.*

Keep following the Grotestraat until the next corner, where you will make a right turn onto the **Muntstraat**. Over at building #10 is the somewhat interesting **Kaarsenmakerij** (Candle Factory) shop where you can either buy some nice-hand made candles, or make your own for only 4.50 NLG per person including instruction. Just next door is the **Mergelatelier Aarts**, a small shop where artisans hand-craft gift items from Marl stone found in all of the nearby caves and quarries. At the end of Muntstraat, pass underneath the 14th century **Grendelpoort** gateway that was once attached to the now ruined medieval city defensive. Once you pass through the gateway you will pass into the Grendelplein square (actually more like an intersection).

Also nearby are the **Fluweelengrot** caves. This is one of several unusual tunnel systems made from quarries where blocks of Marl stone have been carved out of the hillside and used for building forts and villas around here ever since the Roman times. The cave's tunnel system covers well connects via once secret passages to an 200 year old underground chapel, casemates, a gunpowder room, areas covered in old cave paintings, and the connected ruins of the hilltop 11th century **Kaasteel-Ruine** castle that rests on a panoramic hilltop above the town. *A guided tour through the cave, tunnels, and safe passage to the castle ruins is offered daily year round between 10:00am until 5:00pm at 7.50 NLG per person.*

The same street continues uphill for awhile before finally passing the **Steenkolenmijn** coal mines at building #31. Old equipment from former coal mines has been placed in this old section of a Marl stone quarry to give people an idea of what real coal mines are like. You can see a multilingual documentary of mining, and take a self-guided tour through various stages of the coal collection process. Mildly entertaining; some people seem to love this place. *The replica coal mine is open from 10:00am until 5:00pm daily between April and October, and costs 8.50 NLG per person*

Now retrace you steps back to the Grendelplein, and make a sharp left turn to head uphill on the Cauberg. A few steps up this street at building #4 is the **Gemeentegrot** (Town Cave) complex, where tours via foot and tram descend into the fossilized Marl stone quarries once used to shelter Valkenburg's citizens and other refugees during battles since Roman times. These former inhabitants left old murals and carvings in the cave walls that are quite peculiar. *The caves are open 9:30am until 5:00pm daily from April through October, and Monday to Friday from 2:00pm until 5:00pm as well as 10:00pm until 4:00pm on most weekends from November through March. The entrance fee is now 6.75 NLG a person including the tram ride.*

The huge ultra-modern **Thermae 2000** glass enclosed spa center is located another kilometer (0.6 mile) walk uphill along the Cauberg. Here visitors can bathe in the spa's piping hot (90°F/33°C) indoor and outdoor thermal mineral water pools, sit back in a soothing whirlpool, enjoy optional massage and spa treatments, or even order moderately priced healthy meals at their restaurant. *The spa center is open daily around the year between 9:00am and 11:00pm, and costs around 30 NLG per person to enter.*

Now once again walk back down to the Grendelplein, this time turning right to cross under the Grendelpoort gateway and walk along the Muntstraat. At the next corner bear slightly to your right and follow the restaurant-lined **Berkelstraat**. Keep walking along this major shopping street as you pass under the 16th century **Berkelpoort** city wall gateway, and keep going straight as the street name changes to the **Neerham**. A few blocks up this street at building #44 you will notice a station for the **Kabelbaan** (Cable Car) ride that can take you up to the 30 meter (99 foot) tall panoramic lookout at the Wilhelminatoren tower. Nearby there is also a sports park and a fast **Rodelbaan** downhill toboggan slide ride. *Each of these rides costs 5 NLG and runs from sunrise to sunset between April and September.*

Further along this street is the **Themapark Sprookjesbos**, a wooded theme park with a wild west town, theater, laser shows, playgrounds, white water rides, and dozens of costumed popular fairy tale figures that wander around and talk with children. *The theme park is open 10:00am until at least 6:00pm daily between April and September, and costs 10 NLG per person to enter.*

Now turn around and retrace your steps for a few long blocks until turning right onto the **Berkelplein**. Follow this road as it curves to the left while changing its name several times until merging into the **Geneindestraat**. Make a right turn up the **Wehryweg** and follow it back up to the Station Valkenburg to complete your tour.

## GUIDED SIGHTSEEING TOURS

There are several special guided trips offered by foot, bus, and river boat to the sights in and around Valkenburg. The following is a brief listing of the most popular trips, but for a complete listing, contact the VVV tourist information office.

### By Bicycle

Since the Station Valkenburg is too small to have the usual bicycle rental and parking facilities, you will end up renting one from a private cycle store in town. For around 12.50 NLG a day, plus security deposit, you get a comfortable steel bicycle to run around the town and neighboring villages. By far the best means of local transportation, they can be found year round at both the **Cycle Center**, *Oosterweg 26, Tel: (43) 601-*

*5338* or at **Haagman's**, *Nieuweweg 18, Tel: (43) 601-5555*. Make sure to get a *Fietsroute* bicycle path map before you depart town.

## By Bus

The **Stadsrondrit** sight-seeing bus departs Valkenburg's Grendelplein and criss-crosses through the old town streets, and then allows visitors to ride up a second bus towards the town caves and the Thermae 2000 complex. The ride costs 6 NLG per person, and is run by H.Ostermans en Zon at *Oud-Valkenbergerweg 1, Tel: (43) 601-2479*.

## By Horseback

If you can gather up a few friends or new acquaintances for an afternoon outing, try going on a horseback ride. For small groups of five or more people, **Manege Meyer** on *Op de Locht 52 in Kasen-Bunde Tel: (43) 364-1970* can arrange a half day outing in the beautiful Limburg countryside. For around 85 NLG and up a head, it's well worth the price.

## By Kayak

The VVV can help direct you to a local and nearby Belgian adventure outfitters that run seasonal kayak trips along either the Meuse or the Mass rivers. These 2 to 4 hour treks can cost upwards of 95 NLG a person, and must be reserved several days in advance by calling the **VVV-Valkenburg** at *Tel: (43) 601-3364*.

## By Private Sedan

If you want to ride around the picture-perfect villages just outside of town, and either wish to rent a car, or have someone else do the driving, your choices are pretty much limited to **Haagmans Taxicentral** on *Nieuweweg 16, Tel: (43) 601-5555*. They can rent you a late model sedan, and if desired, provide anything up to and including a chauffeur driven classic Mercedes Benz limo.

## By Steam Train

The **Miljoenenlijn** historic steam-powered railroad puffs its way between the nearby cities of Simpelveld, Schin op Guel, and Kerkrade about 15 to 25 kilometers to the south and east of Valkenburg. Operated by the ZLSM regional transit company in Simpelveld, it costs between 7 NLG and 18.50 NLG round trip (depending on the route) and departs Wednesday through Sunday between March and December, and daily during July and August. Reservations can be made by calling *Tel: (45) 544-0018*.

## NIGHTLIFE & ENTERTAINMENT

There are only a handful of good bars and clubs that stay open throughout the year. During the high season, the places to hit are the **Stadscafe** bar, the nearby **Heineken Hoek** pub and live music café over on the Grotestraat, and the **Riverside** and adjacent **Pavillon** discos on the Oranjelaan.

## EXCURSIONS AROUND VALKENBURG

After you have wandered around most of the sights and attractions in the center of Valkenburg, it's well worth the effort to spend a few days touring the nearby area (**Zuid-Limburg**). I have created one possible route past several small villages and farming estates that can be reached via rental car, bicycle, hiking trails, or regional bus service.

For specific details on how to get to these nearby destinations by public transportation, or to get a detailed bicycle and hiking route maps, stop by the VVV-Valkenburg tourist information offices. They also have informative brochures and listings that detail some small family-owned rustic bed and breakfast inns along these (and other nearby) routes. They can also help you plan a bicycle trip or hike from one inn to another, and turn the following 55 kilometer (34 mile) circular excursion route into a fantastic two or three day side trip of unequaled beauty and tranquillity.

### Wittem

The first charming little hamlet that you should visit along this route is **Wittem,** a small and friendly town of 8,000 or so people. It is located nine kilometers (6 miles) southeast of Valkenburg, and accessible by either driving (or taking a bus) down route **N-595 south**, or via several excellent hiking and separate bike trails. This section of the tour marks the beginning of your trip through southern Limburg's most dramatic countryside. Keep your eyes out for rolling hillsides covered in wild flowers, antique half-timber farmhouses, and plenty of small villages.

About a 1/2 kilometer north of town off the Wittemer Allee (route N-595), you can't help but notice the awesome moat-encircled **Kasteel Wittem**, a prestigious little luxury hotel and great gourmet restaurant in a dreamlike medieval castle. Inside the town itself, you can pop inside the lovely Geradus **Kerk** church with its famed Baroque interior.

### Mechelen

From Wittem, the bike paths, walking trails, and small country lanes lead across the pristine landscape towards several of Holland's cutest villages, starting with **Mechelen**, three kilometers (two miles) to the south-southeast. This tiny village is famous for its two operational 18th century

**Waterradmolens** (water wheels) along the **Hoofdstraat**, and an authentic traditional country ambiance that has not been ruined by too many tourists – yet!

About the only thing you can hear while walking through town is the ever-present cowbells coming from small centuries-old half-timber barns just alongside you. You will have no problem finding reasonably priced cafés, restaurants, and family-run bed and breakfast inns.

## Vaals

After spending some time strolling through Mechelen, head about 9 kilometers (5.6 miles) east-southeast to the resort town of **Vaals**. In the town itself you can see the **Kerk**, a 17th century church with a magnificent 13th century tower. A steep road on the edge of town leads past a small forested area and onward to a well-known sight called the **Drielandenpunt**, a panoramic lookout sight on the peak of the country's highest hill. At the confluence of the official borders of Holland, Belgium, and Germany, at just 321 meters (1,054 feet) it is jokingly (but correctly) referred to as "Holland's Highest Mountain" by many locals.

Nearby is the amusing **Drielandenlabyrint**, a box garden arranged in a labyrinth pattern. Visitors try to figure out how to exit the maze, a process that sometimes takes a fair amount of time. *The labyrinth is open daily 10:00am to 6:00pm between April and October only, and costs 5 NLG per person.*

## Epen

When you're done seeing Vaals, carefully continue about 10 kilometers (6.2 miles) to the west via some of Europe's nicest winding country roads (complete with amazing picnic spots!) until reaching **Epen**. Besides taking a peak at the 18th century **Volmolen** water mill and even more half-timber houses, you can also hike to the nearby **Vijlenerbos** forest and see some excavated Bronze Age burial sights.

## Noorbeek, Mheer, Sint Geertruid, Margratan, & Gulpen

Now after departing Epen, keep heading west for another 9 kilometers (5.6 miles) until reaching **Noorbeek**. This idyllic little farming community is most proud of its medieval **Sint Brigid Kerk** church and tower. From here its another 2.5 kilometers (1.5 miles) northwest to the hamlet of **Mheer** that is dominated by a massive 17th century **Kasteel van Mheer** castle.

Further along the same route, another 2.5 kilometers (1.5 miles) northwest, you will pass by **Sint Geertruid**. This village is popular with people who want to visit the **Limburg in Miniature** scale model village over at *Schoolstraat 5*, as well as for those coming to see the 11th century Gothic interior of the massive **Kerk** church.

Now its a challenging 5.5 kilometer (3.4 miles) ride or hike northeast to **Magraten**, the sight of the World War II **Netherlands-American Military Cemetary**, with the graves of over 8,000 fallen soldiers. From here you can finish off the tour by traveling the last 6 kilometers (3.8 miles) north to return back into **Valkenburg**.

## PRACTICAL INFORMATION

**Main VVV Tourist Office** - *Theodoor Dorrenplein 5 - (43) 601-3364*
**Regional VVV Tourist Office** - *Kasteel Den Halder - (43) 601-7373*
**Valkenburg Radio Dispatched Taxis** - *(43) 601-5555*
**Domestic Train and Bus Info** - *(6) 9292*
**Police Headquarters** - *Het Bat 3 - (43) 601-7272*
**Emergency Hotline** - *06-11*

# 19. LEIDEN

The bustling little university city of **Leiden**, birthplace of the master artist **Rembrandt**, is a great place to spend at least a day or two, or perhaps visit as a day trip from the nearby cities of Amsterdam or Den Haag.

Leiden first became a city after Prince WIlliam of Orange rewarded the locals for their many heroic actions taken while besieged by Spanish forces in 1574. His gift was to establish the rather prestigious **Rijksuniversiteit Leiden**, Holland's first and still most prestigious university.

Within a few decades, the city's textile industry grew into a major source of revenue for the region, employing well over 35,000 people (each working 16 hour shifts) in downtown cloth factories. As the area flourished, many of the city's industrialists and merchants built fine gabled houses that still dominate most of Leiden's streets.

It is the combination of the vast student population and the presence of so many dramatic structures that makes this small city a perfect place to wander around and discover your favorite museums, cafés, restaurants filled with students, and great boutiques.

## ORIENTATION

Leiden (also known as **Leyden**) is situated in the north central section of the Netherlands' **Zuid-Holland** province, with a population of 113,328. It lies 36 kilometers (22 miles) south-southwest of the capital city of Amsterdam, and 17 kilometers (11 miles) northwest of Den Haag.

## ARRIVALS & DEPARTURES
### By Air

Almost all visitors flying to this city will arrive here via land links from **Schiphol Airport** near Amsterdam, about 26 kilometers (16 miles) to the northeast.

## By Bus

Many of the bus lines between Leiden and other parts of Holland tend to stop at the depot just alongside the **Station Leiden** train depot on the northwestern edge of downtown. Make sure to call the bus information phone numbers listed in the *Practical Information* section at the end of this chapteri in advance to find out exactly where and when your bus comes in.

Connections between this station and any other point in Den Haag can generally be made by the adjacent public bus or tram stops for 3 NLG per person each way, or via taxi for roughly 10.50 NLG or so.

## By Car

Downtown street-side parking spots are tough to find.

From **Amsterdam**, the easiest way to get to Leiden is to take the **A-10** ring road around until connecting to the **A-4** south for about 32 kilometers (20 miles) before finding the city's "Centrum" exit.

From **Den Haag** you should take the **N-44** north for some 18 kilometers (11 miles) before exiting at the signs pointing to the city's "Centrum" exit.

## By Train

Leiden is linked to almost any other point in Holland and Europe by several major rail lines. The city's main **Station Leiden** is located on the northwest edge of downtown and has an extensive series of daily arrivals and departures. Those arriving here directly from Schiphol Airport can also take advantage of frequent rail service linking these destinations, sometimes via a mandatory change of train at the suburban Den Haag **HS** (Holland Spoor) rail station.

Connections between this station and any other point in Leiden can generally be made by the adjacent public bus and tram stops for around 3 NLG per person each way, via **Treintaxi** for 6 NLG per person, or by taxi for roughly 10.50 NLG or so. Use the train information phone numbers listed in the *Practical Information* section at the end of this chapter to reconfirm, in advance, the exact time and station which you may need.

# GETTING AROUND TOWN

## By Public Transportation

Leiden's **NZH** regional transit authority offers a vast array of public transportation methods to get you safely and easily around town and the nearby suburbs. There are a few dozen bus and tram lines to choose from depending on where you wish to go. They accept **Nationale Strippen Kaarts**.

The normal hours of operation for most of the system is from about 6:30am until roughly 11:30pm. After that your only choices are either to walk or to take a taxi. Locations outside of downtown Leiden, such as the gardens of Keukenhof, will require travel through more than one zone, so you must ask the driver how many blank strips are required.

**By Taxi**

There are about a hundred or so licensed taxis roaming the streets and major passenger arrival points of the city during all hours of the day and night. Drivers here are nice local fellows who tend to use mainly Mercedes, Renault, Opel, and Ford sedans that can hold just a few pieces of large luggage. To find a taxi, either hail an unoccupied cab driving by with its "Taxi" roof light illuminated or go to the taxi stands near the Station Leiden.

Taxis cost somewhere between 9.75 NLG to 12.50 NLG per ride (not per person) between most downtown locations depending on exact distance and traffic conditions. Some of the city's taxi's now accept major credit cards for fare payments.

## WHERE TO STAY

*Expensive*

**GOLDEN TULIP LEIDEN**, *Schipholweg 3. Tel: (71) 522-1121. Fax: (71) 522-6675. US & Canada Bookings (Golden Tulip) 1-800-344-1212. Year round rack rates from 210 NLG per double room per night (E.P.). All major credit cards accepted.*

This modern and surprisingly comfortable 4 star hotel is one of the best equipped and managed properties in the city. Located just down the block from the train station, the Golden Tulip has 50 or so large rooms and suites that all feature deluxe private bathrooms, remote control satellite television, nice furnishings, am-fm clock radio, hair dryers, direct dial telephone, complimentary coffee and tea trays, mini-bar, and either interior or street-side views. Facilities include an outdoor café, a good restaurant, room service, a lounge, available child care, private parking, business meeting rooms, express laundry and dry cleaning, and a good staff.

*Moderate*

**HOTEL DE DOLEN**, *Rapenburg 2. Tel: (71) 512-0527. Fax: (71) 512-8453. Year round rack rates from 145 NLG per double room per night (E.P.). All major credit cards accepted.*

I really like this charming 3 star hotel in a magnificent 15th century patrician mansion, facing the most famous canal in town. There are 14 nice single and double rooms that all feature private tile bathrooms, cozy furniture, remote control color television, mini-bar, am-fm clock radio, and in some cases even superb canal views. Facilities here include a period styled restaurant, intimate public areas, nearby parking, and there is also plenty of ambiance. A rather good choice in this price range.

**HOTEL NIEUWE MINERVA,** *Boommarkt 23. Tel: (71) 512-6358. Fax: (71) 514-2674. Year round rack rates from 140 NLG per double room per night (E.P.). Most major credit cards accepted.*

This nice 2 star hotel is housed in a late 16th century canal-house, and has 40 nice, comfortable rooms with private bathroom, remote control satellite television, direct dial telephone, and simple furnishings. There is also an antique-style restaurant, a traditional bar area, nearby parking, bicycle rental, business meeting rooms, and a friendly staff.

## WHERE TO EAT

*Moderate*

**ANAK BANDUNG,** *Garenmarkt 24a. Tel: (71) 512-5303. Most major credit cards accepted.*

What a great find! This small Indonesian restaurant in the center of town makes superb and freshly prepared exotic Indonesian dishes spiced with peanuts, coconut milk, and sate. The house specialty is called a Rijsttafel (rice table) and includes several portions of assorted meat, fish, poultry, or vegetarian dishes that you select. All items can be made as spicy or mild as you prefer, and a great meal here will cost between 30 NLG and 50 NLG per person, excluding drinks.

**BACCHUS,** *Breestraat 49. Tel: (71) 514-3444. Most major credit cards accepted.*

This delightful and often busy café, bar, and gourmet restaurant on one of Leiden's oldest principal shopping lanes offers an intimate setting for a nice meal. Their delicious menu features carpaccio at 12.50 NLG, wild forest mushroom soup for 8.50 NLG, special salads starting at 11.50 NLG, daily vegetarian specials for 12.50 NLG, pepper steak with spicy sauce at 21.50 NLG, and much more. People here dress fairly well, but you can be comfortable wearing anything you like..

*Inexpensive*

**ANNIES VERJAARDAG,** *under the bridge at Hoostraat 1a. Tel: (71) 512-5737. Cash only - No credit cards accepted.*

Inside and along the terraces of this waterfront cellar you will find a popular bar and a great little restaurant that is packed with students and locals almost every day of the week. After sitting in the fresco topped cave-like dining room, you can order all sorts of items like tomato soup at 4.75 NLG, Greek salad for 8.75 NLG, salad nicoise at 9.50 NLG, ham toasties for 3 NLG, roast beef sandwiches at 4.35 NLG, apple pancakes for 7.75 NLG, tuna salad at 5.25 NLG, burgers for 8.75 NLG, lasagna at 13.75 NLG, and plenty of warm and cold drinks at reasonable prices.

**RESTAURANTE DONATELLO'S**, *Haarlemmerstraat 20. Tel: (71) 514-7938. Cash only - No credit cards accepted.*

When you are looking for an affordable downtown restaurant to have a hearty  meal after a long day of wandering, try this good Italian spot. Their menu features a vast array of pastas with freshly prepared sauces like marinara, white clam, Alfredo, Bolognese, and basil cream. They also offer 12 different types of pizza, and plenty of veal, chicken, fish, and meat specialties made in classic Italian style. The best news is that all of their pastas and pizzas were recently reduced in price to just 8.75 NLG each, a great bargain!

**NEW YORK PIZZA**, *Beestenmarkt 7. Tel: (71) 512-7405. Cash only - No credit cards accepted.*

With a branches elsewhere in Holland, these folks really did their research in New York pizza by the slice. They serve good pizza by the slice starting at 3.75 NLG and by the pie starting at 26.25 NLG, and unlike most other Dutch pizza firms they only use 100% real mozzarella cheese. For a bit more money you can request toppings such as pepperoni, mushroom, ham, pineapple, tuna, broccoli, spinach, tandori chicken, or a vegetarian combo. The crust is light and crispy, and they will be glad to add salads, soft drinks, cappuccino, and great Movenpic ice cream to your order. Ask them about their delivery service directly to your hotel room!

## SEEING THE SIGHTS

• *From Station Leiden through the city and then back.*
• *Approximate duration (by foot) is at least 7 hours, including museum, fortress, church, café, boutique, and side street visits.*

### Towards the Hoogstraat via the Canal-Side Lanes

After leaving the Leiden Station, walk straight through the Stationsplein and head for the city's adjacent **VVV** tourist information office at building #210 of this plaza. Here you should pick up an inexpensive map of the city center, and ask them if they have any free copies of the *Cultur Compact* sightseeing and entertainment booklets available.

Now walk through the Stationsplein and pass by the regional bus depot to continue straight ahead on a street called the Stationsweg. Soon this main street changes its name to the Steenstraat and crosses over a bridge above a lovely canal. Just after crossing to the far side of the canal, cross over to the right side of Steenstraat and keep your eyes open for an entranceway for building #1 that leads to the Rijksmuseum v**oor**

**Volkenkunde** (National Museum of Ethnology). First founded in 1816 as a royal collection of rare Chinese art and artifacts, the government soon bought these private collections and started the ethnology museum in 1883. Since then, the voor Volkenkunde has added over 200,000 unique ethnological items from Asia, North America, South America, Africa, Europe, and elsewhere in the old hospital buildings it now occupies.

For the general visitor, ask for a new floor plan and trying to locate such beautiful objects in their collection such as a vast assortment of antique African tribal masks and sculptures, ancient Peruvian earthenware, 8th century Indian bronzes, a Mexican Aztec skull with a unique mosaic inlay, several American Indian war clubs and garments, 17th and 18th century Japanese porcelain and silk paintings, 19th century Indonesian religious jewelry, a 19th century Tibetan dance girdle made from human bones, Alaskan Inuit ivory pieces, and much, much more.

Recent renovations have also added a restaurant, a great gift shop, new exhibition spaces, a research library, a documentary film theater, and a much nicer surrounding park area. The ethnology museum *is open 10:00am to 5:00pm Tuesday to Friday, 12 noon until 5:00pm on Saturday and Sunday throughout the year, with an admission charge of 6 NLG per person.*

After leaving the ethnology museum, cross over to the far side of the Steenstraat, make a right turn, and a few steps later bear left down the 2e Binnenvestgracht. About a block or so later on the left hand side (near the canal) is the **Stedelijk Molenmuseum de Volk** (Valk Municipal Windmill Museum). This is the only remaining antique windmill in the city, and dates back to 1743. Inside you can walk along narrow staircases leading to seven different floors and view exhibitions including the old miller's living quarters decorated with period furnishings, an antique Delftware-lined kitchen with a cast-iron Dutch stove, a 15 minute audio-video presentation (in English) about the history and functions of windmills, reproductions of a few paintings by Rembrandt who was in fact the son of a local miller, explanations of the grain milling process, scale models of other well-known windmills, original wooden milling gears, and a great panoramic lookout platform. *The windmill is open 10:00am to 5:00pm Tuesday through Friday, and 1:00pm until 5:00pm on Saturdays and Sundays, year round with an entrance price of 5 NLG a person.*

Once you've finished visiting the windmill, walk directly across the street, and this time continue along the Nieuwe Beestenmarkt. About a block or so down, turn left at the near side of a canal and walk down the **Oude Singel**. About half a block down on your left hand side, at building #32, is the **Stedelijk Museum De Lakenhal** (Lakenhal Municipal Museum). Located in the beautiful former **Lakenhal** (Cloth Hall), a striking regal structure that was built in 1640 and housed the opulent headquarters of Leiden's powerful cloth industry executives. In 1869, it was transformed into a municipal art, history, decorative arts, and urban cultural museum with truly powerful collections. After passing through the peaceful inner courtyard and café, you will find three dozen rooms on three separate floors.

The ground floor is best known for the 16th century paintings by Leiden's Lucas van Leyden and Cornelis Engebrechtsz, as well as Delft's Harmen & Pieter van Steenwijck, 17th century masterpieces painted by Rembrandt, Jan Steen, Jan van Goyen, Gerrit Dou, and Saloman van Ruysdael, and exhibits of 17th through 19th century hand-painted ceramics, antique porcelain dishes, one-of-a-kind silver and crystal table settings, engraved glass, finely carved wooden furnishings, and a series of fine portraits and scenic oil paintings.

After passing by several antique maps of Leiden along the circular stairway to the second floor, you can see items relating to local Golden Age textile manufacturing that include paintings of the manufacturing process, small tools used to make fabrics, looms, a reconstructed weaver workshop, swatch books a few wall murals, stained glass pieces, chalices, old photographs, and 16th century paintings of the cloth industry by Issac van Swanenburgh. A final flight of stairs takes you to modern art, with paintings and etchings by artists such as Hendrik Valk, Bakker Korff, Floris Verster, and others. Nearby an historical gallery has several rooms filled with scale models of dikes, statuettes, gold coins, suits of armor, weapons, tapestries, and more before leading to an extravagant chandelier topped staircase leading back down to the ground floor. *The Cloth Hall museum is open 10:00am to 5:00pm Tuesday to Friday, 12noon until 5:00pm on Saturday and Sunday throughout the year, with an admission charge of 5 NLG per person.*

Once you've departed the Cloth Hall, turn right onto the Oude Singel and at the next corner make a left turn onto the Turftmarket Brug and walk along **Turftmarkt**, one of the city's main squares. After you have crossed the canal, turn left onto the Harlemmerstraat, and continue for a couple of short blocks until turning left onto the small Sionsteeg. On the next corner, turn right onto the **Lange St. Agietenstraat** and at building #10 you will find the **Museum Boerhaave**, a former hospice that now houses antique scientific and medical instruments, human skeletons, and other related items belonging to local surgeon and botanist Herman Boerhaave. *The science museum is open 10:00am to 5:00pm Tuesday to Friday, 12noon until 5:00pm on Saturday and Sunday throughout the year, with an admission charge of 5 NLG per person.*

From the strange little science museum, retrace your steps back to the Harlemmerstraat and turn left. After about four blocks, turn right onto a tiny lane called Donkersteeg that merges into the **Hoogstraat** as it crosses over two connecting bridges. Below and alongside these small bridges that form the heart of the Centrum district, there are charming bars and water-side cafés that are well worth a visit for a cold drink. The Hoogstraat also marks the sight of Leiden's great **Wednesday** and **Saturday Outdoor Market** held twice every week from 9:00am until 5:00pm. This is the best place in town to pick up fruits, cheeses, and vegetables for a superb picnic along the adjacent canals.

**Through the Oldest Parts of Town**

After walking across Hoogstraat via the bridges, turn left onto the wide avenue called the Aalsmarkt, and follow it as it changes its name to the Vismarkt as it passes the magnificent steeple-topped **Stadhuis** (City Hall) building. Originally built in the 14th century, this structure was severely damaged by a fire in 1929, sparing only parts of the 16th century facade by Lieven de Key. Although not usually open for tours, you can still ask the building's friendly ground floor city information office for a copy of the *Het Leidse Stadhuis* pamphlet (with an English text supplement). This booklet can show you good quality current and historic photos of the building's council chamber, civic hall, and other areas that may not be open to the public.

Now keep walking along the Vismarkt for half a block until making a left turn to cross over the canal via the Koornbrug covered bridge and head straight ahead on the **Burgsteeg**, a nice lane full of antique shops and respected book sellers. Make a left turn onto the narrow Van der Sterrepad and follow it until it reaches the base of the 12th century **Burcht** fortress ruins. A set of stairs leads past a gate decorated by regal crests, and up to the top of a defensive tower resting atop a man-made hill. Once you enter this strange brick tower, you can sit in the peaceful garden before continuing up to the old arches and panoramic walkway. This is a great place to spend a while just looking out over the countryside and really appreciating how lucky you are to be in Holland! *The tower is open daily year round from sunrise to sunset and is free to enter.*

Once you have finished relaxing up at the tower, retrace your steps to the Burgsteeg and follow it as it crosses the canal via the Koornbrug bridge, and walk straight for two blocks until bearing right onto the wide **Breestraat**, the busy main retail shopping boulevard of Leiden. I have spent hours and hours window shopping here, and have found great sales on designer clothing and inexpensive jewelry here throughout the year.

After walking down the shopping area for a couple of blocks, make a left turn onto an amusing little stone lane called the Pieterskerk Chooersteeg that heads directly into the dramatic **Pieterskerk square**. Surrounded by a series of stunning mansions lining the plaza is the Gothic 14th century **Pieterskerk** church. Now used by the university to give exams, as well as for seasonal markets and concerts, this huge former house of worship contains the burial placques of many famous locals, such as artist Jan Steen and Pilgrim Father leader John Robinson. *The church is open daily from 1:00am until 4:00pm, and costs nothing to enter, but may close at anytime for private special events.*

## Along Beautiful Rapenburg

Now walk along the side of the church via the Kolksteeg, cross the bridge over the canal, and immediately make a right turn onto **Rapenburg**. A few steps later on your left hand side at building #73 is the 16th century **Academiegebouw** (University Academic Building). Inside you can visit a small museum containing items from the Rijksuniversiteit Leiden's colorful history. *The history museum is open 1:00pm until 5:00pm from Wednesday through Friday, and is free to enter.*

Much more interesting is the university's **Hortus Botanicus** (Botanical Gardens), located just behind the Academic building. This pretty garden was started in the late 16th century as a study garden for university researchers. Here you can leisurely stroll past centuries-old trees, including a 350 year old laburnum, view giant rose gardens and cute ponds lined with exotic flowers, and enter several greenhouses. One of the garden's highlights is the **Clusiustuin**, a replica of the walled garden used by Professor Carolus Clusius to cultivate the tulips from Turkey that had never grown in northern Europe before 1593 when he first introduced them to Holland. *The gardens are open 10:00am to 5:00pm Monday to Friday, 12noon until 5:00pm on Saturday and Sunday throughout the year, with an admission charge of 5 NLG per person.*

When you're done at the gardens, continue to walk along Rapenburg for a block or so until crossing over the canal via the next bridge, and walk along the far (right) hand side of the same street. About half way down the street at building #28 is the outstanding **Rijksmuseum van Oudeheden** (National Museum of Antiquities). This is one of the best museums in town, and should be included in a proper visit through Leiden.

As you approach the museum you will see the reconstructed 1st century Egyptian Temple of Taffeh that was donated to Holland by the Egyptian government and can be visited for free. Once you pay the entrance fee, you can walk inside to view two complete floors full of Egyptian mummies and statuary, many fine Greek and Roman sculptures, and several magnificent collections of important archaeological finds from around the world such as glassware, ceramics, gold and ivory jewelry, musical instruments, pottery, mosaics, The third floor is dedicated mainly to prehistoric through medieval relics found in various parts of Holland. *The archeology museum is open 10:00am to 5:00pm Tuesday to Saturday and 12noon until 5:00pm on Sunday throughout the year, with an admission charge of 5 NLG per person.*

Just next door to the above mentioned antiquities museum is the entrance to the **Koninklijk Penningkabinet** (Royal Coin Cabinet) **museum**. Inside there is a massive collection of 18th century coins minted for the Dutch East India Company, as well as Greek and Roman coins, antique paper money, historical medallions, and other monetary related objects, all in pristine condition. *The coin cabinet is open 10:00am to 5:00pm Tuesday to Saturday and12noon until 5:00pm on Sunday all year, with an admission charge of 5 NLG per person.*

### The Long Way Back to the Station Leiden

At this point, keep walking along the Rapenburg for a block and a half until making a left turn onto Noordeinde. About three blocks later, make a right turn onto the **Weddesteeg**. A set of modern low-rise apartments on the right side of this small lane marks the former location of the house where master artist **Rembrandt van Rijn** was born on July 15, 1606 (see Amsterdam chapter). Keep walking along the lane as it crosses over the Rembrandtbrug bridge and walk through the small **De Put Park** that is home to the replica of a 17th century **Molen De Put** windmill, where flour ground on the premises can be purchased. *The replica windmill is open to the public for free on Saturdays from 10:00am until 6:00pm and Sundays from 2:00pm until 6:00pm, costs nothing to enter.*

Now turn left to follow the 1e Binnenvestgracht, where a block later you will see the 17th century **Morspoort**, one of only two remaining old gateways through the city's now demolished medieval fortified walls. Make a left turn through the gateway, cross over over the adjacent Morspoortbrug bridge, and make a right turn onto the **Morssingel** that leads directly towards the Station Leiden rail depot to compete your tour of this fascinating little city.

### GUIDED SIGHTSEEING TOURS

There are several special guided trips offered by foot, bus, and river boat to the sights in and around Leiden. The following is a brief listing of the most popular trips, but for a complete listing, contact the VVV-Leiden tourist information office.

### By Boat

The following cruise is operated by the **Rederij Slingerland** company with ticket and information offices on the *Hoogstraat, Tel: (71) 513-4939.*
• **Leiden Canal Boat Cruise**: This one hour tour starts at the piers near both the Visbrug and Beestenmarkt and continues along the canals to pass along-side some of the city's most famous buildings. Departs several times daily between April 15 and September 1. The price is about 9.50 NLG per person.

• **Kagerplassen Lake & Windmill Cruise**: For about 4 hours you will glide along the nearby rivers to have a brief look around beautiful lake Kagerplassen and some of the regions best windmills. Departures are scheduled at least once per day between April 15 and September 10. The trip costs around 24 NLG per person.

### By Canoe & Rowboat

Over at the Rembrantsbrug bridge near the De Put windmill you can hire canoes and row boats for around 15 NLG per hour. For more information, please contact Jac Veringa at *Tel: (71) 514-9790*.

### By Bicycle

The **Station Leiden** has a great bicycle rental (and storage) facility that charges around 11 NLG per day plus a refundable security deposit. Make sure to learn how these old fashion bikes operate, and do not forget to lock it up every time you leave it alone.

## NIGHTLIFE & ENTERTAINMENT

The best bars and clubs in town are the **Jazz Cafe Duke**, *Ouesingel 2*; the **'t Vattegat** brown café, *Garenmarkt 16*; the de **Bonte Koe** beer café, *Kerk Choorsteeg 13*; the **Bacchus** café, *Breestraat 49*; the historic **De Waag** concert venue, *Aalsmarkt 21*; and **In de Oude Marenpoort** café-terrace, *Lange Mare 36*; the **Societeit Burcht** art society's live concert venue, *Burgsteeg 14*; and the **In Casa** student discotech and concert hall, *Lammermarkt 100*.

## EXCURSIONS FROM LEIDEN

Once you have seen most of downtown Leiden, I strongly suggest heading for a couple of nearby attractions that are rather unique to Holland.

### Keukenhof

I think that more people have asked me about **Keukenhof** than I can possibly count. When the spring season finally rolled in, I could hardly wait to see this most famous of all Dutch attractions. What I found here was easily the largest and most magnificent blooming **gardens** I have ever seen. If you are here between April and May, make sure to include this on your trip to Holland, even if you only are stopping by as a half-day trip from Amsterdam, Den Haag, Rotterdam, or Haarlem.

Situated in the town of **Lisse**, some 14 kilometers (9 miles) north of Leiden, this former 15th century estate was converted into a giant garden in 1949 that now features over 70 acres covered with some 7,000,000 flowers in every size, shape, and color imaginable. You can also wander through pavilions displaying impressive flower arrangements, stroll in an exotic nature garden, and walk along the scenic paths past statues, fountains, swan-filled ponds, and of course enough tulips and narcissus to boggle the mind. Lunch is available at one of three restaurants. *The gardens are only open from late March through late May daily between 8:00am and 7:30pm daily, and costs 16 NLG per person to visit.*

To get here by car, take route **A-44 north** for about 11 kilometers (7 miles) before exiting to route **N-208 north** for another 3 kilometers (2 miles) towards the town of Lisse. By public transportation, take the NZH express bus #54 from Leiden Station to Keukenhof. Those arriving here for day trips from cities further away than Leiden should inquire at any Dutch train station about the discounted Rail-Idea train fare and garden admission ticket – it's a real bargain!

## Aalsmeer

Located 22 kilometers (just under 14 miles) northeast of Leiden, the small city of **Aalsmeer** is best known for its year round **Bloemenveiling Flower Auction**, the largest in the world. Located in a huge auction building, visitors can watch the wholesalers buying up some 13 million plants and flowers every day. *The auctions take place between 7:30am and 11:00am on weekdays only throughout the year, and cost 5 NLG per person to attend.*

By car, the best way to get here from Leiden is to take the **A-4 north** for about 23 kilometers (just over 14 miles). By public transportation, take any train going to the Station Aalsmeer train depot and walk a few blocks to the auction house.

## PRACTICAL INFORMATION

**Main VVV Tourist Office** - *Stationsplein 210* - *(71) 514-1318*
**Leids Convention Bureau** - *(71) 527-5299*
**Police Headquarters** - *(71) 514-4444*
**Medical Emergencies** - *(71) 521-2121*
**Emergency Hotline** - *06-11*

# 20. HAARLEM

The beautiful little city of **Haarlem**, frequently overlooked by many a visitor, has just finished celebrating its 750th anniversary in 1995. Known locally as the **Bloemenstad** (City of Flowers), this captivating community of hard-working residents is full of 18th century canal and town houses, often displaying a beautiful assortment of window boxes and ceramic pots full of blooming multicolored flowers from April through October.

Haarlem has dozens of worthwhile attractions, captivating museums, quaint side streets, reasonably priced boutiques, fine restaurants, and friendly nighttime venues to explore in complete safety. Another great idea is to sample some of the excellent locally available **Jopen** beer, made from a long-lost medieval recipe once commonly used by the 150 breweries that have all since vanished from the city center.

Since this is one of the closest cities to Holland's main Schiphol Airport, and is much more affordably priced than Amsterdam, Haarlem makes a perfect overnight destination to either begin or end your vacation through the Netherlands.

## ORIENTATION

Haarlem is situated in the extreme western section of the lower portion of the Netherland's **Noord-Holland** province, with a population of 151, 238. It lies some 19 kilometers (12 miles) west of the capital city of Amsterdam, and 47 kilometers (29 miles) northeast of Den Haag.

## ARRIVALS & DEPARTURES

**By Air**

All visitors flying to this city will arrive here via land links from the large **Schiphol Airport** near Amsterdam, about 16 kilometers (10 miles) to the southeast.

## By Bus

Many of the bus lines between Haarlem and other parts of Holland tend to stop at the depot just in front of the **NS Station** train depot on the north side of downtown. Those arriving here directly from Schiphol Airport can also take advantage of the inexpensive and frequent NZH bus service linking these two destinations via lines #362, #174, and #236.

Make sure to call in advance to find out exactly where and when your bus comes in. Connections between this station and any other point in Haarlem can generally be made by the adjacent public bus stops for about 3 NLG per person each way, or via taxi for roughly 11.50 NLG or so.

## By Car

Downtown street-side parking spots are fairly easy to find.

From **Amsterdam**, the easiest way to get to Haarlem by car is to take route **N-200** directly from the heart of Amsterdam for 19 kilometers (12 miles) straight past Halfweg and into the center of Haarlem.

## By Train

Haarlem is linked to almost any other point in Holland and Europe by several major rail lines. This city contains two different rail stations, each with its own series of daily arrivals and departures. The large **NS Station** train depot at the north side of the city's downtown section is the major point of mass transport arrivals.

Connections between this station and any other point in Haarlem can be made by foot, via the adjacent NZH public bus stops for around 3 NLG per person each way, by **Treintaxi** for 6 NLG per person, or via taxi for roughly 11.50 NLG or so. Use the train information phone numbers listed in the *Practical Information* section at the end of this chapter to reconfirm, in advance, the exact time and station you may need.

## GETTING AROUND TOWN

### By Public Transportation

While almost any sight within Haarlem is well within walking distance from any point downtown, the region's **NZH** transit authority also offers a selection of public bus lines to get you safely and easily around town. They accept **Nationale Strippen Kaarts**.

Almost all of these buses stop at one point or another in front of the NS Station. The normal hours of operation for most of the system is from about 6:00am until roughly 11:45pm. Locations outside of downtown Haarlem, such as the beaches of Zandvoort or the airport at Schiphol, will require travel through more than one zone, so you must ask the driver how many blank strips are required. To get free copies of the extremely useful NZH public transit system maps for each individual route, just pop into the VVV or NZH offices listed n the *Practical Information* section at the end of this chapter.

**By Taxi**

There are around a hundred licensed taxis roaming the streets and major passenger arrival points of the city during all hours of the day and night. Drivers have new Renault and Opel 4 door sedans (and a few station wagons) with enough trunk space to hold a few pieces of luggage. Drivers are polite, honest, and typically multilingual. To find a taxi, either hail down an unoccupied cab driving by with its "Taxi" roof light illuminated, go to one of the obvious taxi stands throughout the city, or have the nearest hotel or restaurant call for a radio response pick-up on demand.

The main taxi ranks are located at the NS Station, the Raaksburg Station, and near the Grote Markt. Taxis here are metered and charge somewhere between 9.50 NLG to 15.50 NLG per ride (not per person) between most downtown locations depending on exact distance and traffic conditions. A limited number of the city's taxi's now accept major credit cards for fare payments.

## WHERE TO STAY

*Expensive*

**GOLDEN TULIP LION D'OR**, *Kruisweg 34. Tel: (23) 532-1750. Fax: (23) 532-9543. US & Canada Bookings (Golden Tulip) 1-800-344-1212. Year round rack rates from 225 NLG per double room per night (B.P.). All major credit cards accepted.*

Not only is this the best hotel in all of Haarlem, but it is also a great place to spend your last few nights in Holland. Located around the corner from the NS Station, this delightful superior first class property offers 36 nicely decorated rooms, each with large modern private bathrooms, extremely comfortable bedding, remote control satellite television, am-fm clock radio, large windows, direct dial telephones, interior or side street views, and both mini-bars and electric trouser presses in most cases.

This 175 year old hotel has been owned and operated by the charming Hofman family for several decades, during which time they have spend plenty of time and money ensuring the comfort of all their guests. Hotel facilities include a bar, a restaurant, business meeting rooms, nearby public parking, room service, express laundry and dry cleaning, safe deposit boxes, and a really nice staff that go well out of their way to make sure you will soon return. With such reasonable prices for the quality, and adjacent express bus service directly to and from Schiphol Airport, this is a perfect place to stay just before leaving from Holland back to North America. Highly recommended as the most welcoming full service hotel in the heart of Haarlem.

**CARLTON SQUARE HOTEL,** *Baan 7. Tel: (23) 531-9091. Fax: (23) 532-9853. US & Canada Bookings (UTELL), 1-800-44-UTELL. Year round rack rates from 275 NLG per double room per night (E.P.). All major credit cards accepted.*

This towering conference and business-style hotel on the edge of town is perfect for those planning a large meeting or convention in Haarlem. The Carlton has 106 modern double rooms and suites with private bathrooms, direct dial telephone, remote control satellite television, nice art work and new furnishings. Facilities include a bar, a restaurant, a sun terrace, indoor parking, business meeting rooms, child care, room service, and huge reception and conference rooms.

**PALACE HOTEL,** *Burg. van Fenemaplein 2 (Zandvoort). Tel: (23) 571-2911. Fax: (23) 572-0131. US & Canada Bookings (Best Western). 1-800-528-1234. Special package rates from 160 NLG per double room per night (E.P.). Year round rack rates from 200 NLG per double room per night (B.P.). All major credit cards accepted.*

This towering complex on the beach at Zandvoort is worth consideration if you can book one of their inexpensive room rate specials. There are 65 basic sea-front rooms, suites, and fully equipped apartments with private bathrooms, heating, direct dial telephone, and simple furnishings. Facilities include direct access to the beach and the promenade, adjacent parking, business meeting rooms, a bar, and a restaurant.

### Moderate

**HOTEL CAFE CARRILLON**, *Grote Markt 27. Tel: (23) 531-0191. Fax: (23) 531-4909. Year round rack rates from 120 NLG per double room per night (B.P.). Most major credit cards accepted.*

Situated just across the way from the Grote Kerk church in the city center, this simple 22 room inn offers nice basic rooms at reasonable rates. While facilities are somewhat limited, the Carillon has a café, restaurant, nearby parking, direct dial telephones, in-room television, heating, and a nice staff.

**HOTEL INTERLAKEN**, *Van Speykstraat 20 (Zandvoort). Tel; (23) 571-2966. Fax; (23) 571-2966. Year round rack rates from 130 NLG per double room per night (C.P.). Most major credit cards accepted.*

This new ultra-modern 2 star hotel near the center of town is a good bet in this price range. There are 28 rooms with private bathroom, direct dial telephone, satellite television, and comfortable furnishings.

### Inexpensive

**JOOPS INNERCITY APARTMENT HOTEL,** *Oude Groenmarkt 12. Tel: (23) 532-2008. Fax: (23) 532-9549. Year round rack rates from 85 NLG per double room per night (E.P.). Cash only - No credit cards accepted.*

This local firm has some 45 apartments and simple motel style rooms for rent, including some large family-sized units with kitchens. While these are from from deluxe, for this price and location you certainly get your money's worth.

**HOTEL DOPPENBERG**, *Hogeweg 34 (Zandvoort). Tel: (23) 571-3466. Fax: (23) 571-6211. Year round rack rates from 115 NLG per double room per night (E.P.). Most major credit cards accepted.*

The Doppenburg is a nice little family-run inn located in the center of town with 44 rooms that all have private bathrooms, remote control television, and comfortable furnishings.

### Cheap

**NJHC- JAN GIJZEN HOSTEL**, *Jan Gizenpad 3. Tel: (23) 537-3793. Fax: (23) 537-1176. US & Canada Bookings (Hostelling International) 1-613-237-7884. Year round rack rates from 27.50 NLG per person in a dormitory per night (C.P.). Year round rack rates from 70 NLG per double private room per night (C.P.). Cash Only - No credit cards accepted.*

The tranquil river-front Jan Gijzen hostel is situated near the northwestern suburb of Bloemendaal about a five minute bus ride away via bus line #2 from the NS Station. There are about 108 beds in a combination of small dormitories and a handful of comfortable secure private rooms for between two and six people.

Perfect for budget-minded hikers, bicyclists, and backpackers, to stay here you will need a valid Hostelling International membership card (available on the premises). There is both a late night curfew and an afternoon lockout.

## WHERE TO EAT

### Expensive

**DE CAQUELON**, *Ridderstraat 24. Tel: (23) 532-8114. Master cards accepted.*

This is one of my favorite medium-sized French influenced restaurants in town. The intimate dining room is somewhat formal and serves tasty gourmet items such as baked camembert cheese at 14.50 NLG, French onion soup for 8.50 NLG, tomato cream soup at 8.50 NLG, Dutch shrimp with cocktail sauce for 25.50 NLG, grilled scallops at 24 NLG, baked mushrooms with toast for 15.50 NLG, salmon mousse with wine and oyster sauce at 19.50 NLG, tournedos of beef with port and cognac sauce for 39.50 NLG, lamb cutlets with rosemary and honey at 39 NLG, confit of duck for 38.50 NLG, vegetarian special of the day at 28.50 NLG, and a great peach melba for 12.50 NLG.

*Moderate*
**QUATRE MAINS**, *Grote Markt 4. Tel: (23) 542-4258. Most major credit cards accepted.*

Situated just across from the Stadhuis in the city's main square, this extremely cozy and delicious little gourmet restaurant specializes in meals centered around fine wines and cheese. Their superb menu features bouillon with amaretto at 7 NLG, seasoned green salads for 8.50 NLG, grilled goat cheese salad at 10.50 NLG, home made pate for 11 NLG, 1/2 dozen escargot in garlic at 12.50 NLG, gravid lax for 16.50 NLG, salmon in a white butter sauce at 29.50 NLG, grilled shrimp for 34 NLG, swordfish with capers at 35.50 NLG, filet mignon for two at 95 NLG, Roquefort cheese fondue at 26.50, Jopen beer fondue for 27.50 NLG, and a great selection of fine wines in all price ranges. A great place to check out, especially during their 35 NLG per person lunch hours.

**BIERCAFE BRUXELLES**, *Lange Wyngaardstraat 16. Tel: (23) 531-4509. Cash only - No credit cards accepted.*

This relaxing old world bohemian tavern serves up much better than average pub-style cuisine and classic jazz in their simple wooden table lined dining area. Among my personal favorites here are the French onion soup for 5.50 NLG, goat cheese salad at 10.50 NLG, spinach salad for 11 NLG, entrecote with fries at 11.50 NLG, rib-eye steak for 27.50 NLG, rack of lamb at 25 NLG, beefsteak for 18 NLG, chicken sate at 17.50, jumbo shrimp platters for 16.50 NLG, cheese fondue at 17.50 NLG, apple tarts for 4.50 NLG, and over 150 types of beer. A great find in this price range.

**GRAND CAFE & RESTAURANT BRINKMANN**, *Grote Markt 41. Tel: (23) 532-3111. All major credit cards accepted.*

The Brinkmann is the city center's most respected old world-style grand café. Still popular for a casual sunny afternoon lunch and cold beer, this famous eating establishment boasts a fine indoor dining room with huge picture windows facing the lively central plaza. They also setup over 150 seats in Haarlem's best outdoor café area. The extensive menu here includes tomato soup with cream at 6.50 NLG, French onion soup for 7 NLG, chicken filet with curry sauce at 19.50 NLG, New Orleans-style spare ribs for 22.50 NLG, penne with Roquefort cheese and parma ham at 11.50 NLG, tuna salad with feta cheese for 10.50 NLG, mixed grill at 25.50 NLG, pasta with salmon and pesto for 19.50 NLG, lasagna verde at 11.50 NLG, shrimp with garlic for 13.50 NLG, assorted omelets from 11.50 NLG, and a wide variety of pancakes starting at 7.75 NLG.

*Inexpensive*
**DE KAASHUT**, *Grote Hoogstraat 102. Tel: (23) 531-5335. Cash only - No credit cards accepted.*

If you want to grab a great sandwich while walking through town, or prefer to pick up the perfect ingredients for a tranquil picnic, the Kasshut is a wonderful place to check out. You can buy all sorts of fine cheeses and salads by the kilogram, as well as ordering sandwiches such as old Gouda cheese and tomato on a baguette for 4.50 NLG, blue and goat cheese on a hard roll with brie at 5.25 NLG, imported salami and ham sandwiches for 4.95 NLG, cold tuna salad plates at 5.25 NLG, chicken sate platters for 5.25 NLG, liverwurst and sausage on a buttered dark bread at 4.75 NLG, pate for 3.95 NLG, and much more!

**NEW YORK PIZZA**, *Grote Hoogstraat 10. Tel: (23) 532-2223. Cash only - No credit cards accepted.*

This new branch a rapidly expanding Amsterdam-based pizza chain offers really good pizza by the slice starting at 3.75 NLG and by the pie starting at 26.25 NLG, and unlike most other Dutch pizza firms they only use 100% real mozzarella cheese. For a bit more money you can request toppings such as pepperoni, mushroom, ham, pineapple, tuna, broccoli, spinach, tandoori chicken, or a vegetarian combo. The crust is light and crispy, and they will be glad to add salads, soft drinks, cappuccino, and great Movenpic ice cream to your order. Ask them about their delivery service directly to your hotel room!

## SEEING THE SIGHTS

• *From the* **NS Station** *through town and back.*
• *Approximate duration (by foot) is at least 6 hours, including museum, gallery, church, café, boutique, and side street visits.*

### Haarlem's Almshouse Courtyards

Upon arriving, your first point of reference should be the NS Station, the site of Holland's oldest existing commuter rail line (to Amsterdam). After departing the main exit of the NS Station, bear right to pass through the **Stationsplein**. A few steps later you should pop inside the **VVV** tourist information offices at building #1 where the square ends. Here you can get all sorts of free brochures, and for about 10 NLG you can also pick up a copy of the excellent *City Kompas* tourist information map and descriptive booklet.

From the front door of the tourist office, turn left to walk straight back through the Stationsplein for a long block until bearing right at the next corner onto the wide avenue known as the Jansweg. After walking about a block up this avenue, keep your eyes open for the **Het Hofje van Staats**, a mid-18th century almshouse (one of many scattered around the city) with a weathervane topped bell-tower and a remarkable entrance of detailed sculpture work by Gerrit van Heerstal at building #39. Constructed from plans by Hendrik de Werff from funds bequeathed by local merchant Ijsbrand Staats, this amazingly tranquil and dignified complex of tiny cottages surrounding a fine inner courtyard was designed to house 29 old women who took the Dutch Reformed Church rather seriously. Still occupied by over two dozen spinsters and widows, the brass door under the sculpture may be closed, but turn the handle and walk straight into this enchanting oasis of peace and serenity. The S*taats almshouse's courtyard is open daily from sunrise to sunset with no entrance fee.*

After leaving the Hofje, continue heading down the Jansweg. At the next major intersection you will make a left turn onto the Parklaan. Head up the right hand side of this street for a few blocks before turning right onto the Hooimarkt. At the next corner, turn right onto the canal front Nieuwe Gracht and walk a few steps until reaching the entrance at building #2 to the **Het Hofje van Noblet**, an 18th century almshouse designed by Willem Batelaar using funds from the estate of Leonard Noblet, a rich merchant from Amsterdam. The small symmetrical brick townhouses surrounding the garden are still inhabited by twenty old women active in the Dutch Reformed Church, half from Haarlem and the other half from Amsterdam. The main building at the rear of the forecourt features a fine Rococo-style Louis XV sculpted clock and the family crest of the Noblets, while a commemorative reproduction of a medieval sundial and navigational instrument can be found in the center of the courtyard garden. The Noblet al*mshouse's courtyard is open daily from sunrise to sunset with no entrance fee.*

Now exit the almshouse and retrace your steps back to continue along the Hooimarkt and follow it for a block or so. A bridge will take you across the **Spaarne River**, and the street name changes to the **Koudenhorn**. Keep following the Koudenhorn for a few blocks as it curves to the left and then you will find entrance to the **Teylershofje** at building #64, yet another of the city's many 18th century almshouses. These structures were built on the site of a former brewery after funds were donated by rich silk merchant Pieter Teyler van der Hulst. If you walk past the main building's massive wrought-iron gate, you walk alongside two dozen small cottages surrounding a lovely forecourt garden complete with an antique hand pump for fresh water and a sundial. The Teyler almshouse's courtyard is *open daily from sunrise to sunset with no entrance fee.*

**The Teylers Museum**

After departing the Teylershofje, return to the Koudenhorn and bear left. At the next corner, turn left down the tiny lane called the **Valkestraat**. At the end of this lane you will find yourself facing the rear end of the stone block **Bakenesserkerk** church, the oldest house of worship still standing in Haarlem, built and added to between the 13th through 17th centuries. The most impressive feature of the church's exterior is its fine

48 meter (158 foot) tower and elaborate 16th century sandstone clock tower. You can follow along the right side of the building to enter its portal and can get a good glimpse of the beautiful nave and its famous adjacent choir screen. *The church is open only during posted mass hours and special events.*

Return to the rear of the church and turn right onto the Bakenesserstraat. Follow this street until it ends and then bear right onto the river-front avenue known as the **Donkere Spaarne**, and follow it past the beautiful **Gravenstenenbrug drawbridge** and take a good look at some of the awesome 16th and 17th century gabled warehouses and canal houses facing you from the opposite side of the Spaarne River. The street soon changes its name to **Spaarne**, and about another block or so up on the right hand side is the main statue-topped entrance to the amazing **Teylers Museum** at building #16. This is Holland's oldest public museum and was established in 1778 after the rich local silk merchant and science enthusiast Pieter Teyler van der Hulst (the same benefactor as that of the Teylershofje) died and left his mansion and private collections to a special foundation that encouraged public education in the arts and sciences.

Inside this fantastic museum, you will find many separate rooms and galleries dedicated to Cenozoic through Paleozoic age fossils, antique scientific instruments used for measuring everything from barometric pressure to radiation and magnetic fields, an opulent Neo-Classical style two floor "Oval Room" surrounded by glass and wooden cabinets full of telescopes and scientific research tools (don't forget to gaze up at the 16 dramatic stucco ceiling panels), and two rooms full of antique Dutch gold and silver coins, and many 15th through 19th century Dutch and Italian sketches and paintings including a few Rembrandt works and an unbelievable set of drawings by Michelangelo entitled *Studies for the Sistine Chapel.* There is also a complete observatory on the structure's roof. *The museum is open from 10:00am until 5:00pm from Tuesday through Saturday, 1:00pm until 5:00pm on Sundays and holidays, and costs 7.50 NLG per person to enter.*

From the science museum, keep walking along Spaarne for another half a block or so before passing the front of the old **Waag** (Weigh House) at the next corner. Built in the 16th century, this building can no longer be entered by the general public (although a good restaurant inside is now open), but is still worth taking a good look at to view its incredible stone block facade and pinnacle-topped roof. From the Waag, turn right onto the Damstraat and walk a few blocks until it ends at the intersection with the Klokhuisplein square.

### Around the Enchanting Grote Markt Square

From your position in the Klokhuisplein facing the rear of the Gothic cross styled 15th through 17th century **Grote Kerk** (Great Church of St.

Bavo's), follow the small lane called the **Oude Groenmarkt** as it passes along the left side of this huge church until reaching the tiled entrance portal marked "entree" at building #23.

Originally built in 1397, and repeatedly renovated and expanded as recently as 1985, this massive church and its inspiring bell-tower have many fine features that should all be viewed. Among the highlights of the interior are the 17th century wall map of Haarlem in the Southern Ambulatory, the choir's delicate 16th century wrought-iron screens by Jan Fyerens and the nearby lantern-topped tomb of local artist Frans Hals, the archway near the Northern Transept with an old scientific model showing the earth's rotation, an intricately carved medieval Holy Ghost Bench, the 17th century oak pulpit with brass railings in the shape of snakes, the world renowned pipe organ built by Christian Muller in 1738 (actaully played in person by both Handel and Mozart, and still used for summertime concert events) with well over 5,000 pipes stretching in some cases to over 29 meters (96 feet), the high relief sculpted in marble by Jan Baptist Xavery, a couple of antique scale models of Dutch military ships, and of course the towering vaulted ceiling supported by 28 frescoed columns.

The highly decorated 80 meter (264 foot) bell-tower contains a fine carillon with a set of 16th century bells called the **Damiaatjes**. Each evening between 9:00pm and 9:30pm the carillon rings out to commemorate the signal once used to notify local residents of the nightly locking of the town gates through the fortified defensive walls that once surrounded Haarlem. The church is open from 10:00am until 4:00pm from *Monday through Saturday and costs 2.50 NLG per person to view.*

After leaving the church through the same door you entered, bear right and walk a few steps until reaching the bustling **Grote Markt** square, where many outdoor markets and sporting events were held in the old days. Nowadays when you enter this large central square you are much more likely to find hundreds of young people and tourists hanging out on wind-swept tables in front of bars, cafés, and restaurants, such as the well known **Grand Café Brinkmann**.

The plaza is lined by several historic buildings. The first important structure lies just a few feet from the front side of the church and is known as the Vleesshal. This dramatically gabled 17th century masterpiece of Flemish-Dutch Renaissance architecture was originally designed from plans by Lieven de Key as Haarlem's main meat market. The facade is marked by the stone carvings of the heads of a sheep and an ox, and the structure may be entered via a doorway at building #16 known as the **Het Vishuisje**, a small reconstruction of a 17th century home once belonging to the outdoor market's supervisor. Along with the adjacent 18th century **Verweyhal** building, once an exclusive men's social club, this suite of three adjoining buildings was recently converted first to house a city Archaeological Museum, and now has been renovated to contain the **De Hallen Tentoonstellings** (Exhibition Galleries) of the nearby Frans Hals Museum. This annex section of the city's most important art museum contains temporary exhibits of early modern art as well as a series of works by local turn of the century Impressionist painter Kees Verwey. *The exhibition galleries are open 11:00am until 5:00pm from Monday through Saturday, 1:00pm until 5:00pm on Sundays and holidays, and cost 4 NLG per person to enter.*

As you wander further in through the Grote Markt square you will soon be drawn directly to the wonderful 13th through 17th century **Stadhuis** (City Hall) at the far edge of the plaza. The oldest part and most obvious wing of this sprawling complex is the **Gravenzall** (Count's Chamber), once used as the hunting lodge and reception hall of Count William II (before the royal family packed up and moved to Den Haag) and rebuilt after disastrous fires in the mid-14th century.

There are also some other unusual connected wings including the Gothic **Vierschaar** (Trail Hall), where prisoners were tried and condemned before being publicly hung from a protruding scaffold attached to the side of the top floor until the mid-19th century, and a Dutch Renaissance style wing added by Lieven de Key in 1622. A small gothic gateway to the left of the Gravenzall leads directly to the **Prinsenhof**, a 16th century Domenican monastery that was later converted into a residence for Prince William of Orange and is now home to regular city council meetings. The rooms inside *the city hall complex may be viewed on non-holiday weekdays only by advance appointment by calling the Stadhuis office at Tel: (23) 517-1212.*

### Near the Grote Markt Square

After departing the city hall area, turn around walk back through to the center of the plaza where you will make a left turn onto the Grote Houtstra**at**, one of Haarlem's major pedestrian-only retail shopping boulevards that is lined with hundreds of reasonably priced clothing, jewelry, music, and food shops. After walking down this boulevard for a few blocks or so, you should keep your eyes open for the **Proveniershuis** at building #142. Built in 1591, this almshouse style garden complex started life as a monastery and was later used as by the militia before being converted into upscale small cottages for wealthy retired single men. *The Proveniershuis's courtyard is usually open daily from sunrise to sunset with no entrance fee.*

Keep heading up the Grote Houtstraat for one more block until bearing right onto the Kerkstraat. This small lane now leads to straight towards the rear of the **Nieuwe Kerk** (Dutch Reformed Church). This was the first house of worship created expressly for the Dutch Reformed congregation of Haarlem, and was built in 1649 from plans by Jacob van Campen. The lovely Renaissance tower by Lieven de Key rising up some 45 meters (149 feet) is all that remains from an older church that once stood on this spot. *The church is open only during posted mass hours and costs nothing to enter when open.*

From the church's main entrance, walk a few steps up the adjacent Nieuwe Kerksplein and then bear left down Oude Raamstraat. A block or so later this road intersects with the canal front Ramveest where you will turn left. After following the canal for a while, you will turn left on a tiny lane onto the Groot Heiligland. Among the many fine gabled 17th century cottages found on this historic block, you will pass the entrance to the **Frans Hals Museum** at building #62. Originally built in 1610 from plans by Pieter van Campen as an almshouse for retired men including Frans Hals himself, this building was later used as a city orphanage. The museum is best known for its wing featuring a series of eight well-known militia regiment paintings and portraits by Flemish born artist **Frans Hals** (1580-1666), who lived in and painted in Haarlem most of his life.

There is also a section dedicated soley to several fine pieces by other 16th and 17th century Old Masters such as Jan Mostaert, Carel van Mander, Johannes Verspronk, Pieter Claesz, Adriaen van Ostade, Hendrick Gerritsz Pot, Jacob van Ruisdael, and Hendrik Goltzius. Another set of rooms displays a large collection of modern paintings, sculpture, and ceramics by artists like Karel Appel, Jan Sluyters, Contsant, Leo Gestel, and Gerard Blaauw. There are also a handful of galleries dedicated to antique Delftware, locally manufactured silver, hand-made ceramics, period furnishings, applied art, vintage doll houses, and temporary exhibits. *The museum is open 11:00am until 5:00pm Monday through Saturday and 1:00pm until 5:00pm on Sundays and holidays, and admission is 7.50 NLG per person.*

After leaving the museum, continue down the same block for a few steps and pop inside building #47, where you will find the **Historisch Museum Zuid Kennemerland** regional history museum. This entertaining little museum showcases antique photos, paintings, glassware, pottery, rare books, sculpture, coins, scale models, maps, and other artifacts relating to Haarlem and its surroundings. Make sure to take the time to sit and watch the 20 minute multimedia history presentation. *The museum is open 12noon until 5:00pm Tuesday through Saturday, 1:00pm until 5:00pm on Sundays and holidays, and is free to enter.*

When you have had a good look at the history museum, keep walking along the Groot Heiligland while passing by several art and antique galleries. A couple of blocks later the street name changes to the Schaghelstraat and is lined by several upscale boutiques. Keep walking straight as the street's name again changes to the Warmoestraat and leads directly into the Grote Markt square.

Now cut straight through the Grote Markt, make a right turn to follow the square's far side, and pop inside the entrance to the newly opened three level **Brinkmann Passaje Winkelcentrum** (Shopping Center) and multiplex cinema. A few steps further down the left side of the plaza is the unmistakable facade of a 14th century medieval brick house known as the **Hoofdwacht** at building #17. Once used as an 18th century barracks for the city's Civic Guards, the structure may not be visited by the general public.

**The Tiny Red Light District**

From the Hoofdwacht, turn left off the plaza via the Smedestraat and follow it for a few steps before turning right on a tiny alley known as the Noorder Schoolsteeg. Walk along this lane as it curves to the right, and when you reach the Jansstraat you should turn left. A short distance later turn right down another small alley called the **Begijnesteeg**, the heart of Haarlem's miniature **Red Light District**. Besides having several less than discreet brothels on both sides surrounding a nearby church and a small almshouse, this lane is also home to two rather unusual attractions.

The first bizarre sight here is the **'t Steegje**, a small hidden alcove filled with windows displaying young women wearing only lingerie and soliciting thier services. Even more strange is the **'t Poortje** patio in a well marked white house further down the block. This is also an area for working girls to strut their stuff, but here visitors must pay 7.50 NLG each to walk through its alcoves and then be treated to some erotic entertainment, such as pornographic videos and topless dancers.

From the Red Light District, retrace your steps to the Jansstraat and turn right. After a block or so, turn left onto the Ridderstraat and follow it for a block until bearing right onto the **Kruisstraat**, another major retail shopping streets. Follow this wide avenue for several blocks until returning back to the **NS Station** and completing your tour of Haarlem.

**GUIDED SIGHTSEEING TOURS**

There are several special guided trips offered by large and small river boats to the sights in and around Haarlem. The following is a brief listing of the most popular trips, but for a complete listing, contact the VVV tourist information office.

**By Boat**

The following cruises are all operated by the **Rondvaart Rederij Noord-Zuid** company with ticket and information offices at the Gravenstenenbrug drawbridge pier at *Sparne 11a, Tel: (23) 535-7723:*

- **Spaarne River Boat Cruise**: This 70 minute tour starts at the piers near the Gravenstenenbrug drawbridge and continues via glass topped canal boats along the river through several districts of Haarlem. Departs several times daily between April 1 and October 31. The price is about 9 NLG per person.
- **Cruquius Cruise**: For two hours you will glide along the river and have a brief stop at the de Cruquius steam pumping station and water museum. Departures are available almost every day between April 15 and September 15. The trip costs around 14.50 NLG per person.
- **Spaarndam Cruise**: This two hour trip includes a visit to the village of Spaarndam with its famed statue of little Hans Brinker saving Holland from a flood by sticking his hand in a dike, and the summertime only art fair (open Saturdays only) Departures are available almost every day between April 15 and September 15. The trip costs around 14.50 NLG per person.
- **Groenendaal Cruise**: A three hour trip along the river including a stop at an enchanting country estate and a coffee break for just 14.50 NLG per person. Departs most days between April 15 and September 15.

---

### HIT THE BEACH AT ZANDVOORT!

*Many locals spend their free days during the summertime at the major seaside suburb of **Zandvoort**, just eight kilometers (five miles) west of Haarlem. While the small historic town center does have some traditional fishing cottages, much of this heavily developed area is far from quaint. If the weather is good, you can spend a fairly pleasant day here at the 39 pavilions directly on the packed regular and nudist beaches, where water sports, seafood lunches, and cheap alcoholic drinks are plentiful.*

*The town is also well known in Europe for its **car racing** circuit, but there is also a family amusement park called **Circus** and a branch of the **Holland Casino** here as well. To get here by car, take route **N-201 west** from the edge of Haarlem. By public transport, use municipal bus line #80 from the NS Station bus depot.*

---

### By Car & Van

A local outfit called **Sommer Excursions** can provide custom tailored day trips and excursions with their own English speaking guides and air conditioned coaches. While these are designed for small groups, you may want to call and ask them if perhaps they can fit you on with a group, or can arrange a private tour. You can reach them at *Tel: (23) 571-3502.*

## NIGHTLIFE & ENTERTAINMENT

**Bars, Pubs, & Grand Cafés**

    **STUDIO**, *Grote Markt 25. Tel (23) 531-0033.*

The Studio is the best place in Haarlem to hang out at night and meet lots of fun people. This combination grand café and pub has a good selection of over 70 great beers, and just about every type of spirits you could imagine. The place gets packed almost every night after 11:00pm with lots of 20 to 30 year old students and office workers that just want to unwind and listen to great music. Ask for a Jopen beer here; I'm sure you'll love it!

    **IMPERIAL**, *Korte Veerstraat 5. Tel: (23) Unlisted.*

This local pub a couple of blocks away from the Grote Markt has cheap strong drinks, free live rock and blues music several times each week, and a denim and leather clientele of students that stay up late to party.

    **BIERCAFE BRUXELLES**, *Lange Wyngaardstraat 16. Tel: (23) 531-4509.*

With over 150 different beers available on any given day, and some of the best pub food found in Haarlem, this dark, cozy, and spirited old tavern is a great find! Popular with down to earth local residents and commuting students.

    **PROEFLOKAAL DE BLAUWE DRUIF**, *Lange Veerstraat 7. Tel (23) 531-0391.*

If you want a real traditional feel for the city, try an evening gin or two at this fantastic old Dutch-style tasting house near the Grote Markt. It is a real experience!

    **MALIBU BEACH CLUB**, *Smedestraat. Tel: (23) Unlisted.*

This new dance club and bar just off the Grote Markt features large drinks served by half naked male and female bartenders that attract hordes of hormone crazed young people.

    **WILLY WERTOL WORKSHOP**, *Raamvest 63. Tel: (23) Unlisted.*

This converted garage complete with the scattered ruins of old jeeps is now ths city's most entertaining "smoking coffeeshop" and bar. Besides having the best smoke in the region, this place has plenty of pinball machines, fussball tables, a pool table, darts, and a good disc jockey that blasts out classic rock and roll music for the laid-back clients.

    **BIERCAFE BRUXELLES**, *Lange Wyngaardstraat 16. Tel: (23) 531-4509.*

With over 150 different beers available on any given day, and some of the best pub food found in Haarlem, this dark, cozy, and spirited old tavern is a great find! Popular with down to earth local resident and commuting students.

## PRACTICAL INFORMATION

**Main VVV Tourist Office** - *Stationsplein 5* - *(23) 531-9059*
**Zandvoort VVV Tourist Office** - *Schoolplein 1* - *(23) 571-7947*
**Haarlem City Hall** - *Grote Markt* - *(23) 517-1212*
**Domestic Train and Bus Info** - *(6) 9292*
**NZH Municipal Transit Head Office** - *Leidsevaart 396* - *(23) 515-2626*
**Emergency Hotline** - *06-11*

# 21. UTRECHT

Although it is now the fourth largest city in Holland, **Utrecht** has thankfully managed to retain much of its small village ambiance. Graced by patrician mansion-lined canals leading to the nearby **Rhine River**, this energetic university city has enough sights and amusing activities to keep anyone busy for a couple of days.

Besides a series of important churches (evidence to the important role that Christianity has played here since the 7th century), this is one of the best places in the country to hunt for unusual gifts while taking incredible photographs. As you stroll along the canals and side streets of the Centrum, make sure to keep your eyes open for the many old wharfs, almshouses, intimate cafés, and secluded inner courtyard gardens that help make Utrecht so enjoyable for locals and visitors alike.

Among the highlights of any trip here are the city's great outdoor markets, a refreshing walk up to the viewing deck of the Domtoren tower, peeking inside several Gothic churches, a trip by canal boat along the nearby countryside estates, and fascinating tours through museums displaying everything from antique musical instruments to masterpieces of medieval art and modern Dutch furnishings.

After you have exhausted your energy, follow the students as they filter into cafés and pubs, and enjoy a cold drink before picking from one of the dozens of great restaurants here. Be careful not to get run over by a speeding bicycle (something that occurs often here!, and get set for a fun day walking around a beautiful city.

## ORIENTATION

Utrecht is situated in the heart of the Netherland's centrally located **Utrecht** province, with a population of 230,989. It lies 38 kilometers (24 miles) south-southeast of the capital city of Amsterdam, and 49 kilometers (30 miles) northeast of Rotterdam.

## ARRIVALS & DEPARTURES
**By Air**
Most visitors flying to this city will arrive here via land links from the large **Schiphol Airport** near Amsterdam, 36 kilometers (22 miles) to the northwest.

**By Bus**
Many of the bus lines between Utrecht and other parts of Holland stop at the Stadsbus**station** depot, just alongside the **Central Station** train depot on the west edge of downtown. Make sure to call in advance to find out exactly where and when your bus comes in. Connections between this station and any other point in downtown Utrecht can generally be made by the adjacent public bus stops for about 3 NLG per person each way, or via taxi for between 9.50 NLG and 18.50 NLG.

**By Car**
Downtown street-side parking spots are impossible to find.
From **Amsterdam**, the fastest way to get to Utrecht is to follow **A-10** ring road around until connecting onto the **A-2** south for about 37 kilometers (23 miles) until exiting at the city's "Centrum."
From **Rotterdam** you should take the **E-19** rign road north before exiting onto the **A-20** north for about 16 kilometers (10 miles), then follow the **A-12** east for about 39 kilometers (24 miles) until finding the city's "Centrum" exit.

**By Train**
Utrecht is linked to almost any other point in Holland and Europe by several major rail lines. This city has two different major rail stations, each with its own series of daily arrivals and departures. The larger and more conveniently located  Cent**ral Station** train depot at the western side of the city's downtown section is the major point of mass transport arrivals.
Connections between this station and any other point in Utrecht can generally be made by foot, by using the adjacent public bus stops for around 3 NLG per person each way, by Tre**intaxi** st 6 NLG per person, or via taxi for between 9.50 NLG and 18.50 NLG depending on where you are going.

## GETTING AROUND TOWN
**By Public Transportation**
While almost any sight within Utrecht is well within walking distance from any point downtown, the region's **GVU** (Gemeente Vervoersbedrijf Utrecht) public transit authority also offers a selection of public bus lines

to get you safely and easily around town. They accept **Nationale Strippen Kaarts**.

Almost all of these buses stop at one point or another in front of the Central Station. The normal hours of operation for most of the system is from about 6:00am until roughly 11:45pm. After that your only choices are either to walk, or to take a taxi. Locations outside of downtown Utrecht, such as Bunnik, will require travel through more than one zone, so you must ask the driver how many blank strips are required.

**By Taxi**

There a few hundred licensed taxis roaming the streets and major passenger arrival points of the city during all hours of the day and night. Drivers here have new Renault and Opel 4 door sedans with enough trunk space to hold a few pieces of luggage. These drivers are polite, honest, and occasionally multilingual. To find a taxi, either hail an unoccupied cab driving by with its "Taxi" roof light illuminated, go to one of the obvious taxi stands throughout the city, or call *(30) 288-8000* for a radio response pick-up on demand.

The main taxi ranks are located at the Central Station, the NS Station, the Jaarbeursplein, and near the Vredenburg and Domplein squares. Taxis here are metered and charge somewhere between 9.75 NLG to 18.50 NLG per ride (not per person) between most downtown locations depending on exact distance and traffic conditions. There is also a special flat rate of 15 NLG per carload for one way rides within the "Centrum" zone offered by the Utrecht Taxi Service. A limited number of the city's taxi's now accept major credit cards for fare payments.

## WHERE TO STAY

*Expensive*

**HOTEL DE SWAEN**, *De Lind, 47,* **Oisterwijk**. *Tel: (42) 421-9006, Fax: (42) 428-5860. US & Canada Bookings (Relais & Chateaux) 1-212-856-0115. Year round rack rates from 285 NLG per double room per night (E.P.). Special weekday rates from 200 NLG per double room per night (B.P.). All major credit cards accepted.*

This fine deluxe inn and simply amazing gourmet restaurant is located in the quaint village of **Oisterwijk**, a short distance by train or car from Utrecht. This centuries-old inn offers a special blend of charm, luxury, and hospitality. Every inch of this beautiful property is lined with opulent antiques, 17th century Flemish works of art, elegant carpets, awesome crystal chandeliers, marble tiles, and hand crafted wrought iron grillwork. The 18 individually designed rooms and suites all feature private marble bathrooms with gold fixtures, fine art and antiques, direct dial telephone, village or garden view balconies, remote control satellite television, electronic trouser press, mini-bar, and beautiful furnishings.

Make sure to drop by Cas Spijkers' formal gourmet restaurant or informal bistro for the meal of your life (see review below). When weather permits, the hotel's perfectly manicured English gardens are the perfect place to relax and enjoy a sunny day off. If you are looking for a great little place to get away from the big city stress, and still enjoy all the services and facilities of an intimate luxury hotel, this impeccable Relais & Chateaux affiliated property is Highly Recommended.

**PARK PLAZA HOTEL**, *Westplein 50. Tel: (30) 292-5200. Fax: (30) 292-5199. Year round rack rates from 295 NLG per double room per night (E.P.). All major credit cards accepted.*

This modern executive class hotel and convention center is one of the best choices in town for those arriving here on serious business trips. This large full service property in the downtown core offers 120 large and comfortable rooms and suites that all contain deluxe private bathrooms, direct dial telephones, remote control satellite television with pay per view movies, modern furnishings, and much more. Facilities include business meeting and reception rooms, sauna, a bar, a good restaurant, on sight parking, boutiques, and a nice ambiance.

**HOLIDAY INN UTRECHT**, *Jaarbeursplein 24. Tel: (30) 291-0555. Fax: (30) 294-3999. US & Canada Bookings (Holiday Inn) 1-800-465-4329. Year round rack rates from 285 NLG per double room per night (E.P.). All major credit cards accepted.*

This huge modern tower style hotel near Utrecht's giant Jaarbeurs convention center is packed during much of the year with executives attending special congress and large meetings. The 4 star property offers 280 nicely decorated rooms that all feature private bathrooms, direct dial telephone, remote control satellite television, mini-bar, nice lithographs, and comfortable modern furnishings. Facilities include a private parking area, boutiques, restaurants, a nice lounge, room service, business meeting and convention rooms, express laundry and dry cleaning, available secretarial service, and a highly professional staff.

### Moderate

**MALIE HOTEL**, *Maliestraat 2. Tel; (30) 231-6424. Fax; (30) 234-0661. Year round rack rates from 185 NLG per double room per night (E.P.). All major credit cards accepted.*

Located on a tree-lined quiet street on the edge of the city, this deluxe 4 star full service hotel is one of the best places to stay in Utrecht. The Malie is housed in a pair of stylish set 19th century mansions and offers 29 beautifully decorated rooms and suites that each contain large modern private bathrooms, comfortable bedding, remote control satellite television, large picture windows, direct dial telephones, inner courtyard or side street views, plenty of old world charm. Hotel facilities include a bar, a restaurant, business meeting rooms, nearby public and garage parking, room service, express laundry and dry cleaning, safe deposit boxes, and good staff.

**HOTEL SMITS**, *Vredenberg 14. Tel: (30) 233-1232. Fax: (30) 232-8451. Year round rack rates from 178 NLG per double room per night (B.P.). All major credit cards accepted.*

Situated just off the city's main market square, this 4 star modern hotel is one of Utrecht's most welcoming properties. There are 85 spacious and uniquely decorated city view rooms with private bathroom, direct dial telephone, wall to wall carpeting, remote control satellite television, nice furnishings, and sound proofed windows. Facilities here include a good restaurant, one of the nearby parking, business meeting rooms, and a friendly staff.

**TULIP INN UTRECHT**, *Janskerkhof 10. Tel: (30) 231-3169. Fax: (30) 231-0148. Year round rack rates from 175 NLG per double room per night (B.P.). All major credit cards accepted.*

I really like this nice 3 star hotel in the heart of one of the city's most enjoyable café-lined squares. This delightful and well-managed small property offers 43 well decorated and extremely comfortable rooms with large private bathrooms, direct dial telephone, am-fm clock radio, satellite television with pay per view movies, and great bedding. Facilities here include a bar, restaurant, and nearby parking.

### Inexpensive

**NJHC HOSTEL RHIJNAUWEN**, *Rhijnauwenselaan 14, Bunnik. Tel: (30) 656-1277. Fax: (30) 657-1065. US & Canada Bookings (Hostelling International) 1-613-237-7884. Year round rack rates from 26 NLG per person in a dormitory per night (C.P.). Year round rack rates from 74 NLG per double private room per night (E.P.). Cash Only - No credit cards accepted.*

This is a great choice for those who prefer to be just a 15 minute walk, 10 minute bike ride, or four minute bus ride (or drive) from the center of Utrecht, and are looking for great (but still affordable) accommodations in a historic river-front mansion. This superbly managed hostel offers a series of nice yet basic single, double, triple, and quadruple rooms with private bathrooms, as well as a special section of dormitory rooms for up to 20 people each that have semi-private bathrooms and luggage lockers. Guests of the hostel are encouraged to use the available bicycles to visit the adjacent old fortress and make their way into Utrecht via a beautiful winding country lane.

Facilities include free outdoor parking, a nearby bus stop, storage lockers, conference rooms, a good cheap restaurant, a great and inexpensive bar, vending machines, and a nice staff. I really enjoyed my night here, and met plenty of interesting people from all over the world. Highly recommended as the most friendly place to stay, as well as the best value for the money of any place in the Utrecht area!

**PARKHOTEL,** *Tolsteegsingel 34. Tel: (30) 251-6712. Fax: (30) 254-0401. Year round rack rates from 95 NLG per double room per night (C.P.). Most major credit cards accepted.*

This simple family owned and operated inn near the heart of the city is about the best centrally located budget choice. This basic inn features eight medium-sized rooms that all have private bathrooms, television, and direct dial telephone. There is also a swimming pool, private parking, a nice breakfast room, and a good staff.

## WHERE TO EAT

*Very Expensive*

**RESTAURANT DE SWAEN,** *De Lind, 47 (Oisterwijk), Tel. (42) 421-9006. All major credit cards accepted. Member of Relais & Chateaux and also Les Patrons Cuisiniers.*

In every country in the world, there is always one restaurant that stands out among the very best. The famed Restaurant De Swaen Hotel De Swaen (see review above in *Where to Stay*) is a great choice for those who want to experience the absolute finest cuisine available in Holland! This stunningly beautiful formal gourmet restaurant has helped set a standard from which all other dining establishments here should be measured against.

Their ever-present and extremely personable Dutch master chef, Cas Spijkers, has authored outstanding cook books and hosts a weekly television show. He is most often found in the kitchen that bustles with 18 chefs who labor for hours on end each day to create a spectacular array of culinary delights. The cuisine offered here is Mr. Spijkers' own unique blend of French influenced dishes. Dress well here, make a reservation in advance, and you can have an unforgettable 4 or 5 course meal for around 115 NLG a person and up, not including wine.

*Expensive*

**LUDEN,** *Janskerkhof 10. Tel: (30) 232-2344. All major credit cards accepted.*

This restaurant and brasserie on one of Utrecht's most important squares is among the region's most innovative places to dine. For between 42.50 NLG and 80 NLG or so, you can have a multiple course gourmet meal that may include choices like cajun gumbo, salad with lamb and fresh regional herbs, roasted leg of lamb on black pasta, grilled entrecote in a spicy garlic rosemary sauce, filet of sole with pasta and paprika sauce, and Grandma's apple pie al la mode. Dress reasonably well, and if possible, call in advance for a reservation

**TUSSEL HEMEL EN AARDE**, *Oudegracht 99. Tel: (30) 231-1864. All major credit cards accepted.*

For ambiance, few restaurants can beat this establishment's location in the medieval Stadskasteel Oudean city castle. Not only do they serve great meals, but the brew their own beers called Jonge Daen and Oude Daen in the castle's basement cellars.

They have romantic fireside and canal-view dining areas and feature a menu that includes salads with blue cheese and marinated wild onions for 18.50 NLG, fish soup with jumbo shrimp and saffron at 16.50 NLG, cresson and shitake mushroom cream soup for 12.50 NLG, baked filet of tuna served with a puree of pears and apples at 41.50 NLG, filet of lamb with aged cheese and leeks for 37.75 NLG, steamed brill with sauerkraut and Riesling wine sauce at 39.50 NLG, and home-made sherbet in three flavors for 17.25 NLG. By the way, the name of this unusual place appropriately translates to "Between Heaven and Earth."

**D'COONINCK VAN POORTUGAEL**, *Voorstraat 14. Tel: (30) 232-2775. All major credit cards accepted.*

This wonderful gourmet restaurant in one of Utrecht's finest 17th century gabled houses, is located just off the historic Neude square in the historic old city center. Once inside the opulent dining room, patrons are handed a large menu featuring such delicious dishes as salad with smoked salmon for 17.50 NLG, pigeon soup at 10.50 NLG, poached filet of sole with scampi for 41.50 NLG, beef steak with mushroom puree at 22.50 NLG, wild duck with celery for 49.50 NLG, pheasant with caramelized potatoes at 45 NLG, veal entrecote with blue cheese at 42.50 NLG, and plenty of great desserts and fine wines by the bottle. The dress code is not too strict, and reservations are a good idea.

### Moderate

**LA COMEDY**, *Janskerk 22. Tel: (30) 230-4604. Cash only - Most major credit cards accepted.*

La Comedy is a strange little restaurant with imaginative design, lighting, and wallpaper (made from music books!). Early evening dinner here is a quiet and fulfilling event with a good selection of delicious seasonal items like French onion soup with melted cheese at 6 NLG, wild mushroom salad with gorgonzola cheese and nuts for 11 NLG, codfish in a basil-tomato chutney dressing at 24.50 NLG, tournedos of beef in pepper sauce for 32 NLG, and mango ice cream with fresh mango slices at 12.50 NLG.

**STAIRWAY TO HEAVEN**, *Mariaplaats 11. Tel; (30) Unlisted. Cash only - No credit cards accepted.*

This combination restaurant, café, and club offers a diverse menu with huge portions of items such as fried chili pepper steak at 24.50 NLG, marinated spare ribs for 17.50 NLG, chili con carne at 14.50 NLG, jumbo shrimp fried in corn flakes for 28 NLG, fish and chips with salad for 17.50 NLG, a daily vegetarian dish at 17.50 NLG, and apple pie a la mode for 8.50 NLG.

**CAFE ORLOFF**, *Donkere Gaard 8. Tel: (30) 232-1679. Cash only - No credit cards accepted.*

This unassuming little café in just off the Oudegracht canal has a great kitchen that prepares large portions of lunch-time meals such as tomato soup for 5 NLG, vegetarian quiche with salad at 15 NLG, Mexican style meat tacos for 15 NLG, pasta with basil pesto sauce and salad at 16.00 NLG, lasagna for 15 NLG, lamb cutlets with home made mashed potatoes at 14.50 NLG, Indian style curried beef for 15 NLG, and Thai style chicken with sticky rice and salad at 15 NLG.

**DE OUDE MUNTKELDER,** *Oudegracht werf 112. Tel: (30) 231-6773. Cash only - No credit cards accepted.*

This unique old pancake house in a canal-front cellar offers visitors to Utrecht a chance to munch on over four dozen varieties of Dutch pancakes filled with every imaginable type of fruit, cheese, vegetable, and meat. Prices start at about 8.50 NLG and go up from there for a rather filling meal.

### Inexpensive

**DA SOEPTERRINE**, *Zakkendragerssteeg 40. Tel: (30) 231-7005. Most major credit cards accepted.*

As its name suggests, this is the best place in town to head for a home-made soup. Located in converted middle class house, the whole restaurant feels like a cozy living room full of friends. They specialize in their vast selection of vegetarian and meat based soups that cost 6.50 NLG for a cup, and 11.50 for a large bowl, as well as having a regular menu with Greek salad at 11.50 NLG, chicken with curry for 10.50 NLG, quiche at 13.50 NLG, and smoked salmon for 15.50 NLG.

**VICTOR CONSAEL POFFERTJES**, *Neude. Tel: (30) 231-6377. Cash only - No credit cards accepted.*

You just can't leave Utrecht without stopping, at least once, at Hollands only remaining traditional 19th century Dutch *Poffertjes* (fried dough) stand on Neude square in the heart of town – Holland's oldest! The entertaining chefs will have your custom-made fritter ready in 3 or 4 minutes for 3 NLG and up depending on your chosen ingredients.

**IL MULINO**, *Adelaarstraat 2. Tel: (30) 271-7411. Cash only - No credit cards accepted.*

This is not really a restaurant, but rather a great little *gelato* (soft home-made Italian ice cream) shop in the center of town. Just step inside, order a cup of truffle, apple pie, walnut, double chocolate, or pistachio gelato from one of the friendly young women working here, and soon you will forget how long it took you to find this place!

## SEEING THE SIGHTS

• *From the* **Centraal Station** *around the city and back.*
• *Approximate duration (by foot) is at least 5.5 hours, including museum, gallery, church, café, boutique, canal, market, and side street visits.*

**Towards the huge Vredenburg Market Square**

After departing the main exit of the **Centraal Station**, cut through the massive Stationsplein and its adjacent **Moreelse Park**. The vast complex of above and underground buildings that you have just past alongside is called the **Hoog Catharijne**. This is Holland's largest indoor shopping mall and feaures 180 boutiques, movie theaters, restaurants, and department stores that run for over 5 kilometers via connecting tunnels and modern walkways. The m*all can be visited for free from 9:30am until 6:00pm from Monday through Saturday with the exceptions of a late 11:00am opening on Tuesday, a late 9:00pm closing on Thursday, and an early 5:00pm closing on Saturday.*

About a block later you will intersect with a noisy and traffic jammed avenue called the Cathrijne Baan. Carefully cross over to the far side of this avenue and turn left to follow it a short distance until reaching the well marked **VVV** tourist information offices located at building #90 next to the Music Centre performing arts complex. This is a good place to pick up free and inexpensive maps, walking tour booklets, cultural event schedules, and ask a few quick questions before continuing along the same street.

A few steps later on the right hand side is one of several entrances to the constantly active **Vredenburg square**. This large central plaza was named after the 16th century castle of Emperor Carlos V of Spain that once stood here, and is now home to several shops, cafés, and restaurants. This area is also where two of the city's main outdoor markets are, a good place to find good bargains on cheese, fruits, meats, bread, and other picnic supplies.

## THE MARKETS OF UTRECHT

The Vredenburg square has become the site of major local markets such as the **Wednesday** and **Saturday Outdoor General Markets.** Held every Wednesday and Saturday from 9:00am until 5:00pm, this bustling marketplace takes over all of the square with hundreds of small kiosks selling cheese, fruits, vegetables, clothing, fast food, flowers, cookies, and lots of other items to help make for a perfect picnic. On most weeks there is also a great **Friday Outdoor Organic Foods Market** held from 12 noon until around 6:00pm.

For a city of this size, Utrecht is loaded with plenty of great outdoor and indoor markets on almost every day of the year. The following is a brief listing of other entertaining markets that you should attempt to visit while here:

**Monday Horse Market** - 8:00am until 12 noon in the Veemarkethallen - Sartreweg

**Tuesday Outdoor General Market** - 10:00am until 3:00pm on Smaragdplein

**Tuesday Car Market** - 9:30am til 5:00pm in the Veemarkethallen - Sartreweg

**Wednesday Outdoor General Market** - 8:00am til 1:00pm on Oppenheimplein

**Thursday Outdoor General Market** - 9:00am til 2:00pm on the Overvecht

**Thusrday Cattle Market** - 6:00am til 1:00pm in the Veemarkethallen - Sartreweg

**Friday Outdoor General Market** - 9:00am til 1:00pm on Starkenborghhof

**Saturday Outdoor Flower Market** - 7:00am til 5:00pm on Janskerkhof

**Saturday Outdoor Flower Market** - 8:00am til 5:00pm on Oudegracht

**Saturday Outdoor Drapery Market** - 8:00am til 1:00pm on Breedstraat

**Saturday Outdoor Stamp Market** - 12noon til 5:00pm on Vismarkt

**Saturday Outdoor Flea Market** - 8:00am til 2:00pm on St Jacobsstraat

**Towards the Domkerk Tower**

Now walk to the back of Vredenburg square and keep walking straight along the **Lange Elisabethstraat**. All of the side streets intersecting with this bustling lane are filled with fancy boutiques and book shops. A couple of blocks later this street then merges into a pedestrian-only lane called the Steenweg and begins to curve slightly towards the right. After a few short blocks, bear right onto the Hekelsteeg and follow it into a beautiful small plaza filled with 17th century houses and several shops.

At the end of the small plaza turn left onto the **Buurkerkhof**. At building #10 of this lane you will find the entrance to the **Nationaal Museum van Speelklok tot Pierement** (National Museum from Musical Clocks to Street Organs). Inside this 13th century converted church you will find an excellent collection of mechanized musical instruments from the 18th through 20th century including rare examples of pianos, street clocks, juke boxes, music boxes, carillon clocks, mechanical singing birds, old player pianos, street organs, and amusement park orchestrinas. *The mechanized musical instrument museum is open 10:00am until 5:00pm from Tuesday through Saturday, 1:00pm until 5:00pm on Sundays, and costs 7.50 NLG per person including a free guided tour and demonstrations of their odd devices every hour on the hour.*

From the music museum, keep walking along the Buurkerkhof until it merges into the Zadelstraat and then cross over the enchanting Oudegracht canal via the Maartensbrug bridge. Once you have crossed the bridge, the street merges into the Servetstraat and leads directly into the **Domplein** plaza. This was the original site of a fortress when the Romans settled here back in the 1st century, and is now a picturesque plaza dominated by the Gothic 13th through 16th century **Domkerk** church. The partially ruined vaulted church contains several old tombstones, nice stained glass windows, several side chapels, as well as a wonderful 19th century pipe organ. The giant weathervane topped 14th century Gothic **Domtoren** tower with its sweet sounding carillon stands over 112 meters (367 feet) and is considered by some to be the tallest such structure in Holland.

For those with plenty of energy, try climbing up the 465 steps to the impressive tower's magnificent panoramic viewing platform. The church also features tranquil adjacent cloisters with herb gardens, a tea room, gift shop, and free choir concerts on each Saturday at 3:30pm.

*The church is open between May through September on weekdays from 10:00am until 5:00pm, Saturdays from 10:00am until 3:30pm, and Sundays from 2:00pm until 4:00pm, as well as being open October through April on weekdays from 11:00am until 4:00pm, Saturdays from 11:00am until 3:30pm, and costs nothing to enter, but they suggest a 2 NLG contribution! The optional 4 NLG per person guided walk up to the tour's viewing deck takes place every hour on the hour on weekends only between 12 noon and 4pm, as well as weekdays between April and October from 10:00am until 4:00pm.*

Among the Domplein square's additional highlights is the dramatic 15th century Neo-Renaissance **Akademiegebouw van de Rijksuniversiteit** (Academy building of the University of Utrecht) at building #29 where the Union of Utrecht treaty was signed in 1579 by the Count of Nassau, as well several statues and a giant boulder (near the cloisters' entrance) that was donated by the people of Jelling, Denmark, to commemorate their conversion to Christianity.

### Through the Side Streets of the Old City

From the front of the Domplein, retrace your steps back across the canal via Servatstraat and the Maartensbrug bridge, and then bear left onto the Lijnmarkt, one of the city's most unusual lanes filled with upscale boutiques. After following this quaint lane for a block or so, walk over the next bridge on your left that crosses back over to the opposite side of the canal and then immediately turn right onto the canal-front **Oudegracht**. Make sure to take the time to glimpse the houses that line this charming canal, which boasts several waterside wharfs and cellars that have recently been converted into unique restaurants, night clubs, and even a couple of "smoking" coffee shops. Among the most famous places to hit on this street is the **Stadskasteel Oudaen**, a medieval city castle at building #99 that is now home to a restaurant, pub, brewery, canal-side café, and theater wrapped up into one.

Several blocks further down the Oudegracht, as it changes names first to the Tolsteegzijde and then to the Twijnstraat, turn left on the Widje Doelen. A half a block or so along this lane, bear left onto the tiny Schutterstraat which is lined by a series of 19th century almshouses for elderly single women. At the next corner make a right turn onto the Doelenstraat and almost immediately turn right onto the Nicolas Dwarstraat, where at buildings #2 through #12 you can peek at a set of unusual 17th century almshouse-style cottages known as the **Gronsveltkameren** that are occupied by retired single tenants.

At the end of this lane, turn right through the Nicolaskerkhof courtyard as it merges into the Agnietenstraat and at building #1 you will find the entrance to the **Centraal Museum**. This is a fine municipal museum containing a varied array of exhibits relating to art and the history of Utrecht. Among the many displays are an excavated Viking ship, a half dozen amazing rooms furnished in 15th through 18th century trimmings, paintings by local Golden Age masters such as Jan van Scorel and Abraham Bloemaert, additional 19th through 20th century Dutch and French paintings by artists like Vincent Van Gogh, antique costumes, coins, applied and industrial art, and many temporary exhibitions.

The museum also operates the **Rietveld-Schroderhuis** far away from here over on Prins Hendriklaan #50, which was designed as a private house for rich clients of the local de Stijl designer and world-famous modern furniture maker Gerrit Rietveld in 1924. *The museum is open 11:00am until 5:00pm from Tuesday through Saturday and 12noon until 5:00pm on Sundays, and costs 6 NLG per person to enter. The Rietveld-Schroderhuis is open by appointment only for 9 NLG per person including an* *escorted tour of the premises, but you must call in advance at Tel: (30) 236-2310 to be admitted.*

After leaving the Centraal Museum, continue along the Agnietenstraat until the next corner where you can bear left onto the wide canal-front Nieuwe Gracht. A few blocks up on the left hand side at building #63 is the **Rijksmuseum het Catharijneconvent** (State Museum of Catherine's Convent). This former set of Gothic convent rooms located along a fine cloister now contain a superb museum of Christianity in Holland. It features the nation's largest collection of medieval period art, as well as rare 9th through 18th century religious paintings, vestments, sculptures, manuscripts, scale model churches, ornaments, and gold & silver monstrance. *The religious museum is open 10:00am until 5:00pm from Tuesday through Saturday and 12 noon until 5:00pm on Sundays, and costs 5 NLG per person to enter.*

### Back Towards the Janskerkhof and Neude Squares

After departing the religious museum, keep walking along the Nieuwe Gracht for a handful of blocks until it merges with the much narrower Achter St. Pieter. About a block or so later, bear right onto the Pieters Kerkhof that will lead directly towards a peaceful plaza dominated by the famed 11th century Romanesque Pieterskerk. This is the city's oldest standing house of worship and can be visited to view several unique 12th century reliefs near the chancel, old frescoes, an unusual baptismal font, and the crypt of Bishop Bernulphus. *The church is usually, but not always, open 11:00am until 4:00pm from Tuesday through Friday and 12 noon until 3:00pm on Saturdays, and is free to enter.*

Now retrace your steps back down the Pieterskerkhof and at the next corner make a right turn down the Achter St. Pieter. After another block and a half or so you will turn right onto the Korte Jansstraat and follow it straight into the busy **Jans Kerkhof**. The large Gothic church that you will soon see is the 11th century **Janskerk**, while nearby lies the beautiful 13th century **Statenkamer** provincial government building. The entire plaza is lined by several of the city's finest restaurants and bars.

Bear left through this plaza and follow the Lange Janstraat for a block or so until bearing left into the historic **Neude** square. Once the sight of many outdoor markets, this square is now known primarily for the wonderful Amsterdam school style brick facade of the turn of the century **Poostkantoor** (Post Office) at building #11. This plaza is also lined on all sides by much more important examples of Renaissance, Baroque, and Jugenendstil architecture, including the fantastically gabled **Huis d'Cooninck van Poortugael** intersecting the plaza from its position on Voorstraat #11, now a gourmet restaurant.

Bear left through the Neude square and follow the Vinken Burgstraat for a block or so before turning left onto the Weerdzijde. About a block up this canal-side street you will pass alongside a bridge leading past the front of the remarkable 19th century Neo-Classical **Stadhuis** (City Hall). From here you can cross over the bridge and head down the Choorstraat for half a block. Then bear right onto the Steenweg, follow it as it merges with the St. Elisabethstraat, and continue straight into the Vredenburg square before crossing the Catharijne Baan and returning to the **Centraal Station** to complete your tour of Utrecht.

## GUIDED SIGHTSEEING TOURS

There are several special guided trips offered by foot, bus, and river boat to the sights in and around Utrecht. The following is a brief listing of the most popular trips, but for a complete listing, contact the VVV tourist information office.

### By Boat

The following cruises are all operated by the Utrechts Rondvaartbedrijf company with ticket and information offices at the *Bemuurde Weerd 17, Tel: (30) 272-0111.*

- **City Canal Cruise**: This one hour tour starts at the piers in front of Oudegracht 85 and continues along Utrecht's canals. Departs hourly every day of the week from 11:00am until 5:00pm (until 9:00pm on Tuesdays and Thursdays in the summer) year round. The price is about 10 NLG per person.
- **Museum Cruise**: After departing the piers near Oudegracht 85, you will be shuttled by canal boat to the landings near the Centraal Museum and/or the Rijksmuseum het Catharijneconvent, and the be brought back to the Oudegracht, every half hour between 11am and 3pm. The museum boat shuttle operates every Tuesday through Sunday year round and costs 13 NLG round trip.
- **Vecht River Canal Cruise**: This is an extended half-day tour by canal boat that takes visitors on a scenic cruise along the Vecht river to the peaceful town of Oud Zuilen where you will then be escorted through the historic Kasteel Zuylen castle to view its period chambers and collections of art and tapestry. This trip includes a complimentary coffee and pie break and leaves the Oudegraht landing at 11:30am and returns at 4:00pm on Tuesdays, Wednesdays, and Thursdays from May 23 through September 28 only. The fee for these cruise is 30 NLG per person, including the castle tour in English and all admission charges.
- **Kromme Rijn Cruise**: These half day trips go from Utrecht's canals to the picturesque Kromme RIjn river and stop off for an hour at a local

waterfront pancake house where you can either stroll around the quaint countryside estate, or hit the restaurant's great outdoor terrace. This tour leaves from the Oudegracht landing on Wednesdays and Sundays at 9:30am and 2:00pm from May 24 until September 27 only. The price excluding lunch is 21 NLG round-trip.

### By Bus

The **Groen Koetsiers Bedrijf** (Green Coach Company) operates a seasonal 45 minute guided bus tour of eastern Utrecht for 12 NLG per person. They have various scheduled departures daily from June through September, as on weekends only during spring and fall. To find out what is currently being offered, contact them at *Tel: (30) 271-0235.*

### By Foot

Another good way to be guided through the city of Utrecht on your own schedule is to pop by the VVV headquarters and rent a so called "Walkman Tour" audio cassette. This tape allows you to listen to a guided tour (in English) as you stroll past the city's most famous squares, canals, and attractions. The tapes rent for 5 NLG per day, and remember to bring the cassettes back to the VVV offices when you have agreed to, or they will charge you for a second day! For more details, contact the **VVV-Utrecht**, Vredenburg 90, *Tel: (30) 233-1544* or pop by their offices.

### By Horse-Drawn Carriage

There are several horse drawn carriages available for hire just in front of the Domtoren tower in Domplein. For somewhere around 55 NLG per half hour, you can have a ride through the oldest part of the city center. This seasonal service is offered on weekends in April, May, September, and October, and daily in June, July, and August. For more specific information, contact the stables at *Tel: (30) 271-0235.*

## NIGHTLIFE & ENTERTAINMENT

### Bars, Pubs, Clubs, & Grand Cafés

**LA COMEDY**, *Janskerkhof 22. Tel: (30) 230-4604.*

La Comedy is a great combination theater, pub, and restaurant near the Janskerk that features live music and comedy geared for the post-university aged crowd on most nights of the week. Great interior, including stained glass ceilings.

**HET OUDE POTHUIS**, *Oudegracht 279. Tel: (30) 231-8970.*

I really like this cavernous pub and live music venue in the cellar of an old canal-side townhouse. Here you can munch on great pub food, have a few ice cold beers, and watch an up and rising rock or blues band belting out tunes from the small stage. A great place to sit back and watch the crowd at work!

**DIKKE DRIES**, *Waterstraat 32. Tel: (30) 231-8381.*

Popular with the after-office hours crowd, this typical Utrecht pub is a great place for people of all ages to hang out and throw down a few string beers before heading off to the larger venues.

**VANOUDS DE VRIENDSCHAP**, *Wed 1. Tel: (30) 231-8813.*

A cozy dark Brown café where not much has changed in over 25 years. A good place to have funny conversations, and stare out onto the adjacent café terraces full of students enjoying the sunshine.

**'T PANDJE**, *Nobelstraat 193. Tel: (30) 231-8050.*

**DE KNEUS**, *Nobelstraat 303. Tel: (30) 231-8799.*

These two great café-pubs are completely full of beer drinking students until around 4:00am or so on Thursday through Saturday nights. Every one here stands and tries to talk loud enough to converse with members of the opposite sex. Dress down and expect to drink heavily!

**CYRANO DE BERGERAC**, *Kromme Nieuwegracht 16. Tel: (30) 231-2819.*

A good dance club for the fashionably attired 25 and over set that loves 70's and 80's dance music and strong mixed drinks. Set in a comfortable 17th century building with plenty of ambiance. Sometimes cover charges will apply.

**AXL**, *Onder het Stadhuis. Tel: (30) Unlisted.*

Axl is a unique dance club built into the former basement prison of the city hall building and is packed with 20 to 25 year  old locals and students that love to party to the sounds of house and techno music until at least 4:00am. The club costs around 12.50 NLG a person to enter, and the doormen usually don't give anyone a hard time to get in..

**T.A.I.**, *Oudegracht 245. Tel: (30) 231-2455.*

This popular student disco out is actually a multi-purpose venue that features everything from Salsa dance parties to rock concerts in a huge cavernous setting. Admission charges are about 12.50 NLG a person, and you can dress as crazy as you like.

## PRACTICAL INFORMATION

**Main VVV Tourist Office** - *Vredenburg 90* - *(30) 233-1544*
**Municipal Information Center** - *Vredenburg 90* - *(30) 231-5415*
**GVU Municipal Transit Authority** - *(30) 236-3636*
**City Garages and Car Parking Information** - *(30) 233-7611*
**Domestic Train and Bus Info** - *(6) 9292*
**Radio Dispatched Taxis** - *Utrecht Taxi Service* - *(30) 288-8000*
**Police Headquarters** - *Kroonstrat 25* - *(30) 239-7111*
**Emergency Hotline** - *06-11*

# 22. ARNHEM

On the upper bank of the wide **Rijn** (Rhine) **River**, the working class city of **Arnhem** makes a delightful sight for a one or two day visit. Besides being home to dozens of cute squares filled with unique antique shops and designer boutiques, this compact city has a character all its own.

Most North Americans will remember Arnhem as the sight of World War II's disastrous **Operaton Market Garden** in September of 1944. Allied airborne troops retreated after succumbing to massive casualties during an unsuccessful attempt to take a Nazi-controlled bridge over the Rijn river (now called the **John Frost Bridge** in memory of the operation's British commander). The entire region around the city is filled with small towns such as Oosterbeek that regularly pay homage to this heroic effort, and are marked by the graves of the thousands of allied soldiers killed during this horrific nine day battle.

Currently both Arnhem and the surrounding area contain many sights well worth visiting, including the amusing Koernmarkt square with its many bars and cafés, the **Marktplaats** square which is home to a fantastic outdoor market and reconstructed church, several rebuilt medieval houses and monuments, some of the best shopping streets in the country, and a population of hard working people who go out of their way to be friendly to anyone from our part of the world.

Also make sure to take the time to get to nearby sights such as **Oosterbeek**, **Apeldoorn**, the **Naational Park de Hoge Veluwe**, the **Openluchtmuseum**, a few dramatic castles, and many other fun day trip possibilities listed in excursion section of this chapter.

## ORIENTATION

Arnhem is situated in the middle of the Netherland's west central **Gelderland** province, with a population of 134, 613. It lies 85 kilometers (53 miles) east-southeast of the capital city of Amsterdam, and 57 kilometers (35 miles) east of Utrecht.

## ARRIVALS & DEPARTURES

### By Air

Most visitors flying to this city will arrive here via land links from the large **Schiphol Airport** near Amsterdam, 83 kilometers (52 miles) to the west-northwest.

### By Car

Downtown street-side parking spots are fairly easy to find.

From **Amsterdam**, the fastest way to get to Arnhem is to follow **A-10** ring road around until connecting onto the **A-2** south for about 37 kilometers (23 miles) and then merging onto the **A-12** east for around another 58 kilometers (36 miles) before exiting at the city's "Centrum".

From **Utrecht** you should take the **A-12** east for some before exiting onto the **A-20** north for about 16 kilometers (10 miles), then follow the **A-12** east for about 59 kilometers (37 miles) until finding the city's "Centrum" exit.

### By Bus

Many of the bus lines between Arnhem and other parts of Holland tend to stop at the **Busstation** depot just alongside the **NS Station** train depot on the northwestern edge of downtown. Make sure to call in advance to find out exactly where and when your bus comes in. Connections between this station and any other point in downtown Arnhem can generally be made by the adjacent public bus stops for about 3 NLG per person each way, or via taxi for between 8.75 NLG and 13.50 NLG.

### By Train

Arnhem is linked to most other points in Holland and Europe by several major rail lines. This city's major **NS Station** rail depot is conveniently located at the northwestern side of the city's downtown section and is the major point of mass transport arrivals. Connections between this station and any other point in Arnhem can generally be made by foot, by using the adjacent public bus stops for around 3 NLG per person each way, by Tre**intaxi** for 6 NLG a person, or via taxi for between 8.75 NLG and 13.50 NLG.

## GETTING AROUND TOWN

### By Public Transportation

While almost any sight within Arnhem is well within walking distance from any point downtown, the region's **GVM** (Gelderse Vervoermaatschappij) public transit authority also offers a selection of public bus lines to get you safely and easily around town. They accept **Nationale Strippen Kaarts**.

Almost all of these buses stop at one point or another at the **Busstation** just next to the NS Station rail depot. Locations outside of downtown Arnhem such as Oosterbeek, Apeldoorn, the Burger's Zoo, the Naational Park de Hoge Veluwe, and the Openluchtmuseum will require travel through more than one zone, so you must ask the driver how many blank strips are required. The normal hours of operation for most of the system is from about 6:00am until roughly 11:45pm. After that your only choices are either to walk, or to take a taxi.

**By Taxis**

There around a hundred licensed taxis roaming the streets and major passenger arrival points of the city during all hours of the day and night. Drivers here have new Renault, Mercedes, Ford, and Opel 4 door sedans with enough trunk space to hold a few pieces of luggage. These drivers are polite, honest, and occasionally multilingual. To find a taxi, either hail an unoccupied cab driving by with its "Taxi" roof light illuminated or go to one of the obvious taxi stands throughout the city.

The main taxi ranks are located at the NS Station and near the front of the Musis Sacrum. Taxis here are metered and charge somewhere between 8.75 NLG to 13.50 NLG per ride (not per person) between most downtown locations depending on exact distance and traffic conditions.

## WHERE TO STAY - IN ARNHEM

*Moderate*

**HOTEL MOLENDAL,** *Cronjestraat 15. Tel: (26) 442-4858. Fax: (26) 443-6614. Year round rack rates from 115 NLG per double room per night (B.P.). All major credit cards accepted.*

This charming little hotel is housed in a pretty mansion on a peaceful residential street a few blocks away from the center of the city. There are 16 extremely comfortable large modern rooms with private bathroom, direct dial telephone, wall to wall carpeting, and nice new furnishings. Facilities include a great complimentary buffet breakfast, an old world style bar and public sitting rooms, a television room, nearby parking, and the friendliest staff in town. Highly recommended as the most welcoming place to stay inside Arnhem, and well worth the money.

**HOTEL BLANC,** *Coehoornstraat 4. Tel; (26) 442-8072. Fax; (26) 443-4749. Year round rack rates from 135 NLG per double room per night (B.P.). All major credit cards accepted.*

This modern 3 star hotel just a couple of short blocks away from the train station is also well worth consideration. Owned by a friendly young couple, this unique establishment offers 22 beautifully decorated medium-sized rooms that all feature private bathrooms, direct dial telephone, remote control television, nice lithographs, and comfortable modern furnishings. Facilities include nearby parking, a great first floor bar and café, business meeting and convention rooms, and a surprisingly tranquil ambiance.

**POSTILJON HOTEL,** *Europaweg 25. Tel; (26) 357-3333. Fax; (26) 357-3361. Year round rack rates from 175 NLG per double room per night (E.P.). All major credit cards accepted.*

Located just off the A-12 highway on the outskirts of the city, this popular 3 star full service business class hotel is a good choice only for those with a car. The modern Postiljon offers some 84 large and well decorated rooms that all contain nice modern private bathrooms, comfortable bedding, remote control satellite television, large picture windows, direct dial telephones, and lots of sunlight. Hotel facilities include a bar, a restaurant, several business meeting rooms, free outdoor parking, room service, express laundry and dry cleaning, safe deposit boxes, and a nice staff.

### Inexpensive

**HOTEL-PENSION PARKZICHT**, *Apeldoornstraat 16. Tel: (26) 442-0698. Fax: (26) 443-6202. Year round rack rates from 85 NLG per double room per night (C.P.). All major credit cards accepted.*

This good basic 2 star pension a few blocks north of the city center has 15 or so medium-sized rooms with private bathrooms, color television, and simple furnishings. Facilities are minimal, but for these rates they are more than expected.

**NJHC HOSTEL ALTEVEER**, *Diepenbricklaan 27. Tel: (26) 442-0114. Fax: (26) 351-4892. US & Canada Bookings (Hostelling International) 1-613-237-7884. Year round rack rates from 26 NLG per person in a dormitory per night (C.P.). Year round rack rates from 87 NLG per double private room per night (C.P.). Cash Only - No credit cards accepted.*

This is a great choice for those who prefer to be just a seven minute bus ride (or drive) from the center of Arnhem, and are looking for great affordable accommodations in a delightful hilltop inn. This tranquil yet popular hostel offers a series of nice yet basic single, double, triple, and quadruple rooms with private bathrooms, as well as a special section of dormitory rooms for up to about 20 people each that have semi-private bathrooms and luggage lockers.

Facilities include free outdoor parking, a nearby bus stop, storage lockers, conference rooms, a good cheap restaurant, a great inexpensive bar, vending machines, and a nice staff. I enjoyed my stay here, and met a lot of students and fellow travelers. Recommended as a good budget inn with excellent value for the money.

## WHERE TO STAY - NEAR ARNHEM

*Expensive*

**HOTEL DE BILDERBERG**, *Utrechtseweg 261, Oosterbeek. Tel: (26) 334-0843. Fax: (26) 333-4651. US & Canada Bookings (UTELL) 1-800-44-UTELL. Year round rack rates from 255 NLG per double room per night (E.P.). All major credit cards accepted.*

This fantastic 4 star deluxe hotel on a quiet estate on the edge of **Oosterbeek** is certainly the Arnhem area's finest hotel. This modern full service property offers 144 large superbly designed rooms and suites, each with deluxe private bathrooms stocked with amenities, remote control satellite television with pay per view movies, extremely comfortable furnishings, direct dial telephones, hair dryer, an executive desk, wall to wall carpeting, individually controlled heating systems, and in many cases they also have either balconies or wonderful views out over the adjacent countryside.

Facilities include a great restaurant and outdoor terrace, two unique bars, plush lounges and sitting areas, a fireside library, 24 hour rooms service, a game and billiard room, express laundry and dry cleaning, available child care, a heated indoor swimming pool, a health club, sauna, Turkish bath, nearby horse back riding, a sun tanning room, a full range of well equipped business meeting and convention rooms, free private parking, and the best staff imaginable. The Hotel de Bilderberg is highly recommended as the most relaxing and well-managed property in the entire region!

**HOTEL DE KEIZERSKROON**, *Koningstraat 7, Apeldoorn. Tel; (55) 521-7744. Fax; (55) 521-4737. US & Canada Bookings (UTELL) 1-800-44-UTELL. Year round rack rates from 265 NLG per double room per night (B.P.). All major credit cards accepted.*

Located just across the street form the Palace Het Loo, this great 5 star medium-sized hotel is a perfect place to base yourself while visiting the **Apeldoorn** area. The hotel has 100 large sun-drenched rooms and suites with deluxe private bathrooms, heated towel racks, wall to wall carpeting, mini-bars, remote control satellite television, direct dial telephones, delightful hardwood furnishings, and plenty of class.

Facilities include excellent grill-room and a la carte restaurants, one of the region's best buffet breakfasts, free private parking, business meeting rooms, a huge indoor swimming pool, a health club, solarium, sauna, express laundry and dry cleaning, full porterage services, complimentary shoe polishing machines, and available secretarial and child care services. The Keizerskroon is certainly the best place to stay while visiting Apeldoorn!

*Moderate*
**TULIP INN OOSTERBEEK**, *Stationsweg 6, Oosterbeek. Tel: (26) 334-3034. Fax: (26) 334-2011. US & Canada Bookings (Golden Tulip) 1-800-344-1212. Year round rack rates from 185 NLG per double room per night (B.P.). All major credit cards accepted.*

Located just off the main road through town, this friendly superior first class hotel offers 28 nicely decorated rooms, each with large modern private bathrooms, extremely comfortable bedding, remote control satellite television, am-fm clock radio, large windows, direct dial telephones, and plenty of room. Styled like a cozy Victorian mansion, facilities include a bar, a restaurant, business meeting rooms, an indoor swimming pool and sauna, free parking, room service, safe deposit boxes, and a really nice staff.

*Inexpensive*
**PENSION JOHANNA**, *Pieterbergseweg 34, Oosterbeek. Tel: (26) 333-3225. Year round rack rates from 115 NLG per double room per night (C.P.). All major credit cards accepted.*

This welcoming old world converted mansion near the heart of town offers about a dozen or so nice and simple rooms with private bathroom and minimal facilities. While far from deluxe, this is a good place when all you really want is a nice clean room in a friendly little inn.

## WHERE TO EAT

*Moderate*
**HAI CHANG HAI**, *Jansplaats. Tel; (26) 442-3818. All major credit cards accepted.*

This wonderful Chinese restaurant in one of Arnhem's most delightful small plazas is a good place to enjoy a great exotic meal. Once inside the Asian-styled dining room, patrons are handed a large menu featuring such delicious dishes as hot and sour soup for 5 NLG, egg rolls at 4.75 NLG, spare ribs for 8.50 NLG, Schezuan shrimp at 29.75. egg foo young for 16.50 NLG, Singapore noodles at 15 NLG, beef with mushrooms for 23.50 NLG, chicken with peanuts at 21.50 NLG, and mixed Chinese vegetables for 18.75.

**APHRODITE**, *Rijnstraat 76. Tel; (26) 445-9145. Most major credit cards accepted.*

Located near the heart of the city, this delightful and sun-drenched Greek restaurant features a fine affordable menu that includes spinach pies at 9 NLG, mousaaka for 11 NLG, feta cheese and tomato salad at 11 NLG, spiced grilled lamb cutlets for 24 NLG, giros at 17 NLG, souvlaki for 17.50 NLG, mixed grill at 23.50 NLG, a vegetarian special for 21.50

NLG, and plenty of other Greek specialties that are all home-made. They even feature live music on some nights.

**RESTAURANTE DA LEONE,** *Korenmarkt 1. Tel; (26) 442-6964. Most major credit cards accepted.*

This nice Italian restaurant in the city's most happening square offers over 30 varieties of freshly made pizzas and pastas that cost from 9 NLG to 22.50 NLG each. Make sure to check out their daily "Happy Hours" from 4:00pm until 6:00pm when all pizzas are just 10 NLG each and all pastas are just 12.50 each.

*Inexpensive*

**LA CREPERIE,** *Klarestraat 15. Tel; (26) 445-5419. Cash only - No credit cards accepted.*

This casual little restaurant and café in the center of town offers a huge menu with over 45 different types of French styled crepes, salads, and sandwiches that range in price from 7 NLG to about 18.50 NLG each.

**WAIT A MINUTE PIZZA,** *Tel; (26) 351-3999. Cash only - No credit cards accepted.*

After a long day of running around, this Italian kitchen will deliver all sorts of great food directly to your hotel room within 20 minutes of your call. Their extensive menu includes summer salads for 5 NLG, tomato soup at 6.50 NLG, chicken with garlic and cashews for 24.50 NLG, marinated spare ribs at 21.50 NLG, three colored tortellini with ham and cream sauce for 19.50 NLG, lasagna at 19 NLG, and of course all sorts of pizzas from 12.50 NLG to 19.50 NLG each.

## SEEING THE SIGHTS

• *From the* **NS Station** *around the city and back.*
• *Approximate duration (by foot) is at least 6 hours, including museum, gallery, church, café, boutique, canal, market, and side street visits.*

### Towards the Entertaining Korenmarkt

After departing the **NS Station** through its main exit, bear left through the Stationsplein and walk to the corner where you will make your first stop over at the incredibly helpful and friendly **VVV** tourist information center at building #45. Make sure to pick up copies of their great 2 NLG *Arnhem Region* area accommodations and activities guides, one of the 1 NLG *Arnhem Centrum* maps, and grab a few free brochures from the many local museums and attractions.

After exiting the tourist office, turn left to cut through the Stationsplein. At the next corner you will again turn left to follow the wide Utrechtsestraat for a few steps until making a right turn onto the far side of an intersecting avenue called the Nieuweplein. Then at the next corner turn left down a lane called the Korte Hoogstraat and follow it for a block or so until it leads directly into the famous Korenmarkt square. Formerly the site of a corn market, the square still centers around the 19th century **Korenbeurs** (Corn Exchange Building) that has now been converted into the delightful **Filmhuis** movie theater.

Almost all of the old grain storage warehouses that surround the theater on all sides have been remarkably transformed into bars, discos, pubs, and restaurants that have become the center of Arnhem's robust nightlife. During the warmer months, these establishments set up hundreds of outdoor tables and chairs to attract thousands of 16 to 35 year old locals and help to make this one of Holland's most entertaining little squares. Thursday though Saturday evenings here are jam packed with a great crowd.

### Main Shopping Streets

After passing through the square, head for the far right corner and then follow a small lane called the Pauwstraat. At the end of this street make a right turn onto the Janstraat, the sight of several fine boutiques that in some cases have been built on the ground floor of late medieval townhouses (complete with unusual gable stones). After half a block, turn left into the Jansplaats plaza with its statue of a 15th century Duke of Gelderland.

This plaza is also home to a small **Tuesday Outdoor Market** from 8:00am until 12:45pm. As the plaza merges into a street of the same name, on the left hand side you will find the 19th century domed **Koepelkerk** church, built in 1837 from plans by city architect A. Aytink van Falkenstein. Inside there are several Ionic pillars and a fine pipe organ dating back to 1841. Across from the church on the right side of the street you will pass the impressive Neo-Gothic facade of the **Postkantoor** (Post Office) at building #56. Built in 1888 from plans by C.H. Peters, the post office is decorated with colorful enameled bricks and trefoil arches.

After passing the post office turn right down a lane called the Marienburgstraat, and soon you will walk in front of the Louis XV-style facade of the **Marienburg** arts center *(free entry during normal weekday business hours)* to view its ornate interior and staircase that are filled with interesting Rococo ornamentation.

At the end of this lane, turn left onto the Vijzelstraat and follow it for a block until it merges into the Kettlestraat. A couple of blocks down you will find yourself entering the **Land van de Markt plaza** that is surrounded by a branch of a major department store called **Peek & Cloppenburg**.

**Towards the Marktplaats Market Square**

From the Land van de Markt plaza, turn right onto the boutique-laden **Koningstraat** and follow it until it leads straight into the awesome Marktplaats (also known as the Kerkplein) square. This is the sight of the city's best **Friday** and **Saturday Outdoor Market** held weekly from 9:00am until about 1:00pm on Fridays and from 8:00am until 3:30pm on Saturdays.

The most obvious attraction here is the giant 15th through 16th century Gothic **Grote of Eusebiuskerk** (St. Eusebius Basilica). Severely damaged during World War II, this inspiring vaulted house of worship should be visited to view its old communion table, 18th century German pipe organ, the alabaster tomb and 16th century suit of armor belonging to Duke Charles of Guelders, pre-Roman sarcophagi that were found during renovations in 1961, and the east gallery's fine five paneled 16th century mural depicting the way of the cross, the resurrection, and the ascension of Christ. A brand new high speed elevator can now take visitors up the magnificent 73 meter (234 foot) viewing platform of the church tower to see its massive carillon and then get a great panoramic view out over both Holland and Germany. There is also a nice snack shop, exhibitions of photos taken after the damages sustained in the war, and a gift kiosk. *The church is open Tuesday through Saturday from 10:00am until 5:00pm, Sunday from 2:00pm until 5:00pm, and costs 3 NLG per person to enter, the elevator ride up the tower costs an additional 8 NLG per person.*

Just behind the church you will find the new **Stadhuis** (City Hall) building built in 1964 from plans by French architect J.J. Konijneberg. While the city hall building itself is open only to those on official municipal business, its exterior and inner courtyard contain fine works of art by Piet Slegers. Much more interesting is the adjacent 16th century Renaissance-style M**aarten van Rossumhuis**, a former residence of a local general, that is better known as the **Duivelshuis** (House of the Devils) because of the unusual sculpted heads on its facade. The House of the Devils is home to the offices of the mayor and his staff, thus cannot be visited by the public.

From the side of the Marktplein, follow the Turfstraat until turning right down a street called **Markt**. At building #38 of this lane, you will see the 18th century **Stadswaag** built from plans by Henk Viervant. Rebuilt in 1960 after being damaged in the war, this unusual brick structure with several chimneys is now an upscale office building. Continue along Markt as it passes by a few restaurants until reaching the end of the street where you will find the modern **Huis der Provincien** government building that is connected to the much more dramatic **Sabelspoort** fortified gate house. This gateway was originally a 14th century gateway (restored in 1953) through the old defensive walls that once surrounded the city.

**Back to the NS Station**

Now retrace your steps back through the Marktplaats, passing the front entrance of the Grote of Eusebiuskerk church and walk straight ahead onto the Kerkstraat. At the next corner turn left down the **Pastoorstraat** with its many antique shops. A few steps down on your left hand side is a 19th century Synagoge (Synagogue) that is still used by the city's small Jewish population. On the other side of the street at building #1a is a marijuana plant shop with a huge street-side picture window full of exotic flowering pot plants.

At the end of the block, turn right onto **Bakkerstraat** where there are several more antique stores. Note that buildings #19 and #24 of this street have been designated as national monuments of architectural and historical importance. My favorite stop along the Bakkerstraat is the incredible 't **Heerenhuys Decoratie** at building #12b, which is a fine interior designer's shop and romantic café with plush fireside tables. About a block or so up on the left side there is a small lane called the Hemelrijk that leads to a wonderful indoor shopping center of the same name, as well as passing by a tranquil inner courtyard that is home to the fabulous 16th century **Koffiehuis 't Hemelrijk** at building #52 where you can enjoy a fine meal or just a coffee in a wonderful terrace or an old world kitchen setting.

Return back to the Bakkkerstraat and follow it until turning right onto the Vijzelstraat. Keep walking straight as the street name first changes to the Kettlestraat and then merges into the Roggestraat. In a couple of blocks the street ends across from the tree-shaded **Velperplein**, and off to your right side is the massive **Musis Centrum** performing arts center. From your position facing the Musis Centrum, turn left to follow the Velperbinnensingel around the edge of town as it merges with the Jansbinnensingel and leads directly in front of the **NS Station**.

## NIGHTLIFE & ENTERTAINMENT

**Bars, Pubs, Clubs, & Grand Cafés**

**LUXOR THEATER**, *Willemsplein 10. Tel: (26) 443-6955.*

The Luxor is a unique dance club built into a former theater near the rail station. Packed on Thursday through Sunday nights with scantily dressed 17 to 25 year old locals, who love to party to the sounds of house and techno music until the wee hours of the morning. The club also hosts live concerts. Admission costs around 12.50 NLG a person, and the massive doormen usually search clients and/or use metal detectors at the entrance.

**VERGANE GLORIE**, *Korenmarkt 25. Tel: (26) 389-2083.*

Situated on the city's most popular square for partying, this large bar is my favorite place to hang out with casually dressed locals and enjoy a wide variety of great beers and mixed drinks. There is almost never a cover charge, and the doormen let everyone in without a problem. Some evenings there is live rock or blues music here.

**DANCE CAFE LUTHER**, *Korenmarkt 26. Tel: (26) 442-8107.*

Luther is usually a rather crowded bar and disco on most Fridays and Saturdays, as well as offering free (or cheap) live rock and soul concerts on some other evenings. This is a good place to see a mix of people that really know how to drink.

**GET IN**, *Jansplein 39. Tel: (26) 443-4303.*

This crowded bar with a dance floor offers live rock and soul concerts each week as well as a really happening bar scene from Thursday through Sunday until 5:00am or so. Unless a special event is taking place there is normally no cover charge, and the drinks are rather strong here.

**BIERCAFE FLATER**, *Beekstraat 25. Tel: (26) 445-1670.*

This popular local pub and live blues music venue has plenty of great Dutch and Belgian beers on tap and in bottles, and tends to attract a more laid-back crowd of local residents past university age. The live blues and vocalist shows are free of charge, and the people here are really friendly.

## EXCURSIONS FROM ARNHEM

Besides seeing the sights and attractions in the center of Arnhem, visitors could easily spend several days touring the nearby area. I have put together the following brief listings of the most impressive things to do while in the area. You can either rent a car for these trips, take a bicycle ride, or use the region's GVM municipal bus company to get to these nearby destinations.

### *Along the Outskirts of Arnhem's City Center*

Just on the edges of the city, there are a few worthwhile sights that should not be missed by tourists. Among my favorites are the Nederlands Wijnmuseum (Netherland's Wine Museum), located about a kilometer (a bit more than 1/2 mile) northeast of the city center at *Velperweg 23 in Arnhem*. Municipal bus #1 will get you close to the museum.

You can see several rooms displaying rare bottles, glasses, and cork screws that relates the story of how wine is produced and marketed around the world. The museum also contains a giant cellar full of aging wines in barrels, and an adjacent wine shop with good deals on a large selection of famous bottles. *The museum is open from 10:00am until 5:00pm from Tuesday through Friday and 11:00am until 5:00pm during the summer, 2:00pm until 5:00pm from Tuesday through Friday and 11:00am until 5:00pm on Saturday during all other times of the year, and costs 4 NLG per person to visit (including a free guided tour and a copy of Chateaux wine magazine).*

The city's own Gemeentemuseum **Arnhem** (Municipal Museum) is situated about a kilometer (a bit more than 1/2 mile) west of the city center, *at Utrechtsweg 87 and 74* in a small park just above the **Rijn River**. Municipal buses #1 and #6 will get you near this museum. Here you can see exhibitions of Bronze age and Roman archaeological items, antique pottery and glass, medieval ships, rare antique decorative arts such as Delftware and furnishings, 17th through 19th century Dutch paintings, old and recent applied art, antique topographical prints, modern art, sculptures, and more. *The museum is open from 10:00am until 5:00pm from Tuesday through Saturday, 11:00am until 5:00pm Sunday, and is free to enter.*

## Oosterbeek

For a more relaxing half-day trip just outside of the city, perhaps the best place to head for is the small resort town of **Oosterbeek** about 6 kilometers (4 miles) west of Arnhem along route N-225. The town of Oosterbeek and its sights can be reached by public transportation via the GVM regional bus line #1 from Arnhem's NS Station.

You can still see many fine summer mansions of rich merchants and industrialists from large Dutch and German cities, there is a certain affluent feeling to most of the area's restaurants and boutiques.

Among the most famous sights here is the interesting **Airbourne Museum Hartenstein**, off the **Utrechtseweg** at the edge of town. You can first view an audio-video presentation in English about the planning and execution of World War II's disastrous Operation Market Garden airborne assault and the heroic aftermath with Dutch Resistance forces hiding many of the allied soldiers from the Nazis. There are nine rooms filled with weapons, uniforms, medals, photographs, parachutes, abandoned military gear, and a series of precise day by day accounts by stranded American, Canadian, British, and Polish allied troops. A 10 minute walk from here you can also pay tribute to your fallen countrymen over at the famed **Airbourne Cemetary**. *The museum is open year round from 10:00am until 5:00pm between Monday and Saturday, 11:00am until 5:00pm on Sundays, and costs 5 NLG per person.*

Also worthy of mention is Oosterbeek's many less famous sights: the 10th century **Zaalkerk** church on Benedendorpsweg, the **De Westerbouwing** summertime theme park, the action-packed **De Bilderberg** and **Hartenstein** sports park complexes, and the weekly Thursday **Outdoor Market** in the town's central Raadhuisplein from 9:00am until 1:00pm.

## The Burgers' Zoo

The giant **Burgers' Zoo** is located about 4.5 kilometers (less than three miles) northwest of the Arnhem city center via the **Schelmseweg**,

Public transportation is available via Arnhem's NS Station via the GVM regional trolley-bus line #3.

This zoo is different than most other establishments of its kind. Situated on 45 hectares (113 acres) of park land dotted with unusual indoor pavilions and outdoor open areas made especially to simulate a selection of exotic terrain, this immensely popular attraction is almost always packed with families.

You can stroll through the Safari Park section via a series of elevated covered walking platforms where visitors can watch wild African animals such as lions, antelopes, rhinos, zebras, giraffes, cheetahs, and all sorts of other creatures occupying their own separate sections. After this low impact walk past the outdoor areas, you can then head inside the fabulous **Burgers' Bush**, a giant simulated tropical rain forest complete with aardvarks, manatees, otters, birds, frogs, a vast selection of unusual plant life, and plenty of authentic humidity. Nearby, another structure called the **Burgers' Desert** allows you to walk inside a recreation of an Arizona-style sub-tropical desert that contains towering rock formations, cacti, sand plains, and secure viewing zones that contain sheep, bobcats, scorpions, and snakes. Also in the zoo compound there are several pens and tanks with everything from alligators to gorillas, an assortment inexpensive restaurants serving food from around the globe, children's play areas, and walking paths.

*The entire attraction is open daily from 9:00am until 7:00pm during the summer, and daily from 9:00am until sunset during all other times of the year, and costs 20 NLG per person to visit.*

## Nederlands Openluchtmuseum

The **Netherlands Open Air Museum** is situated about 4.2 kilometers (2.5 miles) north of the center of Arnhem along the **Schelmseweg** (close to the Burgers' Zoo). Public transportation via Arnhem's NS Station is provided by GVM regional bus line #3.

This delightful 44 hectare (110 acre) theme park consists of about 80 reconstructed 17h through 19th century Dutch farmhouses and wind-mills taken from various villages around the Netherlands. The idea here is to inform visitors about the way of life that was once common throughout various parts of the nation. As you walk (or take the newly added tram for 1 NLG) through the park, you will find park workers dressed in traditional costumes as they demonstrate the crafts, agricultural methods, folklore, and lifestyles that were used by the former inhabitants of each stunning structure.

Among the highlights here are an old horse-driven oil mill, dozens of antique cottages and barns complete with period furnishings, draw-bridges, gardens, various windmills, a bakery with bread making demonstrations, an old dairy where you can see cheese being made, and an exhibition room with a collection of fine old earthenware. *The Open Air Museum is open daily only between April 4th and October 27th from 10:00am until 5:00pm, and costs 16 NLG per person to visit.*

## The Naational Park de Hoge Veluwe

The fantastic **Nationaal Park de Hoge Veluwe** is a must-see all day trip for all visitors to this region, located about 11 kilometers (7 miles) northwest of Arnhem's city center. Public transportation is available from the Arnhem NS Station via GVM regional bus line #12 from April through October, or via a change of bus at stations in the nearby towns of Otterlo, Hoenderloo, and Schaarsbergen throughout the year.

This is Holland's best and largest public park with some 5,500 hectares (13,745 acres) of pristine nature reserve dotted with fine museums and monumental buildings. Once the private hunting grounds for billionaire industrialist Anthony Kröller and his art collecting wife Helene Müller, this giant reserve of dunes and woodlands was turned over to the government of Holland in 1935 to become a public park, wildlife conservation area, and the home for a new museum for Mrs. Kröller-Müller's amazing collection of art.

The best way to access the park is to use one of the three main entrances near the towns of Schaarsbergen, Otterlo, and Hoenderloo. Once inside the park you can enjoy long hikes, peaceful drives, optional minibus service, or even better yet take advantage of one of several hundred free of charge "White Bicycles" to get around to the countryside lanes as take you past wild animals such as deer, boar, and hundreds of different types of birds. As soon as you reach the park, make sure to first stop over at the **Visitors Center** that can provide you with a copy of the *General Guidebook* that details additional information about bicycle routes, wildlife and bird observation areas, picnic zones, restaurants, museum special events, escorted and self guided hikes, on sight restaurants, and other features of this remarkable area..

Inside the park the most famous attraction is certainly the fabulous **Museum Kröller-Müller** with its unparalleled collection of paintings from master artists such as Van Gogh, Picasso, Seurat, Gris, Mondriaan, and many others. A fine sculpture garden near the museum also features the works of Rodin, Bourdelle, Marini, Paolozzi, and Moore to name a few. This is one of Holland's best art museums, and is busy every day that it opens. Not far from the art museum is the **Museonder**, a unique underground museum complex that has exhibits of living subterranean animals and insects, skeletal remains of prehistoric creatures, explanations of soil and sand conditions, exposed tree and plant root systems, and lots of information about the world that rests below our feet. Even more interesting are the guided tours of the nearby **Jachthuis St. Hubertus**, a mansion-like hunting lodge built for the Kröller-Müller family by famed architect H.P. Berlage in 1920. The lodge features a unique tower, several ceramic brick covered rooms, custom furnishings designed by Berlage, beautiful stained glass windows, collections of fine porcelain, and adjacent gardens and pond areas.

*The park is open from 8:00am until 10:00pm in the summer, and from 9:00am until at least 5:00pm in the winter, and costs 8 NLG per person, and 8 NLG per car to enter including all museum entrance fees and hunting lodge tours. Please keep in mind that the Museums are open Tuesday through Sunday year round from 10:00am until 5:00pm, and that the Hunting Lodge is open during scheduled tours only that are given daily from April through October every half hour between 11:00am and 4:30pm, and daily from November through March every hour between 2:00pm and 4:00pm.*

For more details, contact the park's **visitors center** at *Tel: (318) 591-627* or the **VVV-Arnhem** at *Tel: (26) 442-0330.*

## Apeldoorn's Palace Het Loo

For a longer half-day trip out of Arnhem, consider a 26 kilometer (16 mile) journey north to the city of **Apeldoorn**. Public transportation from Arnhem is via regular train service to the Apeldoorn Station, and then connections onto nearby municipal bus lines #102 or #104.

While the city is pleasant enough, the real attraction here is the lavish 17th century **Palace Het Loo**. Originally built for Prince William III of Orange in 1692 from plans by Jacob Roman, this former royal hunting lodge was later turned into a beautiful summer palace for members of the House of Orange and is now open to the general public as a fine attraction.

Stroll through peacock-inhabited gardens before reaching the "Voorhuis" entrance in the basement. After checking your coats you will pass by an excellent gift shop before starting a self-guided tour of the palace's beautifully furnished opulent old and new dining rooms, several halls, a fine chapel, library, gallery, and private chambers of its former regal residents. Every room is more bold than the next, and each is filled with fine antiques, rare tapestries, period furnishings, and the personal effects of the royal family members that once lived here. The fountain and statuary lined formal gardens just behind the palace are also well worth an hour or two of your time on a sunny day. *The palace is open year round from Tuesday through Sunday between 10:00am and 5:00pm, and costs 10 NLG per person to enter.*

## PRACTICAL INFORMATION

**Main VVV Tourist Office** - *Stationsplein 45 - (26) 442-0330*
**Municipal Information Center** - *Beekstraat 62 - (26) 443-2222*
**NS Station** - *Stationsplein 38 - (26) 351-1280 or (26) 445-1457*
**GVM Regional/Municipal Bus Info** - *Stationsplein 20 - (26) 357-4469*
**Domestic Train and Bus Info** - *(6) 9292*
**Police Headquarters** - *Beekstraat 39 - (26) 442-2222 or (26) 352-4232*
**Emergency Hotline** - *06-11*

# 23. GRONINGEN

**Groningen,** the busy capital of northern Holland, is too often overlooked by visitors to the Netherlands. The city's circular canal-bordered Centrum district is only 1.2 kilometers (3/4 of a mile) in width but still has dozens of fantastic places to visit. During a stress-free trip here you can mingle with thousands of interesting university students, shop in a wide variety of reasonably priced designer boutiques, enjoy one of the almost daily outdoor markets, find hidden gardens, stroll past countless 15th through 20th century monumental structures, try your luck at a great casino, visit fine art museums, and drink with the locals until the sun comes up.

The people of this northernmost major city are very friendly, and will usually be glad to show visitors around the sights known only to natives. Besides the city itself, there are several unusual villages such as **Eenrum, Leens,** and **Houwerzijl** that can be accessed by car, bus, and bicycle from Groningen. From Groningen you can also take a ferry to the beautiful little **Wadden Islands,** not far offshore; I have included a brief excursion in this chapter to **Texel,** one of the Wadden Islands.

If you have a few extra days, give some thought to coming up this way. Your efforts will pay off during your first hour of walking around!

## ORIENTATION

Groningen is situated in the south central section of the Netherland's northernmost province of **Groningen,** with a population of 168,702. It lies 152 kilometers (94 miles) north-northeast of the capital city of Amsterdam.

## ARRIVALS & DEPARTURES
### By Air

Most visitors flying to this city will arrive here via land links from the large **Schiphol Airport** near Amsterdam, 163 kilometers (101 miles) to the south-southwest.

## By Bus

Many of the bus lines between Groningen and other parts of Holland tend to stop at the **Busstation Gado** depot just alongside the **NS Station** train depot on the south edge of downtown. Make sure to call in advance to find out exactly where and when your bus comes in. Connections between this station and any other point in downtown Groningen can generally be made by the adjacent public bus stops for about 3 NLG per person each way, or via taxi for between 10.25 NLG and 15.50 NLG.

## By Car

Downtown street-side parking spots are tough to find.

From **Amsterdam**, the fastest way to get to Groningen is to follow **A-10** ring road around until connecting onto the **A-8** north for about 5 kilometers (3 miles) until merging onto the **A-7** north for 193 kilometers (120 miles) as it crosses over the Ijsselmeer dam waterway and then curves through the provinces of Friesland and Groningen before finally exiting at the city's "Centrum."

## By Train

Groningen is linked to almost any other point in Holland and Europe by several major rail lines. This conveniently located **NS Station** train depot at the southern side of the city's downtown section is the major point of mass transport arrivals. Connections between this station and any other point in Groningen can generally be made by foot, via **Treintaxi** for 6 NLG per person, by using the adjacent public bus stops for around 3 NLG per person each way, or via taxi for between 10.25 NLG and 15.50 NLG.

## GETTING AROUND TOWN

### By Public Transportation

While almost any sight within Groningen is well within walking distance from any point downtown, the region's **GVB** (Gemeentelijke Vervoerbedrijf) public transit authority also offers a selection of public bus lines to get you safely and easily around town and the suburbs. They accept **Nationale Strippen Kaarts**.

Almost all of these buses stop at one point or another at the **Busstation Gado** just next to the NS Station. The normal hours of operation for most of the system is from about 6:15am until roughly 11:45pm. After that your only choices are either to walk, or to take a taxi. Locations outside of downtown Groningen such as Paterswolde may require travel through more than one zone, so you must ask the driver how many blank strips are required.

**By Taxi**

There a couple of hundred licensed taxis roaming the streets and major passenger arrival points of the city during all hours of the day and night. Drivers have new Renault and Opel 4 door sedans with enough trunk space to hold a few pieces of luggage. These drivers are polite, honest, and occasionally multilingual. To find a taxi, either hail an unoccupied cab driving by with its "Taxi" roof light illuminated, go to one of the obvious taxi stands throughout the city, or call *(50) 312-8044 or (50) 313-8999* for a radio response pick-up on demand.

The main taxi ranks are located at the NS Station and near the Grote Markt square. Taxis here are metered and charge somewhere between 10.25 NLG to 15.50 NLG per ride (not per person) between most downtown locations depending on exact distance and traffic conditions. A limited number of the city's taxi's now accept major credit cards for fare payments.

## WHERE TO STAY - IN GRONINGEN

*Expensive*

'T FAMILIEHOTEL, *Groningerweg 19, Paterswolde. Tel: (50) 309-5400. Fax: (50) 309-1157. US & Canada Bookings (Best Western) 1-800-528-1234. Year round rack rates from 310 NLG per double room per night (B.P.). Special Weekend rates from 210 NLG per double room per night (B.P.). All major credit cards accepted.*

Less than a 10 minute drive south of the city center in the suburb of **Paterswolde**, this welcoming lake-view hotel is the best place to stay in the immediate area of Groningen. The delightful deluxe property offers 78 rooms, each with large modern private bathrooms, extremely comfortable bedding, remote control satellite television, am-fm clock radio, large windows, direct dial telephones, mini-bars, and great views in most cases.

This 108 year old hotel has spent plenty of time and money ensuring the comfort of all their guests with all sorts of additional facilities, such as tennis courts, a wonderful large heated indoor/outdoor swimming pool, sauna, three forest and lakeside restaurants, a private pontoon party boat, a lake-front dock and recreation area, complimentary bicycles, a game room with billiard, nearby walking trails, free outdoor parking, a nice lounge and bar area, scheduled children's activities, business meeting rooms, room service, express laundry and dry cleaning, safe deposit boxes, nearby golf, and a really nice staff that go well out of their way to make sure you will soon return. With such a great location, this is a perfect place to stay while visiting the city of Groningen, and is highly recommended a most enjoyable full service hotel.

**HOTEL MERCURE**, *Expositielaan 7. Tel: (50) 525-8400. Fax: (50) 527-1828. US & Canada Bookings (Sofitel) 1-800-763-4835. Year round rack rates from 225 NLG per double room per night (B.P.). All major credit cards accepted.*
This modern 4 star park-view business class hotel on the edge of town is perfect for those with a car who want to be close to the center of Groningen. The Mercure has 157 modern double rooms and suites that all feature private bathrooms, mini-bar, direct dial telephone, am-fm clock radio, remote control satellite television, nice art work, and new furnishings. Facilities include a bar, a restaurant, a sun tanning salon, indoor parking, business meeting rooms, an indoor swimming pool, available child care, room service, and a good staff.

### Moderate
**MARTINI HOTEL**, *Donderslaan 156. Tel: (50) 525-2040. Fax: (50) 526-2109. Year round rack rates from 175 NLG per double room per night (E.P.). All major credit cards accepted.*
The Martini is a modern first-class hotel on the edge of town, only a six minute bus or car ride to the heart of the city. There are 58 nicely furnished double rooms and suites that all feature private bathrooms, mini-bar, direct dial telephone, am-fm clock radio, remote control satellite television, nice art work, and new furnishings. Facilities here include a bar, a restaurant, a sun tanning salon, indoor parking, business meeting rooms, a health club, sauna, available child care, and room service.
**AUBERGE CORPS DE GARDE**, *Oude Boteringestraat 74. Tel: (50) 314-5437. Fax: (50) 313-6320. Year round rack rates from 125 NLG per double room per night (C.P.). Most major credit cards accepted.*
This unique property is located in a beautiful former 17th century civic guard barracks on an historic street in the heart of Groningen's centrum district. I suggest this as the best choice for those who want to be in the middle of the city. The Corps de Garde is more like an inn than a hotel, and features eight pleasing rooms each with private bathrooms, color television, and mini-bars in some cases. There is also a great little restaurant, nearby parking, and a friendly family-style ambiance.

### Inexpensive
**HOTEL FORMULA 1**, *Helsinkistraat 2. Tel; (50) 312-2045. Year round rack rates from 65 NLG per double room per night (E.P.). Most major credit cards accepted.*
This new French chain motel is the only place I know where you insert your credit card into a machine and then a room key pops out! Far from service oriented, this simple 2 star lodging in an industrial area on the edge of town offers a bed to sleep in (up to three people can fit in a room at the same price) and almost no real staff or facilities.

## WHERE TO STAY - NEAR GRONINGEN

*Expensive*

**LANDGOED LAUSWOLT**, *Van Harinxmaweg 10, Beetsterzwaag. Tel: (512) 381-245. Fax: (512) 381-496. US & Canada Bookings (Relais & Chateaux) 1-212-856-0115. Year round rack rates from 275 NLG per double room per night (E.P.). Special Gourmet Package rates from 450 NLG per double room per night (M.A.P.). All major credit cards accepted.*

Situated amidst over 2,500 acres of beautifully maintained English style lawns and gardens in beautiful **Beetsterzwaag** (a scenic 20 minute drive southwest of Groningen), Landgoed Lauswolt may very well be the most charming deluxe hotel in Holland. This superb 4 star Relais & Chateaux member property was originally built over a century ago as a wealthy family's elegant rural manor house. In 1954, it was converted into a small countryside inn and has been extensively renovated several times since. The estate has grown into a fantastic hotel that attracts travelers from around the world.

All of the 58 dramatically decorated rooms and suites here feature huge marble or tile dual basin bathrooms with high quality imported soaps and shampoos, great bathrobes, carefully selected hardwood furnishings, extremely comfortable twin or double bedding, remote control satellite television, am-fm clock radio, fully stocked mini-bar, mini-safe, plenty of closet space, executive style desks, direct dial telephones, giant picture windows with memorable views, individually controlled heating systems, a selection of fine art or antiques, fresh fruit baskets, and in some cases panoramic balconies and working fireplaces. The public rooms at the hotel are equally impressive and are lavishly decorated with priceless 17th century Flemish paintings and soothing color schemes.

Among the full compliment of facilities and services available to all guests are an outstanding restaurant offering three gourmet meals daily, a magnificent wood-paneled bar and billiard room centered around an incredible antique pool table, opulent conference and business meeting rooms, a large indoor/outdoor panoramic swimming pool, a full beauty salon and spa with a full range of hair and skin treatment programs utilizing Estée Lauder hair and skin products, sauna, Turkish bath, solarium, two outdoor tennis courts, rental bicycles, walking trails, available nanny service, and an 18 hole golf course (in use by guests even when covered by snow). The hotel can also arrange for you to experience nearby activities such as hot air balloon adventures, horse-drawn carriage rides, sailing trips on nearby lakes, indoor ice skating, and privately guided custom excursions.

The ambiance here is rather sophisticated yet unusually welcoming for such a famous hotel, and attracts a great mix of international guests, ranging from young honeymooners in search of the perfect hideaway to older executives on short weekend breaks with their family. With a wonderful staff working under the expert guidance of the charming manager (Mr. Johan L.L. Agricola), your complete comfort is essentially guaranteed. There are no strict dress codes to deal with here, and you can walk around feeling like you are staying in a good friend's country house.

The Landgoed Lauswolt receives my highest recommendation as the finest hotel in the north of Holland, and should be included as part of any deluxe trip through this beautiful country.

### Moderate

**HOTEL HET KLOOSTER**, *Damsterweg 8, Kloosterburen. Tel: (595) 481-159. Fax: (595) 481-046. Year round rack rates from 105 NLG per double room per night (C.P.). All major credit cards accepted.*

This unusual hotel is located off the historic old **Cloister of St. Teresa** in the quaint village of **Kloosterburen**, 25 minutes northwest of central Groningen. Owned and managed by a notable photographer who has equipped 14 uniquely designed and comfortable rooms (and two family-size suites) with private bathrooms and nice furnishings. Perfect for active travelers looking for a great place to bicycle and hike, the charming cloister has a good regional restaurant and plenty of ambiance.

**SCANDINAVISCH DORP**, *Oude Badweg 1, Eelderwolde. Tel: (50) 525-6867. Fax: (50) 527-1172. Year round rack rates from 65 NLG per double bungalow per night (E.P.). Cash only - No credit cards accepted.*

This complex of 16 bungalows surrounding a central lodge is a reproduction of a typical Scandinavian resort center, complete with picnic tables, Swedish sauna, wood-burning fireplaces, and a Scandinavian restaurant. Located about a 10 minute drive or bus ride from downtown Groningen, it provides simple wooden bungalows that can each fit up to four persons for the same price. While far from deluxe, it is a good choice for budget travelers.

### Inexpensive

**LOGIES MET ONTBIJT**, *Various Locations. Contact VVV-Groningen. Tel: (50) 313-9774. Year round rates from 30 NLG per double room per night in a private home or farmhouse inn (C.P.). Cash only - No credit cards accepted.*

The Groningen area officially has some 54 bed and breakfast inns that charge between 30 NLG and 40 NLG for a twin bedded room (usually with a private bathroom) with a continental breakfast in an assortment of private homes and farm houses scattered around the region. These establishments accept reservations, and occasionally fill up well in advance during the summer seasons. Contact the VVV for specific details or a copy of their current leaflet called *Logies met Ontbijt* that includes basic information and reservation contact numbers for most of them.

## WHERE TO EAT

*Expensive*

**HERBERG ONDER DE LINDEN**, *Burg. van Barneveldweg 3, Aduard. Tel: (50) 403-1406. All major credit cards accepted.*

Master chef Geerhard Slenema has created an amazing gourmet French restaurant in a picturesque 18th century farmhouse in the village of **Aduard**, eight kilometers (five miles) west of Groningen. You can sit in the opulent dining room or summertime outdoor terrace and enjoy either a la carte or specially designed dinner menus at between 65 NLG and 105 NLG per person. The menus change five times each year but may feature both classic and fusion creations such as cream of curried fish soup, beef consommé with vegetables, salad with grapefruit and pistachio, confit of duck with shallots, salmon steaks with chive sauce, filet mignon with pate, poached mixed fish in white cream, filet of sole with lobster in lobster sauce, veal with tarragon sauce, cannelloni with lobster and seasonal vegetables, and several amzing desserts. Dress well and make sure to call in advance for lunch or dinner reservations!

*Moderate*

**'T FEITH HUIS STADSCAFE**, *Martinikerkhof 10. Tel: (50) 313-5335. All major credit cards accepted.*

This casual but trendy ultra-modern split level café, bar, and restaurant in an historic medieval building across from the most famous church in downtown Groningen is a wonderful place to sit back and enjoy a great meal in an extremely comfortable setting. Open from the early morning hours through the late evening. They offer a full a la carte menu as well as special 3 course dinners at 43.50 NLG and 4 course dinners at 49.50 NLG that usually allow you to select from choices such as mixed green salad with garlic shrimp, Oriental beans with sesame seeds and pistachios served on hoisin sauce, Dutch shrimp bisque, green mustard soup with marcscapone cheese, entrecote with pepper sauce, tuna with curry ginger sauce, marinated spare ribs, fresh fish marinated in balsamic vinegar, asparagus salad, baked lamb filet with honey and goat cheese, and many other innovative dishes. There is also a daily afternoon tea, a less expensive lunch menu, Sunday champagne brunches, and the most relaxing bar in town.

**DE KORENBEURS**, *A Kerkhof 1. Tel: (50) 313-7861. All major credit cards accepted.*

Housed in the Vismarkt square's historic Korenbeurs grain exchange building, this modern café and restaurant prepares really good food at reasonable prices. The menu here features such delicious items as salad with baked salmon and avocado at 16.50 NLG, smoked pigeon salad with green beans for 17.50 NLG, cheese soup at 7.50 NLG, home made fish soup for 9.50 NLG, cheese tortellini in basil and tomato soup at 14.50 NLG, turkey steak with molasses for 18.50 NLG, tuna steak with lemon sauce at 26.50 NLG, lamb filet with cognac for 29.50 NLG, duck breast in casis sauce at 33.50 NLG, and plenty of snacks, sandwiches, flavored coffees, and mixed drinks.

**ABRAHAM'S MOSTERD-MAKERIJ**, *Molenstraat 5, Eenrum. Tel: (0595) 491-600. Most major credit cards accepted.*

Not only is this restaurant situated next to one of the few remaining local mustard factories, but the pleasant 20 minute drive (or 2-plus hour bicycle ride) from central Groningen to the village of **Eenrum** is well worth the effort. In this renovated former windmill keeper's house, chef Freek de Roos puts together hearty and delicious lunch and dinner items that are priced well below what I had expected.

Their large menu includes home-made mustard soup for 6 NLG, fish soup at 7.50 NLG, chicken salad for 9.50 NLG, smoked mackerel at 9.50 NLG, smoked salmon for 16.50 NLG, ham and cheese quiche at 8.75 NLG, baked mussels for 12.75 NLG, spare ribs at 19.50 NLG, beefsteak in mustard butter sauce at 34.50 NLG, chicken filet in curry sauce for 19.75 NLG, mixed grill at 24.50 NLG, fresh fruit salad for 10.75 NLG, and walnut ice cream with bananas and chocolate at 7.75 NLG. No dress code here, and reservations are not necessary most of the time. A great place to enjoy a good meal and then do some serious sightseeing, including a stop by the old mustard factory just steps away.

**'T PANNEKOEKSCHIP**, *Schuitendiep 1017. Tel: (50) 312-0045. All major credit cards accepted.*

This dramatic three mast clipper (an historic sailing vessel) moored along a centrally located downtown canal has been converted into a unique pancake house and restaurant, featuring over three dozen varieties of wonderful home-made pancakes starting from 15.75 NLG that are filled with everything from fresh fruits to meat and cheeses. Also available are many salads and various lunch and dinner items. While far from gourmet, this is a great place to enjoy affordable food in a pretty setting.

*Inexpensive*

**HILLBILLY'S**, *Oude Kijk in 't Jatstraat 14. Tel: (50) 312-5019. Cash only - No credit cards accepted.*

What a strange little place this one is! Situated on a side street near the University of Groningen's downtown campus, this simple restaurant features what Dutch people seem to consider as typical southwestern American food. Their bizarre menu includes such unusual dishes as mock squirrel stew at 18.75 NLG, pumpkin soup for 5.75 NLG, pretzels with butter at 3.50 NLG, Ozark stew for 19.75 NLG, rib-eye steaks at 24.75

NLG, spare ribs for 17.50 NLG, pan fried catfish at 18.75 NLG, fried onion rings for 2.50 NLG, and other hillbilly items.

**EETHUIS ANTALYA**, *Oude Kijk in 't Jatstraat 41. Tel: (50) 312-0219. Cash only - No credit cards accepted.*

When you have been partying all night long in Groningen and need to take a food break, this down-to-earth shoarma restaurant a couple of blocks down from the Grote Markt square is a good place to eat. You can order cheese sandwiches for 3.75 NLG, salami sandwiches at 4 NLG, moussaka for 9.50 NLG, kebabs at 9 NLG, roasted chicken for 16 NLG, shoarma at 9 NLG, and all sorts of combination dishes starting from 17.50 NLG each.

## SEEING THE SIGHTS
• *From the **NS Station** around the city and back.*
• *Approximate duration (by foot) is at least 5 hours, including museum, gallery, church, café, boutique, market, garden, university, and side street visits.*

**From the NS Station to the Groninger Museum**

After exiting the main doors of the 19th century **NS Station**, walk straight through the Stationsplein and turn right onto the canal-front Stationsweg. After a few steps, make a left turn to cross over the bridge that leads directly to the brand new ultra-modern **Groninger Museum**. Recently completed from plans by leading international architects such as Alessandro Mendini, Michele De Lucchi, and Philippe Starck, this strange complex is made up of four separate floating pavilions that center around a golden bullet shaped central treasury.

Inside these structures you will find massive collections of archaeological artifacts found in and around the city, ancient jewelry, fine silver pieces, 15th through 20th century visual arts, applied arts such as Oriental porcelain, modern art by local and famed artists from around the globe, videos and still photographs, and even examples of artistic graffiti. During much or the year the museum features special temporary exhibitions that go further into specific topics. The museum's fine outdoor café is also well worth a visit, and is the perfect place to watch the crowds roll by at rush hour. *The art museum is open year round from 10:00am until 5:00pm from Tuesday through Sunday and costs 9 NLG per person to enter.*

**Through the Heart of Town**

After exiting the museum, turn right to walk across a small bridge and continue straight along the **Ubbo Emmusstraat**. A half block up on the right side of the street is the tiny **Minimuseum** at building #34a, a gallery featuring a selection of historic photos and miniature reproductions of famous artists' works. *The museum is open from 11:00am until 6:00pm daily throughout the year and costs 3 NLG per person to enter.* After heading a couple of blocks further up the Ubbo Emmusstraat, turn right onto the Zuiderdiep. This main avenue is lined on both sides by several boutiques, outdoor cafés, inexpensive restaurants, bars, and even a large multiplex cinema. Keep walking along the left side of the Zuiderdiep for a handful of blocks until you reach a fork in the road where you will bear slightly to the left to then follow the Gedempte Kettendiep. About half a block up on the left side of this street you will find the **VVV** tourist information center at building #6. Stop in to purchase a *Plattegrond Groningen* detailed area map for 2.50 NLG, a *VVV Informatie* multilingual city information booklet for 3 NLG, several free brochures, and then ask as many questions as you need to of the extremely friendly and helpful staff of local experts.

After leaving the VVV, turn left to continue walking down the Gedempte Kettendiep for about half a block. While the **Holland Casino** complex can be visited straight ahead, you should instead turn left onto a small lane called the Kliene Peperstraat and at the next corner turn right onto the Peperstraat. On this street you will pass alongside the **St. Geertruidsgasthuis** (Saint Gertrude's Guest House) with its entrance through an elaboraetly carved archway at building #22. This former 15th century inn for poor pilgrims was later converted into an insane asylum and still features a peaceful inner courtyard lined by an old church, a regent's room, five barreled cells once used to lock up lunatics, and a central garden with lime trees that surround an old water pump. *The old guest house's gateway is usually open for free daily from sunrise to sunset, but if you call the landlady at Tel: (50) 312-4082 perhaps she will give you a detailed tour of the old chambers, guards' rooms, and original kitchen.*

**Towards the Grote Market Square**

After passing by the old guest house, keep walking along Peperstraat until it ends and you are forced to make a left turn down the bar and nightclub-lined **Poelestraat**. This lane in turn leads straight into the bustling **Grote Markt** square. This is where you'll see many student bars and cafés, and is packed with thousands of 18 to 22 year old kids on Thursday through Saturday nights until the sun begins to rise. Among the many fine facades surrounding this central plaza in the heart of the city is the dramatic 18th century Neo-Classical **Stadhuis** (City Hall) building on the far left side. While not open to the general public, its steps are usually occupied by resting locals that just want to take a break in the sun.

Along the far right corner of the plaza is the much more impressive 13th century Romanesque and Gothic **Martinikerk** church. Inside you can view some impressive frescoes and vault panels depicting biblical scenes, a stunning choir, stained glass windows, a fine 15th century pipe organ, and a scale model of the old city center. The church is often rented out to give tests and special events for the city's large university.

The highlight here however is the church's adjacent 97 meter (320 foot) tall **Martinitoren** tower that is topped by a weathervane with a horse motif. Visitors can walk up some 370 steps to a fantastic viewing platform after passing several huge bells and fine 4 octave carillon added by the famed Hemony brothers of Amsterdam in 1662. *The church can be visited Tuesday through Saturday from 12noon until 5:00pm between May 21 and August 31 only and costs 1 NLG to enter. The tower is open daily from 12noon and 4:30pm between April 1 and September 31, and on Saturdays and Sundays only from 12noon until 4:30pm between October 1 and March 31, the fee to enter the tower is 2.50 NLG per person.*

---

### GRONINGEN'S BEST OUTDOOR MARKETS

*This huge square and the adjacent* **Vismarkt square** *are home to several weekly outdoor markets. The following is a brief listing of the best ones to visit:*

   **Tuesday** *9:00am–4:30pm; Flowers, Fruits, Vegetables, Clothing*
   **Wednesday** *9:00am–4:30pm; Fruits and Vegetables*
   **Thursday** *12 noon–9:00pm;Clothing, Collectibles, Odds and Ends*
   **Friday** *9:00am–4:30pm; Flowers, Fruits, Vegetables, Clothing*
   **Saturday** *9:00am–4:30pm; Flowers, Fruits, Vegetables, Clothing*

---

**Quaint Side Streets, Gardens, & Historic Gabled Townhouses**
Once you have exited the church, turn left to exit the Grote Markt square via a street called the Martinikerkhof. When you get to the back of the church, make a left turn into a small plaza where you will find the beautiful turn of the century Neo-Renaissance **Provinciehuis** (Provincial Government Building). This structure is not open to the general public but can still be admired from your position on this small square. Walk though the small square and on your right hand side you will then pass the 17th century **Gardepoort** gateway, where you will turn right to walk through the gateway and then head straight along a quaint lane called the Turfstraat.

At the end of this lane you, bear left onto the canal-front **Turfsingel**. Many of the houseboats that you see moored along this part of the canal are each actually divided into several inexpensive one and two room apartments and are typically rented out to budget-minded university students. A few steps along the left hand side of this street you will turn left to walk through an archway cut into the brick wall. This arch will bring you directly into the incredible **Prinsenhoftuin** garden. The gardens have been here since the 17th century, and you'll find an interesting 18th century sundial, many well-manicured hedges, and a great little tea house. This is the best place in town to grab a bench and just relax for a while in an amazingly tranquil setting. The building next to the gardens is the 16th century **Prinsenhof** monastery that is now used by local government officials and may not be open to public viewing. *The garden is open to the public for free from sunrise to sunset between April 1 and October 15 of each year.*

From the garden, exit through the same archway that you entered and turn left to once again follow the Turfsingel for several blocks as it changes its name to the Spilsluizen. Make a left turn when you reach the intersection of the **Oude Boteringestraat** and follow it past many of the finest historic gabled townhouses in Groningen, many of which are now part of either the State University of Groningen or the Open University.

The first important sight along this street is just on the corner at building #74, and is known as the **Corps de Garde**. This former 17th century civil guard house has an impressive gallery with 15 arches, and is now a moderately priced hotel and restaurant. Other fine structures along this street include the 18th century Louis XVI-style former residence of a local doctor at building #44, the 18th century Court of Justice at buildings #36 and #38, the rococo residence at building #23, the replica of an old wine house at building #19, the English Renaissance townhouse at building #17, and the medieval stone block **Calmershuis** at building #24 that has stood on this spot since 1250! While most of these buildings cannot be entered, a good look at their uniquely embellished exteriors is well worth the effort.

**Towards the Vismarkt Square & the Noordelijk Scheepvaartmuseum**
Turn right down the Broerstraat, a small street just next to the Calmershuis and follow it past the bold facade of the turn-of-the-century Neo-Renaissance **Academiegebouw**. This is the main building of the **State University of Groningen** (Holland's second oldest university), and is covered by fine gables, statues, allegorical figures, and a serious pinnacle-topped clock tower. While the building is not really open to the public, it is relatively easy to just walk briskly past the security guards and get a look as some of the classes in progress.

Continue along the Broerstraat until it ends, and bear left onto the amusing Oude Kijk in 't Jatstraat. After a block or so, the street name changes to the **Stoeldraaierstraat** and leads into the large **Vismarkt** (Fish Market) **Square**. This was once the site of the city's fish auction and is now home to many stalls and kiosks during the **Friday** and **Saturday Outdoor Markets** held here and simultaneously at the nearby Grote Markt square. Besides having several fine bars and outdoor cafés, the most noticeable structure in this plaza is the 19th century **Korenbeurs** (Corn Exchange

Building). This building is still where Tuesday morning grain auctions are held, and has been expanded to enclose a great restaurant and several indoor shops.

From the Korenbeurs, turn right to follow a street called Akerkhof as it passes by the 15th century Romanesque **A-Kerk** church and 18th century lantern-topped tower. The same street then changes its name to the **Schuitemakersstraat** and leads past the side entrance to the **Noordelijk Scheepvaartmuseum** (Northern Shipping Museum). The shipping museum is housed in a pair of the oldest medieval stone houses in town that now display scale models of ships used in this region, items once traded by the Dutch East India Company, nautical navigational instruments, old anchors, life boats, a sail maker's workshop, whaling devices, scrimshaw pieces, fishing utensils, old ship engines, and a carpenter's shop.

The same complex also is home to the adjacent **Niemeyer Tabaksmuseum** (Tobacco Museum) where you can see the history of tobacco use throughout the world and get a glimpse of hundreds of antique pipes. *Both of these museums are open from 10:00am until 5:00pm between Tuesday and Saturday, 1:00pm until 5:00pm on Sunday, and cost 5 NLG for a combined admission ticket per person.*

After leaving the shipping museum, continue along the Schuitemakersstraat until it ends at a canal. Now turn left onto the Kleine Der A and follow the canal along until you pass the Museum Brug bridge and can continue onto the **Praediniussingel**. Building #59 of this wide boulevard will (by the time you read this book) become the new home to the **Natuurmuseum Groningen**, with its fine educational displays of local flora, fauna, geology, landscapes and temporary exhibits relating to regional nature and the environment. *The museum is open year round from 10:00am until 5:00pm Tuesday through Saturday, 2:00pm until 5:00pm Sunday, and is free to visit.*

### Heading back to the Station

From here you can keep walking along the same boulevard until it merges with the **Ubbo Emmiussingel** and takes you in front of the modern Groninger Museum. Take a right turn over the bridge that passes through the museum complex and walk straight across the canal to return back to the **NS Station** to end your tour of this fascinating city.

### GUIDED SIGHTSEEING TOURS

There are several special guided trips offered by large and small river boats to the sights in and around Groningen and the surrounding region. The following is a brief listing of the most popular trips, but for a complete listing, contact the VVV tourist information office.

**By Boat**

The following cruise is operated by the **Rondvaartbedrijf Kool** company with ticket and information offices at the canal-side piers just across from the NS Station rail depot, *Tel: (50) 312-8379.*

• **Groningen Canal Cruise**: This 75 minute tour starts at the canal-front piers just across from the main train station and continues along the canals via glass topped boats to see fine patrician mansions, bridges, monuments, and a few interesting neighborhoods. Departs several times daily from Monday through Saturday between June 01 and August 31 only. The price is about 10 NLG per person.

## NIGHTLIFE & ENTERTAINMENT

**Bars, Coffeshops, Discos, & Grand Cafés**

**WARHOL NACHTCAFE**, *Peperstraat 7. Tel: (50) 312-1350.*

A great small and casual dance club and bar full of students and younger locals who enjoying house and disco music until at least 5:00am from Thursday through Saturday. They also serve up pretty good mixed drinks and usually have either no (or a small) cover charge.

**'T GOLDEN FUST**,*Poelestraat 15. Tel: (50) 312-9159.*

Also extremely popular on Thursday through Saturday nights after 10:30pm or so, this local pub has a welcoming ambiance and plays great rock music from Europe and America. They have good selection of beer, and serve large portions of hearty pub food at reasonable prices.

**DE BLAUWE ENGEL**, *Grote Markt 39. Tel: (50) 313-7679.*

I certainly wasn't ready for what I found happening in this dark basement level pub. It seems that after midnight, they offer beer at only 1 NLG a glass, and attract a huge crowd of 17 to 22 year old crowd of fun loving (often plastered!) students. You bump into so many people here that you're bound to have some interesting conversations if you can talk loud enough. Get here before 11:30pm on weekends and you can avoid the lines. No cover charge, and wear jeans and a tee shirt.

**THE PALACE**, *Gelkingestraat 3. Tel: (50) 313-9100.*

The Palace is pretty much the only mega-disco near the Grote Market. After paying a 10 NLG or so per person cover charge, and then getting hit for a mandatory 2 NLG coat check, you still have to deal with a two drink minimum! All that aside, there is a huge modern dance floor complete with state-of-the-art computerized sound and lighting systems. The music depends on the DJ, but it can range from 1970's disco classics to totally digital house music. While the dress code is not strict, most of the people here look their best.

**CAFE DE GROOTE GRIET**, *Grote Markt 37. Tel: (15) 314-0939.*
**DE DRIE GEZUSTERS**, *Grote Markt 39. Tel: (50) 313-4101.*
Considering most of this massive square becomes totally packed with younger party animals during weekend nights, these two adjacent (and similar) café/bars offer some of the only relaxed and laid-back settings in which to experience this square's unique upbeat ambiance. At either of these two places, consider ordering a strong coffee and then grab an empty seat at a table full of people you've never met before. Besides being included in some esoteric conversations, you can also watch thousands of people passing by through the bars' huge picture windows.
**METAMORPHOS**, *Oude Boteringestraat 53. Tel: (50) Unlisted.*
Probably the best "smoking" coffeeshops in the city. A nice peaceful place to smoke some great herb, and listen to even better music. A nice cozy place to relax and get some alternative views.

---

### GRONINGEN - THE PLACE TO PARTY!

*Groningen has a well deserved reputation as being one of Holland's best places to party. Unlike most other Dutch cities, many drinking establishments are allowed to stay open until the sun comes up. In fact, thousands of university students take to the streets that spoke off the Grote Markt square on Thursdays, Fridays, and Saturdays every week of the year. I've listed several of my favorite places to hang out above, but look or ask around and I'm sure you'll find many more. If you ask the right questions you can easily find out about great private parties or one-time only raves and special events. Good luck!*

---

### EXCURSIONS FROM GRONINGEN

After you have wandered around most of the sights and attractions in the center of Groningen, its well worth the effort to spend a day or two touring the nearby area. I have created one possible route past several small villages and farming estates that can be reached via rental car, bicycle, or regional bus service.

For specific details on how to get to these nearby destinations by public transportation, or to get a detailed bicycle route map, stop by the VVV-Groningen tourist information offices. They also have a listing called *Logies met Ontbijt* that details a series of small family-owned bed and breakfast inns along these (and other) routes, so you can bicycle from one inn to another and turn this into a fantastic two or three day excursion.

Finally, I've included a side trip offshore to tranquil, relaxing **Texel Island**, not far offshore from Groningen.

## *Eenrum*

The charming little hamlet of **Eenrum** is located 19 kilometers (12 miles) north-northwest of Groningen. Accessible either by taking route **N-361 north** until finding the Eenrum exit, or via some of the nicest separate bicycle paths imaginable, or by regional bus service from the Busstation Gado in Groningen, this is quite a nice place to spend a few hours.

Start your exploration at the town's impressive **central windmill** on the Molenstraat. This structure is now home to the impressive **Museum-Restuarant Abraham's Mosterdmakerij** (Abraham's Mustard Factory). Many villages in this region used to have their own little mustard factory, and in the old days several windmills, including this one from the mid-19th century, were used not just for flour, but also occasionally to grind mustard seeds.

Over the past several decades most of these independent mustard makers ceased to turn a profit, closed shop, and let the large multinational companies produce most of the mustard now used throughout Holland. The proprietors of this establishment took over the windmill and started to search for a few of the original recipes. Now they have filled the converted windmill keeper's house just next to the windmill with antique presses, old blending machines, huge wooden vats, and other old tools that are now used once again to create excellent mustards on the premises. There is also a great moderately priced lunch and dinner restaurant open daily (closed Monday and Tuesday during the off season), with a fine chef that creates several excellent dishes based on recipes using their own mustard, and a small gift shop where you can buy a few jars of mustard to take home. *Their museum is open daily from about 11:30am until 8:00pm with guided tours of the production process given in English (if requested) every hour or so. The admission price is 2.50 NLG per person.*

Just steps away from the windmill on the Hoofdstraat is an interesting townhouse (a former bakery) that was converted into the **Grand Hotel de Kromme Raake**. This property is listed in the world record books as "the smallest hotel in the world," and in fact only has one suite for rent at around 300 NLG per night double occupancy. If you ask over at the mustard factory, perhaps you can be allowed to look inside to see the strange collection of turn-of-the-century and deco-style furnishings, the unique closet-bed, and a pair of traditional pajamas that fill every nook of this tiny hotel.

A few steps away on the same little street is another attraction called the **Kaarsemakerij Wilhelmus** (Wilhelmus' Candle Factory), where for 2.50 NLG per person you can watch artisans creating unique and colorful sculpted candles, or for a small fee you can try your skills at making you own candles. *Open during roughly the same hours as the mustard factory.*

Just across the street from the candle shop is the village's **Apotheek** (pharmacy) that doubles as the Eenrum VVV tourist information brochure stand. Make sure to pop inside and grab a few brochures from their racks to pick other good destinations for your day trip through this region. A few blocks away on the Kerkstraat you can take a peek at the 13th century **Romano-Gotische Kerk** (Roman Gothic Church) that has an old pipe organ and an old Romanesque baptismal area.

Additionally, you can stop inside the **D. van der Meulen Klompenmakerij**, a shoe shop on the Zuiderstraat where a good selection of colorful hand-made wooden clogs can be bought for about 35 NLG a pair during normal retail hours. They also give occasional demonstrations of the how they make these traditional wooden shoes. At the back of town off the Handerweg is the **Kwekerig de Kleine Plantage**, an arboretum with gardens and small greenhouses full of roses and other flowers – *open to the public for free visits from 9:00am until 5:00pm on Thursday through Saturday from March 15 through November 1.*

## Borg Verhildersum Recreation Area

From Eenrum, **route N-361** continues to the east, as do the bicycle paths, and at least one regional bus route, and after another seven kilometers (4.5 miles) or so you will find signs pointing to the **Borg Verhildersum** recreation area and estate museum near the town of **Leens**. This beautiful property is dominated by a stately 14th century moated manor house that has been turned over to the local government and has become home to the **Ommelander Museum voor Landbouw en Ambacht** (Regional Museum of Agriculture and Crafts).

Inside you can walk through several fine rooms, chambers, and halls that have been furnished in 19th century Dutch country style and contain displays on what life was like back then on a typical Groningen manor house. There is also an exhibit of antique local costumes in the attic, a converted coach house where fine temporary art exhibitions are held, a fantastic formal garden dotted with sculptures by Eddy Roos, an adjacent barn that now contains a popular café and snack shop, and several nice and well marked walking paths.

A few minutes walk away is the so-called **Museumboerderij Welgelegen** (Farmhouse-Museum), part of the same estate and featuring examples of old farming machinery, saddles, a blacksmith shop, farming tools, handicrafts, and other antique items. *The estate is only open from April through October, and the manor house may be visited Tuesday through Sunday between 10:30am and 5:00pm, while the farmhouse museum is open Tuesday through Sunday from 1:00pm until 5:00pm. Admission to all of the buildings is combined in the 5 NLG per person admission charge. You can also walk around the animal-lined paths, moats, and irrigation canals at no charge.*

## *Houwerzijl*

From the Borg Verhildersum estate and museum, **route N-361** continues further to the east, as do the bicycle paths, and at least one regional bus route, and after another five kilometers (three miles) or so you will find an exit to the town of Ulrum. Cut through Ulrum and follow a small road with signposts that point towards the town of **Houwerzijl**, about seven kilometers (four miles) southeast, via plenty of potato farms and a turn-off at the hamlet of Niekerk.

Once in Houwerzijl keep your eyes peeled for a former church that is now the **Museum de Theefabriek** (Tea Factory Museum) on Hoofdstraat. Some years ago, a Dutch foundation purchased this abandoned church and held a contest to give it away to the person(s) that came up with the most interesting use for the building. A young couple from Groningen that drank plenty of tea then submitted a proposal to convert the church into a tea shop and museum of tea, and then won the competition.

After months of back-breaking renovations on a shoestring budget, the delightful multilingual owners have created one of the best cafés in Holland, complete with a small museum containing an introduction to the history, legends, growth, harvesting, production, packing, shipping, and possible health benefits of consuming various tea leaves from all over the world. The café is open during the same hours as the museum (see below), and offers a tea shop, over 175 different types of exotic hot and cold teas starting at 2.50 NLG per cup, and rather affordable full lunches, excellent scones, light snacks, sandwiches, complete English style afternoon teas, and the best home-made pies in the region.

*The museum and its fine café are open April through October between Tuesday and Sunday from 10:00am until 5:00pm, November through March (closed during January) on Saturdays and Sundays only from 10:00am until 5:00pm, and the museum entrance fee is 3 NLG per person.*

### *Back to Groningen*

Once you're done with the tea museum, continue heading through Howerzijl and take a small road or the bicycle paths that travel about 14 kilometers (9 miles) past the villages of Elektra, Oldehove, Den Ham, and Aduard before either taking the bike paths or driving east on route **N-355** back to the city of Groningen.

## PRACTICAL INFORMATION FOR GRONINGEN

**Main VVV Tourist Office** - *Gedmpte Kattendiep 6* - *(50) 313-9774*
**Municipal Information Center** - *Kreupelstraat 1* - *(50) 367-3000*
**Domestic Train and Bus Info** - *(6) 9292*
**Regional Train Info** - *NS Station* - *(50) 368-1400*
**GVB Municipal Transit Authority** - *Kreupelstraat 1* - *(50) 367-2393*

**Radio Dispatched Taxis** - *(50) 312-8044 or (50) 313-8999*
**Police Headquarters** - *Rademarkt 12 - (50) 316-2222*
**Emergency Hotline** - *06-11*

# EXCURSION TO TEXEL ISLAND

The amazingly beautiful island of **Texel** is one of my favorite places to get away from it all. During the winter the beautiful towns and coastal villages are inhabited entirely by local merchants, farmers, and former city dwellers that gave up on the rat race. As summer approaches, thousands of adventurous tourists from all over Northern Europe pack the ferries and head for week-long package vacations at dozens of cute inns, superb youth hostels, and cheap bungalow colonies near the awesome 16 mile stretch of pristine sand dune beaches.

The island has historically been a major location for sheep breeding and agriculture, but for the past few decades, summer season adventure tourists have brought in most of the money to create a strong local economy. There are all sorts of outdoor sports, regular and nude beaches, strangely shaped old farm houses, fishing ports, dikes, massive polders, windmills, sea bird and marine animal sanctuaries, nature paths (including a special hike for blind people), horseback rides, and plenty more, even in the off season when much of the island goes into hibernation. Make sure to check out some of the locally made *jenever* (gin), as it has unusual properties. Texel is a truly special place, and I strongly recommend a few days here!

**Texel** is situated in the Wadden Sea just off the northwestern tip of Noord-Holland province. It lies 53 kilometers (33 miles) north-northwest of Amsterdam via a 25 minute **ferry ride** from Den Helder.

*Getting To Texel*

No matter how you choose to reach Texel, keep in mind that your travels will include a 25 minute ferry ride from **Den Helder**. Two giant modern ferries are scheduled hourly from sunrise to sunset each day around the year and are operated by the **TESO** (Texels Eigen Stoomboot Onderemung). They depart the Den Helder docks and steam towards the Veerhaven harbor on Texel's southcast end. From there you can take the #27, #28 or #29 public bus for 3 NLG, or a taxi to any desired location on Texel. The ferry fare is about 11 NLG round-trip per person, 7 NLG round-trip per bicycle, and 95 NLG round-trip per car. Teso's offices can be reached by calling *Tel: (222) 369-600.*

While cars are allowed on the island, having one here is not worth the effort. The best bet is to drive to Den Helder and find a safe place to leave the car while you proceed to Texel via ferry. Take the **A-10** ring road until connecting to the **A-9** north for about 47 kilometers (29 miles).

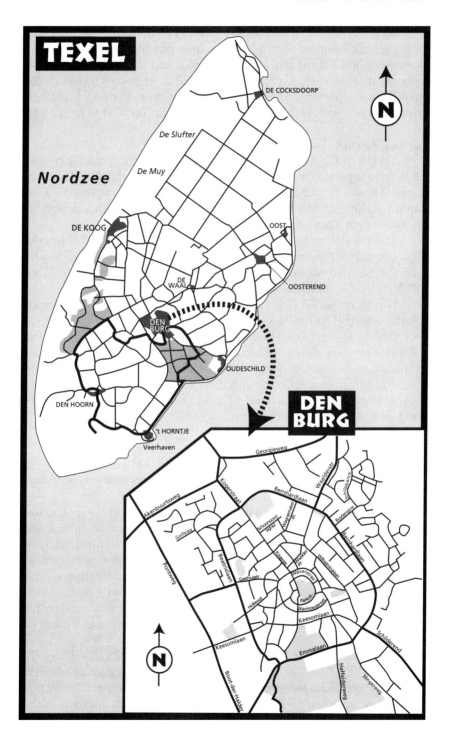

You can also get to Den Helder by train. The train station is just a four minute walk from the ferry pier. The city's tiny **Station Den Helder** is located on just off the harbor in downtown and has almost no services other than an automated ticket dispenser kiosk. Almost all trains arriving here require connections at either Leeuwarden or Alkmaar. From here you take the hourly NZH bus #3 to the ferry port for 3 NLG per person.

### Getting Around Texel

Texel's **AOT** (Autobus Onderneming Texel) transit authority operates three separate circular bus routes to get you around the island. The normal hours of operation for most of the system is from about 6:45am until roughly 9:30pm. After that your only choices are either to walk, or to take a taxi. They accept **Nationale Strippen Kaarts**.

There are also about 60 or so licensed taxis. For just 6 NLG per ride you can take a **Telekom Taxi** between any two points on Texel, but the wait can be up to one hour. Normal taxis will charge between 10 NLG and 23.50 NLG for the same ride, but they will arrive much faster.

For about 65 NLG a day you can rent a moped form places like **Verhuurbedrijf Bruining** in De Koog or Den Burg at *Tel: (222) 317-333.*

Getting around Texel by bike (or foot) is by far the best way to see the island. There are dozens of amazing one to three hour bike and hiking routes that can take you to just about every town, resort, beach area, forest, and rural spot. Check with the VVV for special English bike and hiking route maps. For around 8 NLG per day plus deposit most hotels and several bike shops will rent you a simple bike.

### Where to Stay

**HOTEL OPDUIN**, *Ruyslaan 22 (De Koog). Tel: (222) 317-445, Fax: (222) 317-777. Year round rack rates from 255 NLG per double room per night (E.P.) per week (E.P.). All major credit cards accepted.*

This extremely pleasant 4 star ocean-side hotel is Texel's most deluxe property. Located on the Outskirts of De Koog, it is just a two minute walk to superb dune beaches. There are 90 large rooms and comfortable suites eith deluxe private bathrooms, remote control satellite television, extremely comfortable furnishings, am-fm clock radio, hair dryers, direct dial telephone, mini-bar, and both sea-view balconies and Jacuzzis in some cases. Facilities include a café, a good restaurant, room service, free private parking, business meeting rooms, and express laundry and dry cleaning.

**GLOEDNIEUWE HOTELSUITES**, *Dorpstraat 228, (De Koog). Tel: (222) 317-755, Fax: (222) 327-341. Low season rack rates from 235 NLG per 1 bedroom apartment per week (E.P.). High Season rack rates from 895 NLG per 1 bedroom apartment per week (E.P.) All major credit cards accepted.*

These brand new suite style apartments are among the most relaxing on the island. Here there are 21 different spacious 1 to 3 bedroom that all have private bathroom, kitchenette, balconies, direct dial telephone, cable television, and free parking.

**KAMPERFOELIE VILLA PARK**, *(De Koog). Tel: (222) 317-746, Fax: (222) 327-341. Low season rack rates from 415 NLG per 2 bedroom villa per week (E.P.). High Season rack rates from 1200 NLG per 2 bedroom villa per week (E.P.) All major credit cards accepted.*

I really like this new collection of self standing private houses on the edge of a forest near De Koog. These are really luxurious brick villas with huge modern kitchens, a full size living room, a super deluxe bathroom with whirlpool bath, cable television, direct dial telephone, exceedingly comfortable furnishings, out door patios (many facing water!) and even a private sauna in selected units. This is a great bargain, especially during the months just before and after summer when the island gets expensive!.

**HOTEL DE PELIKAAN**, *Pelikaanweg 18 (De Koog). Tel: (222) 317-202, Fax: (222) 317-687. Low season rack rates from 560 NLG per 1 bedroom apartment per week (E.P.). High Season rack rates from 980 NLG per 1 bedroom apartment per week (E.P.). All major credit cards accepted.*

This modern and surprisingly comfortable 3 star apart-hotel is one of the best equipped properties De Koog. Located next to a forest about 3 kilometers up from Den Burg, the hotel has some 79 or so large one and two bedroom fully equipped apartments that all feature private bathrooms, remote control satellite television, nice furnishings, am-fm clock radio, direct dial telephone, and a small but good kitchenette. Facilities here include a restaurant, a lounge, swimming pool, Laundromat, bicycle rentals, sauna, available child care, and a good staff.

**HOTEL DE LINDEBOOM TEXEL**, *Groeneplaats, (Den Burg), Tel: (222) 312-041, Fax: (222) 310-517. Year round rack rates from 165 NLG double room per night (E.P.). All major credit cards accepted.*

If you want to be in the real heart of Den Burg, try this little inn and café on the unforgettable market square. Here there are several cozy rooms above the famous outdoor cafe that feature nice tile bathrooms, good sized guestrooms, and comfortable furniture. The meals here a quite good too!.

**NJHC HOSTEL HERBERG PANORAMA**, *Schansweg 7 (Den Burg)), Tel: (222) 315-441, US & Canada Bookings (Hostelling International) 1-613-237-7884. Year round rack rates from 31 NLG per person in a dormitory per night (C.P.). Year round rack rates from 82 NLG per double private room per night (E.P.). Cash Only - No credit cards accepted.*

I would certainly select this great hostel as my fisrst choice for budget accommodations. Expertly managed by a fantastically helpful staff, this is what a hostel should feel like. Packed with couple and families in every possible range, each client can grab a bicycle and head off all over the island. The hostel is an excellent choice for travelers that are looking for great (but still rather affordable) accommodations in a typical rural setting just minutes from the beach.

The hostel (and its sister hostel a kilometer away) have nice yet simply furnished single, double, triple, and quadruple rooms with private bathrooms, as well as a special section of dormitory rooms for up to 20 people each that have semi-private bathrooms and luggage lockers. Guests of the hostel are encouraged to use the available bicycles, and book all sorts of available excursions. Facilities include free outdoor parking, a nearby bus stop, storage lockers, conference rooms, a good cheap restaurant, a great and inexpensive bar, vending machines, and a truly inviting ambiance. Highly recommended as the best value for the money of any low priced property here.

**LOGIES MET ONTBIJT**, **BUNGALOWS**, & **SUMMER HOUSES**, *Various Locations. Contact VVV-Texel, Tel: (222) 312-847. Low season rates from just 49 NLG per double room per night in a private home or farmhouse inn (C.P.). High season rates from 875 NLG for a 2 bedroom bungalow or summer house peer week (E.P.). Cash only - No credit cards accepted.*

The island of Texel officially has about 200 bed and breakfast inns, private guest houses, bungalow colonies, and vacation rental homes that can be booked by the day during the low season, and by the week during the high season. Many of the units are also located in an assortment of traditional homes and farm houses scattered around the island. These establishments accept reservations, and usually fill up well in advance during the summer seasons. Contact the VVV for specific details or a copy of their current leaflet called *Gids Voor Vakantie & Vrije Tijd* and *Vacantiewoningen & Bungalows* that include photos plus basic information, rates, descriptions, and more. The VVV is the central booking office for 95% of these types of accommodations.

### Where to Eat
**TAVERNE DE 12 BALCKEN**, *Weverstraat 20 (Den Burg). Tel: (222) 312-681. Most major credit cards accepted.*

What a great find! This small tavern and extremely casual grill room in the center of town makes superb and freshly prepared Dutch and international dishes that are sensational. The menu includes tomato soup at 5 NLG, French onion soup at 5.75 NLG, chicken sate for 18.75 NLG, smoked spare ribs with a serious barbecue sauce at 23.50 NLG, beef tournedos with pepper sauce for 32.50 NLG, entrecote with Roquefort sauce at 26.75 NLG, pork chops in mustard for 24.75 NLG, and a daily vegetarian special at 17.50 NLG. This is my favorite place to eat – and then stay for a few drinks – in all of Northern Holland.

**DE HUYDECOPER**, *Groeneplaats 14, (Den Burg). Tel: (222) 312-041. Most major credit cards accepted.*

This delightful little gourmet restaurant is situated inside a fantastic 14th century home alongside the town's principal shopping and market squares. Make advance reservations for a great informal multiple course meal in a relaxed setting that will cost you around 38.50 NLG a person plus wine.

**HET OUDE VEERHUIS**, *Haven 2, (Oudeschild). Tel: (222) 312-705. Most major credit cards accepted.*

For a fantastic fresh seafood meal in this picturesque coastal village, head straight for this old seaman's house at the edge of the harbor. With a laid back setting and a menu full of fresh fish and lamb items among many others, this is a good place for a good 18.50 NLG lunch on a nice day of bike riding.

**RESTAIRANTE PIZZERIA BELLA VISTA**, *Kikkerstraat 30 (De Cocksdorp). Tel: (222) 316-485. Cash only - No credit cards accepted.*

Inside, and along the terraces of, this cute little Italian joint you can sit down and have a good filling meal for as little as 16.75 NLG a head including salad and pasta or pizza.

### Seeing the Sights

A good place to start out your explorations by bus, bicycle, or foot is over at the peaceful inland village of **Den Burg**, the largest town on Texel. Here you should make a point to visit the **VVV** tourist information offices on Emmalaan at the edge of town, and pick up inexpensive island maps and activity guides. The village has a few hundred cute traditional houses, a great a tiny main square with several cafes surrounding the cute little **Cinema Texel** movie theather, an antiquities museum, and plenty of nice people. The charming **Groeneplaats** square hosts a **Monday Morning Outdoor Market**, and in the summer there is a Wednesday afternoon **Folklore Market**. It will only take an hour to see every street in town, and at night it's a great place to dine and party with locals (some cafes even stay open till 4:00am!)and visitors alike!.

From here it is just a 3 kilometer (2 mile) walk or ride east to the harbor village of **Oudeschild**, a great place to wander around for an afternoon. Nestled between the sea and several large farms, the maritime ambiance is at its best during summer weekends when cutters and beautiful old sailing vessels pull into port. Make sure to check out the 17th century **Zeemanskerk** (Seaman's Church) on the De Houtmanstraat, the sail-maker's shops, the odd **Maritiem en Jutters Museum** sea scavenger's museum, and of course the newly automated windmill. There are fine coastal bike and hiking routes past dikes and fortresses (ask at the VVV for details), all sorts of deep-sea fishing possibilities and water based activities. A great idea is to take one of the twice daily (except Sundays) shrimp fishing excursion offered during the summer aboard the *TX 27* and *TX 10* shrimp boats for just 12 NLG a person, and you even get to keep part of the day's catch. This is the place to go for a fresh fish or seafood dinner.

From here you can head about five kilometers southwest to **Den Hoorn**, a nice town full of flowers and a stunning white parish church. Each summer the town hosts a **Thursday Late Afternoon Market and Fair** with live music. From the town you can walk out onto massive sand dunes and secluded coastal beaches where many people bathe topless and bottomless. There are also fantastic zones nearby such as the **De Guel** and the **Grote Valk**, which have popular trails designed for watching rare wild birds such as spoonbills, tufted ducks, golden eyes, warblers, stone chats, and white throats.

Heading up the west coast for about 10.5 kilometers (6.5 miles), you will pass **De Koog**, a coastal town that has become the center for the budget priced apartment and bungalow style tourist complexes. Totally mobbed during the summer, this is the place to head for the most popular beaches, unusual horse rides, family fun amusements, and a fun summer-only **Tuesday Afternoon Street Fair**.

After heading about 10 kilometers (6 miles) all the way up the fragile beaches and protected park lands of Texel's northernmost tip, stop in at **De Cocksdorp**. This village is best known for its proximity to the **De Slufter** wild bird sanctuary, several great sandy beaches, and is a good place to take a guided walk given occasionally by the Forestry Commission (check with the VVV for details).

There are four unique museums scattered around the island that are all well worth a visit.

The most interesting is known as **Ecomare** and is located two kilometers (1.5 miles) south of the popular coastal resort town of **De Koog**. This is a center for education about the Wadden Sea and the mud flats. There is also a sanctuary where you can watch disabled birds being cared for and the feeding of some 25 seals, a small marine aquarium, and special marine exhibits and guided dune tours. *Open April through October between 9:00am and 5:00pm from Monday to Saturday; admission is currently 8 NLG per person.*

Another great place to check out is the **Maritiem en Jutters Museum** (Maritime and Beachcomber Museum) near the windmill in the coastal hamlet of **Oudeschild**. Inside a pair of converted old grain and seaweed warehouses you will find an odd collection of items found after they have washed up on Texel's shores. *This museum is open year round from Tuesday through Saturday from 10:00am until 5:00pm.*

In **Den Burg** you will find the **Oudheidkamer** antiquities museum on the Kogerstraat #1 in an old house that was once a 16th century inn for tramps and vagrants!. This old gabled house contains a collection of traditional furnishings, coins, decorative art, costumes, and many strange household items from the past. *The museum is open April through October on weekdays only from 10:00am until 3:00pm*

Finally, over on Hogereind #6 in the peaceful hamlet of **De Wall**, you can visit the **Agrarisch en Wagen Museum** (Agricultural and Cart Museum). As its name suggests, there are exhibits of old farm vehicles such as antique horse drawn wagons, a working metal forge, huge plows, and slide shows abouth farming on Texel. *This museum is open April 15th until October 15th between Tuesday and Saturday from 10:00am until 5:00pm.*

*Nightlife*

The best bars in **Den Burg** are the **12 Blacken** on Weverstraat, the **Nachtbar Casino** on the Zwaanstraat, and the **Question** dance bar on Zwaanstraat.

Over in **De Koog** you can walk along Dorpstraat, where you should visit the **De Jutter Café**, the **De Beerekuil**, **Tiffany**, the **Onder de Pomp Café**, the **Metro** disco, and the **Café De Kuip**.

---

### MARITIME FUN OFF TEXEL ISLAND!

*Shrimping Aboard a Shrimp Boat - This 3 hour tour starts at the of Oudeschild and continues along open sea as it sets and retrieves nets for shrimp in the time tested method. Passengers are allowed to take a share of the dayŌs catch at no extra charge. It leaves 10:30 am and again at 2:00pm Monday through Saturday during summer, and 2:00pm on Wednesdays during the rest of the year, and the fee is about 12 NLG per person. For more info please call the TX 27 boat at Tel: (222) 313-806 or the TX 10 boat at Tel: (222) 313-639.*

*Sailing Trips aboard vessels such as the Zeester and Grote Jager depart on most summer days and charge upwards of 27.50 NLG per person for 2 hour baot trip. Contact the VVV-Texel for specific details.*

*Deep Sea Fishing - For about 21 NLG a head you hop onto a large fishing vessel and test your skill. Departures are scheduled at least once per day between April 15 and September 15. Please contact the VVV - Texel for details.*

---

*Practical Information for Texel*
**Main VVV Tourist Office** - *Emmalaan 66 (Den Burg) - Tel: (222) 314-741*
**The Teso Ferry Office** - *Tel: (222) 369-600*
**Telekom Taxi** - *Tel: (222) 322-211*
**Emergency Hotline** - *06-11*

# 24. USEFUL DUTCH PHRASES

## Numbers

| | |
|---|---|
| een | 1 |
| twee | 2 |
| drie | 3 |
| vier | 4 |
| vijf | 5 |
| zes | 6 |
| zeven | 7 |
| acht | 8 |
| negen | 9 |
| tien | 10 |
| elf | 11 |
| twaalf | 12 |
| dertien | 13 |
| veertien | 14 |
| vijftien | 15 |
| zestien | 16 |
| zeventien | 17 |
| achtien | 18 |
| negentien | 19 |
| twintig | 20 |
| een en twintig | 21 |
| twee en twintig | 22 |
| dertig | 30 |
| veertig | 40 |
| viftig | 50 |
| zestig | 60 |
| zeventig | 70 |
| tachtig | 80 |
| negentig | 90 |
| honderd | 100 |

| | |
|---|---|
| duizend | 1000 |
| miljoen | 1,000,000 |

**Days of the Week**

| | |
|---|---|
| maandag | Monday |
| dinsdag | Tuesday |
| woensdag | Wednesday |
| donderdag | Thursday |
| vrijdag | Friday |
| zaterdag | Saturday |
| zondag | Sunday |

**Months of the Year**

| | |
|---|---|
| januari | January |
| februari | February |
| maart | March |
| april | April |
| mei | May |
| juni | June |
| juli | July |
| augustus | August |
| september | September |
| oktober | October |
| november | November |
| december | December |

**Time**

| | |
|---|---|
| dag | day |
| morgen | morning |
| middag | afternoon |
| avond | evening |
| gisteren | yesterday |
| vandaag | today |
| morgen | tommorow |

**Colors**

| | |
|---|---|
| zwart | black |
| wit | white |
| rood | red |
| blauw | blue |
| groen | green |

## Useful Words

| | |
|---|---|
| ja | yes |
| nee | no |
| goed | good |
| slecht | bad |
| ingang | entrance |
| uitgang | exit |
| open | open |
| gesloten | closed |
| omhoog | up |
| naar beneden | down |
| links | left |
| rechts | right |
| vroeg | early |
| laat | late |

## Greetings

| | |
|---|---|
| hallo | hello |
| Tot ziens | goodbye |
| goed morgen | good morning |
| goede nacht | good night |
| Hoe gaat het ermee? | how are you? |
| por favor | please |
| dank u | thank you |
| sorry | I'm sorry |

## Descriptions

| | |
|---|---|
| klein | small |
| grote | big |
| deze | this |
| die | that |
| dichtbij | close |
| ver weg | far |
| warme | hot |
| koud | cold |
| goedkoop | cheap |
| duur | expensive |
| gratis | free |
| hier | here |
| daar | there |

## Queries

| | |
|---|---|
| wanneer | when |
| hoe | how |
| hoeveel | how much |
| wat | what |
| waar | where |
| waarom | why |

## Transportation

| | |
|---|---|
| wagen | car |
| bus | bus |
| trein | train |
| taxi | taxi |
| avion | airplane |
| metro | subway |
| station | station |
| airport | airport |
| eerste klas | first class |
| tweede klas | second class |
| enkeltje | one way |
| retourje | round trip |
| brug | bridge |
| parking | garage |

## Services

| | |
|---|---|
| politie | police |
| dokter | doctor |
| ziekenhuis | hospital |
| apotheek | pharmacy |
| postkantoor | post office |
| bank | bank |
| hotel | hotel |
| restaurant | restaurant |
| toiletten | bathroom |
| telefoon | telephone |

## Accommodations

| | |
|---|---|
| hotel | hotel |
| pension | guest house |
| jeugdherberg | youth hostel |
| logies met ontbijt | bed & breakfast inn |
| appartementen | apartment |
| camping | camp site |

| | |
|---|---|
| eenpersoonskamer | single room |
| twees persoonskamer | double room |
| met bad | with private bath |
| met twee bed | with 2 beds |
| met een king bed | with a king size bed |

## Sights

| | |
|---|---|
| stad | city |
| provincie | province |
| centrum | city center |
| plein | a town square |
| grote plein | the main town square |
| brug | bridge |
| gebouw | building |
| kasteel | castle |
| stadhuis | town hall |
| kerk | church |
| museum | museum |
| VVV | tourist information office |
| tuin | garden |
| straat | street |
| markt | marketplace |
| park | park area |

## Beverages

| | |
|---|---|
| fles | bottle |
| glas | glass |
| kop | cup |
| water | water |
| ijs | ice |
| mineraalwater | mineral water |
| thee | tea |
| koffee | coffee |
| expresso | expresso |
| koffeemelk | cream |
| melk | milk |
| verse jus | fruit juice |
| bier | beer |
| rode wijn | red wine |
| witte wijn | white wine |

## Dining

| | |
|---|---|
| kaart | menu |
| ober | waiter |
| juffrow | waitress |
| wijnkaart | wine list |
| betalen | the bill |
| ontbijt | breakfast |
| lunch | lunch |
| diner | dinner |
| mes | knife |
| vork | fork |
| lepel | spoon |
| broodje | sandwiich |
| dagschotel | daily special |
| vegitarisch | vegetarian |
| brood | bread |
| boter | butter |
| zouwt | salt |
| peper | pepper |
| suiker | sugar |
| olie | oil |
| azijn | vinegar |
| mosterd | mustard |
| soep | soup |
| ei | egg |
| eieren | bacon |
| patate fritas | french fries |
| broodje | sandwich |
| | |
| vlees | meat |
| biefstuk | steak |
| varkensvlees | pork |
| eend | duck |
| ham | ham |
| worst | sausage |
| lamsvless | lamb |
| klafsvlees | veal |
| konijn | rabbit |
| kip | chicken |
| | |
| vis | fish |
| kabeljauw | cod |
| tonjin | tuna |

| | |
|---|---|
| bot | flounder |
| forel | trout |
| rodaballo | turbot |
| zalm | salmon |
| paling | eel |
| haring | herring |
| makreel | mackerel |
| schaaldieren | shellfish |
| oesters | oysters |
| garnalen | shrimp |
| langostinos | prawns |
| krab | crab |
| kreeft | lobster |
| | |
| groenten | vegetables |
| rijst | rice |
| uien | onions |
| aardappelen | potatoes |
| worteltjes | carrots |
| spinazie | spinach |
| champinons | mushrooms |
| komkommer | cucumber |
| knoflook | garlic |
| bonen | beans |
| sla | lettuce |
| kool | cabbage |
| tomaten | tomato |
| asperges | asparagus |
| | |
| fruit | fruit |
| sinaasappel | orange |
| citroen | lemon |
| melon | melon |
| druiven | grapes |
| kersen | appel |
| peren | pears |
| | |
| nagerecht | dessert |
| kaas | cheese |
| oude kass | aged cheese |
| taart | cake |
| ijs | ice cream |
| chocola | chocolate |

## Cooking Methods

| | |
|---|---|
| gegrild | grilled |
| gebraden | roasted |
| gerookt | smoked |
| gebakken | fried |
| gestoofd | stewed |
| gekookt | boiled |
| gepocheerd | poached |
| | |
| doorbaken | well done |
| medium | medium |
| rare | rare |

## SOME COMMON QUESTIONS, IN DUTCH & ENGLISH

| | |
|---|---|
| *Sprecht u engels?* | *Do you speak English?* |
| *Waar is....?* | *Where is.....?* |
| *Hoe kom ik naar....?* | *How do I get to....?* |
| *Hoeveel kilometers is het naar....?* | *How many kilometers is it to the ...?* |
| *Hoeveel kost dat?* | *How much does this cost?* |
| *Ober, kan ik betalen?* | *Waiter, could we have the bill?* |
| *Wat kunt u aanbevelen?* | *What can you recommend?* |
| *Neemt u credit cards aan?* | *Do you accept credit cards?* |
| *Zijn er nog kamers vrij?* | *Are there any rooms available?* |

# INDEX

*Thanks for traveling with **Open Road**! If you have any comments about this guide, write the author care of Open Road Publishing, 45 West 60th Street, Suite 27 D, New York, NY 10023.*